Advance Praise for Nurturing Adoptions

Deborah Gray, once again, addresses the primary issues that parents and professionals confront when they become involved with hurt children. She has something for just about everyone in the adoption world! Her detailed examination of many cogent issues will help anyone whose life is touched by children and adolescents who have lost so much prior to their adoptions and yet have so much to gain in their new families. Reading Gray's work will leave no stone unturned.

Gregory C. Keck, Ph.D.
Founder/Director of The Attachment and Bonding Center of Ohio
Co-author of *Adopting the Hurt Child* and *Parenting the Hurt Child*
Ohio

Deborah Gray thinks like a child, both imaginatively and yet very concretely. That's why *Nurturing Adoptions* is filled with creative ideas and practical suggestions that bring a fresh approach for traumatized children learning to love and trust in an adoptive family. I started to mark the pages of *Nurturing Adoptions* that contained especially useful ideas and soon found myself in a blizzard of bookmarks. Too much good stuff!

Mary Ann Curran, M.A.
Director of Social Services at
World Association for Children and Parents (WACAP)
Washington State

Nurturing Adoptions is a "must read" for anyone providing therapeutic services to adoptive families. Deborah provides a wealth of information based on current research that enables therapists to help children and their families heal and develop positive relationships.

Patty Jewell, L.C.S.W.
Therapeutic Foster Care and Home Run Program Supervisor
Bethany Christian Services, Indianapolis Branch

At last there is a "how to" book for professionals working with children with the scars of abuse and neglect. Deborah Gray lays out the foundations of research in this field, explaining how and why children respond to stresses of their early lives. From these foundations she helps professionals and families to create a milieu that will build self-esteem, address trauma and grief, and work towards resiliency. Therapists with little experience in this field may not recognize the many issues that are impacting the child's behavior. Often I find that these mental health professionals are at a loss, incompletely understanding the impact of a child's early trauma on their emotional development. Here, as well, is a toolbox to help both adoption professionals who are new to adoption and those with years of experience. This book will be quoted over and over again to my patients, therapists in my community, and even in my home. I plan to have two copies—one to share with families at work, the other to refer to as a parent as I nurture my own children towards coping with their pasts.

Deborah Borchers, M.D.
Pediatrician specializing in adoption and foster care medicine
Adoptive Mom
Cincinnati, Ohio

Deborah's work in *Nurturing Adoptions* identifies the importance of considering the biological impact of trauma and neglect in children. She bridges the physiological and psychological effects of traumatic stress that can develop into lifelong emotional or attachment issues. Deborah has the unique ability to give practical context to the challenging outcomes that are reflective of stress, trauma and neglect in children. Her sensitive, insightful writing style draws the reader into her work with ease. Whether you are a parent by birth, adoption or foster care or a professional working with children you will benefit from Deborah's expertise and dedication to families!

Cindy Haftner, Executive Director,
and **Leah Deans**, Resource Director
Adoption Support Centre of Saskatchewan Inc.

This is an essential book for professionals and parents! Deborah Gray reviews and explains valuable, current and applicable research. She then goes much further and clarifies the "whys" and "hows." Why are we seeing children and families in such distress and how do we assist them? *Nurturing Adoptions* offers skill building in assessment, treating, placing, parenting, teaching and loving traumatized and neglected children.

Parents and professionals will find important information about building the resiliency of children, of families and of professionals. The vignettes used to describe research, techniques and strategies are so thorough and encouraging they can be visualized.

Deborah, what a gift you've given to those of us that are committed to and have claimed hurt children. Thank you for sharing your passion with this optimistic resource. As soon as it is available, *Nurturing Adoptions* will be on my list of "must haves."

Yolanda Comparan, M.S.W.
Owner/Operator
Adoption Referral & Information Service
Mom by Adoption
Washington State

Deborah's book made me sigh with relief. Finally there is a resource that lets us see the big picture. There is risk to focus only on what is diagnosed "on the surface". For example, a child adopted internationally may have RAD or sensory integration disorder. Deborah enlightens us that children are not that simple. She fosters one to stop and think about the child as a whole, how the child was wired in the womb and how the child's world to date has left an enduring impression. She blends the scientific biomedical research with hands-on easy to understand therapeutic approaches to children who have experienced trauma. Both parents and professionals will find this book a blessing.

Julie K. Keck, M.D.
Neurodevelopmental Pediatrician
Director of the International Adoption Clinic
at Riley Hospital for Children
Indianapolis, Indiana

People sometimes do not understand that attachment work has many facets. Deborah Gray's *Nurturing Adoptions* helps parents, therapists, and social workers integrate trauma, loss and grief into attachment work. As always she uses clear language, case vignettes, and is able to take complex issues and break them down for easy understanding. This should help all concerned view attachment as a process not an event which, depending on the family, has many issues that need to be addressed. Thank you Deborah for this contribution.

Regina M. Kupecky, L.S.W.
co-author with Gregory C. Keck, PhD *Adopting the Hurt Child* and *Parenting the Hurt Child*, author of curriculum *My Brother My Sister: Sibling Relations in Adoption and Foster Care* co-author with Arleta James and Gregory C. Keck of curriculum *Abroad and Back: Parenting and International Adoption.*

Nurturing Adoptions

Creating Resilience after Neglect and Trauma

Deborah D. Gray

Jessica Kingsley *Publishers*
London and Philadelphia

Front cover image source: Can Stock Photo®. The cover image is for
illustrative purposes only, and any person featuring is a model.

Table 2.1 from Cook, Blaustein, Spinazzola, and van der Kolk, 2003 on p.37 is reproduced by
permission of Joe Spinazzola.
Epigraph from Marianne Williamson on p.411 is reproduced by permission of Marianne Williamson.
Epigraph (Never doubt that a small group of thoughtful, committed citizens can change the world *)
from Margaret Mead on p.427 is reproduced by permission of the Institute for Intercultural Studies.

This edition published in 2012
by Jessica Kingsley Publishers
73 Collier Street
London N1 9BE, UK
and
400 Market Street, Suite 400
Philadelphia, PA 19106, USA

www.jkp.com

First published in 2007 by Perspectives Press

Library of Congress Cataloging in Publication Data
A CIP catalog record for this book is available from the Library of Congress

British Library Cataloguing in Publication Data
A CIP catalogue record for this book is available from the British Library

ISBN 978 1 84905 891 9
eISBN 978 0 85700 607 3

Printed and bound in the United States

Dedication

To Joseph

Acknowledgments

Such wonderful people I have the privilege of thanking!

My first thanks goes to my family, who encouraged me and believed in the worth of this project. Thank you, Joe, Summerlea, Tricia, and Joey. You have been supportive in those personal ways that mean the most to me.

This book required a science editor. How grateful I was to Patricia MacKenzie, neurobiologist, who edited this book from a scientific point of view. She smoothed awkward sentences while she worked. This book gained in accuracy and grace because of her generous time commitment. And what a helpful attitude as she worked! She made this information useful to readers, thinking of helpful aids like charts and glossary. She was a terrific partner: scientific, efficient, and genuinely helpful.

The children and families with whom I have worked have taught me much about solutions that work, attitudes that transcend challenges, and commitment. On so many levels, I am in debt to them for the lessons that they have taught me. I hope to share their gifts in passing their insights on to readers.

Special friends encouraged the thinking and development of this book's work. Mary-Carter Creech, my friend at Nurturing Attachments, generates fresh ideas. Her enthusiasm to support families kindles my desire to do more. My thanks to Yolanda Comparan of Adoption Resource and Information Services, Tony Collis, of Antioch University, and Brian Andersen, Cascadia Training— Northwest Adoption Resources. Mary-Carter, Yolanda, Brian, Tony, and I talked through what today's adoptions required of professionals and parents. Many of the book's ideas were first trotted out during trainings with Brian. We discovered what audiences found useful. Brian is always companionable in planning trainings and forward-thinking in conceptualizing ways to support families.

Mary Ann Curran, my long-time friend, helps to keep me abreast of the changes in the adoption field and helps me to evolve in response. Mary Ann works with excellence and compassion, giving me a model for best practices in-home and in casework.

Child and adolescent psychiatrist Robert Fleming has shaped the way in which I am able to think about complex children's problems. Bob, thank you for your clarity, advice, and wisdom in cases over all of these years. Your imprint, fortunately, is on the cases described in this book. Similarly, Vera Fahlberg, M.D. shaped the way in which I practice. But especially in the section on moving children and the effects on their personalities, the seminal ideas are hers. By using her concepts, so many children have had caring moves and better outcomes.

The University of Washington's Center for Adoption Medicine and FAS clinic staff have been so generous in sharing their information and in collaborating. Thank you Julie Bledsoe, M.D., Julian Davies, M.D., Heather Lickenbrock, and Cyndi Musar.

The participants in the certificate programs in foster care and adoption in both Seattle and Portland have been amazing teachers even as I have taught. The resultant consult groups are keeping us all sharing and growing. Thank you for the insights and resources that we have all shared—and your encouragement in writing this book.

Gwen Lewis helped me to understand executive dysfunction in a manner that I could apply—as well as the subsequent best practices in homes and education. Than you for those lunches, Gwen.

On a personal note, like the children I treat, I yearned for the promise of adoption—a spiritual one, into a family in which I could leave fears and defenses and be loved authentically. But like the children in this book, I have struggled. Is it too good to be true? Coming home spiritually into the family of God, through experiencing the love of Christ, has brought me home. My heart was broken long ago by life, and by children's sufferings. I am grateful for God's love that fills my heart and shines through my brokenness.

Lastly, I have met new friends through Jessica Kingsley Publishers. Thank you, Stephen Jones, Senior Editor, for your eye for excellence and your positivism. Thank you for contributing to children's well-being through publishing books that will help us all to help children.

Deborah Gray
Seattle, WA.

Note to the reader:
Facts in the anecdotes and vignettes have been altered to protect the confidentiality of clients.

Table of Contents

Introduction

This book is a guide for the parents and professionals charged with the task of helping children affected by neglect and trauma. Research with people who have suffered neglect and trauma confirms that those who have grown up without appropriate professional and family interventions continue to exhibit trauma in adulthood. This book details interventions that create hope and resiliency in children post neglect/trauma. The challenge for the adoption and foster care communities is to first identify the symptom clusters of neglect and trauma, and then to select home and professional practices that move children into healthier developmental arcs.

When I first presented material on trauma and neglect, an adoption professional friend of mine said, "I had a visceral reaction to what you were talking about. My daughter's struggles played as a mental slide show as you talked. I realized how many problems were related to maltreatment. But how do I get a therapist to understand what she needs? I went home feeling sick—for my family and for so many others. We have to get help to families and also to therapists who relate to our children."

This experience compelled me to begin my journey of organizing the information into a user-friendly format. This book provides a practical manual for professionals, reflecting advances in brain processes shaped by early stress, neglect, trauma, and exposure to substance. It applies theory and research to professional protocols in both therapy and casework. Parents can also use this information to understand the effects of neglect/trauma and to employ in-home processes to create a hopeful future for their children.

Neglect and *abuse* are commonplace terms in the histories of children being adopted through domestic foster care programs or from overseas institutions. As adoption has changed, and these terms appear more frequently, there has been a tendency for professionals to treat these potent words as if they were insignificant—almost innocuous. Abuse and neglect are far from innocuous. The truth is that, by itself, placement into stable, loving families cannot be sufficient treatment for problems stemming from chronic maltreatment.

Routinely, children who have been maltreated suffer from high rates of traumatic stress symptoms, anxiety, social problems, aggression, and hopelessness. They will need professional treatment in order to recover.

Traumatic stress is best understood as a health condition, needing early treatment for best results. It stands in the way of a person's ability to develop close personal relationships. It becomes the silent shaper of everyday life, a lens that superimposes the helplessness of trauma on the meaning and pleasures of life. It leaches away life's joys.

In addition to the emotional costs, a study by V.J. Feletti and colleagues demonstrates the relationship of childhood maltreatment to many of the leading causes of illness or death in adults. People who had been maltreated in childhood had a four to twelve times greater risk of developing alcoholism, depression, and drug abuse and of attempting suicide than people who had not been abused or neglected in childhood. They had a two to four times greater risk of smoking, of having at least fifty sexual partners, and of acquiring sexually transmitted disease; a 1.4 to 1.6 times greater risk for physical inactivity and obesity; and 1.6 to 2.9 times greater risk for ischemic heart disease, cancer, chronic lung disease, skeletal fractures, hepatitis, stroke, diabetes, and liver disease (1998).

Secure attachments act as vehicles for the transmission of healthy stress regulation systems. Without healthy stress regulation systems, children are especially vulnerable to the shocking biological effects of trauma on their memories, attention, concentration, anxiety levels, and social responses. Children who lack secure attachments during the time of trauma are particularly at risk for developing traumatic stress disorders. The type of traumatic stress that they are prone to develop is the type that is particularly hard to treat—complex post traumatic stress disorder. With the exception of newborns carried and delivered out of healthy pregnancies, children coming into placement rarely have secure attachment histories. But these children are placed as if the trauma has not shaped their brains or their lives, or as if their rates of distress post-trauma are the same as distress rates in children who have had continuous, secure-base attachment histories.

Neglect has even more misunderstood implications than does trauma. The effects of neglect on mood, empathy, and emotional understanding of others can be long-term. As a group, children who have been neglected show distinct vulnerability in developing empathy and/or the ability to balance their own points of view with the interests of others. This balance is essential in social relationships. Laurie Miller, M.D. has conducted studies of children adopted from Eastern Europe. These children, ages 8 through 11, are notably quite similar in characteristics to children adopted from the North American and Western European foster care systems. One-half of the children in Miller's study were identified by schools or parents as requiring social skills classes. Yet, the group's average age at adoption was just 21 months, with 66% of the children adopted at under 8 months old (2005).

It is remarkably common for new adoptive parents to be sent home with good information on adoption as a lifelong process, but with no information at all about the dangers of untreated traumatic stress—a potentially serious long-term threat to their children's mental and physical health. No specific plan is being made for post-placement treatment of traumatic stress. Far too often, placement professionals themselves are unaware of its potentially lifelong repercussions. Furthermore, placement professionals who know that therapy is essential often have difficulty finding therapists who understand the simultaneous treatment of attachment, trauma, and grief. The result is, in my opinion, a growing public health disaster.

For the treatment community, *Nurturing Adoptions* provides treatment outlines and case examples for therapists who are treating the related issues of traumatic stress, attachment, and neglect issues for children. Therapists who look at their cases strictly through a trauma lens describe having treatment failures when children in treatment have never developed a beginning attachment that permits the emotional stability to begin doing trauma work. They recognize that play therapy alone is not helping these children resolve issues. Instead, the trauma themes are played out, over and over and over again. No mastery or de-sensitization seems to occur.

Therapists who focus only on attachment describe the frustration of continuing to treat for attachment issues for long periods of time, making gains and then seeing them erode. They have never included trauma work in their treatment models. Trauma keeps eroding attachment relationships until the trauma is treated. This book reflects the growth in the field in terms of understanding the interrelationship between trauma, neglect, and attachment. It gives detailed case descriptions of updated treatment processes.

This book includes the theory and the practicalities of therapy for children who are coming into families after maltreatment. I have a specialty practice in adoption and foster care, and, as a result, children and their families have taught me to adapt my therapy processes to fit their specific needs. I have incorporated these lessons into this book. Additionally, I have liberally cited the beautiful research that has been done by workers in the trauma and neglect fields to assist the understanding of how best to help children. The vignettes in the therapy section should also help parent readers recognize the process of change in families like theirs.

Nurturing Adoptions describes therapeutic techniques and case examples for children who have early neglect. Many neglected children have difficulties later with anxiety, emotional regulation, emotional attunement, and reflective thought. Ways to stretch brittle emotional states and to develop reciprocity are detailed. This book describes ways to understand how neglect has altered the development of such children. Then it describes ways to remediate this.

Attaching in Adoption (Gray, 2012) was written for parents, with the understanding that professionals could also use and enjoy it. The material in *Nurturing Adoptions* does not duplicate the information in *Attaching in Adoption*. Instead, they are companion books, *Nurturing Adoptions* giving an updated map for successful professional practices—bringing children in the placement journey all the way home. It is understood that parents will be reading over the shoulders of professionals throughout these chapters.

All too often individual parents are forging trails to services, feeling like lonely pioneers, burdened with finding appropriate services in a timely way. All the trail markers are written in a different language, i.e. psychobabble. Many commonalities shared between parents in terms of problems and resource needs are described in this book, as well as the professional supports necessary to undergird success in these families.

Child welfare workers have not been left out. *Nurturing Adoptions* covers not only the issues of neglect/trauma, but also goes on to discuss how to move children, prepare parents for placement, and make assessments during home studies. Templates are provided for community mental health workers who may be seeing children from the foster care system who will be adopted by their foster parents. The methods suggested in this book fit well into typical outpatient mental health practices.

There is no question that an increase in adoptions of maltreated children is a societal advance. *Nurturing Adoptions* assists the child welfare field's trend by updating practices in therapy and casework that respond to the changing adoption population. For placement professionals, this book identifies capacities needed by adoptive parents who will be parenting children with trauma and neglect and methods of assessing those capacities in home studies. It provides parent preparation guidance for placement professionals as they help families to identify and use capabilities that provide long-term benefits for children.

Theoretically, psychodynamic and cognitive behavioral approaches co-exist. Family systems approaches are used with families. Developmentalists will see approaches best described as applied developmental psychology. Evidenced-based practices are used as the preferred treatments throughout the book. Readers familiar with coercive techniques will find them singularly absent from *Nurturing Adoptions*. The reasons go beyond widely shared ethical concerns. Coercive techniques are contraindicated due to the effects that neglect and trauma have had on the brains of the children about whom this book was written.

Vignettes and case examples are used throughout the book to capture the flavor of the successful parent-professional teamwork that makes for best practices for children. The stories give a voice to children who are on a healing path. Their voices give encouragement to all of us in the field, reminding us to give them not just a good start in their families, but an excellent future.

PART ONE

The Issues of Neglect and Trauma in Today's Adoptions

In a survey by Harvard University and the Casey Family Programs, foster teens were observed to move into adulthood with post-traumatic stress disorder (PTSD) at a rate that was five times that of PTSD in the general population (Pecora, et al., 2005). This surveyed group is similar to the group from which many parents will be adopting. The compounding effect of early neglect with other types of maltreatment seems to be potent in reducing resiliency in children. Part One explores these interrelationships that are critical to address when helping children.

Part One details the reasons why children need to be helped as quickly as possible after trauma. A "wait and see" attitude in seeking professional help for trauma defies research and experience. It plays to the illusion that children can get over and forget anything—especially since they are so young. On the contrary, children are especially impacted—because they are so young.

Nurturing Adoptions has been purposefully divided into two sections. The first section defines the problems of neglect, trauma, and complex trauma often seen in children adopted after multiple moves or from institutional settings, and details the reasons why children need to be helped as quickly as possible after trauma.

The chapters in the second half of the book will look at methods of working, given these interrelationships. Individuals whose learning style leans to learning the "how to" before the "why to" are welcome to turn now to the second half of the book, reading the two sections in reverse order.

CHAPTER 1

The Changing Nature of Adoption

A doption, both domestic and international, has changed dramatically in just one generation. Increasing numbers of children enter new homes after having experienced trauma and neglect in families or in orphanages throughout the world. Trauma and neglect are not adoption issues by themselves—indeed they are pre-adoption issues—but they are of special interest to the adoption community because of their prevalence in today's adopted children. In the same way that triad issues were of special interest thirty years ago, resulting in new and developing literature at that time, issues stemming from early maltreatment[1] undergirds modern, developing adoption literature.

Domestic Adoption in the Early 21st Century

According to a 2006 report by the North American Council on Adoptable Children, about 140,000 children are adopted in the United States annually. About 10% of these children were infants whose parents made voluntary adoption plans. Semi-open or fully

---

[1] Throughout the book the term *maltreatment* will be used. The term refers to one or more of the following: neglect, physical, emotional, and sexual abuse.

disclosed adoptions are more common than confidential adoptions (NACAC, 2006).

Contrast these numbers with 1970's adoptions, when there were 172,000 children adopted in the United States. Almost all were infants whose parents made confidential, voluntary adoption plans. There were few children adopted after trauma and neglect, since adoptees were mostly newborns.

Since the 1970s AFCARS Reporting shows that the rate of newborn adoption has dropped steadily, while the adoption rate from foster care has surged. AFCARS, or the Adoption and Foster Care Analysis and Reporting System, is a federal data collection effort that provides child-specific information on all children covered by the protections of Title IV-B and Title IV-E of the Social Security Act. On an annual basis, all states submit data to the U.S. Children's Bureau, concerning each child in foster care and each child who has been adopted under the authority of the state's child welfare agencies. The AFCARS databases have been designed to address adoption and foster care policy development and program management issues at both the state and federal levels. About 50,000 children were adopted from foster care in 2003. The reporting of final numbers comes in slowly, but statistical sampling shows that that level seems to be holding steady. The average age of children being adopted from foster care in 2003 was 7.0 years and the median age was 6.1 years. Showing public policy commitment and hard work on the part of social workers, that number had climbed from 36,000 children adopted from substitute care in 1998. Of the children adopted from the foster care system, 87% qualified for a special needs assistance package.

There were 119,000 children waiting in foster care to be adopted in the United States in 2006. Their average age was 8.6 years, and the median was 8.7 years old. Today the number of children waiting for adoption is at a relatively steady level, with one child becoming legally free for adoption as another one child is adopted (AFCARS, 2006, pp. 3-10).

While poly-drug and alcohol abuse have always been issues for child welfare, the successive epidemics of cocaine, crack cocaine, and methamphetamines have escalated the rates of severe maltreatment in young children. Children, as a group, are entering the foster care system with more serious neglect than in generations past.

International Adoption in the Early 21ˢᵗ Century

There have been similarly dramatic changes in international adoption. About 23,000 children were adopted internationally in 2005. The number of internationally adopted children has tripled over the previous fifteen years.

These selected years show the trends in the number of international adoptions in the United States.

Table 1-1

Number of Children Adopted to the U.S. from Other Countries by Fiscal Year			
FY 1990	FY 2000	FY 2004	FY 2005
7,093	17,718	22,884	22,728

During this same period, the countries of origin have also shifted.

Table 1-2

Top Six Countries from Which Children Were Adopted to the United States	
FY 1990	FY 2005
2,620 Korea	7,906 China
631 Columbia	4,639 Russia
440 Peru	3,783 Guatemala
421 Philippines	1,630 Korea
348 India	755 Kazakhstan
302 Chile	441 Ethiopia

International adoptions, like domestic adoptions, show a trend towards children being adopted later in infancy/childhood. However, internationally adopted children, as a group, are markedly younger than children adopted from foster care. Of the total children internationally adopted, 10,113 children were between 1 and 4 years old and 3,537 were older than 5 years old. (The differences in the manner in which statistics were collected do not allow for an average age.) Additionally, the gender differences were remarkable, with about two girls adopted to every boy (U. S. Department of Homeland Security, 2007).

There are uncertainties about how the international Hague Convention Treaty guidelines and the 2007 implementation of those guidelines under rules set by the United States may impact the numbers of children coming to the U.S. through international adoption.[2] The House of Representatives Hearings on International Adoption Guidelines held on November 14, 2006 revealed that agencies were quickly preparing for the new regulations (Barry, Scialabba, 2006). The trend towards adoption from countries without a tradition of family foster care and with third world health conditions continues.

Changes in Adoptive Families in the Early 21st Century

During this same period there have been substantial changes in adoptive parents. Social changes are prompting people to build families later. There is an increase in treatment options for older women, so that couples adopting due to infertility are significantly older than they were a generation ago. The rate of divorce and second marriages as well as the related increase in the age differential within married couples means that it is not uncommon for one or both potential adoptive parents to be in their late 40s and up to late 50s. Sometimes there are much older half siblings connected to very young adopted siblings.

Age can contribute to whether singles or couples choose to adopt independently as opposed to from private agencies, whether they

---

[2] Specifics of the 2007 Hague Convention accreditation and approval regulations may be found at www.gpoaccess.gove/fr/search.html and entering, "Hague Convention on Intercountry Adoption" in the search field. Social workers and parents are encouraged to review this website.

choose to adopt internationally as opposed to domestically, and, when adopting internationally, can influence from which country they choose to adopt.

About 80% of families who adopt internationally do so after infertility (AFCARS, 2006). Families who are adopting internationally are building families. They will look at another option if opportunities for international adoption dip because of changes in the international guidelines. The probable result is that the number of families adopting domestically from foster care is likely to increase if international adoption opportunities decrease. About half of two-parent families adopting from foster care are doing so after issues of infertility. And, half of the parents adopting older children are first-time parents (AFCARS Report, 2006).

The trend toward kinship care, or placing at-risk children with grandparents, aunts, uncles and other relatives after they are re-moved from abusive or neglectful environments, represents about 25% of adoptions from foster care. This is another contributor to an older cadre of adoptive parents. This group tends to be less prepared or supported in facing the challenges ahead (AFCARS Report, 2006).

More singles are adopting than ever before. Notably, now over 30% of those adopting from the foster care system are single par-ents. This means that the support systems that include an automatic passing of the baton back and forth between two parents needs to be intentionally bolstered for single parent families

While there have been gay and lesbian people adopting for some time, most adopted as single parents in a "don't ask, don't tell" en-vironment. Today more and more agencies are placing children in two-parent openly gay and lesbian families.

Changes in Adoption's Impact on Child-Placing and Mental Health Professionals

The statistics from both domestic and international adoption give a clear take-home message for professionals working with adoption issues:

- The children being adopted include many older children who have had and lost parent figures. They will have grief issues, having lost attachment figures.
- These children's rates of neglect and maltreatment are higher than rates in past decades.
- Many of today's adoptive parents are single parents. They need more intentional supports built into their parenting plans.
- Many adopting parents will have parented biologically before. Their expectations about the value of their parenting skills with traumatized children may be unrealistic.
- Parents need to be prepared for the effects of neglect/trauma and familiarized with the treatments for problems caused by neglect and trauma.

As adoption has become far more complex, therapists and caseworkers have had to master specialized practice areas including prenatal exposure, trauma, and attachment, in addition to their adoption-specific expertise.

The child welfare community is struggling to develop a proactive approach for families who are parenting children placed after trauma and neglect or other influences that have altered children's developmental pathways. But the issues surrounding trauma and neglect are complicated. Even after understanding the consequences of trauma and neglect, creating practical suggestions for families can seem overwhelming to agencies and to therapists.

It is imperative that user-friendly information about trauma and neglect become available to parents as part of the placement process. It is also necessary for child therapists to be aware of and use therapies most effective for this population. Major findings of the Casey Project were that many children were not getting mental health treatment at all, or they were not treated appropriately with evidence-based therapies, such as using cognitive-behavioral approaches for traumatic stress (Pecora, et al., 2005).

Therapists must adapt their therapy models to include therapies suitable for children who have been prenatally exposed to substances and/or deprived of attachment-producing and sensory-stretching relationships by neglect. While children's psychotherapists do have sound information about trauma treatment in children, most have less exposure to specific information about later-placed adoption. *They struggle to understand how to integrate specific attachment-related or adoption-related information into treatment models which were originally developed for use with children in the continuous care of their biologic families.*

Child placement experts, on the other hand, are much more likely to have mastered the issues of adjustment in later-placed adoptions and know some techniques for forming attachment. But they are less likely to recognize the ominous symptom clusters of trauma and traumatic stress. They are missing signs simply because they do not know what to look for.

At the same time, all children's specialists are attempting to get up to speed with the emerging literature and practice area of neglect.

As a first step toward the overall goals of laying out information for effective work for both specialties, a foundation must be laid for an understanding of trauma and neglect as they impact development in children and their families. The next chapter describes trauma and traumatic stress from the unique perspective of children who are affected while they are also changing homes or have attachment challenges. It intentionally builds a bridge connecting the trauma issues with reduced capacities to tolerate stress in children who are entering new families after maltreatment in other care settings. Other chapters will successively build on this base.

CHAPTER 2

Trauma, Stress, and Post Traumatic Stress Disorder— Interrelationships

"The concept of trauma, which is by definition psycho biological, is a bridge between the domains of both mind and body."   –Allan Schore

"The longstanding nature versus nurture debate is obsolete...the question is...how early experience and genetic predisposition interact."   –Paul Wang, M.D.

Why do so many children show extreme feelings and behaviors, even after years of placement in stable, loving families? Why do their families seem so exhausted by their children, struggling to establish the simplest of daily routines? Why do children with early maltreatment make poor progress in therapy? What makes some children so past-oriented and fearful, and others so lacking in self-reflection or insight? What issues are agencies missing in their preparation of parents-to-be during the placement process?

This chapter demonstrates that trauma shapes the developing brain as well as early personality development in a dramatic and negative manner. The chapter establishes a foundation for the intentional and focused methods for helping children, as described in the rest of the book.

Stress and Stress Regulation in Infant and Child Development

What is "stressful"?

How do children cope with stress?

How much stress is too much stress for a child or an adult?

The answers to these questions are common sense "no brainers" for people who have been raised in relatively healthy homes. Their own childhood experiences tend to give answers that will guide them in parenting. But the answers become complex, and it is difficult to understand stress and its effects on a child who has been traumatized and/or neglected. Some of the common sense solutions just do not work well for these kids, or they do on some days and not on others. How do we best help these children? A working knowledge of stress and its effects undergrids skillful placements, therapies, and parenting.

Stress regulation simply means controlling stress levels. The concept of *regulation of stress* usually refers to a person's meeting the challenge of a stressful event without becoming overwhelmed. Some stress is positive, and well within normal limits. Examples of positive stressors are biking, going to a birthday party, running a race, or finishing a report.

Stressors become negative when they involve unpleasant events, overstimulating events, or when they require mental or emotional capacities that exceed a child's developmental stage. Widely experienced negative stressors include hospitalizations, immunizations, humiliating sports mistakes, academic struggles because of learning issues, chronic pain, arguments, financial problems, and emotional losses like death and separation. Optimally, people will have a support system around them during these experiences. Optimally, they will not have too many negative stressors occurring within a short time period.

But children in adverse settings experience many stressors. Often one becomes the final straw. Lily, age 8, described one such event.

> "I was with my mother and sisters when my mom got really mad at Bill, her boyfriend. He left with our car. We were camping then because we did not have a place to live that summer. We camped—even when it rained. We had to keep moving campsites because they would kick us out. But after Bill left, we didn't have a car. So we had to carry everything down the road to this new place. I had to carry a whole lot of stuff and when I dropped it, my mom and sisters got really mad. I couldn't carry the bags any more. Sometimes I think that that was when my mother was like, 'This is too much. I can't take care of Lily.'"

Another child described the stress of living short-term with a relative who was related to his brother, but not to him. Kyle, who was 7 years old, said,

> "I wanted to know if they would give me some money for school lunch and school supplies, too. I asked my brother to ask them because they liked him better. They said, 'No.' So I didn't know what I would do without any backpack or lunch. My brother just said to go to school and see if they would give me a backpack. Instead, I said that I forgot mine, because I did not want to tell them all the stuff about where my parents were. I kept getting in trouble for forgetting."

Typically, stressors cause people to become emotionally aroused and able to release a reserve of energy in order to meet the challenge of the stressor. But people's tolerance to high-stress is time-limited. They need to find the ability to cope with the stressor, and return to a comfortable, less stressed state within a reasonable length of time. Hurrying to catch a bus or plane are examples of typical stressors that are time-limited. But in the examples of Lily and Kyle above, there is evidence of a longer-term chronic stress. Even though the children are mobilizing to meet stress, the parent figures are not reducing the stress levels for them so that they develop biologic regulation. They are feeling stressed because they cannot depend on adults to keep them within a tolerable limit.

In interviewing a 15-year-old girl in my office with experiences similar to Kyle's and Lily's above, I asked how therapy in her early elementary years had influenced her development. "If I didn't get it, I bet I'd be mean. I was hurt so I was just passing it on. I'm a lot nicer now. I used to be scared, well, all of the time. I'm able to relax now and enjoy my life—except for chores, that is."

This chronic stress with the accompanying fear and anger is typical for maltreated children prior to treatment.

Stress and Neural Firing Patterns in Infancy and Early Years

Our society collectively understands that children do not have a mature resilience to stress. They need some help in tolerating stress even on typical days. Naps, a cuddle on a parent's lap, a drink of juice, or recess are all ways of handling stress. In healthy homes, a significant part of a parent's day includes buffering children from, or calming after too much stress.

Optimally children are kept in a regulated state by their parents. Separations from caregivers are typically stressful for children. Children are immature in their abilities to be away from the person who helps "recharge" them. A 4-year-old is often unable to tolerate the stress of full-time school that 7-year-olds take in stride. As childhood progresses, the capability for managing stress without a parent matures, allowing for longer school days and more time outside of the parents' care.

In optimal situations, emotionally healthy and sensitive parents positively shape their children's stress regulation systems. Infants' or children's neural firing patterns are met by the parent's regulated neural firing patterns. As the adage goes, neurons that fire together, wire together. Over time, the parent's neural firing patterns are imbedded into the infant's developing brain. As Schore says, "Parents download their neural firing patterns...limbic system to limbic system" (2002).

Infants who have the good luck to be with a sensitive and emotionally healthy parent learn a comfortable up and down, zigzag pattern of arousal. Emma, aged two, is an example of this.

> Emma goes to the children's zoo. She crows at seeing the donkey, approaches it while being held, touches the donkey's back, takes a delicious, deep breath, looks at her parent's face and eyes, shares the feelings of excitement and joy, laughs, and then turns away to calm down. She repeats the sequence with her parent.
>
> On the walk to the car, she gets irritated by the dreaded portable stroller, arches against it, wails, responds a little to the parent's urgent soothing, howls in earnest, reaches the car, and gets picked up and soothed. Then she sighs and smiles weakly, tears still on cheeks. She sucks on a sippy cup, with the parent saying something in a rhythmical manner, like, "There, there, you're all right. Did you have a big day?" Again, the parent and the child share the experience and their feelings.

Throughout these experiences Emma is learning to anticipate her parent's help in calming. She learns to stay within her ability to tolerate stress. In time, the parent's vocal tones and comments will be incorporated into part of the self-soothing in Emma's developing brain.

Trauma and Stress Regulation

Trauma stuns, shatters, or shuts down a person's abilities to comprehend, feel, or process. In traumatic stress reactions, people describe feeling as if they are out of their bodies, as if time has slowed down, and as if they are watching and re-watching the traumatic event over and over. They note feeling powerless and helpless. Traumatic events do not integrate well or positively into a person's schema of how life works. People need a lot of support and processing to comprehend what happened to them and why.

A traumatic stress reaction is a normal reaction to an abnormal event. The American Psychological Association describes a traumatic event as "an event that is outside the range of usual human experience and that would be markedly distressing to almost anyone" (APA, 2000, p.468).

Trauma leaves a symptom cluster that includes four main components:

- Intrusive memories, night terrors, or flashbacks—flashbacks (being defined as frightening memories, images, or feelings related to memories) keep occurring even though they are unrelated to what is current reality.
- Emotional numbness or dissociation—dissociation means that individuals stop processing or integrating their feelings or the meaning of events because they are overwhelmed. They may have reminders of trauma that swing them into being overwhelmed. Children look frozen, dazed, or "spacey."
- Affective dysregulation—this means that a person's moods fluctuate more than daily events explain. Moods swing widely. This includes aggression.
- Somatization—this is defined as feeling bodily distress that signals that something is wrong. Yet, there is no physical explanation for the headaches, stomach problems, and other ailments.

Often caseworkers do not know, and therefore cannot teach parents, that this is a symptom cluster that means that the child's development has been dramatically and negatively impacted. Each of the symptoms above will be described in Chapter 4.

And all of the damage is not summarized in the symptom list; trauma leaves people with reduced abilities for meaningful connections and emotional attunement. Children are so contracted by their efforts to escape danger or reminders of danger that they cannot open themselves up for close relationships. Significantly, if children are under the age of 5 when they are traumatized, then the rates of symptoms in the above four symptom areas are all measured above the 90th percentile by the time they reach adulthood (van der Kolk, 2002).

In other words, trauma at an early age remains and shapes personality and development over successive years. The passage of time for these little ones does not in itself reduce trauma's impact to a bearable level. The rates of symptoms in children who have been traumatized by abuse under the age of 14 include the following:

- 77% reported affective dysregulation or anger problems
- 80% were dissociative
- 54% described chronic pain
- 66% reported being or having been suicidal
- 75% experienced hopelessness (van der Kolk, 1994).

(Statistics were gathered prior to treatment.)

Why are these rates so high?

One reason is that the trauma is occurring in a personality that is not yet formed. The trauma contaminates the meaning of life and is part of early personality formation. It influences how people think of the world and themselves.

Neurobiologically, trauma shapes the developing brain. Early high stress is especially damaging because brain development is in such an early stage. (This is discussed in more depth later in the chapter.) Many children experience not only isolated traumatic events, but a life filled with daily traumas. As one 8-year-old boy said to me,

"Every night someone tried to take my blanket. Big kids jumped on my back and laughed. I cried. They took my food. I took other little kids' food and their blankets. I was afraid and mad all of the time."

Yet another reason behind the profound impacts is that these children don't have parents who are helping them with safety and calming before, during, or after trauma. And, in fact, the children are often traumatized by the very person who is to be providing safety. The next section summarizes some of the effects on children's views of themselves in early developmental stages.

Chronic Trauma, Complex Trauma, and PTSD by Definition

Trauma, by definition, is an event or series of events that shatters the threshold of tolerance for people. Traumatized people feel that they are in danger, or that they are watching someone else in acute danger. It is a sensory shattering. Our eyes, ears, skin, or nose are conveying information that we cannot stand to process.

An *acute trauma*—a one-time event like a weather disaster, a car wreck, a rape, witnessing a murder, and so forth—is what most of us think about when we think of trauma. Acute traumas are expected to give symptoms both during and after. By definition, people who experience acute trauma have cleared most of the symptoms that are giving them trouble with day-to-day functioning in one month. The ones who do not tend to bounce back are people with earlier traumas and/or backgrounds of maltreatment. These people tend to move into a post traumatic stress disorder (PTSD).

Some of the children we are talking about here have had acute traumas. Many of them instead, or in addition to, have had chronic trauma. *Chronic trauma* is a lifestyle that is marked with traumatic events. Children who have been in domestic and international placements have often experienced chronic trauma. Children who have been in homes in which the parents beat on each other, used children as sexual partners, contain psychologically wounded family members without emotional repair, or physically abusive family members when drunk or under the influence of meth or crack, have experienced chronic trauma. Children who have been hungry, cold, handled roughly, or sexually assaulted at night in unwatched orphanage wards have all endured chronic trauma.

The National Child Traumatic Stress Taskforce defines *complex trauma* as "exposure to multiple traumatic events that occur within the family and community systems…that are chronic and begin in early childhood" (Cook, Blaustein, Spinnazola, and van der Kolk, 2003, p.3). Complex trauma has far reaching effects on child development. It is the outcome of chronic trauma and/or exposure to multiple traumas. A chart by the researchers cited above demonstrates the pervasive impairments.

Table 2-1

A Summary of Impairments of Children Exposed to Complex Trauma as Reported by the Complex Trauma Taskforce in 2003 *(Cook, Blaustein, Spinazzola, and van der Kolk, 2003, p.2)*	
Attachment	Boundary problems Social Isolation Difficulty Trusting Others Interpersonal Difficulty
Biology	Sensorimotor Developmental Problems Hypersensitivity to Physical Contact Somatization Increased Medical Problems Problems with Coordination and Balance
Affect Regulation	Problems with Emotional Regulation Difficulty Describing Emotions and Internal Experiences Difficulty Knowing and Describing Internal States Problems with Communicating Needs
Behavioral Control	Poor Impulse Control Self Destructive Behavior Aggressive Behavior Oppositional Behavior Excessive Compliance Sleep Disturbance Eating Disorders Substance Abuse Re-enactment of Traumatic Past Pathological Self Soothing Practices
Cognition	Difficulty Paying Attention Lack of Sustained Curiosity Problems Processing Information Problems Focusing on and Completing Tasks Difficulty Planning and Anticipating Learning Difficulties Problems with Language Development

A Summary of Impairments of Children Exposed to Complex Trauma as Reported by the Complex Trauma Taskforce in 2003 *(Cook, Blaustein, Spinazzola, and van der Kolk, 2003, p.2)*	
Self Concept	Lack of Continuous and Predictable Sense of Self Poor Sense of Separateness Disturbance of Body Image Low Sense of Self Esteem Shame and Guilt

Children will need intentional home and professional care to redress the areas described above. There will need to be much more support for these children than for people who are processing a single trauma.

One father, traumatized as a young adult, did his trauma counseling soon after the trauma and finished his process in about six months. He concluded his work with some desensitization and reprocessing through a technique called EMDR, which helped with a few resistant reminders of trauma. It was hard for him to understand why his son could not follow the same course. Guided by the internet, he sent his son for EMDR to an individual who was not skilled in other relevant issues. The young teen needed help with traumas of sexual abuse, abrupt and traumatic placements, physical abuse, and domestic violence. The teen found that EMDR was not successful in reducing the pain, but pot, alcohol, and then cocaine were. The teen had to attend a residential treatment facility to treat addiction and then move back into appropriate therapy.

Complex traumatic stress, or complex PTSD,[1] denotes the presence of chronic or multiple traumas, especially with attachment

---

[1] The definitions that are included in the *Diagnostic and Statistical Manual*, or DSM IV-TR reflect that the foundational work on traumatic stress has been traumatic stress in adults, not children. Children experience trauma differently, so can be significantly distressed without meeting the current definition for PTSD. There is work being done to redress this problem, including the efforts by the cited task force.

challenges, and their effects on the development of personality and neurological makeup. Recovering from complex traumatic stress necessitates the type of help that includes ample support and guidance in building personal connections, stress regulation/reduction, transforming the meaning of trauma to the sense of self, creating problem-solving strategies, de-sensitizing to the reminders of trauma, and expanding reflective thought. This is a daunting list. It takes time to successfully treat this type of complex trauma.

> As one parent said after we discussed the treatment plan, "Deborah, it's a good thing that we get along well, because it seems like I will be seeing a lot of you over the next two years with my boys!"

While I certainly believe that children should not have to be in therapy indefinitely, any treatment plan should address the issues as described in the chart above. It is helpful to avoid comparing children who have chronic trauma to those with simple trauma. I typically suggest that parents avoid subjecting themselves to people who have no experience with complex traumatic stress, but who still freely dispense advice based on experience with people from dissimilar backgrounds.

What Predicts Success in Recovering from Trauma's Effects?

The quality of close relationships is the factor that most accurately predicts which people will go on to develop the long-term symptom patterns of PTSD after a trauma (van der Kolk, 2002). Children who experience a sense of safety with a parent learn to calm with that person. They borrow from their caregiver's coping abilities, and use that person as a base as they calm and feel safe. Even if the parent is not available, they remember the soothing of their attachment figure and use that to reduce their stress level right after the trauma. This soothing is part of the early imbedding of the parent's stress regulation, as discussed earlier.

The key to determining who recovers after trauma, then, lies in the ability to control levels of emotional arousal. In other words, the person who can calm herself down or talk herself through situations is likely to recover. The key determinant behind this capacity is early attachment experiences. Those with competent parent figures in early childhood develop early competence in calming themselves, thus controlling emotional arousal. In stressful situations, including trauma, these people are using the skills learned in early childhood to calm themselves (or not) and to reassure themselves (or not). They are also are more likely to reach out to others for support and help.

Children who are the subject of this book rarely have had secure attachments with parent figures prior to placement. Adoptive parents must understand that they will have to teach their children soothing, calming, and emotional regulation through their attachment relationship. Therapists should be assisting that developmental process. Caseworkers will have the obligation to place children into homes that are prepared for and competent to help in these emotional processes.

Differences in Resilience after Trauma

People who have had relatively safe lives, with competent caregivers to help them develop reasonable stress regulation systems, are more likely to have the capacity to gradually process awful events and to incorporate them without personality damage. "What distinguishes people who develop PTSD from people who are merely temporarily stressed is that (the former) start organizing their lives around the trauma" (van der Kolk, 1996, p.6).

Children with PTSD lack the ability to handle the event mentally and therefore must avoid reminders of the trauma. This causes extreme problems in dealing with daily situations such as having a teacher who reminds the child of the emergency room physician who treated their arm broken by abuse, having a police officer at the school grounds who reminds them of the night they were picked up by Child Protective Services, or being served the dinner similar to the menu served the night of the trauma of seeing their mother beaten.

Even children who had a competent caregiver before being traumatized are at special risk after trauma because their stress regulation systems are not fully developed. In fact, their stress regulation systems are thwarted in their development due to exposure to trauma.

Traumatized children arc off onto a developmental pathway that is one of dysregulation rather than continuing the normal process which would result in increasing amounts of self-control as they grow older. Traumatized children's knowledge about themselves is not developed either. They incorporate trauma into their self-identity. They think, "I am the kind of person that things like this happen to. There is something about me that draws these events."

Another potent distortion after early trauma is the assumption that "They must be right and I must be wrong, since they are so powerful. I should not regard my own feelings, but instead should be observant of their feelings." This is a set-up for future high-risk situations and/or relationships. And, in fact, Cloitre's work has shown that 65% percent of rape victims have been maltreated as children (2003). By focusing on the feelings of others as a survival mode, traumatized people miss how interactions relate to their self-interest. They ignore their feelings about whether they are safe and comfortable, or scared and anxious, or whether they are being set-up or treated with respect.

Additionally, often the trauma has been layered with meanings related to their relationships and sense of self. It is critical to recognize that it is not just the traumatic event that needs to be addressed in treating traumatized children. *It is the meaning of the event to the child's sense of self and to the fabric of relationships in children's lives.* The example of nine-year-old Natasha in describing an event two years earlier shows the complexity of trauma.

> "My father was drunk. He kicked my little brother in the back. Then my mother yelled at him, 'Stop!' She put Dad's picture in the fireplace. It was burning up and she said that she was leaving with the baby. Dad chased her and hit my mother on the head with a board. I could not move. My mom was crying and ran down the road that night with the baby. She left us with Dad. In the morning Dad got in his truck,

locking my brother and me outside. My mother did not come home. It was still winter and we were freezing. It was getting dark. We heard dogs barking and howling, so we hid under the boards of a shed that fell down. We stayed there all night waiting for Dad to come home.

"We were starving and my little brother was crying because his back hurt from where my dad kicked him. I told him, 'Be quiet! The dogs will hear you and come get us!' We heard my dad's truck the next morning and ran to the house. He said nothing! Nothing like he was sorry. He spent all of our money and didn't bring any food. He was drunk and went to bed. I walked a long way to our neighbors and asked them for food and where was my mom? Then guys from the orphanage came and got my brother and took us in a big van to the orphanage. People could see us. My dad came to visit me and cried for what he did. I would not look at him. My mother came to see my brother, but did not come to see me."

At this point, I asked her, "I am wondering if you are worried that part of this is your fault somehow?"

Natasha's eyes filled with tears and she choked out, "I think that it was my fault for going to the neighbors. We were starving and I was mad at my parents. But I wanted them to get in trouble, not to go away forever. Now I will never get a chance to say goodbye to my mom." Natasha's adoptive mom held her close while she cried.

This vignette illustrates the multi-layered meaning of children's traumas. The traumas are interwoven with feelings about close relationships. The source of the trauma can be the very person who was supposed to be keeping the child safe. Traumas may occur early in life, before children have a good sense of how the world works. They involve complex relationship issues. Their experience is usually full of information potent to their sense of self. For example, Natasha perceived herself as a "failure" as a sister and as a daughter. She had not acted effectively as a surrogate mom. Usually there are mixed feelings, like anger and regret after "telling" on parents.

Natasha's initial telling of the story to her adoptive parents had been numb and wooden. She had not integrated the feelings of the event. In fact, her adoptive father had said, "I think that she's pretty tough. I don't think that she lets it get to her."

Sadly, the reality was the opposite. The experience had been so overwhelming that Natasha was robotic in describing it. She could not revisit any of the feelings without believing that she was back in the event—re-experiencing the trauma. Additionally, she was filled with grief and shame at her part of the story. When her helplessness in enduring the event had turned to initiative, it had resulted in the permanent loss of both parents. Natasha's conclusion was that she should not show initiative. In her daily life, she was better at enduring than at trying hard. After two years in an orphanage, that initiative was further reduced.

While children certainly suffer even without adoption and foster care, the case above illustrates the layering of meaning when adding placement issues to trauma. Natasha had never developed a sturdy stress regulation system. She reported that her birthmother left her alone for days or even a week at a time. She was already compromised in her capacity to withstand stress. She learned an adaptive response of just waiting helplessly, rather than showing initiative. When she did try to vary the pattern, she lost her birthparents.

Natasha felt fear and shame around her maltreatment and her adjustment to a new family. She needed to learn and to meet expectations in the family, even while she was limited by a pattern of dissociating or avoiding life challenges. She had never learned how to problem-solve, or to receive help when dealing with the frustrations of life. Natasha chose instead to avoid the issues that came up. This resulted in an annoying avoidance that ranged from lying and hiding wet underwear to throwing away difficult schoolwork.

Avoidance of trauma-related themes and frustrating problems is characteristic of maltreated children coming into adoptive families. They do not expect that they can go to adults in order to calm down or to get help when life exceeds their capabilities. And, even when they do go to adults, it is harder for them to calm themselves with parents since they are still learning to trust in their parents' capabilities.

Talking to children about the role of parents as helpers should be done in a scripted, specific manner, not just a general one. An example of this scripting:

"Come get me or call if you are having a bad dream. I want to help you feel safe again. So, what are you going to say?"

The child may answer hesitantly, "Ah, come please."

The parent says with emotion, "Yes. But yell a little louder. Like, '**Come here. There is the ghost from Scooby Doo under my bed! I'm scared.**'"

At this they might both giggle, then the parent says, "You try it."

The child says, often putting some of her own fears in the exercise unwittingly, "**Dad, there is a bad guy. Come quick and save me from this stinky guy.**"

These scripts help to lock the "parents as helpers" concept into the memory system.

Effects of Trauma on Children Stage by Stage

The following developmental stages are laid out successively with approximate age ranges in months. The range of months is meant as a guide. When children have been previously moved and/or neglected, they may be in the age range for the stage, but will show delays. They will be emotionally younger, not having reached the emotional development typical of their chronological age. Readers can correct back by looking at the needs and milestones of an earlier stage.

The significance of this information is of great interest to a variety of disciplines. As Schore writes in his seminal book, *Affect Dysregulation*, "A body of interdisciplinary research demonstrates that the essential experiences that shape the individual's patterns of coping responses are forged in the emotion-transacting caregiver-infant relationship...We are beginning to understand, at a psychobiological level, specifically how beneficial early experiences enhance and detrimental early histories inhibit the development of the brain's active and passive stress coping mechanisms" (2003, p.185).

Phase I: Birth through 7 months of life

This stage produces children's first adaptations to the world. Babies are wired during this stage to be welcomed, soothed, and socialized—or to be worried, fussy, reactive, frozen and watchful, or "still-faced." *Still-faced* describes an early form of dissociation, also called *conservation withdrawal*, in which infants freeze in silence so that they are not noticed and can avoid detection.

Ideally, parents organize children's feelings on a micro level at this early stage. They are micro-organizing beacons of orientation for
- attention-focusing
- affective-transmitting
- social referencing.

In other words, children look to parents to know
- what is important to attend to
- what to feel about it
- what to think and feel about other people and themselves.

Parents give emotional meanings to daily events. This information transmission happens even if the parents are sharing material which is overwhelming and stressful or traumatic for children. If children do not have parental attention, they do not get the benefit of a parent's organization of feelings, their help in focusing attention, or their guidance in reaching out to one another socially. Whichever areas are missing during these crucial months of development will become the areas that must be intentionally brought along later in childhood by adoptive parents and professionals. (This theme is explored more in Chapter 3 on neglect.)

An infant's needs at this stage include
- parent(s) who are socially responsive—wiring the baby for social and emotional interactions
- a buffered, or protective, setting. When the baby's hunger, loneliness, fear, tiredness/overstimulation, or pain are met by an effective parent, this helps to reduce these problems

- the feeling that she is safe and that her parents are as well
- the ability to learn to be curious and playful, by having parents who are able to be engaged and responsive
- parents who can increasingly move the little one into a settled routine over the first few months of life.

The infant's neuroendocrine levels are kept in regulation with his or her primary caregiver's neuroendrocrine levels during months three to six. A sudden move from the caregiver will result in massive disequilibrium in their neuroendrocrine levels (Dozier, et al., 2006). Certainly this does not mean that such children should not be moved out of situations of maltreatment, but <u>sudden</u> shifts are to be avoided. (See Chapter 10 on moving children.)

The child who has been traumatized, whether by neglect or abuse, will not have regulated moods, even by the standards of this early age. He will already show *conservation withdrawal*. After trauma, babies will startle easily, seem anxious and wary, freeze easily, and often show eating and sleeping problems. They may withdraw and seem harder to connect with. Parents who are trying to form attachments with children of this age do best with built-in, intentional support systems so that they can continue to be sensitive and patient (Bates, Dozier, 2002).

Phase II: 7 to 18 months

This is typically the stage in which an exclusive attachment to a parent forms. It is also a time of increased vulnerability to developing borderline/PTSD personality disorder. (Please see the appendix for this definition.)

Babies at this stage need

- a consistent and nurturing parent who is emotionally available to the little one. Separations of more than a day should be avoided unless they are emergencies.
- a parent who can be patient with the baby's need for proximity during this stage
- a safe home with parents who are neither frightened nor frightening
- parents who can celebrate the baby's movement into more mastery—standing, crawling, and speaking

- parents who are "in synch" at least 30% of the time—the definition of the "good enough" parent. That is the percentage that the parents need to aim for when creating an emotionally healthy environment (Fosha, 2004).
- parents who can stimulate language by speaking with and responding to their babies
- parents who continue to provide buffering and soothing, as well as play and social experiences.

In a safe environment that includes continuous care from nurturing caregivers, children feel safe and insulated from danger. Children who are traumatized at this stage learn to ready themselves for constant danger. In a curious adaptation, some babies and toddlers begin to adjust by lowering their level of alertness. They may have a low arousal level, which means that they do not seem to respond to normal stimulation. It takes much more to get their attention and involvement as compared to a baby without chronic trauma.

Other traumatized infants have high arousal; that is, they are always somewhat overstimulated and stressed. They move quickly into overarousal. They tend to show anxiety, quick startle, and anxious scanning. By the end of Phase II they feel shame.

By this stage, normally developing babies form a sense of attunement, or a feeling of being "in-synch" between family members and infants. They can easily share the same feelings, or affects. In nurturing contexts infants effectively use parents to help get back into balance. In adverse settings they follow parents' dysregulated states or enter their own dissociative states in response to an overwhelming world.

Trauma symptoms at this stage include

- sleep problems,
- over and under eating,
- growth problems caused by cortisterone's (CORT) inhibition of growth hormone (see Chapter 4),
- a dazed or shocked look, with rigid body, arched back, feet up to kick, elbows out,
- head butting instead of nestling when being held,
- night terrors and many large motor movements at night.

Phase III: 18 months to between 30 and 36 months

This is the stage in which most children begin to explore their worlds, moving out with curiosity! They are developing autonomy and a beginning sense of their own identities. They say "no" quite a bit, and love asserting their preferences. In nurturing settings they can use parents as a secure base from which to explore. They continue to need their parents to help organize their feelings and provide nurturing.

Toddlers think of themselves as good or bad by the end of this stage. Almost all maltreated children think of themselves as bad. In spite of the many positive things that people may say about them in terms of later accomplishments, trauma and neglect tend to be foundational in developing a poor self-image.

Needs for children at this stage are for

- close nurturing relationships with parents in order to support increasing exploration
- rules, so that children begin the process of learning limits and staying safe
- limits and expansion of empathy so that children learn to care and contain aggression
- new experiences that enhance mastery in play, speech, and social interactions with peers
- shared enjoyable activities between parents and children
- assistance from adults in building a positive gender and self identity as "good" and as a valuable family member
- opportunities to make choices or to say "no"
- the ability to retreat to parents or trusted adults when life feels overwhelming.

Trauma at this stage may lead a child to excessive protest or a learned helplessness. Sometimes children decide that cooperation doesn't work. Other children decide that opposition doesn't work either. They learn to display a freeze-and-surrender mode around adults or other children. Rituals and order are soothing to normal children in this stage. Play develops in this stage. Both play and rituals may become inhibited or exaggerated after trauma.

Behavioral symptoms of trauma at this developmental stage include

- nightmares
- avoidance of gaze
- difficulty calming
- freezing in place
- difficulty engaging socially
- difficulty knowing where her own body is or what it is feeling
- aggression: hitting, feet up, elbows out
- dissociation
- avoidance of certain trauma-related places or situations, i.e. the bath, belts, loud voices.

Phase IV: 30 to 36 months through 48 to 54 months

By this stage children have formed their beginning sense of self, and most are ready to enter the social world. They tend to have internalized their style of attachment and can form words that describe some of this mental schema. They may say things such as
"Will you play with me? We'll have fun."
"I want a hug!"
"Molly and me are friends. We like each other and play nicely."
"You are invited to my birthday party."
"That boy is crying. Where is his mommy or daddy?"

Or, they may observe,

"Ouch, don't hurt me."
"Molly touches my stuff."
"You can't come to my party if you don't stop that."
"Did his mommy hurt him? He's crying."
(There is more elaboration on attachment in Chapter 5.)

Compliance usually works well for children who feel that they are in a safe place with caring people. Alternately, when they are not in a safe environment, children tend to oppose, control, threaten, or hide, depending on their attachment pattern.

Children of this age are egocentric. Their world view is that "Everything that happens is because of me!" Therefore, they tend to incorporate any trauma into their identities. "I made this happen. I am the kind of person that things like this happen to."

Gender identity develops during this stage. Traumatized children may feel that being a boy or girl is "bad." Children think in terms of *big* and *little*. When traumatized, they often decide that big people are brutal and equate *big* with *mean*. After trauma children have more difficulty with peers. They often withdraw or control and bully. If trauma is a lifestyle, rather than an event, peer problems are particularly severe.

Children's needs at this stage include

- nurturing and sensitive parents who can help foster a positive self-identity
- a simple "what's different" for traumas that occurred. For example: "Scary people are not allowed in our house. We don't let them in. It's our rule. Your birth family did not have that rule. I'm sorry that you were scared there"
- support of children's exploration—following their lead in play
- rules and structure so that children continue the process of learning limits and staying safe
- expansion of empathy so that children learn to care, compromise, and contain aggression
- experiences that enhance mastery in play, speech, social interactions with peers
- shared enjoyable activities between parents and children
- assistance from adults in building a positive gender and self identity as "good" and valuable family member
- opportunities to make choices or to say "no"
- ability to retreat to parents or trusted adults when life feels overwhelming.

Trauma symptoms include

- more marked difficulty in social contexts with aggression in play
- nightmares with real themes related to traumatic incidents
- talking about or acting out sexual themes not typically known by children this age

- bullying behavior of peers or adults
- angry tantrums that are more frequent than other children's tantrums
- frenetic over, activity when remembering traumatic material.

Trauma symptoms from stages above which may also be present include

- avoidance of gaze
- difficulty calming
- freezing in place
- difficulty engaging socially
- difficulty knowing where her own body is or what it is feeling
- aggression: hitting, feet up, elbows out, head butting
- avoidance of certain trauma-related places or situations, i.e. the bath, belts, loud voices.

By this stage it is clear that trauma is shaping the way children are developing their sense of themselves—as good or bad—how they view their gender, whether they feel confident socially, or whether they will fight, give up, or problem-solve.

Often children with early neglect and trauma who have now been adopted into safe homes will dream about being separated from their parents and being hurt or neglected again. This is an intrusive memory, which is trauma-related. Unlike dreams that are more typical bad dreams, these dreams may recur several times per week, and the return to sleep is often difficult. Children may be up for one to three hours after such dreams. They are afraid of the dreams so may avoid going to sleep.

Phase V: 4½ through 6½ to 7 years of age

Children in Phase V increase in identity formation. Typically they are mastering language, play themes, and are eager for social relationships. They may hope to have a romantic relationship with an opposite sex parent.[2] Children of this age need a life story that has a

---

[2] Some children are already showing the development of a gay orientation and will demonstrate this preference.

"why" in it, but their life stories are quite concrete. They may want to know more about the events that happened pre-adoption in a search for what explains their feelings.

Children at this age need

- support for speech and learning skills as they enter an academic setting,
- continuation of a nurturing, sensitive relationship with parents,
- safety,
- the ability to retreat to parents or trusted adults when life feels overwhelming,
- a simple "why" for the events that have shaped their lives. For example, "Your birthmother did not have enough money or any food for herself or for you. She knew that we were all ready for a child. That is why she and the judge decided that you should come be our boy. She wanted you to have a family with lots of good food, love, and a warm house,"
- therapy for trauma that they experienced,
- help in handling their feeling extremes, (Please see the last half of the book for practical suggestions.)
- buffering and soothing help when they need to retreat to their parents for a cuddle, comfort, props, or ideas,
- social experiences that help them to develop peer relationships. These experiences may need to be coached for success,
- basic chores so that they contribute to the family,
- structure in going to bed, brushing teeth, etc., along with consequences to maintain this structure,
- positive statements about their gender, their accomplishments, and their value to the family,
- help in organizing their life story, social contexts, and increasingly complex worlds.

Phase V children are grandiose, and think that they have triggered incidents. Children who experience traumatic events during this stage tend to be melodramatic in their understanding of trauma. If they are not treated, they tend to maintain this dramatic all-or-nothing perception of their worlds. There is often a romantic cast to their trauma themes. Children are noted to be "drama queens or kings" by their parents. However, these references made by parents are not made with a permissive doting smile. Adults who are parenting traumatized children tend to make such references with wan expressions and sighs. Parents are ready for the play to be over!

If children were sexually or physically abused, they will probably act out the abuse at this stage. They may romanticize the characters. One parent, requesting an appointment for her 6-year-old, reported, "She was playing that she was Barbie getting married…but was really explicit about the honeymoon. Ken gave quite a performance!"

Reflecting the grandiose manner that is common for all children at this stage, lots of children decide that they are unstoppable, unmanageable, sooo cute, and so forth. They may even believe that these qualities are the reasons why their trauma occurred. As in the stage before, their self-explanations for having been traumatized are egocentric and have little to do with the person who caused the trauma. But, this at least gives them a sense of predictability. They feel better knowing why something happened—even if the "why" is negative about themselves (Briere, 2002).

Some children may refine role reversals in attempts to control parental performance and to get care and protection.

As a 5-year-old girl wistfully described to me her plan to return to her birthmother, "I will bring her all of her food, take care of her. She won't need to get a mean boyfriend again. I can take care of her. She can sleep in. We will be best friends. I will take care of her and she will take care of me."

Children with this adaptation will feel a vivid sense of failure that they were not able to take care of their parent. They will need to process this in therapy. Trauma symptoms at this stage include the earlier listed behaviors, plus

- night terrors
- dissociation at reminders of trauma
- quick startle reflex
- social withdrawal or heedless approach of strangers
- playing out trauma themes in playtimes

- identification with the brutal "victor" who might be an abuser
- complaints of body pains (somatization)
- avoidance of gaze or staring
- difficulty calming
- freezing in place
- difficulty engaging socially or highly controlling social behaviors
- difficulty knowing where her own body is or what it is feeling
- aggression: hitting, feet up, elbows out, head butting or verbal aggression
- avoidance of certain trauma-related places or situations, i.e. police, sirens, angry adults
- sexually acting out if there has been sexual abuse or exposure to sexual material.

Traumatized children may confuse simultaneous events with cause and effect, for example, erroneously drawing such conclusions as "He slapped my mother because I was so loud at the table." Or, "Because I was just so cute when I sat in his lap he did that bad touching." Or, "Because my bother and I were so wild, those foster families couldn't handle us."

Phase VI: Ages 6½ to 8: How am I the same and different as other children? Ages 8 to 10: Joining in and finding my place

Though often considered two separate stages, there is so much overlap in tasks of normal development and as well of trauma-related behavior, that they are described together in this section.

Children entering these stages of development are rigid in defining what is normal and what standards they use for group inclusion. This development causes children to compare their lives to the lives of others. In their rigid self-assessment they realize that they are different after trauma, neglect, or having had to change families. Unless they have had sensitive adults as compassionate helpers in their lives, they may avoid any talk about trauma or other painful topics.

By this stage of development, children who have experienced trauma usually have a sense of shame about who they are, related not just to traumatic incidents, but also to early neglect. Who wants to talk about shame, feeling even more shame, they reason. Helping professionals will have to explain to seven- to ten-year-olds the merits of using therapy to reduce their pain and stress. (Chapter 10's vignettes demonstrate talking to children about therapy for trauma and neglect.)

This is an age of mastery and social development: finding one's place, cooperating with groups, and accomplishing tasks. Children, after trauma, often miss social cues or may misinterpret cues as threatening. The abilities to share, to join ideas together, to compromise, to feel one's feelings and to be simultaneously aware of another's feelings, are all processes that may not have developed in children raised in foster care or orphanages. They must to be taught during this stage. Since children are aware of the need for friends, they tend to be open about to receiving help when it is described as having an explicit goal, such as being a better friend and or having more friends.

Needs at these stages are for
- safe, nurturing homes and parents,
- experience-rich lives that help them to develop a sense of mastery
- academic successes, either with or without accommodations and school support
- social successes giving them friends and a fit with their same-aged peers. Social support in the way of social skills groups and/or counseling may need to be given to assist in this development
- a life story that helps them cope with adoption issues and trauma/neglect issues. It should both give facts and corrects any distortions
- therapy that helps them to process and de-sensitize to trauma and shame
- building of moral, spiritual development, and empathy
- structure and discipline in order to move smoothly through the cycle of the day and necessary chores

- help in handling feeling or behavioral extremes. Consequences are given to help enforce limits.

Trauma symptoms at this stage include
- exaggerated startle reaction
- difficulty with friendships
- knowledge of adult sexual information or sexual acting out
- night terrors
- body symptoms (somatization)
- paranoid thoughts (such as worrying that people are watching her through the windows)
- worries that an abuser will return
- bullying of small children or pets and worries that others may victimize him
- anxieties that are specific to the trauma
- generalized anxieties
- concentration and memory problems that interfere with learning
- loss of optimism about the future
- emotional dysregulation including aggression.

Children who are too busy keeping themselves protected have difficulty connecting with others. It interferes with their close relationships, including those with other children. For that reason, among many others, it is helpful to begin therapy during this stage if children have not started already.

Regulation, Arousal Levels, and Behavioral Indicators

It is helpful to chart out regulation, arousal levels, and behaviors in an interrelated manner. It is beneficial to look at several aspects at one time. Please note that this chart does not include the influence of developmental delays that have not been accommodated.

Table 2-2

Regulation of Stress and Stimulation				
Arousal Level	Possible Explanations/ Diagnoses	Behavioral Resemblances	Behaviors if Stress or Boredom are Not Reduced	Results
Under-aroused	Attention Deficit Disorder, and/or neglect, and/or long-term chronic trauma (Note that neglect and trauma will appear at the underaroused and overaroused end.) Depression a possible issue.	Irritable with stimulation level that would maintain attention in others. Distractible and/or hyper-focused. Has organizing problems.	Does not direct focus well. Has a hard time shifting focus. Learning process is impeded. Motivation suffers. Feels like he is not meant for school.	Academic problems. School frustrations. Problems with daily chores. Messiness. Losing work. Transitions are hard. Needs organizational help, accommodations, nurturing classroom. Medication may help.
Low Normal Range	A little distractible. Needs a routine.	Has a hard time getting down to business in school or chores.	Tends to respond to structure and consequences.	Needs a structured and nurturing teacher.
Normal Range	Typical. "My focus, attention, and senses are suited for my age tasks!"	School is made for me!	Needs few reminders to achieve and focus.	May need less structure and nurturing support.
High Normal Range	The intense, anxious or shy child	Give me routines and quiet down—please!	Tends to have trouble with focus if too much pressure occurs.	Needs nurturing teacher and some emotional calming. Benefits from learning response flexibility.

Table 2-2 (continued)

Arousal Level	Possible Explanations/ Diagnoses	Behavioral Resemblances	Behaviors if Stress or Boredom are Not Reduced	Results
Over-aroused	Neglect, and/or trauma. Could be on the continuum of autistic spectrum disorder, or have some sensory processing issues. Bipolar or FASD are other possibilities. Referrals to neurologist or psychiatrist for diagnosis.	Anxious, wary, will have a hard time focusing or remembering because of anxiety. Needs predictability and set routine.	Can move from irritability to yelling, ranting, or aggression if sensory overload is not reduced.	Needs nurturing teacher, structured and probably accommodated classroom. Needs help with sensory and emotional demands of day. Benefits from skills training in handling feelings and sensory input.

(MacKenzie, Gray, 2007)

The chart shows these issues of sensory and emotional arousal as a range. Many children who have lacked early experiences with regulation spend a lot of time at both the underaroused and over-aroused area. They have diagnoses of both attention deficit disorder as well as anxiety. The parents and professionals are working with these children to expand their time in the normal range. They are trying to calm the oversensitized brain at the same time that they are helping children to focus their attention.

Neurobiology and Stress

This section gives a basic overview of the interrelationship between high stress and children's neural development. My perspective is to inform end users: people like me who need to know the "why" in order to understand and design some practical interventions. This section underscores why "hardball" approaches that intentionally raise stress in children are contraindicated for this population. It gives reasons why children may struggle with eating, sleeping, calming, learning, and behavioral patterns.

Studies discussed in this section are ones that pertain to the subject of this book—children who have been in situations of maltreatment and who are entering new families. The studies cited have results more technical than the summaries in this section and are referenced for further reading.

Formally defined, "*stressors* are anything, actual or perceived, that threatens to disrupt the homeostasis, i.e., the optimal biological functioning of an organism" (Sapolsky, 1992). These stressors result in a stress reaction that can be within or beyond the normal coping abilities. Dr. Megan Gunnar has studied stress in babies and children in healthy versus maltreating homes. A seminal article that she and Dr. Carol Cheatham wrote describes stress reactions and development. Notice how they tie the stress response to growth.

"The *stress response* is a cascade of hormonal and biochemical events that has evolved to restore homeostasis and promote survival. The main systems of the stress response are the norepinephrine-sympathetic adrenomedullary (NE-SAM) system and the hypothalamic-pituiary-adrenocortical (HPA) system. The HPA system produces glucocorticoids from the cortex of the adrenal glands." In humans the glucocorticoids are steroid hormones, mainly cortisol, referred to as CORT. "The NE-SAM and HPA systems work to restore the well-being of the organism by **increasing energy resources through increasing heart rate, metabolizing fat and protein stores, inhibiting digestion, inhibiting the immune system, and inhibiting the growth system**. In the brain, NE and CORT operate to support the cognitive and emotional processes important in promoting immediate survival in the face of threat" (Gunnar, Cheatham, 2003, p. 196). [Note: bold type added for emphasis by D Gray.]

In the quote above the researchers are clearly describing a shift from normal daily living into a survival mode. When children are always reading themselves for survival it is at the expense of normal processes.

CORT is always present in our systems, rising and falling throughout the day according to a circadian rhythm. Typically, *CORT rises in the morning, promoting eating, learning, experience-seeking, and memory consolidation. It falls by evening, allowing us to calm and to sleep.* Sensitive, interested, and committed parents who are available for attachment help children to establish normal circadian rhythms and levels of CORT.

Infants who move early from a neglecting home to a caring one tend to respond quickly to their safer surroundings with a drop in CORT. As a group children who are adopted by four months of age show no differences from their peers raised in nurturing families. Those adopted after eight months in deprived care and those adopted after twenty months in orphanages formed different groups. They had CORT levels that were high in comparison to their peers in control groups with consistent caring parents. The group with twenty months in the orphanage had higher CORT levels and more behavioral and developmental issues (Gunnar, Morison, Chishom, 2001). Dr. Dana Johnson has described developmental delays and growth disturbances--as much as one month of linear growth loss for every three months that children remain in an orphanage (2000).

High CORT, Low CORT, and Reactive CORT levels

A concerning development occurs when children have been under high stress for a long period of time. The CORT levels actually drop into a subnormal range for some children. This drop is unlike that of children whose CORT drops into a normal range because their life events have improved. Instead, their systems have become so worn that they show a further dysregulation in their systems. This is a secondary, or "stress stage II" problem, stemming from unrelenting high stress. They are oversensitized to stress. These are low CORT children.

Normal CORT helps children meet the day's challenges for alertness, learning, getting up for school, eating, and participating in social events. Lower is not better. Children with low CORT are not getting the biological-based energy to support these normal activities. Nor are they particularly advantaged in dealing with stress. A little stress hits them hard. Their CORT levels are reactive, and spike from too low to too high. These are extremely fragile little people. Research is being done to determine what causes children to hit this tipping point and how to correct these systems.

Children may have circadian rhythm CORT issues. It rises in the evening rather than in the morning so they are wakeful at night and lethargic in the mornings. Those children are not being signaled to eat, learn, and remember newly learned information.

Researchers describe a process of moving from uniformly high CORT to a low CORT system that can escalate quickly because it has become a reactive system. "CORT is 'down-regulated' through a negative feedback system at the level of the hippocampus. But when the level of CORT stays very high with prolonged stress, the system responds with fewer receptors, sending a message to the hypothalamus to halt production of Cortisol Releasing Hormone (CRH), a critical organizer of fear/anxiety and stress…the capacity to organize stress responses and to contain the stress response (turn it off) can be compromised, and even mild stressors may produce prolonged elevation in CORT" (Gunnar, Cheatham, 2003, pp. 200-202). These children calm down slowly after a stressful event.

Mary Dozier and her group are pointing out that neuroendocrine systems dysregulate every time we move babies/children from primary caregivers. (The neuroendocrine system includes CORT levels.) After moves there are home interventions that help to bring children's systems towards normal levels. These settings include high commitment to children by parent figures, positive and effective parenting strategies, and extra support for the parents. These are qualities that effect positive changes in children's CORT (Fischer, Gunnar, Chamberlain, Reid, 2000).

High stress has an effect on working memory, behavioral inhibition, and logical reasoning—areas known as executive functioning. After stress in early development, the levels of CORT are detected by the hippocampal CORT receptors. CRH (Cortisol Releasing Hormone) is a hormone and neuroactive peptide produced in many of the neural systems that are involved in regulating fear and anxiety, notably in the amygdala. High levels of CORT over long periods appear to increase the development of receptors for CRH-producing amygdalar cells. This neural structure appears to play a critical role in processing emotion-related stimuli and in tagging events as emotionally important. As Gunnar instructs, "the amygdala has many connections with areas of the frontal cortex (involved with what has been broadly termed executive functions, including working memory, effortful inhibition of behavior, and logical reasoning), as well as connections with the hippocampus (important in the laying down of memories for unique or specific events) and with the areas of the brain involved in the stress response" (Gunnar, Cheatham, 2003, p. 206-209). They conclude:

> "There is evidence in both clinical depression and post-traumatic stress disorder of disturbance in both basal and stress activity of the HPA system. Furthermore, for both of these clinical disorders, relationship loss, emotional deprivation, and early maltreatment have been implicated in their etiologies, perhaps especially for individuals who bear genetic vulnerabilities for these disasters" (pp. 198-201).

The summaries of research depict children whose CORT levels are too high, high and low at the wrong times, or too low and reactive. Looking at the overview of the studies to date, Gunnar concludes that the amount and length of neglect and maltreatment early in life appears to be related to abnormal levels of stress hormone present later, even after children's lives have improved (p. 207).

The application of this section is that children who have been through trauma will not only be affected by memories of specific events. Instead, the very circuitry of their brains has been altered. They will have a harder time concentrating, waking and sleeping, feeling safe, or steadying after stresses. Children will need positive experiences in order to shape their brains in a more positive manner. The techniques described in Chapter 8 are especially helpful in teaching parents, professionals, and children skills to work towards better stress regulation. Please notice that the executive functions of the brain are impacted by stress. This will be explored in some depth in successive chapters. It has implications that affect every area of life.

Multiple Traumas and High Stress over Time

There is a popular myth that children somehow become "expert" at coping with trauma, or, that it does not bother them as much because they experience it as a way of life. Trauma research does not support this. Rather than "becoming used to it" in a way that would show resilience or coping, children who are repeatedly exposed to the stress of trauma become more sensitized to it, becoming even more dysregulated by successive traumatic events.

Children who are exposed to new traumatic events after having a background of abuse and neglect are particularly vulnerable to developing post traumatic stress disorder. One of the symptoms of PTSD is numbing after trauma. Numbing can look like the person does not care about the event. The successive damage caused by the myth of "being used to it" is described in Destiny's situation.

> The judge reviewed the department's plan to file a petition for termination of parental rights. Both birthparents had left drug and alcohol treatment. The abuse suffered by 6-year-old Destiny was documented by eighteen CPS complaints, several failed reunification attempts, and numerous police and hospital emergency room reports. Destiny became frantic and then pale and wordless in visits with her birthfather. The visit supervisor's notes said that Destiny looked "out of body." The visits were discontinued as a result.

> The judge reversed the caseworker's decision saying, "I am ordering visitation with both parents weekly. That way, you can bring the effects in to the Court for the termination hearing." When the shocked social worker tried to advocate for Destiny, the judge replied, "This will make your termination case. She's been through worse."

> Destiny was driven to supervised visitations with her birthfather. She was sure that her foster mother had betrayed her. After two weeks of visitation the Department did come in with documented effects—Destiny's hospitalization in a children's mental health residential facility. But her trust in the foster-adopt parents never fully returned.

"But why did you give me to him?" She would query—even years later. No answer satisfied her. She *knew* that she had been given to her torturer by the people who promised to protect her. Her parents tried to explain the reality of a court order and the sequence of events: that no one knew that he had raped her. "But you knew that he broke my arm and burned me with a cigarette! Why didn't you hide me? I can't trust you!" While the Court had Destiny's best interests in mind with a logical plan, sometimes the adage, "beware the helping hand" is all too true.

In summarizing research findings, Jon Allen from the Menninger Clinic concludes, "The more severe the psychological abuse, the higher the risk of depression and suicidal behavior…the higher the number of types of maltreatment (psychological, sexual, and physical abuse; neglect), the higher the likelihood of depression and suicidal behavior. Although psychological abuse was often confounded by other forms of maltreatment, it bore a stronger relation to depression and suicidal behavior than any other childhood adversity" (2001, p. 29).

In the efforts to understand the meanings of trauma in working with children, it is imperative not to miss the impacts of psychological abuse on children's sense of self.

As one woman said to me, "I could clean up the messes when my mother got drunk and smashed things. I could wear long sleeves when she shoved and grabbed me. But I lived the shame of hearing what a disappointment I was to her…I believe it now."

Those psychological insults need to be carefully processed with children and countered during therapy and at home. Caseworkers should be documenting these statements in the record. They may need to process this type of abuse with children during preparation for placement.

Trauma, Sexual Abuse, Early Development

Trauma that includes sexual abuse has an impact on sexual hormones and sexual development in girls. Sexually abused girls were a topic of research by Bessell van der Kolk and his colleagues. They found that sexually abused girls are developing earlier. Their level of sex hormones is remarkably elevated, approximately five times higher than the levels of their peers who were not sexually abused. And more specifically, the sexual hormone androstendione, which governs sex drive, was three times the level of their peers (van der Kolk, 2002).

Parents whose children are emotionally immature are then faced with the dilemma of teaching children to understand and contain sexual desire at an early age. Most parents hope to avoid talking to their teens about sexual desire in concrete terms. They prefer the use of metaphors when possible. Of course, this is not effective for children whose thinking is so concrete. Parents must help youngsters understand the sexual feelings in their bodies. Many have to help their daughters learn to handle having their period in the 3rd grade.

The work of Patrick Mason looks at early sexual development in girls adopted internationally. He has found the change from poor nutrition to ample nutrition seems to kindle early sexual maturity (Mason, 2003). His findings are similar to studies done in other countries. Girls are starting sexual maturity a little early, and are completing the process in a little over a year instead of a little over two years (Mason, 2003). In the process they end up losing height, and also have to deal with the results of a developmental task and hormones much earlier than expected.

The take-home message from this section is, once again, a call to reduce stress in children so that as much repair as possible can take place. Clinicians and placement specialists need to be aware that early sexuality is a reality for which families parenting traumatized children need careful, direct and realistic preparation that placement specialists can feel certain these parents have heard and understood.

Calming after Trauma:
For the Brain's Sake

High stress kills children's brain cells, making them even more vulnerable in stressful events. Adults who have survived abuse as children show reduced hippocampal volume and, in some instances, memory impairments. Why is this? There is a neurotoxic effect of circulating glucocorticoids, which are present due to high stress, on the hippocampus, a structure rich in receptors for stress hormones that also plays a key role in memory.

Exposure to corticoids is also involved in the inhibition of cell division in the brain. So, not only is there destruction of cells, there is also a reduction of new cells. The take-home message that I use with families is *to avoid the danger of brain cell death, children who have been traumatized need to learn techniques to calm themselves down as quickly as possible.* Screaming and tantrums are bad for kids' brains. Their mouths, which are emitting the loud noises, are closest to their own ears!

On the way home from a family session a boy started yelling because he did not get something he wanted. His brother interrupted the mounting tantrum, coaching his brother: "Save your brain. Don't scream at Mom. It's bad for your brain cells! Calm down… Breeeeeathe."

Often adoptive parents of previously traumatized children complain that their children only listen when yelled at, threatened, or when highly stressed. These methods of stressful confrontation give short-term gains at the expense of longer-term health. While high-stress, coercive methods may appear to work initially, they inevitably backfire as children deteriorate over time. Children who receive help developing calming techniques and self-reflection ultimately respond much better behaviorally. Suggestions for children should always include calming techniques as part of interventions. Such interventions are included in successive chapters of this book and are also a part of *Attaching in Adoption* (Gray, 2012).

Stress Regulation Enhances Coping

Stress regulation, in emotional terms, means that "one can regulate the flows and shifts of one's bodily based emotional states either by one's own coping capacities or within a relationship with a caring other" (Schore, *Affect Dysregulation*, 2003, p. 250).

Essentially, people with a sturdy stress regulation system have an inner assurance of their capacities to meet the demands of the day. But they do not necessarily believe that they must meet those demands alone. This balance is a source of healthy optimism. Not only are people with good calming abilities able to meet challenges without undue distress, they also can surpass individual limits. They believe that others will help them in times of need. Their scope of exploration and interest can be wide since they can rely on others.

Alan Sroufe's work shows that "attachment can be understood as the primary mechanism to regulate stress and emotion, and is developed in the right brain. The early developing right brain largely dominates during the first three years of life" (2002). (See the chapter on attachment and the stress regulation system.) But many adoptive parents have not even met their children by ages three or four. And others could not have fathomed the earlier traumatic events that changed their children's lives forever. Still others are parenting children whose earliest parent figures were the instruments of trauma. They inflicted the trauma that shaped their children's world. The "next" parents are left to try to set right a broken beginning relationships with parent figures.

Therapy and therapeutic home techniques enhance children's stress regulation and coping so that they do not go through life so vulnerably. These techniques are described in more detail in Chapter 7 and beyond. The vignette of Kelli illustrates the change that occurs in children who are in therapy and using therapeutic parenting.

> Kelli was 8 years old when she nearly broke her brother's arm because he had touched her game. She tantrumed if her mother spent time alone with her brother, including bedtime stories or Boy Scout activities. Adopted after almost

four years of neglect, she always felt that she was in danger of being cheated or pushed aside. After some therapy, which not only improved her connection with her mother, but helped her to calm herself, she shared with her brother for the first time. Later that day, she said to her mother, "If you want to put Ryan to bed first, I won't yell and say that I need you."

I asked her what had changed for her. She said, "There's enough sugar to go around." She had a sweet smile on her face that matched a new peace in her life. "I can count on my mom. She won't forget me. And Ryan is not a bad brother. He can be fun."

Kelli was able to rework her view of life so that she had people she could count on. She was not alone, grasping, and desperate in life. She could calm down and play. This is the essence of internal work with children that improves stress regulation.

Repairs after Stressful Events

It is impossible to totally meet the needs of another. There are always little missteps during which children become stressed. Parents who intervene in a timely and effective manner after a dysregulating event bring their children back into regulation. These parents respond to their children's distress in a manner that recognizes the problem and meets the needs of the situation promptly.

This gives children a belief in the validity of their needs. It gives them the beginning template of how to solve problems with another person. They know that their needs are real and that the other person finds their needs worthy of attention and effort. The parent is able to reconnect with them after a disappointment. The example below describes a typical misstep and repair for a 4-year-old.

Jerry, anxious to be home, unbuckled his own car seat and wriggled out of the car as his mother commanded, "Wait! Come out the other side!" Jerry's father, struggling with grocery bags, slammed the car door against Jerry's leg. Immediately Jerry's father dropped the bags, his face full of concern, mirroring Jerry's pained expression. He examined the leg and then scooped up Jerry into his arms. They ran into the house for ice, Jerry howling against his dad's chest.

His mother applied the much-used bag of frozen peas. Mom crooned, "Sorry, Buddy, Daddy didn't know that your leg was in the door. That's why Mommy told you to wait." Within ten minutes, Jerry was back in action, in spite of a growing bruise. Parents neither ignored nor overly shamed Jerry for the missed "wait" command. Jerry and his mom and dad worked together to bring in groceries. The family moved back into its rhythmical, healthy pattern.

In the example above, Jerry's parents gave a *contingent* response. That is, a response related to the problem. If their responses were usually unrelated, he would have learned odd, and not helpful, pairings. For example, if they had spanked Jerry he would have learned that getting hurt means that he gets punished. Or if they had fed him, he would have learned an association between pain and getting fed.

An important part of stress regulation includes the child's ability to identify an internal state correctly, and an effective, sensitive response to the situation from the parents. When infants signal distress, excitement, anger, or fear, the responsive neural firing pattern of the caregiver becomes imbedded into the infant's brain. If parents can sooth distress, for example, the infant will imbed the soothing responses. Over time she will have neurological structures developed for self-soothing. If she becomes excited and social and is met with a parent who amplifies these feelings with her own responses, she becomes a child who finds that a positive stimulation is met and excelled by the caregiver. She can initiate something positive that is met, matched, and exceeded with positivism—and then calmed. After a period of play, parent and child can break off, "resting" from the emotional intensity of the moment before they interact pleasantly again. The child learns a pattern of engage, break, engage, break, all the while staying within a comfortable level of interest and alertness.

Children whose parents do not respond with this engage and rest, engage and rest pattern may shift to either end of the arousal spectrum. At one end they may shut down, refusing to process any more information. They may look like they have a still, frozen face. They do not trust the parent to modulate the amount of stimulation. On the other end of the spectrum, they may ask for attention incessantly, as they do not trust the parent's availability to re-engage. Some children will use both techniques with confusing inconsistency.

Over time, parents' abilities to provide a combination of safety, emotional support, and permission to explore helps build a stress regulation system into their children that tolerates variety in life. Children become confident in their abilities to cope with both positive and negative events. They look for challenges that stretch their interests and capacities. When parents provide secure attachments and effectively buffer their children from highly stressful events during the first four years of life, they provide a measure of resiliency for life.

Children moved to foster care or adoption after abuse or neglect most likely have not had these healthy learning experiences. Instead, they have been left alone, experienced feelings of overwhelming frustration or loneliness, and been hurt or yelled at when exploring. The delight in sharing mastery of skills, new experiences, and closeness with a family member has been absent. They do not know how to use parents as a safe base for exploration or for help. As a result, they need real life experiences that are intentional in order to use their new sensitive and available parents effectively.

Initially children may not want to engage with parents, or they may want to control parents so that they do not risk becoming overwhelmed or frustrated. Rather than dismissing this as, "He's just independent," be aware that this child needs experiences that are attuned, fun, playful, and sensitive in order to make the connection that parents are secure bases of help and joy. Being specific about the parent's job as a helper who is sensitive to the cues of children helps build a pattern of using the parent as the touchstone for positive emotions, soothing, and exploration.

Learning to Calm Before Tackling Trauma Therapy

Parents have a reasonable expectation that children will put energy into adjusting to their new family. Actually, the first task for children is to form a beginning sense of safety in their parents' care. Traumatized children, of course, will have symptoms of trauma that will interfere with attachment, including emotional numbing, dissociation, and emotional modulation problems. They will only become really available emotionally when they have worked through trauma. They will work through trauma best if they form some attachment and trust in parents. This gives them the ability to soothe and to regulate the emotional upset during trauma work. Parents report another increase in attachment after children have worked through trauma issues. Emotional numbing decreases, safety increases, and children have more interest and energy to put into an attachment relationship.

Until children have the ability to calm down, they should not move on to trauma work. It is too overarousing. When people are overaroused, they cannot think through what has happened without feeling like they are in the throes of it again. When they are flooded with emotion and overaroused, they feel as if they are re-experiencing the traumatic event or as if they are being re-victimized. And, in fact, they are being damaged in such a situation. Going over and over the event, and re-experiencing the same feelings of helplessness and terror, is emotionally and physiologically damaging. It deepens the footprint of trauma. Often, traumatized people become so overaroused that they lose their capacity to speak and thus to organize and to process the earlier traumatic situation (Cloitre, 2003).

Children adopted later in infancy or after maltreatment are in the category of those most likely to become overaroused. Why is this? It is because they have not usually had the opportunity to build a good calm-down system before experiencing a traumatic event. Children develop the resource bank necessary to do trauma work when they learn to calm with their parents and look to their parents for assistance in calming.

Unresolved Trauma—
Effects on Functioning

After examining the lists of trauma symptoms and effects in various stages of childhood as discussed throughout this complex chapter, and after reading examples of how trauma and neglect have affected children who have been moved from negative circumstances to stable adoptive homes, it should be obvious why we must seek and provide treatment for children who have been neglected or maltreated. They are miserable symptoms to live with! In summary, the costs of unresolved childhood trauma to children are these:

- Shame is integrated into their identities. "I'm identified with my maltreatment."
- Their meaningful relationships have been diminished. "I feel wary or numb. I have a hard time connecting with your feelings."
- They feel alarming body symptoms. "My body is putting off false positives like I am in physical danger."
- They have mood problems. "It's hard when I feel fight-and-flight energy not to fight or withdraw into anxiety or depression."
- They show a bias towards using dissociation rather than coping. "This is my option when I have no options."
- They lose a simple belief in a loving God. "I am outside of the group that God protects or cares for."
- They have difficulty finding their places in the world. "It's hard to fit in when I'm constantly afraid."
- They cannot find safety or comfort. "I am afraid of being alone and even more afraid risking getting close."

The goal of each successive chapter is to identify ways to heal these children and help them to lead normal and happy lives.

 # Neglect

"Neglect breaks the implicit contract that caregivers
have with children—that their basic needs will be met."
– Deborah Gray

C hildren who have experienced chronic hunger or pain, who
have been left alone, and denied holding and touch have all
been neglected. Children who have been in either institutional care or that of alcoholic or drug-addicted parents have almost
always experienced neglect. While it is often the abuse that institutes
removal from the home, neglect causes the most long-term destruction. It drives home messages like, "You can depend on no one," and
"It would be better if you did not exist." There is a cranky, irritable,
low mood state common to children and teens after neglect.

Neglect is a form of trauma. It is important, though, to make a
distinction between the effects of trauma caused by events as opposed to trauma resulting from neglect. Abuse dramatically *over*-
stimulates the developing psychobiological systems in infants and
children. In contrast, neglect massively *under*stimulates the developing psychobiological systems. The difference between these traumas
is often summarized as "abuse is in the 'sins of commission' while
neglect is in the 'sins of omission.'"

Over time, neglect leads to an irritable, depressive state. Children
seems to get "stuck" in this state. Andrei's mother describes this state
in her previously neglected 4-year-old.

"In the morning he would never be hungry. He stayed in
his bed until I got him. We'd start the morning and after a

while I would find him sitting somewhere, zoned out. Playing always seemed to be more my idea than his. I had worked as a teacher for twenty years, and I said to myself, 'This is the wierdest kid I have ever met. He doesn't even know how to be a kid!'

"I didn't tell anybody about it because it seemed disloyal to say that your own child is offputting. But I felt strange being home with such an odd kid. I went on antidepressants at the end of the first year. That helped. Sometimes I thought that I should just read a novel all day. He wouldn't have noticed. Finally, after the first couple of years, he started playing and acting more naturally. He woke up."

Andrei's brain and personality were shaped by the four years he had spent in an orphanage. There, he had grown accustomed to waiting for the potty, waiting for meals, waiting to get dressed, and waiting for all of the children and their needs. He constantly waited. He was irritated by the high level of interaction expected in his new home. It was unlike anything that he had ever experienced. It was overwhelming, and it made him cranky.

Andrei's mother had a rough and lonely time adjusting to specialized parenting. As in many neglected children, Andrei's daily rhythm had been disrupted. He was sleepy midmorning, awake at night, and never hungry at mealtimes. His low mood carried into the family placement. Within a year, his mother was regulating herself to his low mood—instead of the reverse!

Competent caregivers meet their children's needs in a prompt and effective manner. This type of response is considered *contingent*. That is, the child's needs directly relate to the caregiver's response. When children begin life with competent caregivers, they learn that expressing their needs results in contingent, positive attention. But when caregivers ignore or respond to expressed needs in a confusing manner, children learn to mute their needs or to hold back, unleashing anger later. Alix, age 8, describes his earliest memories.

"There was a store in the bottom of our house. They took me down there in the morning and left me there until late at night. An old man would sell things to people. I was in, like a wood box. I would stay in it all day. I had a dirty doll and only half of a gray-colored bottle. In the evening I would get to go upstairs to the house. That was better, but my mom was never happy to see me.

"No one picked me up or talked to me all day. Sometimes I can't get the feeling of how much I hated that out of my brain. Why did I have to go there? Why didn't they pick me up? I have bad dreams about that. I wanted to scream at them. I don't know why I didn't yell. It probably wouldn't have done any good. I felt like I was garbage.

"I think of taking a knife and cutting people apart—laughing while I do it. It scares me to want to kill people. I don't know if I will ever change."

Alix struggled to have any form of hope in his life. His rage became separate from its source: the events and memories of his maltreatment. This made treatment more difficult in general, because he still practiced the mental habit of separating his feelings, or affects, from the events that were tied to them. He preferred to show his rage indirectly, pointing it toward the unsuspecting. He broke off pencil points and dropped them around the pool area. He giggled when people would hurt their bare feet on these points. He clogged toilets on purpose and blamed it on his toddler brother. He broke pens, spilling the contents on books, upholstery, or drawings. He released this rage daily, but he would not register the cause of his anger. In psychological literature this is known as "isolation of affect from event." It is a troubling sign, because the person may hurt others without feeling emotion.

He began to show progress when he recognized his anger was the beginning point of his plans for payback. He said of one incident, "I was jealous of my brother. That must be why I stepped on his toy later." This natural connection was a self-discovery for him. He started to let himself feel anger and process it with me or a parent so it was not so intense.

He said, "I used to think that someone should get hurt if I got mad. Now I can get over being mad without hurting someone." Later, he was able to feel anger, report it, and talk through the situations that had made him so angry. Prior to this work Alix just thought that he was a mean and angry kid, unlikely to ever improve. He said, "I'd like to be a farmer and take care of the animals, feeding them and watching over them."

Hopelessness, as a part of disappointed expectations, can become a set point for children. It is easier to stop hoping and trying than it is to face continual disappointment. Children who have been neglected learn to expect that their actions will have little to do with what happens in their lives. New parents of previously neglected children must understand that. While they automatically expect their children to show initiative and hope, these expectations constitute a radical cultural change for these children.

Some children, in fact, refuse reward systems. They refuse to be involved in a system that challenges their negative view of the world. They may find rewards anxiety-producing. Systems also force them to accept responsibility for their actions. And, while children may be shame-filled, they typically have a difficult time accepting responsibility following early years filled with neglect. They react to having to accept appropriate amounts of guilt.

Trevor, aged 11, was asked to practice friendly behaviors. When he showed friendly behaviors, parents remarked on the behaviors and gave him a star. The stars were rewarded with things that Trevor liked, including having a friend over.

Trevor actually decreased his number of friendly behaviors with the reward system. In sessions with me and his parents, he said that he did not like that they could hold anything over him.

"I don't like all the pressure when it's up to me," he said. "I would rather have everybody give up on me. I know it's wrong, but I liked it better when I could blame somebody else if something went wrong. Even though it sucked, it was easier."

In the same vein, another child told me that he felt far behind other children. Trying hard bothered him because he felt that he would never catch up to his peers. In each of the cases, it took several therapy sessions to convince the child to accept a reward system that would help him notice his positive gains. Focused efforts at home and in therapy helped these children understand that they could change their lives, could have friends, and could put forward efforts success- fully. Before these discussions each boy thought that he was being set up for another failure.

Neglect and Emotional Intensity

Neglect results in dramatic understimulation during the devel- opment of psychobiological systems, impairing the normal develop- ment of the emotional brain. These psychobiological impairments result in, among other things, limitations in the ability to process and to tolerate intense experiences. Chronically neglected children are often characterized as having a difficult time processing vivid positive and negative emotional experiences. Laura Jane's father de- scribes this below.

"We seem to be so rigid. Sometimes I wonder if it's just us. After all, don't all kids get excited over birthday parties? So we try to ease up. But Laura Jane and her brother are ob- sessed with the treats in the cupboard. It's not like they are toddlers. For heaven's sake they are 7 and 8 years old! By the morning of the party, they are almost hysterical and actu- ally banging into things. It takes the joy out of many of our experiences."

Many adoptive parents give up and simply stop trying to help their children process their positive and negative emotions. Instead, they work on a containment model. That is, they try to limit their children's range of experiences to those that will not exceed their ability for smooth processing. Of course, the outcome is boredom.

In my waiting room, a brother and sister were coloring in coloring books, obviously bored. I asked if they could kick the soccer ball in the fenced yard behind the office. "No, no," their father said. "My wife wouldn't like that at all. They would be too wound up to learn anything in home schooling today!"

Parents can feel constantly torn between trying to maintain stability in life and trying to stretch their children's ability to tolerate more excitement. In my practice, I encourage parents to gradually vary the experiences available to their children. This process usually requires parents to temporarily increase their own level of discomfort.

Parents can become overwhelmed at first when I suggest this extra work. However, the goal is not for the children to get better at living in their parents' homes, but for them to develop the abilities required to cope successfully with life's richness—life outside of their parents' homes.

If parents are resistant, I make two suggestions. First, I recommend increasing their level of available support. This gives parents enough time to allow their children to become a little out of control. It also helps parents plan and then implement means for their children to process intense emotions. Second, I ask parents if they really want children who need parental structure to the extent that they cannot leave home. Usually, tired parents find motivation in the second alternative. They begin the process of helping their children tolerate more experiences. Seven-year-old Celeste demonstrates this.

Celeste's birthday activities had been restricted to cakes the first two years in her new family. Still, she became so overexcited by the cakes that she ran around wildly, hitting her brother and mother sometime between the candles and the serving. She yelled at her father as he hauled her off to bed.

This year, her mother pondered whether she should even tell Celeste that it was her birthday at all. I recommended working on helping Celeste have a more typically positive birthday experience instead.

First, we reviewed deep breathing techniques with Celeste. "In through your nose, out through your mouth." (The most important part is the steady breathing *out*.)

Then we described the steps of a party by drawing them out in four comic book-type frames. Celeste practiced each part of the party through role-play several times at home. Celeste loves the water, so she invited three friends over for a swimming party. We also planned and practiced breaks that Celeste would take in her room throughout the birthday. These breaks from stimulation would allow Celeste to stay within her range of tolerance.

While the birthday had included some redirecting, it was a success. The family brought in pictures, showing them off proudly. "We actually felt like normal parents. Looking back, we had a *great* time! When Celeste needed help, we said, 'What's your plan?' She got it together!"

Celeste's eyes shone brightly as she beamed at her parents.

Early Neglect's Impact on Moods and Reflective Thought

Early neglect compromises the development of positive emotional states. As aptly described by Alan Sroufe in his book, *Emotional Development*, the brain is experience-expectant and experience-dependent (1995). Neglect deprives the experience-dependent brain of the experiences that help develop the brain structures required to support and stretch positive mood states. "At ten months of age, 90% of maternal behavior consists of affection, play, and caregiving." Children usually build up a tolerance for joy and excitement before moving out of the parents' laps. As they move into the walking stage, parental admonitions continue at an average rate of once every nine minutes. The positive structures that were formed earlier form a positive base for little ones as they learn beginning limits (Schore, *Affect Dysregulation*, 2003, p.17).

Attunement with a parent helps children tolerate strong emotions through following the parents' guide. This attunement then "act[s] as a mechanism that maximizes and expands positive affect and minimizes and diminishes negative affect." (Schore, *Affect Dysregulation*, 2003, p.18). Early neglect deprives children of the experience-dependent events required to stretch affects (feelings). Neglected babies do not build the structures in the brain that allow for calming or smooth processing through highly arousing experiences. Additionally, new parents must set limits while simultaneously building more positive states and brain structures because most children are coming into the home mobile, rather than on the lap.

The key to building these brain structures is in the development of a relationship in which the parent is sensitive and the child is referencing, or looking to the parents for signals or cues. Using the sensitive parent as an empathetic base, children can be encouraged to learn how to stretch their limits and also to calm themselves.

It is equally as important to process positive emotions with children as it is to process negative emotion. That's an important concept that bears repeating: *It is equally important to process positive emotions with children as it is to process negative emotions.* Processing positive emotions enhances the capacity to seek out and tolerate such experiences. The work of Diana Fosha teaches that, after processing these emotions with an emotionally attuned person, the child is able to store the memories as part of their schema of themselves (Fosha, 2004). Without that careful processing with another person, an individual may not store a positive experience, even though it has occurred. The child then retains impressions that remain true to their initial core self-concept. In the case of Celeste, in the vignette above, her initial self-talk might have been, "Nothing nice ever happens to me." After her reciprocal positive experience with attuned parents, however, her stored memory becomes a happy and exuberant one, "I had a *great* birthday when I was seven!"

Early Neglect's Impact on Self-reflection and the Continuous Sense of Self

People are conscious of their own existence. The ability to think about how something affects us or about who we are is fundamental to the way people experience their own lives *subjectively*. Awareness of self provides a means to stand outside of experiences in order to think and reflect. This self-awareness allows for healthy adjustments, making moral decisions, enjoying life, or understanding confusing situations.

Many people with backgrounds of neglect do not have a

continuous sense of self. While moving through their day they can go into a state of "automatic pilot." They may experience these lapses several times a day. If you say, "What are you thinking about? What are you feeling?" They may honestly answer, "Nothing," or "I don't know," or shrug. Sometimes they seem to be collecting and processing information about themselves in a disconnected manner—as if their lives were happening to someone else. They seem to experience life in the third person rather than the first person. And, in fact, sometimes children will actually speak of themselves by name or as *he* or *she*, rather than using a personal pronoun. For these children, the self is an objective rather than subjective experience.

People lacking a subjective sense of self have difficulties representing their own needs in life. They tend to sway into asking, "What do you think?" rather than balancing their own feelings and thoughts with that of another. They forsake their own interests, moving into the perspectives and needs of others in place of their own. Alternately, children may flood with emotions when their interests are at stake. They cannot blend their thoughts and feelings. They become either all feeling or all thought.

Parents project bleak futures for these children, as shown in Madison's case. Madison, at 11 years old, had been in her family eight years, after entering it post neglect.

Madison followed her older brother around, desperate for his attention and approval. She shadowed her parents, needing attention constantly. She never initiated activities other than television. She would invariably chime "I don't know" if any family member asked her what she wanted to do.

"Her closet is filled with gifts and crafts that she never touches," her mother said. "When I tell her that she needs to give me breathing space and ask her to go to her room, she will push and shove me. Other than that, she is just pleasantly there—ALL OF THE TIME! Sometimes her brother asks her to do things that she hates to get her to leave. But she will smile and dust his room, or take out his garbage."

Madison heard this description in my office with her parents. She looked at me with a fixed smile, "But I don't mind," she said. Simultaneously, she twisted her fingers backwards.

A few minutes later, in private, Madison's father said,

"Can you imagine what is going to happen to her in adolescence? She's a set-up for some jerk to take advantage of her. I don't mind telling you—I'm scared!"

Other individuals have "dead spots" in their continuous sense of themselves. They do have a subjective sense of themselves, but they seem to lose it temporarily. Neglected children are especially prone to going blank after experiencing an emotionally overwhelming event. This is described in Isaac's case.

"How did your day go? How was your field trip?" Isaac's mom said as he came in from the school bus.

"O.K.," said Isaac absently. Isaac, at age twelve, looked a little "flat" to his mother, but not so different than his brother had looked at that age. Maybe he was growing again.

A few minutes later the phone rang. It was his friend's mother wondering if Isaac had recovered. She described him getting upset, holding his head, and then yelling for a full fifteen minutes on the field trip bus.

"Why didn't you tell me?" Mom asked Isaac.

In all honesty, Isaac replied, "I forgot."

Children seem to lose their subjective sense of self when they get extremely bored or overwhelmed. This looks like dissociation, which is described in depth in the next chapter. However, the look as related to post neglect is peculiar and unique. The look is a flat look. These children do not have a clear sense of themselves during this time.

In a fundamental way, neglect impairs the self-help process that is part of self-reflection. When individuals lose their continuous sense of themselves, they also lose their capacity to think about their situations and problem-solve. They cannot experience their feelings or coordinate them with thoughts about themselves. The capacity to step back from events and analyze them with a sense of perspective is called *reflective thought*. This ability is regularly missing in children after neglect.

The capacity for self-reflection is the one variable most closely linked to achieving successful results in therapy (Fonagy, 2002). The development of a continuous and subjective sense of self is a critical and often overlooked area in working in the home and professionally with children coming from foster care or adoption. Methods for working on the sense of self are presented in Chapters 8 and 10.

Summing up, after neglect, the tasks are

- to stretch children's positive moods
- to help children connect their thoughts to their feelings
- to assist children in thinking about the feelings and thoughts of others at the same time that they think about their own feelings and points of view (Below age 6 this is normally difficult, but after that age should be an emerging skill.)
- to connect children's feelings in their bodies with their thoughts
- to teach children how to read the faces of others in real time, and to relate to the feelings of others
- to develop in children both optimism and a sense of mastery
- to encourage in children an attitude of being in charge and responsible for having a satisfying life.

CHAPTER 4

Traumatic Stress— The Symptom Clusters

"The core issue of post traumatic stress disorder (is) dissociation, i.e. 'a disruption in the usually integrated functions of consciousness, memory, identity, or perception of the environment'"   –John Nemiah

What constitutes evidence of trauma? What recurrent problem areas afflict people who go through appalling events? This chapter details the major areas of daily life which are influenced by trauma. The focus of this book is on children who have been adopted or who are being fostered, and, as such, the examples used are specific to these children. The children who are a focus of this book are unlike children who may have had just one overwhelming event occur in an otherwise advantaged childhood, in that they experience the complications associated with repeated relationship disruptions and attachment challenges interrelated with trauma.

Dissociation

Dissociation is evidence of a developmental catastrophe. Dissociation allows children who cannot handle the stimulation entering their world to freeze in place. They can be physically present without having to process what is happening to them. It is a "freeze and surrender" tactic. It is the defense when there is no defense.

What does dissociation look like? Children who are dissociating often look "zoned out," as if they are thinking of something else. Adults may say, "He looks like he is daydreaming." Unlike a daydreamer, however, children who are dissociating are not easily brought back to the present. Dissociating children often seem lost in time. Superficially some children may look fine because they appear to be smiling. People who know the child well may recognize the dissociative state as marked by a fixed smile. However, the eyes and the rest of the face are certainly not relaxed and smiling. The body is frozen-looking.

Dissociation appears to be an adaptation that allows children to freeze during high-risk times in order to prevent injury. Many children describe dissociation as working in just this way. Kyle, aged 10, described a scene that he remembered from when he was 3 years old.

"My mother was standing between me and the door to the apartment. Two men, one I called 'Dad,' but it turns out he wasn't my dad, were fighting. One man came toward my mother. He had a knife and I thought he was going to stab her. She was crying. I was on the floor. I didn't move or make any noise. I could hear the cars outside. I listened to the cars. Then the guy made a phone call and left. I didn't look up. I don't know what else happened. But suddenly, everyone was gone except for me, my sister and my mother. My mother was watching T.V. like nothing had happened. There was blood on the floor and in the sink in the bathroom.

"I think about the fight sometimes when I think of my birthmother. Then someone says something like, 'Nicholas, Nicholas, why aren't you getting ready for school?' I get ready for school and then I have a bad day."

Dissociation allows children to live through experiences that are unendurable. They simply stop integrating the experience into their life schema, i.e. their view of the world. For example, children may dissociate through the experience of being beaten by a mother who says through words or looks, "I am going to kill you." Through dissociation, that same child can approach the parent in a half-hour saying, "I love you, Mommy. May I have a drink?" Because traumatized children have to remain in highly threatening situations, they need to be able to "not know" the meaning of events that would put them into an intolerable conflict.

Traumatized children do not integrate feelings and thoughts from traumatic events into their life story, and they often seem to be—and are—illogical. Claire's example illustrates this type of discrepancy.

> Claire used to ask to be returned to the abusive home from which she was removed twice due to sexual abuse by an older sibling. While working on trauma with me, she remembered how her mother had leaned against the doorway, watching the abuse with a slight smile. Claire had been told that her mother had a serious drinking problem, but our session was the first time that she had been able to integrate the facts and feelings about the drinking with her abuse.
>
> "So that's why they don't let me go back to live with her. Now I get it," she said. "I kept thinking that I should go back and take care of her. She needs me. But she lets bad things happen to me when she is drunk. That's not fair!"

Integration allows children to find their own feelings and to update their thinking in a realistic fashion. Children who are dissociative are not happy. It might seem as if children would be better off not thinking about unpleasant past events. But the truth is that not acknowledging these events and integrating them puts them in more long-term jeopardy.

Dissociation's Long-term Disadvantages

The advantage to processing traumatic information, by thinking it through and determining its relevance to your life, is that processed information feels like it is in the past rather than in the present. Processed feelings are not as vivid. When feelings have not been processed, traumatized children can become dissociative to the memories of trauma and the situations of threat that produced them. As a result, they stop processing these memories.

Dissociated memories are kept out of the normal processing of information by the toxic nature of trauma. If these memories are not processed, then the information remains toxic. Children will become afraid to even think about the original incident because doing so makes them feel like it is happening all over again. They become phobic of their own fear! Children need security, good pacing, and guidance in order to think through traumatizing events; they need calming and comforting afterwards.

Dissociation allows children to have lapses in place of integrating highly threatening information into their senses of self. But until children are able to integrate the information safely, they will have a compartmentalized approach to life. Sadly, the compartmentalization that originally helped them will gradually make them more vulnerable to successive traumas.

Children who have integrated their trauma can pick up danger signals, integrate these signals, and make a plan to avoid dangerous people or places. In contrast, children who have learned to dissociate make no such plans. Children who "zone out" later in life consequently lack the ability to forge a protective strategy. Instead, they use a primitive strategy of avoidance. Studies that measure heart rate and levels of the stress hormone cortisol in dissociating children show that they can register risk signals on a physiological level. However, they keep these signals out of their consciousness (Freyd, 2002).

Mind-Body Connection Uncoupled

Until individuals can integrate traumatic events into their lives, they cannot form the strategies necessary for adequate protection. For example, a woman who was sexually abused in childhood might begin to pick up cues if her boyfriend is staring at her daughter sexually. If she learned to dissociate from trauma as a child, the memories and reminders of trauma may keep this new information out of her conscious awareness. She may recognize that she is agitated and has a faster heart rate, but she will not know why. She will not be able to use protective strategies for her daughter. People who dissociate have learned to disregard some of their body's danger signals. The physical symptoms, such as faster heart rate and anxiety, are compartmentalized. The mind-body connection becomes uncoupled.

The uncoupling of the mind-body connection becomes a daily problem for children who are dissociative. They simply do not know where their bodies are. They are so poorly connected that they seem amazed to find where their limbs have gone off to. This is another way in which the initial dissociative adaptation becomes problematic later in life. As trauma expert Bessel van der Kolk describes, "You just cannot get by in life without knowing where your body is in space and time" (2002, 2006).

Traumatized children are prejudiced toward using a dissociative defense in place of healthy coping skills during highly charged emotional or physical life circumstances. This is one of the reasons why trauma work is essential to the future well-being of these children. They need a lot of work, not just to treat the trauma, but also on a practical level. Moving away from a dissociative defense serves to protect both themselves and others from additional trauma.

Dissociation's Domino Effect

A bold statement was made earlier in this chapter: *dissociation is evidence of a developmental catastrophe.* What are the devolving components indicative of this damage? The following is a list of successive repercussions of dissociation.

1. Early use of dissociation is evidenced as causing enduring changes in neurobiological organization (Schore, 2002).
2. These neurobiological changes will lead to a bias toward using dissociation as a defense in other frustrating or overwhelming emotional/interpersonal situations (Schore, 2002).
3. Dissociation occurs when children cannot endure external pain or overwhelming stress. In situations of maltreatment, it also occurs when they cannot endure internally induced pain, for example, when their memory systems are triggered,

causing them to remember some of their former traumatic life events. So, when people start to experience feelings reminiscent of the trauma, instead of connecting the events that are occurring in their lives in the present with their associated feelings, they dissociate.

4. Traumatized children begin to organize their lives on parallel tracks. Their unconscious brain recognizes danger, but they do not react to the danger by thinking about it and responding with a coping strategy. Instead, they use their early defenses—dissociation or denial.

5. This parallel way of operating in the world predisposes them to high-risk situations. They do not respond to highly charged emotional information by seeking help or by leaving. Their bodies show that they are under stress, but they are not be able to recognize the source of the stress or even acknowledge any more than a sense of jitteriness, numbness, or disorganization.

6. Dissociation uncouples the mind-body connection. It isolates the feelings of emotional or physical danger from the cognitive functions that allow people to determine whether or not they are in danger. In this way, dissociating people stay in a dangerous or high-risk situation instead of coming up with a course of action.

Often parents who have been abused and learned to dissociate will leave their children in situations thick with the ominous predictors of abuse. Why do these parents ignore the danger signs? This phenomenon is explained by dissociation's effects on functioning. Parents begin to dissociate when their memory systems are triggered by these high-risk situations. They do not respond to their internal pain and dread with action or insight. Instead, they dissociate from these trauma-laced events. Parents who are living a life of parallel tracks may make dinner or lie down with a headache while their child is being sexually abused in the living room.

The public health implication behind early and successful trauma treatment for children is that we, as a society, can prevent successive generations of abuse. Children are far less dissociative after receiving treatment. Their inability to connect bad events with their feelings can be repaired. Emily illustrates this.

Emily, age 13, had been left beside a freeway with her sister and brother when she was 5 years old. On many occasions she had been left in the home alone. Before treatment for trauma, she was marked by dissociation. After treatment for trauma following her adoption at age 8, she became far less dissociative. She began problem solving. At age 12, she wrote an essay on taking responsibility for her life.

One morning, after picking up Emily and her sister in her car, Emily's babysitter ran into the house to make a phone call, telling Emily to catch her school bus as she left, and leaving Emily's newly adopted baby sister in the car outside in the driveway. Emily took action. Rather than getting on the bus to school, she stayed outside beside the car, right beside her sister. She called her mother on her cell phone, even though she knew that the sitter would be angry. She stayed outside with her sister for twenty-five minutes.

"I won't ever let that kind of thing happen again," she said. "Anyone could have taken my sister. She wasn't safe."

The mother left work to pick up both children. The babysitter was fired. Emily was praised for her clear thinking.

Sometimes parents or professionals want to assess the degree of dissociation that a child demonstrates in day-to-day life. Reliable and valid scales for dissociation in children, by Frank Putnam, and for adolescents, by Judith Armstrong, Frank Putnam, and Eve Carlson, are included in the appendix of this book (no copyright restrictions apply). They are excellent tools for parents and professionals. There are more assessment tools that include ways to measure dissociation listed in the Resource List. "The Trauma Symptom Checklist for Children" by John Briere is particularly helpful.

Working with Dissociative Children in Therapeutic Tasks

Children who have learned to "zone out" rather than to put their lives together into a smooth story are difficult to treat in therapy. Their abilities to learn ways to cope are underdeveloped in many ways, including in receiving emotional help from parents or therapists. They need help learning how to calm themselves and slow down stress reactions, also known as affect regulation.

These children will often flood with emotions during their first attempts at working on integration with therapists or caseworkers. It is imperative to teach calming, methods of getting help, and pacing as part of integration work. It is equally important not to believe that children are "fine" even after they are found to be unable to think about vast sections of their lives.

> One mother said, "My son was adopted at 11 years old. They said that he might not go to college, but other than that, he was fine. Of course, he was a time bomb after all of the abandonment that he had been through. We had some good years before he went off completely. We try to hold onto those years."

In defense of this boy's caseworker, she probably wanted to believe him when he told her that he was fine and never thought about his mistreatment. Of course, he did not mention that he was actually unable to think about any of it. Or, that he became enraged when faced with situations that evoked memories.

The take-home message for dissociation is that an increase in dissociation in a child is always balanced by loss of true coping. The self has mortgaged the future to survive in the present. The balloon payment will come due—usually in teen years.

Affective Dysregulation

Trauma has such an impact on psychobiological systems that it limits the capacity to sustain even moods. Mood swings make social contexts difficult. Children who become too excited to sit on the bus during the field trip, or who react with extra sensitivity to daily events, for example, can be taxing to friends. While there is typically some tolerance among friends, it is limited.

> A 12-year-old described his friend's behavior during the sixth grade class movie, *Old Yeller*. "We looked forward to the movie because our class had read the book. During the deer and fence part, Simon started to get really sad and to cry a

lot. He's my friend, so I told him, 'It's just a movie,' and gave him some of my desk tissues.

"Then, Simon kept crying harder and put his head down on the desk. Finally he cried so much that it was just awful. He cried more than anyone in the class. I gave him all of the tissues in my desk. Then he used the teacher's box up, so we had to go get another box from another sixth grade. It was so embarrassing. All the kids were looking at me like, 'He's your friend. Help him.' I didn't know what to do. No one did."

Simon had exceeded the typical limits of his friend's tolerance. In our complex society, the ability to balance moods is essential. Even if family members can look past outbursts and highs and lows, in institutional settings, such as school systems, medical clinics, and the workplace, others will not. For the short-term, it is helpful to provide more buffering or accommodations for traumatized children in school. However, long-term, effective therapy and teaching traumatized children the rudiments of emotional intelligence are essential to their future.

More of the practicalities of teaching emotional intelligence are described in the case examples provided in subsequent chapters. Parents and therapists can teach these abilities during the therapeutic process by aiding the sense of perspective, describing the importance of the big picture rather than the details, explaining things through the viewpoint of another's interests, and so forth.

An excellent reference book on developing emotional intelligence, including affective regulation, is *Relational Development Intervention (RDI)* (Gutstein, Sheely, 2002). This book is referenced in the Resource List. The inventory in the back of *RDI* delineates the progressive development of social and emotional skills. It refers the reader to matching exercises that may be used in the home and classroom. Older children can be helped using *Navigating the Social World*, a manual by Jeanette McAfee, also referenced in the Resource List. Even through both references were primarily developed for children with autistic spectrum disorders, they are still extremely helpful for the children in this book. A cognitive behavioral approach to affect regulation is described well in Bloomquist's latest edition of *Skills Training for Children with Behavior Problems* (2006).

Aggression

When people feel that their lives are in danger, they tend to freeze, fight, or flee. The section above on dissociation describes the freeze or "flight when there is no flight option." Fighting, or aggression, is part of the expected symptom pattern for many children and adults after trauma.

Post-trauma victims tend to over-interpret life events as threatening. This is particularly the case when the trauma has occurred during early stages of brain development. The trauma experience causes more receptor sites to form in the developing brain. These extra receptor sites prejudice the brain toward interpreting new information in an extreme and paranoid manner.

Often these extreme responses occur so quickly that children do not have the opportunity to rethink the situation. Instead, they kick or hit. The case of Mia, adopted at fifteen months, exemplifies this early shaping.

> Mia came in with her mother within three weeks of her placement. She had a fixed gaze on her mother's eyes and batted at her mother's face. She was all knees and elbows on her mother's lap. She fought to hold food by herself. Her mother queried, "Do you think that she is just independent? I think that she is exploring my face. But it is hurting me quite a bit." In fact, the mother had several bruises on her arms and scratch marks on her cheeks and around her eyes.
>
> Mia and her mother left with appropriate instructions on self-preservation and soothing care. These instructions included having Mom hold Mia's hands and feet away from her mother's head and telling Mia, in simple words and with exaggerated facial cues while demonstrating on a doll, that Mom and Dad would not hurt her. The parents spent time cuddling the doll and stroking its face to indirectly invite Mia into their laps. (It probably should be noted that she angrily pushed the doll to the floor in order to climb up for her cuddles.) The parents described a rapid decrease in aggressive behavior.

Mia reappeared in my office five years later. Now 6 years old, Mia was kicking, hitting, and scratching schoolmates when she perceived scarcity or physical aggression. Defending herself, she described, "That girl was taking the last pencil! If she had let me go first, I would not have kicked her. She should have moved!"

When asked whether it bothered her that she had kicked the girl in the face, Mia said flatly and patiently, "But she took the last pencil. She should have moved. It wasn't fair."

Aggression is amplified in traumatized children because they feel that their survival is at stake. In Mia's case, aggression was part of her earliest makeup. While Mia responded beautifully to treatment over the course of the next eighteen months, the process required helping her to become aware of her fear, to notice and interpret the feelings of others, and to improve her attachments and her resultant sense of safety was methodical and even tedious.

By the age of 5, most children go through a developmental window that allows them to successfully inhibit physical aggression. While there are lapses, these lapses occur in small numbers in normal children. Often the lapses are with siblings, in the school bus line, or at recess. There tends to be restraint even within the loss of control. The aggression is a push, an open-handed slap on an arm or back, or tripping.

Children who are mentioned in case reports as "aggressive" tend to present significantly more serious physical lapses that can include punching in the face, kicking in the genitals, throwing rocks, or pulling out plugs of hair. Parents who adopt children who have been traumatized and neglected need to have special help with building a parenting plan that will help manage their child's aggression. Notably, this is an area where most of the parents I see have expressed a lack of support from adoption professionals.

Parents, and the caseworkers who are working with them, tend to be motivated by a desire to help children find safety and connection through adoption. They are compassionate and see children as victims. The flip side of the neglect/trauma coin is that children who have been victims can be victimizing as well. Aggression is discussed more in terms of home and therapeutic plans in Chapters 8 and 10.

Aggression Turned onto the Self

Aggression unleashed onto the child by herself is a common theme in traumatized people. Children find that by inducing pain on themselves, they can interrupt their internal flow of distressful thoughts and feelings. In sessions with me, children often say that it does not really hurt when they slice themselves. The traumatic images with the accompanying horrible feelings, or the anger with which they are seething, are much more distressful as compared to their self-harm. Hurting themselves gives children a way to stop the flow of images, or to deal with painful feelings. A 12-year-old boy described this to me.

> "When my mother gives me a consequence, sometimes I think of my birthmother sexually abusing me. I feel like I want to die. But if I poke a pencil into my legs—above my shorts—no one sees it. Then I feel better. When I look at the marks, I am sorry for myself. I cry in my room. My mom sees the scabs when my shorts ride up. I know that it makes her mad and sad. That makes me feel a little bit sorry, and a little bit like, 'Ha, ha, ha. She can't stop me.' I know that I shouldn't do it, but I need a way to get my mads out."

Of course, any parent who is attempting to help a child with typical parenting consequences anxiously weighs the consequence's potential for self harm. Children need more structure and more behavioral interventions after neglect/trauma. Parents have to struggle to help children accurately interpret their parenting interventions.

In the case above, a lengthy course of therapy helped assuage the internally-produced images. Processing the meaning of discipline was also helpful. This was accomplished by describing the parenting intent. Parents need to give consequences or negative feedback at times. We made a careful distinction between abuse and discipline.

His parents and I emphasized that the discipline was not a "payback," but a way for him to learn new behaviors or to do restitution. The boy walked through the pattern of receiving discipline, roleplaying it twice. Then, he received the consequence in earnest with a de-briefing just after the discipline. (Discipline tended to be writing a letter to the aggrieved person, doing a chore for them, missing television, and so forth.) This, over time, arrested the aggression he felt towards himself. He learned to modulate his intense feelings. He did this by learning how to accept his parent's non-verbal and verbal messages rather than using painful injuries.

One of the driving forces behind aggression toward self is the child's belief that he may have caused the abuse. Most children prefer being the cause of the abuse or rejection over putting the control into someone else's hands. Life feels a little more predictable when they think they have identified the error that caused their trauma or traumatic treatment. Part of the therapeutic process is helping children disengage from being the cause of trauma. Children who can accept safety and protection from their new families tend to be the most successful at working through a trauma that contaminates their self-identity. This work helps reduce the drivers for self-injury.

Benefits to Treating Aggression through Parental Support

After summarizing the psychobiological effects of early relational trauma, the literature comes back to the efficacy of one-on-one relationships in which children learn to regulate strong emotions. "Through secure attachments, children's neurobiological maturation of the right brain is facilitated...which is centrally involved in the adaptive regulation of motivational states, including aggressive states, and in enabling the individual to cope with stress" (Solomon, Siegel, 2003, p. 148).

The key to successfully resolving aggression is in providing training and support for parents. It is the parents who must maintain an emotional connection with their children in the midst of aggression. Parents need coaching and practice using specialized techniques in order to continue to deal with traumatized children. These techniques allow children to connect with the parents' safety and resources. Parents trump the situation by using their caring and sense of regulation, all the while preventing their children from injuring anyone. Without instruction and support, parents are only occasionally effective in performing well when faced with out-of-control children. They need encouragement and nurturing in order to continue on with the process of helping their children.

Of course, the always attractive option that simultaneously frightens parents is to distance themselves from their children. Emotional disengagement can appear to be an easier choice as compared to completing the above process. While stepping back just enough to be thoughtful with an aggressive child is an effective strategy, if parents disengage, then children will feel further abandoned and even more dysregulated. Additionally, children cannot receive a stress regulation template from a parent who just does not care. Chris, aged twelve, illustrates an effective alternative to distancing.

> Chris was a sneaky, sometimes raging, and regularly frustrating child. His parents were aware that Chris spent a lot of time throwing sand in the family's gears. He also spent a lot of supervised time repeating a routine "right" twice—like putting his wet towel in the dirty laundry, not the clean laundry. Repetitions of these daily events could cause two hours of tantrums. But if the parents avoided the task, another daily event would become the fodder for the next firestorm. Chris would scream about how much he hated his parents. They would respond to him by affirming that he would "come along" and that he was an important and valued member of their family.
>
> Logic did not appear to touch Chris. Over time, his parents' steadiness did. He concluded, "I yelled at them that they were the worst parents in the world, but underneath I was saying that I was the worst kid in the world. And I always knew that they loved me, but I couldn't accept that they loved me. I felt like I wanted to fight them. But I really didn't. I'm glad that they didn't give up on me."

The body and brain are influenced so much by threatening circumstances after trauma that they become oriented toward aggression. The therapist, caseworker, and parents must team up to show children the route away from the battleground. Good therapy helps children develop the belief that they can lay their weapons down: that they are safe. Parents must model and instruct with a safe, nurturing, protective, and appropriately structured home life. Caseworkers must coach parents, offer support groups, and deliver post-placement services so that aggression behaviors can be matched by excellent care.

It is helpful to investigate why each instance of the aggression occurred at that time, in that setting, or with that theme. Sometimes it is because the child has had a traumatic memory or a flashback. This is difficult to track, since children may dissociate first and then become extremely aggressive afterwards. It is well worth the effort in tracking. I like to try to figure this out with children/teens and their parents. It helps them on the road to making sense of their reactions and coming up with alternatives.

Intrusive Memories and Flashbacks

Intrusive memories interfere with the daily joys of life. Therapists must treat trauma in children practically. There should be a dialogue about what the child experienced and how to handle it. The story of Ki, a 10-year-old, describes this direct approach.

Ki's father said, "Ki wanted to go to a haunted house for Halloween. On the way there, he wanted us to stop the car to get something to eat. We were in a friend's van, so we didn't stop. When we got to the haunted house he became impossible. He was whining, mean, selfish, and picky. I had him wait outside with me because he was ruining it for everybody."

"Fine," Ki ranted at his father. "You are such a bully! You ruin everything. Our family would be better without you. Why are you always sleeping over? (This dumbfounded Ki's father, who was in his 20th year of married life.) I hate you!"

In the therapy session that followed this incident, we found out that Ki had looked at the brochure on the way to the event. It contained frightening images. Ki had had a flashback in the car. It lasted for several miles. He could not speak. He remembered being transported in another van by his mother's boyfriend and ultimately being sexually abused. When he regained his ability to speak, he did not know how to signal his panic to his father. He just asked to stop for food. When his father did not stop, he was too far gone to think of another idea.

We made a plan for what to do if he had another flashback. He would say that he had to vomit. Then, his father could calm him down and together they could figure out a next step.

We worked on the trauma trigger in therapy to reduce the incidence of intrusive memories. However, over the next four years, Ki only needed to use the "throw-up" excuse once. Having the plan simultaneously brought the memory into better integration. As therapy concluded, Ki hugged his father and apologized for being so hard on him. "I was confused. I started to think that you were my birthmother's boyfriend. I know that you are not like that. But, I do get mad at you when you make me do things that I don't want to do."

"I know, Ki," said his father. "I'll always help you, but I will still make you do jobs for me if you act disrespectfully. I want you to grow into a good man."

The balance of accountability and sensitivity to trauma shown to Ki by his father is a healing combination.

Therapists need to help children establish a pattern of working through intrusive memories or flashbacks. Children tend to avoid trauma issues until they have experienced help and comfort a number of times. Therapists need to be explicit. "I will be responsible for helping you to calm down before you leave today. I will not bring up too much in the sessions. I will not leave my job or move away while we are in the middle of this work," and so forth. This teaches children that the therapist will support them during trauma work so that they can feel better-connected and less afraid of the work. Of course, giving children practical techniques to deal with flashbacks and traumatic memories helps them to establish a sense of mastery. These techniques are described in the cases sections in Chapter 10.

Somatization

Somatization is the term used to describe a feeling of genuine physical distress caused by psychological issues. It can be thought of as an overactive alarm in the body. The brain becomes preoccupied with the drama of survival after trauma. It keeps checking the body over and over again to determine whether something else might be going wrong. Somatization, then, is the act of taking psychological distress into the body as pain or distress.

Children who have been traumatized often have stress-related complaints of ailments such as headaches, stomach aches, itching, body aches, and so forth. Often these ailments help induce a cycle of receiving much-needed care. However, the medical care provided for physical distress does not, over time, increase feelings of security. Every day the bucket is empty again. Caregivers get weary of the complaints. Advising them to ignore the physical does not help to rebuild their child's mind-body connection. Therapy for trauma asks children to notice their bodies' feelings. We cannot simultaneously tell them to stop complaining.

Therapists do well when using a psychoeducational approach with these parents and children. When children or teens understand somatization, they become better detectives themselves. They begin to look for ways in which they are feeling threatened. They practice other methods of asking for closeness and attention during times of stress.

It is imperative when treating trauma to help the person to feel more safety, connection, and mastery in the world, reducing the incidence of these types of painful body experiences. Within the context of treatment, working on physical symptoms can be discussed in a caring, rather than dismissive, manner.

In summary, the issues of trauma mentioned above are ones that form an important symptom cluster. These areas will need specific attention during therapy and also in daily life. Adaptations to trauma that are distressing to children and the families who love them are both symptoms of the trauma, as well as problematic in themselves. A motivator to get treatment and to use specialized parenting is to see a decrease in the severity of the distress that children experience in these symptom areas.

> As one teen boy said, reflecting on his early trauma work with me, "I was hurt in my early life, and I was passing it on, hurting others. I set goals in therapy and met those goals. I could tell that I was changing. I'm not scared all the time now. I am a caring person."

CHAPTER 5

Early Relational Trauma, Traumatic Loss, and Effects on Development

"I want to conquer my dad, just dominate him! It would give me so much pleasure. I think it has something to do with being hurt by my birthfather."

–John, age 11

Trauma caused by caregivers in the early years has long-term and complex effects on child development. Trauma within the caregiving relationship is the most destructive early psychological insult. These relationships place children in a particularly cruel dilemma. They are unable to be safe without the parent; yet they are not safe with the parent. As a consequence, their stress levels are unendurable at times. Rather than building a pattern of attunement, with some mild mis-attunement and effective repair, children are faced with massively overwhelming experiences. Their figure of safety is also the source of their fears. Their source of food, nurture, and connection is also the source of their terror. They need to approach and they need to flee. They need to open up for attention and they need to withdraw for safety. It is an unendurable psychological conflict. This chapter lays the foundation for the coming chapters that give strategies for helping children with these conflicts.

An individual's predisposition towards resilience following stress is one positive product of having relationships with competent caregivers.[1] The ease and comfort with which people approach each other for friendships and connections are other important endowments from experiencing early safe relations with caregivers.

Early relational trauma by a caregiver has a malignant effect on brain development. As noted earlier, children's moods are largely co-regulated with their caregivers during the first eighteen months of life. When children are traumatized by their parents, the unregulated negative emotional states of the caregiver become the co-regulation standard for the infant in place of optimal brain wiring. As Allan Schore describes,

> "In traumatic episodes, the infant is presented with another affectively overwhelming facial expression, a maternal expression of fear-terror…the infant is matching the rhythmic structures of the mother's dysregulated states, and that this synchronization is registered in the firing patterns of the stress-sensitive corticolimbic regions of the infant's brain that are in a critical period of growth.

> "In light of the fact that many of these mothers have suffered from unresolved trauma themselves, this spatiotemporal imprinting of the chaotic alteration of the mother's dysregulated states facilitates the downloading of programs of psychogeneses, a context for the intergenerational transmission of trauma" (2003, p. 252).

Parents do not necessarily have to be abusive in the traditional physical sense to pass this effect on to their children. Instead, they can have this effect by being frightened and frightening. For example, a parent places his child into chaos when, with the baby/child in his arms, he is fighting with another adult, weeping uncontrollably, or experiencing states of terror and rage.

Children who are receiving rough and dismissive orphanage care also show evidence of damage from early relational trauma. They are

---

[1] Genetics also play a part in resilience. Children who are genetically predisposed to anxiety or mood disorders are more likely to see these issues emerge, or to become more severe, if they have experienced adverse life events. Some experiences that dysregulate, like abuse or trauma, will set off a series of other dysregulating processes triggering problems in a person already genetically predisposed.

attempting to connect with these caregivers. Often, however, there is a complete lack of attunement between the children's states and those of their caregivers. This lack of attunement is evident in Tasha's description below.

> "I used to smile at the mamachkas to try to get them to play with me or take me to the market with them. They would only take me if I smiled. If I cried, they would not pick me up. I was really mad at them a lot. I did not show them how I felt. I did not trust them and used to take things out of their purses when I could."

Tasha's example shows the lack of authenticity in these relationships. She could not get attention when she was in an authentic state. She correctly perceived that the caregivers had no interest in meeting her tender needs. Later, she was remarkably good at trying to figure out what people wanted so that she could get what she wanted. She had also become a lonely girl who could not let her parents get close without feeling extreme anxiety. She anticipated rejection with every authentic interaction.

What do reactions to parents look like in children who have been maltreated in earlier relationships?

- Often children will wince when parents come close physically.
- They avoid eye contact so that they do not have to attune to the parent's emotional states—anticipating that sharing emotions will be painful.
- They regularly keep their feet up at waist level—ready to kick out to protect themselves.
- They experience gastric distress when they get physically and emotionally close to a parent. They begin passing gas or have to use the bathroom.
- They may try to control parents, using words, body language, or through role reversals.
- They control when it is time to disengage in a hug—and panic or fight if the parents do not immediately comply. (As a note, parents should allow children to disengage from hugs or affection, especially if they become agitated or frightened.)

Parents often go through tremendous soul-searching in response to these reactions, wondering how to attune to their children. They realize that many of the things that they are doing seem to be traumatizing their children. Sadly, it is the association with parent figures in and of itself that feels traumatic to children. They are simply afraid of parents. One 4-year-old in therapy typifies this reaction to parents.

Sophia had been in her family for a year. She avoided her father and only hugged her mother in a curled position, with her head tucked, eyes shut, and face strained. She could get down any time that she wanted, which she did a number of times. We encouraged her to try to stay in her mother's lap, because she really did crave the affection that her siblings got. After a few therapy sessions, in which she was assured of safety, she was able to turn her face up and look into her mother's eyes for a count of ten. Her mother's loving face was pointed out to her, so that she could recognize a safe, friendly face. Within a few weeks she was cheerfully receiving hugs and snuggles without fear.

In spite of encouragement, she simply could not approach her father. She tried, but froze. I complimented her for trying, reflecting that when she felt safer, she would be able to cuddle with him. Fortunately, her father was able to accept the lack of resolution and did not force or press her.

By the fifth session, Sophia described being burned by a cigarette by a father figure—as well as violent fights in her birthfamily. She would have been just under 3 at the time of the abuse. As she progressed in therapy over the next six sessions, she no longer avoided her father. She began to be his buddy, dogging his steps, and giving and receiving hugs. "He is not the hurting daddy," she told me earnestly. "He is my good poppa. I love my poppa. I love my momma."

Early Relational Trauma and Low Arousal

After early relational trauma, children are prone to "a greater right than left resting frontal activation at 3 years...Greater right than left resting frontal activation at 3 years is associated with a lack of empathy and by 4½ years with oppositional defiant disorder"[2] (Solomon, Siegel, 2003, pp. 138-9). This brain pattern is that of a low arousal brain. Children with this brain pattern seem to need more stimulation in order to feel optimal or normal levels of arousal. Aggression and/or exposing the self to high-risk situations are examples of stimulation-seeking behaviors, which are accompanied by a lack of empathy. This is the type of brain development seen in antisocial personality disordered individuals.

Allan Schore, an oft-mentioned researcher in this book, describes the types of negative caregiver environments that would bring out the most aggressiveness/dysregulation in traumatized children and adults. One environment listed is that of pre-and/or postnatal maternal alcohol or cocaine use. Another would be maternal neglect followed by paternal abuse and humiliation (Solomon, Siegel, 2003, p. 138).

Of course, these are precisely the patterns of early relational trauma that adoptive and foster parents often face with their children. Brain and developmental experts recommend remediation through programs of emotional rehabilitation—helping children develop attunement to safe adults, positive attachment experiences, and ample opportunities to work on calming and self-regulation.

In spite of the complexities associated with the earliest effects of maltreatment, the rehabilitation is characterized by stark simplicity. Parents who are sensitive, who are able to model and teach calming and self-regulation, and who are given enough support to keep connecting with difficult children form the healing milieu at home. Professionals need to be skilled both at supporting parents in these

---

[2] Oppositional Defiant Disorder is defined in the Glossary section at the end of this book. Briefly, such individuals display a number of the following: annoyed easily, angry and resentful, spiteful and vindictive, defies rules or requests of adults, blames others for own errors, argues with adults, and loses temper (DSM IV-TR).

activities and also able to help them explore and overcome obstacles in attachment, as in Sophia's situation detailed in the section above.

It helps to speak to children with low arousal states about tolerating and enjoying a less arousing environment. I usually speak to them about how exciting, but how frightening, some of their experiences have been. They recall a few of the experiences, for example, hiding in closets, or shopping for groceries with money pulled from the pants of a passed-out adult. These experiences were both thrilling and scary. We go on to discuss giving up some of this excitement for safety.

Children can relax into a safe feeling and recall feelings associated with some other emotionally rewarding experiences with their present parents through further discussions. Examples that children have shared with me include being up to bat and hitting a ball, knowing that their parents are watching and feeling pride and joy; or waking up in the morning and being told that their parents are taking them to Disneyland; or wrestling with a playful and dramatic parent. Children begin to store these memories as part of their new schema of themselves. Thinking about these memories boosts their mood.

I also try to identify extremely arousing activities for some children. One family hung a harness and a pulley between two large trees. Their teens loved the thrill of the climb and the ride. Other children play a sport in every season and have skateboards, horses, or other high intensity activities that they can do daily. One teen said to me, "Deborah, if I can just make it through the time between kayaking season and snowboarding, I know that I will be all right. I can make it through a school week if I know that I'll be on the water or on the slopes by the weekend."

Prenatal Stress

Often families describe their children as looking quite anxious even though they have never been through a known trauma. Some people describe this in personal terms, making comments like, "I think she knew from the womb that she was not wanted." This book does not try to analyze those beliefs. But I will point out the informative studies that suggest prenatal influences on the developing brain. There are human studies summarized in the *Handbook of Infant Mental Health* by Charles Zeanah showing the effects of maternal stress on the development of the fetus' brain (2000, pp.37-55). There is interesting research being done on rodents on the influence of stress on the developing brain as well.

Prenatal stressors are important considerations in placements. They are critical to the way society views and supports expectant mothers. Highly stressed women have high levels of circulating glucocortocoids. These glucocortocoids are thought to influence the prenatal brain, causing structural differences in the unborn child by 26 weeks gestation (Nelson, Bosquet, 2000, pp.43-46). It is important to examine the areas that are most likely to be affected, which include the areas of the brain associated with anxiety, attachment, memory and executive functions. Maternal stress may affect fetal brain development via hyperactivity in the maternal hypothalamic-pituitary-adrenal axis (HPA axis). Other areas of the brain with high numbers of glucocortocoid receptors, and thus more likely to be shaped by prenatal stress, include

- the cingulate gyrus, which is thought to be involved in conscious attention, inhibitory control, and self-regulation of emotion and behavior
- the amygdala, which has been implicated in fear and stress reactions
- frontal lobe regions, which have been implicated in attentional attributes (Nelson, Bosquet, 2000. p. 44-45).

Prenatal stress is also shown to be related to changes in serotonin levels in rat brain studies. Normal serotonin levels are critical to maintaining both a positive mood and a desire for social interaction.

This section raises more good questions than it answers, such as whether parenting techniques for prenatally stressed children should be altered right from the beginning, with an increase in soothing and gentler transitions. It also raises questions as to whether and to what degree the high rate of attentional difficulties in adopted children are related to the stress of an unplanned pregnancy.

The take-home message here is that there seems to be evidence of shaping by the prenatal environment. Certainly providing better support for all pregnant women, so that they are not under such duress, is not only a moral matter, but a practical one. Placing high stress on pregnant women may force unborn children to pay part of the price. Child welfare workers often wonder whether to use a confrontational model or supportive model with pregnant women. The information about stress and prenatal development should help guide practices.[3]

How Trauma and Neglect's Emotional States Become Emotional Traits

Sometimes there is a discrepancy between a child's reactions to misfortune and how we predict they will fare in life. When examining which children will recover from traumatic stress symptoms, the twin factors of neglect and separation from parents are two of the most ominous risk factors (van der Kolk, 2002). Children who have negative moods as altered by loss, trauma, and neglect tend to become negative adults, often troubled by depression and withdrawal. Sadly, the greatest predictor for being a highly anxious adult is being a highly anxious child, another common attribute in children who have been maltreated (Sroufe, 2002).

The moods and defenses stemming from early trauma gradually become what others perceive to be the core personality. Powerful intervening variables for children include forming loving connections and providing assistance in order to heal from the effects of maltreatment. The children most likely to recover are the ones who feel safe and have confidence in handling life stressors. In the vignette earlier, we met Natasha, whose parents' neglect had resulted in an orphanage placement.

---

[3] A study compared the effectiveness of models that provided support and resources to parents involved with Child Protective Services. The take-home message is that these parents did best with help in understanding how their own life events related to their treatment of their children. The outcome measures were assessed, in part, by children's views of their parents after the interventions. A model with extra resources and stricter accountability/tracking was less effective (Toth et al., 2002).

With the help of her parents and the therapist, Natasha developed the capacity to reflect on her life. In other words, she could stand back from events in order to think about the experience without feeling the full impact of the trauma again. She developed a sense of perspective. She reduced her sensitivity to the trauma but could still work through the feelings of shame and loss, and the meaning of those events in her own life.

Natasha described, "Sometimes when my dad plays with my brother, I remember my birthdad and how he kicked my brother. When my brother yells, I start to get mad and hide. But then I relax and say, 'Calm down, Natasha, they are just playing around.' I used to listen for noise because it meant that I was in trouble or that my brother was. Now it's different. The only time that it's quiet in the house is when those two are gone, but no one is getting hurt when it is noisy."

Fear of feelings and avoidance of therapy

Children who do not have reliable caregivers to soothe and buffer them do not go on to develop the capacity to think about abuse and neglect without having the sensation that they are re-experiencing it (Fonagy, 2002, p. 343-371). Consequently, these children tend to be exquisitely sensitive to reminders of the traumas as well as to information about the meaning of trauma to their sense of self.

They tend to be terribly frightened of bringing the issues around trauma to the surface. They do not want to work on the issues, since this seems too overwhelming. It feels to them that they are back in the original situation. They project an experience identical to the original experience, one in which there is no reliable person to work through issues with them. They think that they will be alone in the experience again. In not working through the issues, however, their lives become trauma-contaminated. The very meaning of their selves and their relationships become organized around the trauma.

Parents who are working with children who have been neglected will need to rebuild the capacity for reflection. The capacity to calm is a core self quality. As Schore describes, "The orbital cortex matures in the middle of the second year… The core of the self is both non-verbal and unconscious, and it lies in patterns of affect regulation. This structural development allows for an internal sense of security and resilience that comes from the intuitive knowledge that one can regulate the flows and shifts of one's bodily based emotional states either by one's own coping capacities or within a relationship with a caring other" (*Affect Dysregulation*, 2003, p. 250).

Confidence in the ability to handle shifts in moods and reactions gives children an incredible freedom to explore life and its challenges. Reflecting on life, and making plans for life, is part of the process of exploration. Children and adults can reach out for help as part of their plan. This will be discussed more in Chapter 8.

Abuse and the Coordination between Thoughts and Feelings

Abuse, and particularly emotional abuse, tends to result in thinning of the corpus callosum, the structure that connects the right side of the brain with the left. The thinning makes the individual more prone to emotional flooding. Why is this a problem? Language abilities are contained in both the right and the left cerebral hemispheres. It is the left cerebral hemisphere, however, which contains structures like Broca's and Wernicke's areas, and that dominates this function. Communication requires that both sides of the brain are functioning and connected to each other; during emotional flooding the right hemisphere dominates and shuts out input from the left side (MacKenzie, 2007). When people flood with emotion, it means that they cannot access the parts of the brain that control language, self-control, problem-solving, and a sense of time (van der Kolk, 2002).

As a result, the linguistic left brain is not able to use language as effectively, including self-talk, auditory sequencing, or descriptions of the content of emotional distress. This has enormous implications for people who are trying to help children after trauma. When children flood, they are not able to maintain themselves as problem-solvers or sequence the events that they have experienced, while simultaneously accessing the soothing self-talk that helps them calm down.

The result is that they can feel a great deal, but they are not able to think about this at the same time. Or, they can think about what happened without feeling it. The next time that something happens to trigger the same feeling, however, they cannot remember the discussion. Memory systems are "hot" memory systems. The "heating up" part is the feelings. That is, people need some feelings to relate to in order to remember earlier feelings and events. But, when children who are prone to flooding recall memories, they tend to remember in an overwhelming, counterproductive way. It takes time and a keen sense of pacing to help these children remember some of the feelings around trauma without becoming overwhelmed, and then make sense of the feelings and events simultaneously.

Parents will often say, "But we talked about this! I cannot believe that we are back to the same behavior. I know that she understood!" Unfortunately, children may not have a connection to that discussion when presented with emotionally-charged information. They may move into a "feelings only" mode. And, when the discussion occurred, they probably were in a "thinking only" mode. This is why there is so much emphasis in therapy on pacing, making plans, and thinking and feeling together in a well-regulated manner when processing good trauma work.

John Briere describes the effects of abuse, in terms of the ability to stay within a comfortable emotional state, as having three main components that act to impact affect modulation. Those three components are

- interference with the development of attachment and trust for others
- decreased self-awareness due to hypervigilance
- less exploration of the world (2002).

The practical implications of this are that

- the child stops trusting as a safety precaution—but ultimately is more anxious because she does not have people to help her and has to rely on herself
- the child looks around constantly in order to keep himself safe. But, he misses the cues from his own body that would help him detect that he was feeling scared

- the child is so preoccupied with safety that she cannot explore. As a result, she knows less of the world and is not as masterful, which reduces her options and adaptability.

All of these areas will need to be redressed in the home and in a therapeutic setting.

The take-home message from this section is that there are brain-based reasons why abused or neglected children have difficulties thinking and feeling simultaneously, literally reacting to stress in an "unreasonable" manner. They need therapeutic approaches that allow for gradual increases in their coping skills. Parents and therapists should not take these children's differences in development personally. However, they should proactively help these children learn stress-reduction techniques. Template after template should be developed for problem-solving.

Great appreciation should be shown any time children are emotionally upset and yet make attempts to calm themselves enough to solve problems in their lives. All of these processes can progress only if children are placed into homes that are safe and with parents able to teach models of soothing, calming, and respectful problem-solving. And, any lapse must be met with a discussion that includes emotional repair as well as suggestions for the next time.

CHAPTER 6

Trauma and Neglect— Double Insults

"I've been dumped by two families, abandoned by my birthfamily, and abused. I feel like I've had to climb Mt. Everest to get to where I am today—and I'm still climbing. My friends just took a helicopter. " −13-year-old Kellen

Neglect and trauma regularly occur together. Yet, as Jon Allen points out in his book *Traumatic Relationships and Serious Mental Disorders*, "Abuse is often compounded by neglect. Whereas abuse generally consists of acts of commission, neglect generally consists of acts of omission" (2001, p. 31). While neglect tends to result in fewer official reports to child protective service systems, it still achieves the distinction of representing the largest component of official cases of child maltreatment confronting our child protective services systems today.

Compounding Effects

The *compounding effect* mentioned by Jon Allen is a serious consideration for anyone working with maltreated children. The *reflective capacity* described in Chapter 3 represents a major issue. People who have this reflective capacity can stand back from their experiences and think about the past or present. When they think about an experience they are not "in it," or feeling it with the same intensity as the original experience. This helps them to modulate their emotions and to regulate stress. Neglect negatively impacts this process. It results in an impoverished state of the mental resources needed to deal with trauma. It promotes a "defensive withdrawal from the mental world" (Fonagy, Target, 1997). The outcome of this is that neglected individuals tend to have poor outcomes when in therapy for trauma. The rebuilding of reflective thought will have to be undertaken as a part of therapy and home life.

When children are very young, it is protective for them not to know the mental state of abusive or neglectful caregivers. Instead of exploring the mind of others and oneself, children choose to "not know" their parents' episodic hate, contempt, boredom, and detachment. It is too fracturing to their developing personalities to acknowledge these states. Instead, they avoid learning about others' feelings in relation to themselves or their own feelings as they relate to their best interests. The outcome is simple and dramatic. Children cannot think and feel at the same time. The add-on is that they can feel their emotions and the others' emotions but not both at the same time. This interrupts the healthy process of perceiving their impact on the thoughts and feelings of another. This knowledge about their own thinking and feeling process, as well as that of others can be called *mindsight* (Siegel, 2006).

Basically, mindsight allows to people to see themselves reflected in the heart and mind of another. This is an essential in any close, two-way relationship. This process is stunted during neglect. Children are afraid to begin the process again because of the information that "knowing" gives them. As Chris said,

> "My birthmother treated me like garbage. She put me in my room all day. I hated that. Why did she hate me? She punched me in the stomach at night. Why? What did I do wrong? Why?"

After placement, Chris was afraid to even acknowledge his feelings. But he would explode when told "No." He folded into the fetal position when he started to get sad. He could only begin to face his sad and frightened feelings, and then begin his trauma work, after he learned to calm down on his mother's lap. Chris, his parents, and I had to repair some of the self-regulatory damage caused by neglect before beginning the trauma work. Of course, we did this through the vehicle of attachment. (This case is described in more detail in Chapter 10).

Neglect negatively affects moods, as described above. Neglect also steers children towards self-destruction. It is almost as if neglected people agree with the notion that they should not have been born in the first place. "I think that I must have been a mistake," is a comment that I often hear in therapy. "I think that that my family adopted me and ruined their lives," a 12-year-old abused and neglected girl told me. Antonia Bifulco and Patricia Moran found that neglect in childhood more than doubled the rates of adult depression in their sample (1998).

Bessel van der Kolk and his colleagues found that, while the trauma of sexual abuse was most likely to result in self-destructive behavior, neglect in childhood was the most potent predictor of failure to give up the self-destructive behavior (van der Kolk, Perry, and Herman, 1991).

Because neglect inhibits mindsight and eventually attunement, children have a hard time knowing how others might react to events. This raises their anxiety, since they are unable to predict what other people might think or do. Of course, their anxiety is also high, since trauma raises anxiety. Part of the necessary work, then, is on rebuilding the capacity to think and feel and, at the same time, reflect on how others might think and feel. These needs are so basic that often social skills groups do not include them. They need to be folded into therapy sessions and home routines.

Resources originally developed for children with autistic spectrum disorders or Fetal Alcohol Spectrum disorders are helpful for guiding children in the process of becoming aware of the feelings of the self and others, and using that information in real time. The books by McAfee and Gutstein, previously mentioned and also in the Resource List, are ideal for use in the home, school, or with a coach.

Any methods used to promote social skills with children are taught best in real time and in spontaneous situations, whenever possible. Feelings need to be actually transmitted to promote brain development. Many social skills groups are simply manners classes, operating under the premise that children don't know the manners used to connect. Children who have been traumatized by neglect will learn to recite rote rules and point to faces on a feelings chart after attending these groups. They will still be unable to read faces and respond empathically, to understand the feelings of others, or to acknowledge the viewpoint of others in real time. They are not connecting in a meaningful way. Stanley Greenspan has described a variety of techniques for helping children with learning differences with these skills for emotional attunement and empathy. Please see his resources, which are also found on the Resource List.

Play and Neglect

One of the magical ways that children express mastery of their world is through play. Neglect interferes with the ability to project thoughts and intentions on another, resulting in a tendency for disrupted play in neglected children. Many adoptive parents complain that their children do not know how to play. Some children do not even understand that events have a "why." Other children are avoiding "scripting" of the characters that is a natural part of play. Children often need a parent to play with them in order to tolerate putting thoughts and feelings into the figures.

Sometimes children will become anxious and controlling of their parents during this process. A common parent gripe is that their children become so controlling of them during play that they cannot build reciprocity. As in the section above, the goals should include both shared ideas and feelings so that parents enter and share their children's worlds. Some parents get very serious when they are not connecting. Getting down and having fun is a much more effective way to involve children.

One man, completely shut out of his 5-year-old son's world, came in for some help with connecting. He was employing a Socratic method of play, peppering his son with a number of interesting questions. His son treated him with the same interest as the pillow on the couch upon which Dad sat.

In therapy, Dad was given his own trucks to drive alongside his son's trucks—on the floor. I showed him how to become involved, driving his trucks quickly beside his son's trucks, and then overtaking them. His son responded with a chase scene. Within about twenty minutes, they were playing chase with the trucks. At one point, the dad lifted his son off the ground. The boy was laughing and managed to get his truck a few inches ahead of his dad's—even when aloft. The son's eyes glowed with excitement. He revved up the trucks for another chase scene.

The goal was to begin to have fun together, making play a way to enjoy each other. The father was encouraged to keep having fun, even though his son shut him out at first. Rather than becoming serious, heavy-hearted, and dejected, this man was encouraged to play. Fortunately, he was lithe and spry. Dad continued to pull his son in by developing his interest in Dad's state of mind and how that combined with the boy's.

"Oh no! Oh no. I'm losing," he whispered. "What will I do? I might have to cheat a little. Will my boy notice? Oh! He did. I'm busted. I have to start all over. I'll take a deep breath; I think that I might cry." This was all spoken with exaggerated expressions that were quite appealing to observe. At the word *cry*, the boy gave his father an expression of empathy. He patted his dad's knee lightly, but then commanded, "Don't cheat. I'll let you win next time."

The play was interesting, attuning, and a great contrast to the dad's initial hurt observation, "Oh, I guess you want to play by yourself." It certainly drew in the boy more effectively. "This is really fun," the dad said at the end of the session. "I can do this!"

The concept of play is well-utilized in play therapy. Many therapists, however, describe a repetitive, disorganized, and fruitless play in children who have neglect and trauma backgrounds. Some children just make chaos from the materials—over and over again. These children need more help organizing their therapy than can be provided in a non-directive or loosely directive type of play therapy. Otherwise, therapists describe that no particular progress or interpersonal joining occurs in the therapy, even after using a variety of play settings. Chapters 8 and 10 address methods that help these children.

In concluding this chapter, the take-home message is that children will be processing differently when they have experienced both neglect and trauma. They will need attention to the minute building blocks of self-reflection, stress regulation, mindsight, and connection of the self with others. Only as these building blocks are assembled can therapists and families cope with the challenges of recovering from trauma.

CHAPTER 7

Attachment and Trauma/Neglect

"The crucial point is this: the precursors of attachment in mother-infant interaction that initially foster physiological regulation lay the foundation for attachment that subsequently promotes emotional regulation."

– Jon Allen

What is the role of attachment in trauma/neglect? While the interrelationship between attachment and trauma and neglect was mentioned in previous chapters, this chapter will define the interplay in a more specific manner. *Attaching in Adoption* describes the attachment-building process in detail, emotional stage by emotional stage. This book describes the role of attachment, or the lack thereof, in promoting emotional regulation, endowing resilience, and providing support in overcoming life's difficulties.

Readers who have healthy attachments can relate to the important role attachments play in life. Who do we call when we are hurt, scared, sick, confused, or bereft? With whom do we celebrate good news, exciting changes, and personal successes? Readers with secure attachments have a short-list of go-to people. These are the people to whom we are attached. They are present not only in our day-to-day lives, but also in our minds and hearts. We hold onto their memories while we are away from them or if we lose them. We cannot experience attachments without emotions. In attached relationships, we fall in love, grieve, enjoy each other, worry, get angry, feel proud, and experience peace.

Upcoming sections will explore working concepts of attachment and how it relates to the brain, regulation, neglect, and trauma. But first I will cover guiding concepts about attachment.

Attachment Is the Means through which Children Develop a Stress Regulation System

It is through our early attachment relationships that we develop stress regulation and emotional regulation. Depending on the type of attachment, this may be for better or for worse. The early developing right brain, where attachments develop, is largely dominant during the first three years of life (Schore, 2003). It contains the initial and lasting template for stress regulation. Revisions to this template will require intentional efforts.

The neural firing patterns that make up the primary caregiver's stress regulation system become imbedded into the developing infant brain through the vehicle of attachment (Schore, 2003). In this way, the caregiver's stress regulation system forms the template for the infant's stress regulation system, or neural firing patterns. The parent-child attachment acts as the mechanism behind this shared firing pattern.

Attachment Relationshps Are Built over Time

Certainly there is "attachment in the making" from the time parents begin to interact with an infant. However, an attachment relationship takes about six to seven months to form in infants placed as newborns or soon thereafter. After infants are moved, they may begin transferring their previous attachments to the new person, that is, they begin relating using the patterns of attachment they already know.

Babies will often begin to attach again within weeks if they have had a first healthy attachment to a person, lose it just once, and then recognize the same warmth, care, and concern in the next parent figure, especially if they are moved carefully. Successive moves, however, decrease the ability to attach. Toddlers and children who are moved often will take months, not weeks, to form new attachments. This does not mean that infants and children not yet attached can be moved easily! Each move is disruptive to "attachment in the making" as well as to the baby's emotional stability and identity formation.

Babies and children who have never had an attachment before should show signs of exclusive attachment—that is, attachment to their parents above anyone else—within a year of coming into the new home. Parents may feel attached before children do, and vice versa. Children may also have attachments to figures they have lost in addition to their attachments to current parents. (The upcoming chapter on moving children suggests time frames for forming new attachments, stage by stage).

Attachments Are Always between Two People, because They Are Relationships

It cannot be determined ahead of time whether a particular child has the ability to attach if that child has never had the opportunity to enter into a relationship that would allow for attachment. Sometimes the parents I see use the internet to access controversial information on reactive attachment disorder. They will decide, within three weeks of becoming parents, that they have a child who is in trouble because she has not attached. In fact, it would be remarkable to see any growth beyond adjustment and bonding in only three weeks after placement in a child of any age. Children must be in relationships before anyone can see whether they are forming attachments to the people in their home.

Temperament Has Little to Do with Attachment Quality

Child welfare workers often assume that temperament comprises a major factor in attachment. The research on attachment does not support this concept (Sroufe, 2002). Temperament tends to be a modest variable, unless parents are low in resources (Cassidy, Shaver, pp.198-225). Neurobiologist Patricia MacKenzie describes why this is so.

"This confusion about temperament is often precipitated by the biological aspects of stress. When people are stressed, they release high levels of cortisol. Cortisol acts to activate the sympathetic nervous system, or to prepare body for a "fight or flight" response. Long-term or extreme stress changes cortisol regulation enough to change the activities of other structures, like the HPA axis, as well as to turn on cortisol's gene targets. The changes in gene expression can prolong the stress response. While these biological changes are meant to serve as protection and preparation for danger, they are outwardly perceived as grouchiness, agitation, or anxiety. It is important to remember that stress genes and reactions are present in everyone, and that they will come out of dormancy during a stressful situation.

"However, the difference in children, as opposed to adults, is that, since they have experienced these changes from such an early age, it may seem as if these behaviors are an expression of their personality. In fact, they are undergoing a very similar biological process as seen in adults. An adult who lives through a violent rape, a bad divorce, or a war-related injury, for example, is expected to go through a period of anxiety and distress, or bad moods, following the stressful incident. Only proper care, emotional support and processing, and a safe environment will return their cortisol to normal levels. It takes time for the body to regulate back to its pre-stress state; the body wants to make sure that the danger is gone before it lets its guard down. In children, this same process should be expected. Even if the core personality has always been masked by the stressed state, it is still there. While stress during child and fetal development may present some lasting challenges for children later in life, stress reactions do not constitute the core personality" (2007).

Children who are negative due to trauma, loss, and neglect are often difficult to deal with. While these difficulties, rejections, anger, and avoidance cannot be considered "temperament," they certainly can make for a daily challenge. Parents will need extra support so that they can continue trying to connect with neglected or traumatized children.

Secure Attachment Relationships Promote Emotional Regulation and Positive Moods. They Have a Psychobiological Effect on Children's Development

Many children who do not have early experiences of proper care also lack proper physiological and emotional regulation. This is because both of these regulation systems are developed through an attachment relationship. As Jon Allen explains, "In the early months, there is a psychobiological synchrony between babies and parents, which means that interactions entrain the infant's physiological and behavioral rhythms. Thus the infant's capacity for physiological self-regulation depends on synchrony with a caregiver…The crucial point is this: the precursors of attachment in mother-infant interaction that initially foster physiological regulation lay the foundation for attachment that subsequently promote emotional regulation" (2001, p.45).

While the concept of a "critical window of time" for attaching was once major theory in forming attachments, this concept has proven to be false. Certainly attachments are more difficult to establish when the opportunities for attachment relationships are coming later in childhood or if the child has lost several prior attachment figures. However, research shows that almost all children *can* attach.

The process of leading the dance of attachment can be more difficult for parents when children have moods that are shaped by neglect or trauma. Of course, it is easier to attach to children who are not withdrawn, angry, aggressive, or irritable. Children, however, are likely to be in these states more often after neglect and trauma. In fact, their moods have been shifted by their experiences, many of which have been negative.

Babies' and children's positive moods are stretched and encouraged when they are in homes where their needs are met in a sensitive and timely way, when there is ample time spent in smiles and play, and when they are soothed and distracted when they are upset. Frustrated or overwhelmed moods are encouraged instead when they are often left in these types of situations. Over time, these experiences become physical structures in the brain; they comprise the "mood" or emotional wiring. If experiences are largely positive, the correlating positive structures will be developed; if largely negative, the negative structures will be more developed.

Experiences promote emotional wiring. Maturation of the brain, including the development of emotion and emotional regulation pathways, is "experience-dependent;" that is, social interaction directly influences central nervous system development (Sroufe, 1995). Parents and professionals, then, need to encourage as many positive experiences as possible following placement.

The brain is also "experience-expectant." That is, it is hardwired to expect certain signals, such as eye contact, kind touch, rocking, loving voice tones, playful interactions, and assistance from others during sickness or distress. Those signals stimulate social responses. Attachment techniques that include age-appropriate signals are taking advantage of the experience-expectant brain. The following schedule describes the actual experience-dependent process of brain development as conceptualized by K.M.B. Bridges and Alan Sroufe. These are the brain structures that support feelings.

Developing emotional structures in the brain

0-3 months

- Early care helps early brain development so that the baby is either adapting to a hostile environment with high anxiety and wariness, or regulating for a safe environment, with increasing physiological regulation.

3 months

- Excitement branches to delight.
- Emotions present: excitement, distress (frustration), delight.
- Babies show active laughter. They begin to regulate tension showing increasingly positive affect in nurturing, safe settings. They have a frustration reaction.

6 months

- Distress branches to distress, fear, disgust, and anger.
- Emotions present: excitement, delight, distress, fear, disgust, and anger.
- Babies show the development of reciprocity. They participate actively. They show both joy and anger.

12 months

- Delight branches to delight, elation, and affection.
- Emotions present: excitement, delight, elation, affection, distress, fear, disgust, and anger.
- The 12-month-old baby can explore and master tasks. He can show angry or petulant moods. He shows anxiety to immediate fears, and shows elation, as well.

18 months

- Distress branches to jealousy; affection branches to affection for adults and affection for other children.
- Emotions present: excitement, delight, elation, affection for adults, affection for children, distress, fear, disgust, anger and jealousy.
- This is the age for emergence of the self. Children can demonstrate that they like themselves. Shame is a major emerging emotion at this stage, as are defiance and rage.

24 months

- Delight branches to delight and joy.
- Emotions present: excitement, delight, elation, joy, affection for adults, affection for children, distress, fear, disgust, anger, and jealousy.
- In a continuation of the self development above, children go on to develop pride, love, guilt, and the variation of anger and frustration—intentional hurting. (Sroufe, 1995, pp.172-191).

The take-home message is that when children are attaching in positive settings, they are literally being wired to become positive people. Their brain development is tilted in a positive direction. When children are moving into new homes, they will need to experience a highly positive and nurturing home environment in order to overcome their past and to take advantage of the plasticity of the developing brain. Children who have previously been abused or neglected may have been wired to be negative. Unless they experience something very different, nothing will change. Parents need to be deliberate in order to counteract their own disappointment with the mood difficulties their children may be having. They should be aware that they may have to create positive moods—and that they cannot take negative moods personally.

Attachments Come in Styles, or Types

When most people think of attachment, they visualize secure attachment. Secure attachment is, in fact, the healthy pattern that most people hope to enjoy when they enter relationships. It is also, however, only one style of attachment. Attachment comes in different styles or types, each one defined by a pattern of behavior. There are ten subtype patterns of attachment. The major types are listed in this book as are the relationship between parenting styles and children's styles of attachment. The impact of trauma on attachment styles will be discussed more in this section.

When children move into a home, they will use the patterns of attachment that they already know. However, these patterns are malleable. They can change over time as a result of increased support, resources, or therapy. Parents will want to direct children into secure base attachments. Children cannot develop patterns of attachment that are of the secure base style unless the parents themselves are capable of this type of attachment.

Secure Attachments and the Child's Internal Working Model

What does a "secure" attachment look like and what does it teach? The formation of a secure attachment can be seen as the development of an internal working model that informs children of how to look at themselves and at others (Bowlby, 1969). The template that securely attached children use when looking at themselves and the world includes elements of built-in security.

- My parents come back. They are reliable.
- I am worth coming back to.
- I can depend on my parent(s) and people they entrust to educate and spend time with me.
- My affective states (feelings) are mirrored back to me, so that I can get help knowing how I feel, and how others feel.
- I want to please my parent(s) most of the time.

- I am rewarded for becoming competent, for my curiosity, and for my positive states.
- I can get help with psychologically overwhelming events and feelings.
- Parents will teach me how to cope with problems and how to solve them.
- Intimacy is enjoyable.
- My needs are routinely met in a timely, sensitive manner.
- Repairs to relationship disruptions are empathic and prompt.

The especially striking characteristic of a secure-base attachment is that it provides a basis for self-confidence that is literally wired into the core self. Schore describes the development of the orbital cortex and the core self in his book, *Affect Dysregulation*. "The core of the self is both nonverbal and unconscious, and it lies in patterns of affect regulation. This structural development allows for an internal sense of security and resilience that comes from the intuitive knowledge that one can regulate the flows and shifts of one's bodily based emotional states either by one's own coping capacities or within a relationship with a caring other" (2003, p. 250).

People derive a tremendous sense of security just through knowing that they can normally handle the frustrations and challenges of life without falling apart, becoming overwhelmed and feeling worthless, or yelling at people. They feel secure knowing that they do not have to provide solutions alone, but can depend on others to help them solve problems. Within the secure base attachment relationship, children's brains develop the abilities to calm themselves and to seek help.

Insecure Attachment: Avoidant Attachment Style and Dismissive Parents

In avoidant attachments, children have their needs met, but they have learned that they cannot trust their parents to meet their needs in a reliable or sensitive manner. Children who have an avoidant attachment style do not know whether they will be hugged or hurt a little (but not abused) when they express needs. They conclude that it would be safer and better to become self-reliant (Sroufe, 1995). Children who have developed this style of attachment have not experienced trauma, neglect, or abuse. Rather, harshness and lack of sensitivity in these parents characterizes the way in which they relate to their children.

These parents are denoted as "dismissive." That is, they react in a dismissive manner in response to their children's tender needs. It is interesting to note that these are often parents who cannot remember their own childhoods, or present an idealized view of their own parents even though the facts do not support this view. This parental style will be discussed in more depth in an upcoming section on the Adult Attachment Inventory.

Children entering new homes after having a dismissive parent will usually react in an avoidant, self-protective manner towards their new parents. Sensitive but structured parenting, as described in Chapter 8, helps these children. Adoptive parents who are insensitive cannot help their children move into a secure base attachment pattern (Bates, Dozier, 2002).

Insecure Attachment: Anxious, Clingy or Resistant Subtypes, and Preoccupied Parents

Children who have someone whom they love but are afraid of losing show this anxious, clingy attachment pattern. They may show love and trust in a parent, but they are always "in the moment." They seem to believe that the parent will disappear once out of sight. Children tend to show this anxiety in their attachment style after experiencing neglect in the first half of their lives, or after care by rotating orphanage staff. Children who have been moved suddenly, early in their lives, also show this pattern. These children are not certain whether they can trust their parents to come back, or trust them to attend to their needs. Their controlling behavior tends to be focused on separations or getting needs met.

Parents who are preoccupied with their own past attachment experiences are prone to form this pattern with their children. Parents who invest their energies in the past and are still brooding, resignedly passive, or angry over their own childhoods, may be present for their children in body, but "not there" emotionally. Their children, then, become anxious and cling or may move into angry resistance. They may try to bring their parent's focus into the present by drumming their legs against the parent, pulling and whining. Sometimes children will behave ambivalently towards the parent, as if resenting them. They will push them away to punish them for their lack of emotional availability, yet alternately desperately want them.

These children seem distressed even before separations. They seem unable to settle and find comfort in their parent's presence. They have difficulties using the parents as a secure base of regulation or exploration. They continue to cry even after their parents return after a short absence.

Parents can help these children decrease their anxiety by remaining emotionally present for their children, and by acting calm, steady, predictable, and nurturing. One of the vignettes in the upcoming therapy chapter describes the process of helping anxious children develop more security within the attachment relationship.

Insecure Attachment: Ambivalent Subtype

An ambivalent attachment is the style in which the child alternately clings or pushes the parent away. This child switches between the traits of the anxious, clingy or resistant attachment pattern and the avoidant attachment pattern described above. In my experience, children who exhibit this style in their new homes have often had prior parenting experiences that include changing caregivers and/or perfunctory, insensitive care. Children who are resolving trauma/neglect issues also often loosely fit into this pattern when moving from the disorganized style described below. The goal for this style is, once again, to help parents to remain steady and nurturing as they move children into a secure base pattern.

Disorganized/Disoriented Attachment Style and Disorganized/Unresolved Parental Style

This style describes children who exhibit parts of the secure, avoidant, and anxious styles arranged in a disorganized mix. Significantly, trauma is interlaced into the way in which these children relate to their parents. They become fearful, frozen, and disoriented (Solomon, George, 1999, pp. 3-28). Children who have been abused and neglected will show this style over 80% of the time. Children who have been undernourished because of poverty will begin moving into this style of attachment even if parents have good intentions and adequate parenting skills (Waters, Valenzuela, 1999, pp. 265-285).

Children with disorganized attachments tend to have a sense of helplessness in their relationship with parents. The parents who raise this type of child often demonstrate these attachment traits themselves, reporting feelings of helplessness about their relationship with their child (Solomon, George, 1999, pp.3-28).

When distressed, these children are often more upset by the arrival of the parent than comforted. Parents of children who have disorganized attachments typically have been frightening or alarming to their children in the past. Often these parents have repeatedly set up the child for overwhelming situations, and then responded with rejection, abandonment, or in a frightening manner.

The fragmentation, or the "disorganized" element characteristic of this style, is adaptive for children during maltreatment. Fragmentation allows children to smile and get close to a parent, asking for food or comfort even if the parent was angry with them only minutes before. Or, it allows children to freeze when their parents look frightened. This adaptation helps the child escape notice during domestic violence incidents. In a few minutes, the child might turn to hug the violent person, saying, "I love you." This is a successful, short-term strategy. But over the long term, as mentioned in the chapters on trauma, this lack of integration prevents children and adults from avoiding future high-risk situations.

Children with disorganized attachments respond to parents' terror or threats by showing a "fear versus approach" conflict drama. This conflict is part of their core. Fear of abandonment and fear of proximity take turns in this pattern of attachment.

Children with disorganized attachments tend to be highly controlling. They also dissociate much more frequently than other children. They show a long-term vulnerability in making emotional and social adjustments, with high rates of psychopathology (Stafford, Zeanah, Scheeringa, 2003).

What happens when children with disorganized attachments move into new homes? Some of the old feelings around attachment become activated[1] when new parents get close to them. "In situations that activate a disorganized attachment schema, children can become chaotic, with visceral activation and disruptions in their sense of self" (Schore, 2003). Those "activating situations" are those that ask children to become close, dependent, or cooperative. When children are trying to do this they can feel like they are breaking apart inside. Or, they can feel as if they have an upset stomach or have to go to the bathroom. (Readers beware. Even if they have just gone to the bathroom fifteen minutes ago and fifteen minutes before that, these children may very well have to go again due to a fear response. Let them go.)

These reactions make it difficult for previously maltreated children to connect closely with adults. The children experience distressing feelings when they are asked to come near to or to calm and co-regulate with the parent. They may have visceral reactions that cause them to withdraw. Because of their past experiences, they fear that they will be hurt or startled if they relax their guards.

Parents who themselves have a secure state of mind towards attachment, who can stay regulated and can help children learn to calm and connect, will gradually help children with disorganized attachments move into a secure base attachment. Therapy for grief and trauma also helps these children.

On the other hand, parents who have unresolved grief and trauma in their own lives, especially in family relationships, are likely

---

[1] *Activation* is a term that means that the "memory pot" is being stirred, or emotions are emerging because of unresolved conflicts.

to have disorganized/disoriented states of mind toward attachment. Children who enter the homes of such parents have a poor prognosis for any real change in the way they relate to parents. There are neuronal pathways that enable children to feel a little of what the parent is feeling when they look into the parents' eyes. If their parent is frightened or remembering trauma, children will respond with the mixed strategies of freezing, avoidance, and disorientation and anger when they are around the parent. They will not want to connect with their parent's state of mind. It is too overwhelming to feel the parent's feelings.

All Types of Attachments Are Equally Strong

It is important to note that attachment does not have to be a secure attachment in order to be strong; any type of attachment can be strong. Anyone who has lived with or worked with children who have lost parents knows that children grieve when they lose parents to whom they were attached—even if the attachment was of an insecure or disorganized style.

In fact, it seems easier to grieve a secure attachment. It was more easily understood than a style in which anger, fear, shame, and a sense of failure inhibit the grief process.

Attachment's Ripple Effect

Children's security of attachment to their caregiver can be assessed using the Infant Strange Situation. Alan Sroufe's team at the University of Minnesota has followed a sample of 280 families over thirty years of research. The classifications of attachment translate into home and school behaviors (Sroufe, 2005).

In schools teachers begin to treat children with secure attachments with more nurturance or patience than their peers with insecure attachment styles. The children who learn how to manage their stress and to co-regulate move on to use these qualities to succeed in group work. Their peers who lack these qualities begin to fall behind because they cannot work as well in groups. Since children learn from each other, this impacts academics.

Teens with secure attachments were shown to be more successful in interactions with adolescent peers. They tended to be self-confident and socially competent, with greater social involvement. As teens they were more likely to have friends or a best friend (Sroufe, Egeland, Carlson, Collins, 2005).

Sadly, it seems that children who have already gotten a poor beginning are more likely to get the short end of the stick once they encounter schools and friendships.

The Adult Attachment Interview— Lessons for Casework and Therapy

The Adult Attachment Interview (AAI) is a tool that has been used in research projects for over twenty years. It assesses the correspondence between parents' states of mind toward attachment and the style of their attachments with children. The AAI was developed by Mary Main, N. Kaplan, and Carol George in 1984, 1985, and 1996. A fine chapter on the AAI is authored by Erik Hesse in the *Handbook of Attachment* edited by Jude Cassidy and Phillip Shaver (1999). This will be referenced frequently in this section.

By assessing "state of mind toward attachment," the creators of this tool mean to understand both how the person values close relationships as well as how he or she integrates the importance of these close relationships with their development and functioning. The AAI is a structured, hour-long interview. I have included descriptions of the interview because it will help therapists and caseworkers as they interview their clients. The questions used in the homestudy section in the next chapter are informed by the AAI. The AAI is a research tool at this point. We can use the information from the AAI in interviewing and understanding factors potent to success.

The AAI questions explore the following issues about the participants' past relationships.

- Recall the family in which the person grew up, starting with earliest memories.
- Provide adjectives to describe the family in which the person grew up, and associated memories to support each adjective.
- Describe memories of rejection by parents, reaction to rejection, and opinion as to whether the rejection was recognized by the parents.
- Describe which parent one felt closest to, and why.
- Recall whether parents threatened or frightened them.
- Reflect on how childhood affected the adult personality.
- Discuss any childhood or adult loss of parents or loved ones, including how that affected the individual.
- Contrast how the family relationships and perceptions of relationships changed between childhood and adulthood.
- Summarize the current relationship between the subject and parents.

Trained assessors use the taped interviews to identify critical factors. Their results predict which style of attachment the parent is capable of—even before children enter the family. The AAI does not attempt to capture factors such as parenting skills, support, or financial resources. Yet, it can predict the *style of attachment* that parents will form with their children about 80% of the time. This prediction provides important information when making initial placement decisions or when assessing the support and therapy needs for a family.

The AAI has been replicated reliably in several different countries with a variety of populations. In all of these cases, adults are interviewed about close family relationships in their growing up years. Then, the adults' synthesis of their attachment history is assessed, but not the attachment relationship itself. Note that the assessment is not looking at how "lucky" the individual was or was not in relationships. Instead it focuses on

- the development of a cohesive narrative, or life story
- the degree of insight
- the integration of emotions with narrative
- the resolution shown from losses and traumas, and
- the current attitudes towards close relationships.

The interviewers who use the AAI are carefully trained over a two-week period. The purpose in this book is not to equip individuals to become AAI interviewers for research purposes. Instead, the purpose of discussing the AAI is to sensitize readers to the concepts behind the AAI in order to inform their therapy, placement decisions, and personal knowledge.

Classifying Adult Attachments Using the AAI

The adults evaluated using the AAI are classified as Secure/Autonomous, Dismissing, Preoccupied, and Unresolved/Disorganized. The first three categories are what Mary Main has described as the organized qualities. That is, they show a particular strategy that is organized into how people describe their states of mind in relation to their attachments (Hesse, 1999, p.399).

Secure/Autonomous Parents

As was mentioned previously, secure/autonomous parents correspond to securely attached children. When interviewed, these individuals demonstrate that they value their attachments, "but seem objective regarding any particular event/relationship. Description and evaluation of attachment-related experiences are consistent, whether experiences are favorable or unfavorable" (Hesse, 1999, p.399).

The striking information about this category is that the individual's life narrative demonstrates an internal consistency that governs her external behaviors, i.e. her later behaviors toward a child. Even if she has a background of maltreatment, her narrative demonstrates resolutions—resulting in resolved, sensitive behaviors toward her infant and children. It appears that the tendency to protect, soothe, and care for children is what comes most naturally to adults who have a secure state of mind toward attachment, even if they have a history of maltreatment.

Dismissing Parents

Individuals classified as being dismissive are likely to have children who form avoidant attachments. Their AAI transcripts are not coherent. They tend to idealize their own attachment figures or to claim that they cannot remember their childhoods. Their answers are too brief and/or do not contain examples that support their conclusions. Their examples tend to contradict their global statements.

One study assessed mothers' sensitivity to their babies by interviewing 18-year-old parents with the AAI and also assessed their infants in the home at 1, 8, and 24 months. "The mothers of the thirty-five dismissing 18-year-olds (i.e. those who normalized or presented an idealized portrait of their parents, often while insisting on lack of memory for childhood) were found to have consistently received the lowest sensitivity scores" (Hesse, p.415).

Dismissing adults idealize their parents rather than viewing their relationships objectively and reflectively. Professionals involved with these parents may feel like things are not quite adding up. This theoretical position comes to life in therapy practices.

One parent, Megan, described her own mother as "fantastic, magnificent." Megan moved on to talk about the close connection she had to her mother during her teenage years. Then, she begin to weep as she described being lonely in high school after her parents moved four times. "There was no one to turn to," she said. She concluded by saying that she wished she'd been sent to an out-of-state boarding school.

Megan's descriptions did not support her claim of having a close connection with her mother at all. Interestingly, Megan routinely placed her own child into situations that were overwhelming, showing a lack of sensitivity to her child's needs. Her child was easily overstimulated. Megan regularly took her to a succession of loud, crowded events, missing bedtimes, and then complained bitterly of the child's behavior problems. The lack of coherency in her life narrative was echoed by her lack of applied insight when planning for her child.

Preoccupied Parents

The preoccupied category is characterized by the parent's preoccupation with past attachment relationships and experiences. The transcripts from these interviews are marked by excessive length, irrelevant and incoherent information, and vague usages. "In many cases…the memories aroused, rather than the intent of the question itself, appear to draw the subject's attention and guide the subject's speech. Often these speakers are angry, fearful, or passive" (Hesse, p. 399). These individuals show a corresponding resistant or ambivalent pattern of attachment with their children. Jonathan, described below, is such an example.

Jonathan was a stay-at-home dad, raising his second family. Jonathan came in for help with his 4- and 5-year-old daughters, who were anxious and hard to move into a routine. They moved around his legs like water, constantly moving, and never stopping to calm.

His girls talked to their dad as he was talking to me, asking him for help, drinks, attention, attention, and attention. As he gave them juice or handed them a toy, the girls would as often refuse the toy or resist the drink as take it. He would say, "Oh, I guess you don't want that after all. Oh well." During the intake session Jonathan said, "I'm not that great at this, as you can see. I can remember my dad telling me that I would forget my own head if it weren't attached. Sometimes he would say these unbelievable things to me…Like maybe he should get me a prostitute to get the ball rolling because I was socially retarded." Jonathan looked away, lost in thought, and said earnestly, "Why would someone say that to their son? What was he thinking?"

Meanwhile the girls kept insisting, "Dad, Dad, help please." When Jonathan did help them they simply moved to the next request. "Oh, I guess that you didn't want that," Jon said. One of the girls knocked a toy out of Jonathan's hand roughly, even though she had insisted that she wanted that particular toy. She glared at Jonathan but he hardly noticed as he continued to talk.

Jonathan said, "I can't remember that it was this hard

with my other children. But then, I don't remember much about it. It seems like a blur. I remember my dad always said that he thought I had ADD. Why do you think he'd say something like that?"

In this vignette Jonathan was clearly emotionally distracted by the past. His girls felt his limited emotional availability and were unhappy over it. While they had their own contributions to the attachment relationship from early orphanage care in China, Jonathan was not moving them toward a secure attachment. Fortunately, Jonathan took the time to work through some of his issues in individual therapy. The clarity with which he connected with his daughters post therapy was remarkable in contrast with the earlier sessions. They settled when he offered them comfort, drinks, or attention. He was connected to them and seemed to "finish" every interaction with them instead of fading off.

Disorganized/Unresolved Parents

The category of disorganized/unresolved is one in which parents seemingly cannot come up with a coherent and consistent approach to attachment. Instead, they show lapses in reasoning and conversation during discussions of "potentially traumatic events…significant loss experiences, or abuse" (Hesse, p. 388). These individuals might fit the above categories, however, their lapses into prolonged silence, descriptions of a person they have lost as if they are still present, and lack of coherency when faced with the topics of abuse, constitute the disorganized/unresolved categorization (Hesse, p. 399).

This category corresponds, not surprisingly, with the child disorganized/disoriented category. These infants and adults do not have a strategy that works consistently. Infants with these parents tend to freeze in trance-like behaviors, clinging while crying hard and leaning away with averted gaze. These children will often mirror the inconsistencies in their reactions to their parents; they reach up, then freeze with the face averted. *Caseworkers should note that this is not a typical reaction in children.*

Fear of abandonment and proximity alternate in people who are both afraid of their caregivers and also abandonment. This conflict creates drama between many children and parents in abuse and neglect situations. Adults in this category have histories with an abundance of unresolved grief and traumas. As one adoptive mom described,

> "Our stepfather would strike me without warning. But my mother would never intervene. She said that we could not survive without him." Going on to describe her emotionally abusive, alcoholic husband, she said. "How could I leave and take my son away from his father? My son has already lost his birthparents. I don't think that he could survive the loss of his father."

> Her issues replayed from generation to generation. In the latter case the parent said, "What am I saying? I've had contempt for my mother's weakness yet repeat the pattern." She made some necessary changes to protect herself and her son.

Cannot Classify

A last category in parental attachment styles is a "cannot classify" category. It is often found to be "associated with adults' histories of psychiatric disorder, marital and criminal violence, and sexual abuse" (Hesse, p. 398). Recently a caseworker told me that there had been a "secure attachment" between a child and her father. The child had been sexually abused by her father over a period of two years. (A secure attachment and this type of sexual abuse are contradictions by definition!) That type of situation may fit into this category if not into the disorganized category.

Children Can Develop Different Attachment Styles with Different Parents

Because attachments are relationships, children will form attachments based on the type of relationship possible with a particular parent. Beyond the issues related to a child's history, children and parents form attachment styles based on how they relate to one another. Some children will have a secure base attachment with one parent and another style with their other parent. In a two-parent family, children may choose one parent for their initial attachment. Fathers are frequently chosen as the favored attachment figure, either because of unresolved loss issues towards a mother figure or because of past maltreatment when in the care of a female.[2]

Some adoptive parents have questioned me; they think that efforts in attachment by both parents may detract from the quality of attachment to one parent. On the contrary, both parents should work on building their relationships with their children simultaneously in two-parent families. Children who have secure attachment patterns to two parents are twice blessed.

What changes attachment styles?

Categories of attachment can change in response to improved or deteriorated circumstances. For example, placement into a safe home with caring parents can help children move into a secure base attachment. Mary Dozier and her research partners show that these placements are effective when parents have a secure attachment style (Bates, Dozier, 2002).

Research from Sroufe's group shows that new secure base relationships and more support for parents can help shift parents and parent-child dyads into different patterns of attachments. Particularly, the study mentioned the benefits to single, low-income women when they had the assistance of a stable partner (Sroufe, 2002). Parents can avoid overwhelming and dysregulating their children with their own grief and trauma states by working through these issues. Dan Siegel, Peter Fonagy, and Allan Schore have described the importance in working through parental grief and trauma issues in terms of helping children feel close to and regulated around their caregivers—leading to a secure state of mind towards attachment (Fonagy, Siegel, Schore, Stern, 2002).

Research done by Jay Belsky and R.M. Pasco Fearon shows that decreasing stress, adding new secure base relationships, improving support for attachment relationships, and helping with grief and

---

[2] Work has been done showing that the experience of feeling protected by the father and cared for by him contributes to a lifelong sense of safety (Blos, 1984).

trauma all help shift people into secure base attachments (2005). In fact, that is precisely what good therapy should be facilitating in adoptive parents. For a period of time, therapists add a supportive relationship, support the budding attachment relationship between parent and child, decrease stress, and help with grief and trauma.

Attachment categories between children and adults tend to be stable, but can change with improved or deteriorated circumstances. People who enter into the family's lives and support the parents, encouraging them to behave in a consistent, sensitive, nurturing and emotionally available fashion tend to comprise an important factor in supporting dyads' movement from an insecure to secure status. Some of the following vignettes will describe supportive interventions.

The vignette below describes a transition between Sheila and Chad and their daughter, Liliana, who was 7 years old.

> Chad and Sheila came in describing anxiety issues in their child, Liliana. Sheila had worked hard in therapy to resolve her maltreatment experiences from her own childhood. She had lovely parenting skills with their daughter, Liliana, but she also expressed being afraid of Liliana. Chad said, "It's like Sheila goes away for a while sometimes. I walk into the room, and Liliana is yelling and Sheila is frozen with a little smile on her face. I'm like, 'Hello, is anybody home in there?' She's like, 'Huh? What?' You'd have to see it, Deborah. I'm sure there's some explanation. But it looks crazy to me."
>
> In therapy sessions, Sheila would begin dissociating when Liliana became demanding and loud. In order to establish a different pattern, we role-played and made videotapes where she played the daughter and I played the mother (Liliana handled the camera). Over a series of sessions Sheila internalized both the soothing manner and the firm limits necessary for their daughter. She also stopped dissociating, which calmed Liliana down.

In the vignette above, Liliana was frightened by her mother's affect. Her mother was frightened of her daughter's affect. However, this family was doing well within several months. Sheila was no longer triggered by her daughter's anger after she tried role-playing and received some support through therapy. They were also able to move into a more organized pattern of attachment. A follow-up session showed that Sheila and Liliana were still maintaining their progress years later. These relationship patterns are capable of change.

Parents engaged in role reversals put tremendous pressure on their children, even if the parents describe the relationship as "close." This is the case with 14-year-old Shelby, who was part of a disorganized/disoriented dyad.

> Shelby came in as a new client. She was having nightmares after having to listen to her father's threats of suicide. Her parents had been divorced for years. But her father stopped by often, entering the home without knocking and sometimes threatening her mother.
>
> In therapy, Shelby told her mother her fears—that he would shoot himself during a visit or shoot her mother. Her mother smiled in a beseeching, childlike manner. When I pointed out that Shelby was asking for protection, the mother leaned sideways, ultimately placing her head on her daughter's chest. Shelby looked over her mother's smiling head at me and exclaimed, "No wonder I'm anxious all of the time!"
>
> Her mother sat up and responded, "I don't know what she wants from me. She is always criticizing me."
>
> Shelby's mother not only became childlike when presented with this emotional crisis, but went on to ask her daughter for protection. Then she complained about being criticized—in a teenage tone. The mother's body automatically moved into a posture true to her mental schema. The mother kept breaking into a dazed grin throughout the session.

In the first vignette with Sheila and her daughter, the relationship showed improvement as Sheila took advantage of therapy to help her to regulate herself and set limits—even with Liliana got loud. She stopped acting like her daughter's noise was a trauma trigger. The sessions with the camera were effective in de-sensitizing her.

There was not as much hope for Shelby and her parents. In the second vignette Shelby made progress by getting clearer about why she was so anxious. She realized that she had been put in a position of being responsible not only for herself but also for the welfare of both parents. She was encouraged in therapy to get better support outside of her home from an uncle and aunt. She also began to set limits with the help of the therapist.

The father dropped out of Shelby's life to a great extent after she would no longer listen to his phone threats. She told him that she would call 911 for help the next time that he expressed a suicidal threat or action against her mother. Rather than missing him, Shelby expressed relief.

Her mother got a new door lock, a visitation schedule, and caller ID to give some predictability and boundaries. "You know, though," the mother said to me, "this means that all of the pressure will shift back onto me." The mother was not interested in altering her role reversal, but did make some moderate changes since Shelby no longer cooperated with the adult tasks put on her.

She stopped being her mother's confidante and said, "I'm not the person you should be talking to about this. Call a friend!" When her mother described her fears, Shelby said, "I think that I should sleep at a friend's tonight." Shelby described herself as less anxious, but longing for the protection of parents. "Why do I have to have pseudoparents?" She said mournfully.

This disorganized/disoriented category is not just a classification, it is predictive of big difficulties in relationships! There is frequently not an easy or happy ending for these types of attachment patterns.

In summary, the take-home message from this chapter is that attachment styles in parents and children are affected by issues of fear, sensitivity, and safety. Unresolved trauma in parents tends to replay in their children's patterns of attachment. And, after children are traumatized, adoptive parents with a secure state of mind toward attachment are those most capable of helping children gain comfort and regulation, often transforming children's attachment styles to secure ones, especially if children are also given therapy to help with trauma. Secure base attachment relationships help regulate children emotionally and physiologically. These attachment relationships help give them the strength and regulation to work through trauma issues. That, in turn, helps children's attachments to become more secure. This transformation helps children mature into adults capable of forming secure attachments with their children.

Summing Up Part One

Children who have experienced trauma, traumatic loss, and neglect also experience cumulative effects on every area of their development. These children will need therapy not only for a specific traumatic event, but also to help them with basic skills like knowing where their bodies are, maintaining a sense of hope, discovering the emotions in their bodies and thinking about what might make them feel that way, understanding the feelings of others and what might make them feel that way, and understanding the events in their lives and what those events mean or do not mean. It is imperative that they receive the assistance of caring people who can help children remain in an emotionally regulated state while working with them in their contexts.

Parents who have a secure state of mind toward attachment will be working to build a secure pattern of attachment with their children. Through this attached relationship they have the opportunity to build qualities of resiliency: optimism, calming, empathy, motivation, attunement, and mindsight. The next section will give practical guidance for parents, caseworkers and therapists who are helping children to create resiliency and bounce back from neglect and trauma.

PART TWO

Putting the Pieces Together—Restoration after Traumatic Stress and Neglect

This second half of *Nurturing Adoptions* provides the hands-on application of the information learned from the first half. Part Two begins with a chapter offering activities, interventions, and techniques that parents and professionals alike will be doing in children's lives. Casework that reflects the foundation laid in Part 1 will be discussed next. Finally, therapeutic processes will be covered.

In Chapter 8 professionals and parents will learn to create a milieu that helps children develop coping and problem-solving skills, stretch their positive thoughts and moods, build self-confidence, and develop better patterns of relating after trauma/neglect.

Chapter 9 moves into the casework processes that are essential in helping today's adoptive or foster-adopt families. Moving children in a developmentally appropriate manner is described in detail—from the processes used in preparation, to the age-by-age time frames that best serve children's interests. The homestudy that prepares parents and is attachment-oriented is described, along with the research that supports why this approach works. Again, this chapter is written in a practical manner, adding to caseworkers' skill bases as they read.

Chapter 9 also includes some cautionary tales so that social workers are familiarized with troublesome signs in placement processes.

Chapter 10 covers therapeutic intervention. It describes classic cases of anxiety, trauma, and neglect, along with the detailed therapy interventions that achieve good results. The chapter also includes a protocol for intervention when children have a combination of attachment, trauma, and grief issues. An organized and research-based approach is described, along with interventions that are appropriate for children whose brains were shaped by trauma/neglect or prenatal exposure to alcohol or drugs. Again, this chapter is quite practical in giving skills for intervention. A description of differential diagnosis is also included, so that clinicians may look at several contributing factors at once, or one at a time.

Chapter 11 looks at ways to support professionals who are dealing with the complexities of planning for and treating today's adoptive families. Methods of stretching resources, caring for oneself, forming collaborative groups, and pacing oneself are described in a manner specific to work in this practice area.

The book's capstone is a chapter that brings the topic of resiliency full circle, looking at ways to build resiliency not just in children, but also in their families. Chapter 12 is written for professionals and parents alike. The book models a positive message as it concludes, encouraging beliefs that develop resiliency after adversity.

CHAPTER 8

Common Ground: What Parents, Caseworkers, Teachers, and Therapists Can Do to Help

Throughout every second of every day there was change abroad in the world, change due to the impact of mind on mind; teacher and pupil, parent and child, world leader and citizen, writer or actor and the general public. Yes, each one of us carried seeds for change. Seeds that needed nurturing to realize their potential.
—Jane Goodall, *Reason for Hope* (1999)

What home and school settings bring out the best in children? What critical activities should parents and professionals do together to restore hope after neglect, trauma, and attachment loss?

This chapter describes practical methods for bridging the gaps created by maltreatment. It offers techniques for modulating extreme moods and reactions in children. The concepts discussed here will assist parents in helping children respond to their new safer and kinder settings, rather than continue to act out the lessons learned through maltreatment. While discussed in the context of helping children who have suffered the traumas of abuse and neglect, these suggestions are also appropriate for children who have problems resulting from prenatal exposure to drugs and alcohol.

Restoring Hope/Counteracting Shame

Children and teens who have successfully overcome the obstacles posed by early abuse and neglect will say things like this:
- "My parents never gave up on me."
- "My teacher said, 'I believe in you. You'll get through this.'"
- "I had a therapist who saw something in me besides the way I was treating everybody and myself."
- "My mother believed in me—even when I would have given up on myself."
- "I would have given up, but I didn't want to disappoint the people who invested their hope in me."

People drift towards depression and hopelessness following early neglect and/or trauma experiences. Children who have been traumatized tend to believe that they were not worth being cared for, or that they deserved abuse. Restoring hope is one of the most significant and ongoing tasks when working with children and teens after neglect. Children without hope will not even bother trying to change.

A crucial aspect of the process of building hope is receiving support from professionals. One girl wrote to me after years of treatment.

"Thanks for all that you've done all these years. When I fell, you were another person ready to catch me or pick me up. I let you in my life and I opened up. There were so many days when I felt like that all that was left of me was what I pretended to be. I would act like I was fine when inside I was so broken up. So thank you so much. You changed me so much. Thank you a bunch. I feel more alive. Not that you could find that really possible with all my energy. But I wanted you to know. And this letter isn't half of what my gratitude is towards you. Thank you a billion times ten."

Initially this girl had been desperate, although her Teflon veneer indicated otherwise. Her letter demonstrates the nurturing effect of rekindling hope through the care of others. This letter has a key phrase: *another person to pick me up.* My helping her to connect with others, most importantly her mother, enabled her to have meaningful support and connections—a life with hope.

When parents lose hope, children and teens respond with bitter anger. After all, if your own parents have lost hope, then you are in a sorry state!

One teen, Chloe, resisted her mother's positive and appropriate comments and activities. She was disrespectful and surly, well beyond any normal teen tendencies.

While in session with me, she was finally able to verbalize her feelings, "She thinks that I will turn out wrong. She thinks that I am going to get pregnant like my birthmother, kill myself, become an alcoholic, or drop out of school. I hate her!"

Even though her mother had never directly said any of these things, her mother was in fact thinking and worrying about these outcomes. Facial expressions and wry asides conveyed these negative messages, effectively outweighing all of the positive comments that Chloe's parents tried to convey.

Once they recognized how profoundly their lack of hope had demoralized their daughter, the parents were able to express positivism and hope both verbally and nonverbally. Chloe's mom reflected that her own mother had never expressed much positivism. She had been acting out a familiar pattern. Chloe was able to calm down and began to accept affection and spend time with her parents again. While there were still some tasks left to do in therapy, the teen could find the energy to face them through the confidence her parents and I shared in her future.

What language promotes hope?

Helpful phrases include these:
- "That was a thoughtful comment! Smart choice!" (Compliment thinking.)
- "You have a strong sense of fairness." (This is especially good for the person who likes to talk about what is unfair.)
- "You have a sensitive heart. I know that your heart was hurt before. You know how others feel when in similar situations and will be able to help them when you get older." (This shows how pain can be transformed into a source of empathy.)
- "I am so interested in seeing how your gifts will develop as you get older!" (This shows optimism about the future.)
- "You have a nice touch with that tool."
  "You have a sense of style!"
  "You are definitely the best with the paintbrush!"
  "You drew that? Wow!" (These emphasize mastery themes.)
- "I believe that you have a good heart. I wonder what was going on with Person X who just didn't see this?" (This comment shows that the maltreatment belonged to the other, not to the child.)
- "I think that you can let the love into your heart and share it with others."
- "I couldn't help but find you loveable. There's just something about you." (This shows intrinsic worth. Some children will find this too strong. Temporarily skip this and the rest of the list if the child acts out in order to prove you wrong!)
- "I believe in you. I think that you will be a caring teen and adult. I will be here to help you along the way."
- "I liked how you did that! Wow! You are growing up!"
- "You care for others."

Comments such as these help children and teens think about and become curious about themselves in a positive way. This positive self-exploration, with hope, constitutes a great breakthrough for young people who are convinced that they should hide themselves and be ashamed.

Hopelessness promotes deception—
setting goals for recovery

Some children with little hope feel that they cannot compete with other children on a level playing field. They feel marred by maltreatment. Kellen, 8 years old, described his internal feelings.

"I feel like a monster. Other kids shouldn't want to be my friend. I'll pretend to like them. Then I'll take their stuff or maybe hurt them."

After Kellen had worked on attachment with his parents and felt more empathy for others, he said, "I've been doing the wrong thing so long that I am too far behind the other kids to do the right things. I am great at stealing and lying. I am terrible at being nice to friends!"

I agreed with his accurate assessment of the problem. We drew a picture of a road. We drew mileposts along the road: playing a game fairly, telling the truth when there were problems, caring about others' feelings, giving other people choices, and keeping his hands off of others people's stuff. We put in incremental positive outcomes next to each milepost: acting kind most of the time, having one friend, having several friends, getting invited to birthday parties, giving back money or possessions that a friend dropped, etc.

We drew swamps on either side of the road, and a pig standing in reeds in the swamp. Stealing, making fun of others' weaknesses, lying, sneaking, and intentional temper tantrums were also in the swamp. Kellen and I made a route out of the swamp so that he could quickly get back on track after missteps. The route was labeled "apologizing and restitution." (He learned these words and concepts in session.) He also rehearsed how he wished that he had acted after he had had mishaps in order to plant alternatives in his brain.

Kellen liked looking at his picture and visualizing his progression. He celebrated with me and his dad when he got invited to his first play date. It was the hope that he could do better that allowed him to get on the road in the first place. When he got his first birthday party invitation, he delighted in sharing a realized hope with his dad.

Explicit and Implicit Memory and Giving Up Old Defenses

The type of memory that is consciously used is called *explicit memory*, or *declarative memory*. Explicit memory stores facts and events. These include autobiographical, verbalized memories, such as, "When I was about 4, I rode my pony alone for the first time. My father gave me the reins and I rode the Shetland around our five acres. I remember the excitement, the pony's big eyes, and the handful of coarse mane that ran through my hands. I remember my dad's voice when he hoisted me into the saddle." This is typical explicit memory. There might be only a few memories from a particular year, most stored only because they were vivid or meaningful.

In contrast, *implicit memory*, or *nondeclarative memory*, stores information such as perceptions, feelings, and motor movements that is used unconsciously. Implicit memory is the first type of memory stored in the developing brain (Briere, 2003). It is nonverbal, although sometimes early memories and feelings can be accessed through verbal discussions. Implicit, early memories store the *schemas*, or internal representations, of how life works in regard to close relationships.

The lessons from earliest attachments, then, are stored in implicit memory, at the nonverbal level. At this young age, explicit memory storage systems are not yet capable of storing narrative memory; the structures that hold explicit memories have not yet functionally developed. The way in which children approach the world is largely based on the intrinsic, implicit memories formed in the first 18 to 22 months of life.[1]

Children may enter their new, loving families at any age with stored implicit memories of early abuse or neglect. These early schemas may, for example, prompt children to raise their elbows to ward off physical contact. Or, these children may routinely arch off their parents' laps and squirm out of hugs. Parents may ask, "Why did you

---

[1] Memory may also be described as explicit (declarative) and implicit (nondeclarative). Explicit memory is further split into episodic (autobiographical) and semantic (factual). Explicit memory is stored in the temporal or frontal lobe; implicit memory is in the neocortex, striatum, hippocampus, amygdala, motor/somatic planning areas (MacKenzie, 2007).

do that?" Since these children are acting out their reactions to unconscious memories, they will have no idea why they react in these ways.

Most children feel shame about reactionary behavior. They are sure that there is something wrong with them or their parents that explains the inexplicable. It is important to remember that these physical withdrawal or resistance reactions are not consciously thought out. Children need help understanding that their reactions are based on early, intrinsic memory systems, as in the case of Kira, age 8, below.

> Kira used to explode whenever she rode in a hot car in the summertime. "You're trying to kill me," she accused her mother.
>
> "Everyone is hot," her mother would reply, "not just you. We are in a traffic jam!"
>
> "You hate me! Why did you bring me here? I want to go home!" Kira ranted.
>
> When Kira came into the office, we went through her early history. Her mother remembered that the orphanage Kira came from was beastly hot in the summertime.
>
> "It was the hottest that I have ever been in my life," Kira's mother recalled.
>
> I told Kira that I thought that she was responding to an early memory of the orphanage. She and her mother and I talked about the heat. Kira was asked to do something to help herself the next time she got in the car. She accomplished this by collecting a "car pack" which included a wet washcloth for her forehead and a small icepack from the freezer for her feet. She never "melted down" again. Even when she forgot her items she said, "I know that my heat reaction is just a memory. I can sit here just like the rest of the family."

I used a cognitive behavioral therapy with Kira, even though she did not really have cognition, but rather a "feeling memory." (A more thorough discussion of cognitive behavioral therapy for feelings is included in *Mindfulness and Acceptance* [Hayes, Follette, Linehan, 2004]).

Often, giving children good background information about themselves helps them to identify a "why" for their feelings or behaviors. This suggests and aids making plans for coping with early intrinsic memories. Sometimes, when specific background information is not available, I tell children that something happened, but we don't know exactly what, that scared them or made them mad. Then I ask them to try acting in a different way, since the old situation is not happening now. For example, could they return a hug without throwing an elbow, since they really do like their parents? Or, might they try serving the tray of cookies instead of grabbing at them, since there are enough cookies for everyone?

Stress impacts executive functioning

Stress during early childhood shapes the brain. Children who experience early stressors also exhibit high rates of executive functioning problems, or executive dysfunction. This means that children will be prone to
- forgetting or being preoccupied versus using working memory
- inhibiting inappropriate behaviors in favor of exhibiting appropriate ones
- making impulsive choices instead of using logical reasoning
- giving quick, random responses to memories and events instead of organizing memories and events
- scanning of the surroundings instead of devoting attention to the task at hand
- responding to a situation "in the moment" instead of remembering the reason why they came into the situation.

Some of these behaviors overlap the symptoms in the diagnosis for attention deficit disorder (ADD). And, some of these children may indeed have ADD. Executive functioning issues caused by early stressors, however, are more extensive than those seen in ADD.

Many of the activities in this book redress the damage caused by high stress in the earliest years. These activities allow adults to provide structure, which acts as the executive brain for children who need extra work on focusing, logic, understanding context, and organization. At the same time, these activities offer them templates for refocusing, finishing tasks, allowing time for thinking, and practicing the routines necessary in daily life so that these processes are eventually done automatically.

Children with fetal alcohol spectrum disorder (FASD) may have permanent brain injuries that will prevent them from developing executive functioning. In these cases, parents and teachers will need to practice activities in order to supplement the executive control and judgment that teens will lack.

Memory systems and understanding life as "then" and "now"

Children cannot give up protective reactions, or ways to defend themselves, until they are given valid reasons for doing so. These reasons should be in the format of clear "before" and "after" messages (Siegel, 2005). That is, the explanations and reasons must provide their brains with a recognizable "then" and "now." An adult may assist this process by saying something like, "I can see that your elbow is up. You had to protect yourself from people a long time ago. Can you feel that you are in a friendly place now with a parent who wants a hug? Let's try that again while you remember that I am a friendly dad who is giving his son a hug."

The following vignette shows this "then" and "now" with a 9-year-old girl and her 8-year-old sister. Both girls wanted friends, but routinely teased, stuck out their tongues, laughed at others' expense, and mugged at their parents with derisive looks and comments.

"I know that you want friends," I said. "but when you were little you learned that you needed this big shot way to protect yourselves. Now that you are safe, you are still keeping people away." I made motions with a scowl and strong palm out to demonstrate. "And you're lonely. I'd like to work on friendship with you. We can work on friendly behavior with your parents and your sister so that it will come naturally at school and with your neighbors." I illustrated by drawing their friendly faces under the word *now* and the push-away, surly faces under the word *before*.

Following a year of work, the parents got their first hugs after four years of placement. I continued to work on the before and after themes weekly. Both girls would often ask their parents where they had been before their adoption. This was confusing to them, as there had been a time gap between when the parents had first visited their orphanage and when they were able to finalize the adoption and return to Russia to pick up the girls. The parents' previous explanations had been too abstract for the girls to understand. For example, they might have said, "The workers did the best that they could. International adoption is complex and takes time to process."

In one session, I mentioned that they could trust their parents. The older girl blurted, "But I don't trust them! I'm mad at them! They just make excuses. They left me in that place. And probably went out to dinner," she added with an imaginative flourish. Her sister nodded.

"Oh, I didn't leave you there," their mom said, while their dad choked with tears. "We wanted you to forget the hard times and remember the great parts about Russia. When we heard that you could be our girls, we came right away." The parents continued with "claiming" memories—mentioning how they showed the referral pictures, how they called every friend to share the good news about their daughters' coming, and how they worried about whether the girls would have enough to eat and whether they were too hot or too cold until they were able to make the trip to bring them home.[2]

These parents had assumed that their daughters had the information required to make clear inferences about their love for their children. In fact, the girls had not integrated important facts about

---

[2] "Claiming" themes in adoption are powerful in demonstrating parental bonds. Claiming means that parents are giving notice to family members—including the newly adopted children—and to the community that they have brought a new member into the family. The claiming activities include notice and celebration with friends and the community, giving of special gifts, and engaging in bonding activities.

their parents, so they continued to use the same defensive position until our sessions.

Hot memory systems

The intrinsic memory systems that store early and/or stressful memories are "hot" memory systems (Briere, 2004). By "hot," we mean that it is difficult to access the memory systems and make changes unless the feelings and reactions are activated by experiences. The girls in the vignette above knew that their caregivers had changed. But they still held onto their early beliefs about caregivers that taught them not to trust their parents. Only in the heat of the session did the intrinsic memory of their belief emerge.

I might not have seen the issues had I not asked the girls to engage in experiences that would bring out the memories and beliefs. The sisters might have simply agreed that they had good parents. If I had not asked for them to engage in interactions, in real time, the memory systems that included potent information about neglect, abuse, and attachment would have remained inactive. There would have continued to be a lack of integration. The emphasis on working in the present, in real time, with actual experiences, ensures activation of these memory systems.

Auditory Processing Issues

Quite a few of the children on which this book focuses have limited auditory memory recall. That is, they cannot remember what has been said to them accurately, in context, for a normal length of time, or with the proper complexities implied in the content. This auditory limitation includes difficulties remembering and understanding detailed instructions given in both the home and school.

Most people can relate to these processing and memory lapses. They often occur during stressful times. Or, things that are part of short and long-term memory recall are simply forgotten. For many children who have been neglected or abused, these lapses constitute a habitual state. Furthermore, their neurodevelopment has been shaped by stress to the extent that their memory systems may never be robust, even after they move out of the stressed state.

I recommend that adults use some simple techniques when speaking to young people who have abuse and neglect related auditory processing limitations.

- Use words sparingly.
- Pretend that you are paying by the word.
- Be concise.
- Go slowly.
- Say your main point at the beginning of the conversation.
- Use phrases like, "the main point is," or "the most important thing is."
- Make sure that they understand how your point relates to the "big picture," or overarching idea.

People tend to use lengthy verbal explanations, providing supporting evidence and building up to their case before stating the main point. This places the most important information at the end. But by the end of a discussion, a child's brain may be flooded with too much information. They can seem impatient because we have exceeded their processing loads, not because of our content. Our personally interpreted "resistance" is just the physiological reality for that child. This is demonstrated by one teen, Jean, with an auditory processing problem.

Jean's mother was used to giving long lectures. The first part of her discourse included all of her thoughts, feelings, and explanations. Jean was overloaded by the time her mother began the second half of the discussion on what she wanted to have happen. Even though Jean had an IEP in place at school, her home dialogues were unaltered. Jean and her mother's mismatch in style were summarized by their complaints after the discussion.

"Too many words," Jean said. "It hurt my brain. All I could think about was how to get Mom to stop making that noise."

"She doesn't care about anyone but herself," her mother said bitterly.

"I never understand her. She's always complaining," Jean

said. "Why doesn't she just say what she wants instead of telling me all this other stuff?"

Organizing Memories

Early neglect/trauma can impact the ability to organize memories, as described in Chapter 2. Sometimes memory recall is also more difficult.

- It may take more time for the brain to find information, especially for children with prenatal exposure to drugs or alcohol.
- Children may need more clues in order to bring back memories.
- Children may not recall information in a way that relates it in sequence and priority.

Learning templates help these children develop patterns for organizing the information that they are retrieving from memory. The following phrases help children learn patterns of organization:

- "Tell me what happened first? Then, what happened second? How did it end?"
- "Who was there?"
- "Where were you?"
- "Where did this event happen?"
- "Was it in the morning or after lunch?"
- "Were you indoors or outside?"
- "Who said what? What was the important point in what they said?"
- "What part of the story is most important to you?"
- "What is the part of your story that you think that I'll like the most?" This can be followed with, "You are right! That is my favorite part!"

Pictures are especially helpful for children trying to sequence and get all of the parts together. When I prompt them to form templates for organizing memories, I often ask children to get a picture in their heads first. They tell me about their memory, starting with where they are in the picture, what time of the day it is, who else was there, what action occurred, and then the relevance of the information to them and to me.

Children with FASD are not able to retrieve information unless the keywords or images precisely match the words or images in the brain's storage system. This is because FASD limits their abilities to generalize and search for similar and overlapping words or images. A common miscommunication may look like this.

> The parent will say, "You said that you would go to bed after the program was over."
> "No. I did not," says the child.
> "Yes. You did," says the parent.
> Actually, it turns out that the parent said. "Get your teeth brushed and change into your pajamas so that you are ready to get to bed after the program is over."
> The child did those things. He did not generalize that he had to go to bed after the program was over. Huge arguments can break out over this type of mismatch.
> The child will say, in an injured tone, "She never told me to go to bed."

A number of children have told me about abuse even after formerly denying this abuse in interviews with another professional. Sometimes their decision to disclose later is an issue of timing, trust, and safety, but sometimes the wording of an interviewer simply did not match their recall systems. When I ask about the interview, children will mention what the interviewer said and then the overly literal way in which they interpreted it.

Children's difficulties with organizing their memories have immense implications for therapists. Most of the modalities used in children's therapies presuppose that children can organize their memories in a meaningful way. The indirect methods used in play therapy and talking therapies give most children a medium and the emotional support necessary to work through issues. Children with difficulties organizing their memories, however, will need some special help. They typically need more assistance organizing the space, the plan for therapy, and in understanding how the information about the events in their lives and their feelings fit together.

To compound this issue, children with prenatal substance exposure have difficulty moving information from one part of the brain to another. Children who work on issues during play therapy will not necessarily substitute the new information for the old by moving it to different parts of the brain so that they are provided relief. Much more intentional, concrete methods must be used when working with these children. This is covered in more detail in the chapters on therapeutic approaches.

Rebuilding the Mind-Body Connection

Children cannot continue to feel what they are feeling when they are in physically and/or emotionally overwhelming situations. They have to stop the feelings. In doing so, they stop "knowing" the sensations in their bodies. This provides a temporary respite for them. Long-term, however, it is problematic; it is impossible to get far in life if you do not know where your body is or what it is feeling.

Children who become numb like this have felt overwhelming feelings before, while having no reliable person to calm them or to intercede at the time. They were forced to come up with a device to stop the frightening feelings before they became unendurable. Even after they have parents and a safe daily routine, these children continue to use these defenses so that they do not risk being alone with unmodulated feelings. For example, at the first sensation of loneliness, fear, shame, or grief, they may use diversions such as

- eye-rubbing
- skin picking
- finger stretching
- knuckle cracking
- changing subjects
- kicking items
- unraveling loose threads in upholstery, and so forth.

When I first noticed children engaging in these activities in my sessions many years ago, I went home and experimented with these habits in order to try to understand why they were doing these things. I poked and rubbed my own eyes and I pulled my own fingers

backwards just to the point of pain. In an "ah-ha" moment, I realized that these physical sensations stopped my brain from processing
anything else. It was like putting an eraser to my mind. I encourage
you to try this yourself, so that you can understand what your child
is or is not feeling and why.

While I was accustomed to dissociation from trauma, I was not
used to these physical reactions from children who had endured
overwhelming neglect in their backgrounds. I soon realized that they
had simply needed to find some way to deflect the unendurable when
left without needed attention in crack houses or orphanage cribs.

When children in my office engage in these defenses, I will often
ask them what they are feeling. They often say, "I don't know." They
are so right. They will have no idea why they are pulling their fingers
back, for example. I then point out that they do this every time we
bring up a difficult subject. I do not shame a child, but in bringing
their attention to the connection between the behavior and the difficulty they are feeling, I point out that while that activity might have
been a comforting option when they did not have attentive parents or
a caring therapist, the action is holding them back now.

Sometimes children are not convinced it is helpful to know their
feelings. I like to give examples that support my position. What follows is a true story that I offer children as an example.

Mia told me that when her dog died everyone in her family felt bad and cried. She felt weird because she did not feel
anything. She knew in her head that it was sad, but it really
did not feel bad. She thought, "Oh well. I guess the dog won't
be there after school every day." Every time she started to feel
sad, and I could feel some of her sad feeling within her, beginning in her chest, she would pull her fingers back. No wonder
she did not feel anything. She was stopping her feelings.

We worked together so that she stopped pulling her fingers back and let her feelings come out. She got to know that
when she felt the beginnings of sad feelings in her body, in
her chest and throat, that it was OK to let those feelings come
up within her.

When she came back a couple of years later, as a teenager,
she told me that she was sad for a friend who had been left

out of something. She helped her friend. I asked her how she knew the friend was sad. "I just knew," she said. "I could look at her face and I felt bad for her."

"Where in your body did you feel this?" I asked.

"In my chest and heart and a little in my head," she said.

Then I can say to the child in my office, "Do you think that it was better or worse for her to know her feelings?" Usually the child can describe both the positive and negative aspects of knowing feelings. It is always interesting and informative to hear their answers and subjective responses. It helps me get to know them better. More importantly, these exercises help children in therapy come to know themselves. They understand why it is helpful to know their own feelings.

Parents and therapists can help children who are shutting themselves off from their feelings find the sensations they have in their bodies. Neuronal pathways that focus on mirroring allow children to sense these same feelings in adults as we work with them. While I do not want to overshadow clients with my own sensations, I can ask if they are feeling certain sensations in their bodies, or if it is just me. They can answer appropriately.

When working with an 8-year-old boy, I found that I was breathing high in my chest when I was with him. I asked him if he had a hard time getting a deep breath into his belly. He told me that he was scared that relaxing was the wrong thing to do. He felt that something might sneak up on him. He agreed that he could relax in the office with me.

When we did some deep breathing, he told me that he had been increasingly tense, feeling the need to get ready to run, over the last two weeks. We connected this to when he had looked at some pictures of birth relatives who had exposed him to domestic violence.

As children are able to identify their feelings, they are able to begin to put their thoughts together with the feelings. They are restoring the loop between mind and body, the relationship between thoughts and feelings. That will help them to make meaningful connections so that their lives seem more coherent and integrated.

Parents and professionals need to mirror children's feelings, describing them and the other person's corresponding feelings. Use every opportunity to align with them. This is helpful in building emotional attunement and fundamental in forming meaningful relationships with others.

This following list of steps summarizes the route for helping children rebuild mind-body connections.

1. Interrupt children who are stopping their feelings.
2. Give them support with finding the feelings in their bodies. Help them to see the value of feeling. Share the feeling you have when mirroring them.
3. As they share their feelings, explore what might cause any normal person to feel such feelings. Help them to get comfortable with having normal feelings. Promise to help them with feelings if they become uncomfortably intense. Make a plan to handle the contingency of intense feelings (deep breathing, getting a drink, getting a hug, taking a walk, etc.)
4. Connect and support their conclusions as they put thoughts and feelings together. Share examples of situations where knowing feelings helped people act on their own behalf.

Many adults want to rush in, offering a child interpretations and conclusions. While it may be necessary to give hints, clues, guesses, and examples, it is best to limit involvement to supporting a child or teen as she puts her own meanings together. Remember that the child is the one who needs to develop mindfulness. Her initial steps are more important than an adult's most elegant reflections. It is better for her to gain skills than for adults to look wise.

Make plans for the day and for important events

Children who have executive functioning difficulties will often respond to daily events impulsively. Writing out a plan for their day allows them to rely on that plan and stay on task.

One boy wrote a plan for his grandparent's visit.

When he started to insist on a side trip to a pet store, his parents said, "Please review your plan."

He settled down after he checked his plan. "I forgot," he said. "No stops. We have people coming over for dinner."

Plans can be made in picture format for younger children. These plans also supplement short-term memory abilities, which have been impacted in many children. Children can review the plan anytime throughout the day. It calms children by helping them to feel a sense of predictability.

Mari, aged 6, drew her plans every morning. Part of the planning was to draw how she wanted to feel that day. Daily, Mari drew herself as "happy!" and "sparkly-dressed!" In drawing herself, her mood shifted to happy. This was an astonishing transformation for Mari, who was formerly described as "anxious and grumpy" by loving but worn parents.

Regulation patterns in oversensitized brains

The example above contains an important concept: long-term stress oversensitizes the brain, making it prone to blow-ups, tantrums, irritable behavior, and negative responses.

Children can develop more positive, regulated mood patterns when parents help them maintain calm, happy states. Techniques used with these children, then, should promote positive and regulated moods. These new, positive patterns eventually become the ones that seem familiar. They become the new "normal" for children.

On a practical basis, I like children to practice thinking and reflecting on their lives. Children can initially receive help in figuring things out, as needed. Parents can do this by writing out questions about the child's feelings or thinking, and then asking them to respond with pictures and writing. The mental wheels will begin to turn.

An example of this was in the case of Isaac, a 10-year-old, who had been argumentative all day—his brother's birthday. The questions given to him were, "Why is this day hard for you? What are you feeling inside? What are you thinking that gives you this feeling?"

Isaac responded with things that others had done that made him feel overlooked. As he warmed up he mentioned that he was feeling unloved. People were making preparations for his brother's birthday. He was thinking that his parents loved his brother more—just like at the foster home. As Isaac worked he concluded. "It still hurts my feelings that our foster parents wanted to keep my brother and not me. I heard them say that I was a lost cause."

This exercise took about one hour, with parents checking about four times to reflect on what Isaac was writing while encouraging him to continue. The conclusion was reality-based. Isaac had thrived in the home, but needed consoling over the hurtful comments made in the past. Isaac agreed that his brother should get a good birthday. He needed help with the pain of rejection. He did not need to ruin a birthday for his brother.

Reflect on the Positive

Make sure that children are processing and storing their positive memories. Just because they have fun with you and share important events does not mean that they will remember them later. The brain's schema, or life pattern, acts as a filter, choosing what to remember and how it is remembered. The work of Diane Fosha describes this in some detail (2004). Unless we spend a significant amount of time talking with abused or neglected children and reflecting on positive experiences with them, these experiences will often be filtered out.

Children need to be able to share the positive parts of their lives with another who is caring, well-regulated, and positive. This sharing allows them to start changing their life schema, and, thus to hold onto positive memories. Therapists and parents need to spend time carefully working on positive events, breakthroughs, and memories so that they are stored in memory systems. Otherwise, the efficient and stressed brain deletes the positive content in favor of high-stress, negative information, which is required for survival.

This change in the life schema is a crucial part of the process by which children become more mentally positive. Spending time with children in every therapy session describing gains, or reflecting on accomplishments in home and school helps consolidate these memories so that they can change their life views.

Mastery is one important factor in building resilience into personalities—especially after stressful life events. Describing the tasks as they are accomplished in therapy and noting children's successes will build this sense of mastery and shared positivism.

One little boy, Alex, crowed to me, with his arms outstretched, and his face glowing, "Guess what? A great week! No swearing, no touching my brother's penith (*penis* said with a lisp), and no punching anybody!"

His mom said, "He's been waiting all morning to tell you this." We cheered and then he swept into her arms for a big hug. That high excitement and shared enthusiasm set this memory in his brain and will change the way Alex experiences life.

Going on, we stretched the experience a little more. "How does it feel to share this with me and with your mom?" I questioned gently.

"Really, really nice," Alex said, sighing a little. He was calm and relaxed, making full eye contact.

"It's been great for me to share this with you," I said quietly, "Really a privilege."

His mother nodded, with a sweet smile on her face. He connected with the expression on her face, improving in his attunement abilities.

In that way, Alex not only integrated his achievements, but also knew that he shared them in an attuned way with me and his mother. He integrated events and experienced closeness, or a positive attachment pattern, in the same interaction.

Keep a calendar of positive events

Both neglect and trauma have a depressing effect on children, and, as a result, they frequently remember only the negative parts of the day. It helps to mark one or two positive events on a calendar every night. Review the calendar frequently, recalling some of the positive memories with the child. One 8-year-old boy responded well to this, remarking, "My life has turned from bad to lucky." A sense of optimism such as this allows children to open up to the opportunities in front of them.

What Does the Home Look Like?

Unhurried homes

The children/teens described in this book do not do well with family stress. One of the easiest stressors to avoid is a hurried and hectic home. While maintaining a hectic home may be the norm for today's young families, parents must defy this trend in order to be successful. Children will also need parents who have the mental energy to do some of the positive, reflective activities in the book. Parents must maintain large margins of available time in order to do this important work.

One family I see did this by reducing their outside and inside commitments. Their young son gave them a big payoff when he said, "Our family is so comfortable. I like just being at home with you guys."

Children who have traumatic stress symptoms or prenatal exposure to harmful substances tend to have some days that are more difficult than others. Their brains simply do not work the same way every day. Allowing for their variations reduces the amount of discipline required.

Predictable and structured settings

Settings for previously traumatized children and teens in therapy, at home, and in school should all be predictable and structured. Their brains have been shaped by high stress, and, as a result, they will enjoy predictability, because it lowers stress levels. Structure that is built into experiences helps kids who are having difficulties organizing their attention and efforts. These are consistent features in the young people described in this book. Built-in structure also helps children learn patterns of structure in everyday life.

In therapy, I like to talk to children first about what we will work on and then how we will work on it. Often I draw or write with them at the same time so that they can use a visual modality. We can talk about the time frames, as well, and include how we can work together.

This "pre-learning" helps children see the big picture as we are putting the pieces into place. The children like knowing what comes next. Their brains enjoy recognizing the familiar parts as we move into them. It is similar to recognizing and appreciating a familiar chorus in a song or a repeated phrase in a symphony.

Young people who have executive functioning issues, as described earlier, live in worlds that seem disjointed and full of meaningless details. Pre-learning helps them to organize information, relate the parts to the whole, and understand what will be coming next.

High-stress children often do best in homes with schedules. The schedule does not have to be boring, but it should be a touchstone of regulation. Posting the daily schedule on a white board is easy to do. Families describe much better results, especially in the summertime, with children who have developed regular and predictable schedules.

When the structure and schedule of school are missing in the summer, I like to go beyond just forming a schedule to implementing a "theme of the week" for children. So, for example, a child might have Tropical Fish Week. Activities, books, meals, and decorations could all involve this theme. This is fun for the child, and it keeps their minds in the positive present. It helps them focus on something pleasant, encouraging curiosity and creativity. Since many children have reduced play skills due to early neglect, it also solves the problem of "What now? I'm bored."

Teachers who post daily and weekly schedules and run an interesting, but regulated, classroom find that the children have more energy available for learning. They are not constantly scanning for "what's next?" They always know what is next.

Train children through role playing and repetition

Prepare children in advance when they need to learn an important new activity. Teach it to them in real time by first making them do now what you want them to do without prompting later. For example, if you want them to get into the car in an organized fashion, then practice getting into the car several times before you actually have to drive somewhere. Or, if you want them to put their dishes in the dishwasher, practice this a few times before dinner. Teach children the skill before they will have to use it.

Overlearn activities

Any opportunity to practice activities of daily life is an advantage for children or teens. Practice will lead to storing these activities in the "automatic pilot" of motor-behavioral habits. At some point, they will no longer have parents coaching them. It is far more important for them to learn how to accomplish tasks independently than it is for them to learn how to listen to their parents. After all, they will not achieve in life because they are excellent at living under supervision in their parents' homes.

As mentioned previously, children who have traumatic stress, ADD, or FASD all have "off" days. Overlearned activities tend to stay with them even on these off days.

> It was clear from a neurodevelopment evaluation and medical history that 15-year-old Nik had been impacted by prenatal exposure and massive neglect. However, he had practiced the routines in his life so well that he looked quite capable. His daily routine was regular, well-practiced, and rather slow. It afforded him a time margin on hard days. He did his homework regularly and achieved good marks in school. Nik's excellent outcome was due to well thought-out home processes implemented by both parents. For six years they had followed the recommendations that were given in his previous neuropsychological assessment with excellent results.

Minimize background noise

Most children with backgrounds of neglect, traumatic stress, and FASD will become easily overstimulated, flooding with too much input. Some children may function just fine in the presence of background noise, in spite of their backgrounds, or they may have developed effective capacities for screening it out. But most children appreciate a calm, quiet setting, finding that this makes them feel more relaxed. When children are getting loud and out-of-control, they are often acting out the sensory modality that is overstimulating them the most. Reducing background noise will have a calming effect on such children.

The reality is that random background noise is too much for most traumatized children. Eliminate background noise by putting all the televisions in a room with a door and keeping the door closed. Turn off the television unless someone is specifically watching a program. Make it a rule that when family members want to speak to one another, they must find each other and converse within the same room, rather than yelling throughout the house. Yelling raises the tension level in the home—exactly what parents are trying to avoid.

Screening out background noise requires energy. Often children will do horribly on the school bus, especially at the end of their school day. The loud bus can be massively overstimulating. Many children do much better if they can avoid riding the bus. One parent said that until she deleted the bus, she did not realize how overwhelmed her child became when riding it. "I'd rather pick him up after school every day than have him scream at us after school," she said.

Be nurturing and friendly in speech and body language

Children do best when they feel safe and cherished. Use friendly non-verbal cues and vocal tones. Some parents and professionals, because of their own stresses and frustrations, begin to use a commanding dog-obedience type of tone and posture. This approach works well with pets and less well with children. A harsh approach may effectively convince children to behave and get back on track in the short term; over time, however, they will become more defensive and disorganized. They will feel as if they are back in a hostile setting, and, as a result, they will return to using their old defenses.

While parents do not need to conceal their irritation or frustration at all times, they should certainly reflect a positive and nurturing attitude overall. Their bodies and voices should show the child respect and promote a sense of safety. Sarcasm should not be used. It tends to be a way to one-up or get back at children and teens in a veiled and hostile manner.

Reward and discipline in small increments

Behaviors should be backed by reinforcements, so that children pay attention to these behaviors, either by avoiding or repeating them. When I explain reinforcements to children, I describe just that.

> One boy said. "I get it. You just don't want my brain to learn that when I take a short-cut by lying about doing my chore that it turns out well. You don't want me to get into bad habits." He got it precisely.

When working on behavior shaping, put the behaviors into a context so that children can understand how the shaping operates to their benefit. In the example above, this 10-year-old was ready to accept consequences because he understood its connection to working towards his eventual well-being.

Interventions work in two parts, first through changing the thought process, and then through developing specific daily goals. So, for a boy who hits or calls out names, who refuses to get up, go to bed, pick up socks, and so forth, first begin by helping him with his inner thought process. Discuss the thoughts and feelings that occur when he does these angry behaviors. Typical culprit feelings include these: that's not fair, they're mean, poor me, I can't, it's too hard, etc. Help him substitute these thoughts with helpful ones:

- I'll try.
- I don't like it, but I'll do it anyway.
- I'm not stupid.
- They aren't mean.
- They need my help.

- I'll feel better once I get started.
- I'd rather have friends than to fight over the rules.

Help children identify how their anger is affecting their bodies, as well.

- I feel my face get hot.
- My stomach gets tight.
- My fists go up.
- I feel my head pound and I get dizzy.
- My chest gets tight.
- My chin goes up and my mouth drops open to yell.

Michael Bloomquist's 2006 manual (see Resource List) provides an excellent treatment of this approach, complete with handouts and training sheets. I also make my own worksheets with children, and you can, too. I ask them to identify how their bodies feel and what they are thinking. Then, we substitute a more helpful thought. We practice ways to calm down through thinking of the helpful thought.

Second, we write up some objectives and measure them every day. I like to reward positive behavior and have children do restitution or pay a fine for misbehavior. I tell children and teens that the rewards are meant to teach their brains to pay more attention to the new pattern. The child can earn some reward every day.

There are many interventions that need to occur, so only give minute bits of rewards, privileges, loss of privileges, or restitution for each. Parents will say to me, "We've already taken away her TV program, her later bedtime, and her treat—and it's only 9:00 a.m. We don't have anything left for the day. What else can we take away when she gets home from school?"

For example, Jon, aged nine, listed not hitting, not throwing, not screaming/yelling, not calling names, and not raising a fist as good brain training behaviors. For two weeks he was to work on these problem areas, earning fifteen minutes of screen time (TV, Xbox, computer game) for daily success in each of these five areas. Jon did quick math and realized that he could earn 75 minutes of screen time per day.

Jon had to do restitution for any misbehavior. So, when he hit his sister, he did her laundry. When he threw bark at his brother, he was fined $3. The fine was arbitrary since the parent did not want to supervise restitution at that time. Jon had to do his job or pay his fine before he could redeem his screen time.

He wrote up a plan every day that included what would be happening that day and his behavior chart. At the end of the day, he could redeem the screen time he had earned. Even with slip-ups, he began feeling that he could change and overcome his difficult behaviors. By not taking away rewards, but simply postponing them until he did restitution, he could keep working all day long.

Another family used a reward system based on dimes for their boys who were accomplished whiners and name callers. Every time that there was quick compliance, as opposed to aggrieved arguing, the children gained a dime. Positive behaviors like calming intentionally, saying something supportive, being cooperative, and remaining silent at the appropriate time all earned dimes. The boys could take their dimes to the store every few days. Negative behaviors had different, non-monetary consequences, so the dimes kept coming. That way, the children did not get disheartened.

Two sisters had survived extensive physical abuse and domestic violence prior to their adoptions. They specialized in calling their parents derogatory names. Their father, who taught at the same school his daughters attended, was routinely referred to as "dumb ass" in front of his co-workers.

"Hi!" he said in one call to his wife. "It's me, dumb ass." Both parents laughed morbidly.

"It's yo bitch to you," she rejoined. "I don't think the kids will change. We might as well accept our new names."

This was the general level of coping in the family almost four years post-adoption. After I had worked with both girls on their thoughts and feelings, they agreed that their early modeling had been in aggressive behavior. They viewed this behavior as the successful way of getting what people wanted—especially in situations in which they also saw slapping and kicking. When they heard "no," they felt like it was time to threaten.

With some processing, they agreed that this was not a behavior that they wanted to continue. They agreed to use jobs for restitution, but earned daily dimes and a big reward when they did not swear or hit anyone for two weeks. They came in, proudly carrying their prizes, after about three months of consistent work. This combination of connecting their thoughts and feelings and a reward/restitution system worked well.

A teen of 15, Benjamin, described, "I'm in lock down. I wish my parents were not so conservative! I drank a little vodka and then I stayed home for three months—grounded. I got off restriction for a few months. Then I got caught posting some rude stuff on MySpace.com and one of my mom's friends said that she saw me drinking. I got busted again. They also found some beer cans in the recycling. Why do they think that they are mine?

I have my permit now. I can hardly wait until I can drive!!! Even if they restrict me every other month I'll have a good time half of the time! I think that they should let me make my own mistakes."

The parents said, "How do we parent him? We either keep him home or get these terrible phone calls. We have been at the police station twice! He posted enough information on MySpace.com to give a map to any predator of where and when to reach him—and his younger sister. If he drinks and drives, he could kill someone. We had an alcohol assessment done and made him go to an all-day workshop. They said that he did not have an addiction problem. But he has been caught with booze three times. When we restrict him he gets depressed but does not really learn anything from the restriction. He became suicidal at the end of the last three months. It's really like we are sentencing ourselves when we restrict him."

In sessions we worked with this teen on his identity. Who was he really? What were his values? Of course, those are questions for any teen, and are especially pertinent to teens who have questions about birth parents, as Benjamin did. We discussed the ways in which his behavior kept him close to his parents. His behavior was keeping him in a child-like stage. We also talked about whether his friends were helping him to be his best or dragging him down.

"My friends are my family," Benjamin said. "My dad said that they are losers. He's kind of right. Actually, a couple of them are losers. I might need better friends. Some of my friends are cool, though." Through discussion we actually started to break the issues down together. That is, Benjamin moved beyond an all or nothing point of view.

We next talked about what he wanted for himself—routing a path to success for him. Then, we got together with his parents, discussing what they expected in a teen of his age. We worked on teaching Benjamin to stand up for his position without blaming, becoming defensive, or fighting. I noticed that he had a pattern of acting out behavior when he felt powerless and angry. I wanted him to learn to negotiate—within safe boundaries.

Instead of taking away privileges, we began with a zero base. Parents and Benjamin agreed that they all valued a family with little fighting, safe computer use, and substance-free peer relations. Every day that he showed those qualities, he earned some time learning to drive the car. This was highly motivating. Every waking hour at home that he acted like a friendly and honest family member, he earned ten minutes of computer time. (Benjamin was in activities to the extent that this time was not excessive.) His computer was equipped so that a log of his activity was kept.

However, because he did need contact with friends, Benjamin's cell phone was not confiscated. But his text messaging was periodically reviewed. Benjamin continued to have access to his friends in the home and at supervised school activities—whether or not he was in trouble. But he had to earn the ride to those events and any spending money through being current on chores and being friendly to his family. Usually a friendly day would result in a friendly ride—with chores done. Sometimes Benjamin would use the ride earned from the previous day.

Benjamin was not permitted to go places with friends unless he could describe how his parents could be comfortable that he was remaining substance free. That meant that Benjamin had to make a plan to come home when booze showed up at a party. After two weeks of respectful family behavior and abiding by house rules with friends, computer, and substance, Benjamin could try his first outing with friends. This actually took Benjamin about six weeks to get together.

Benjamin avoided a friend who always got him in trouble. "I'm tired of paying the price for his mistakes," Benjamin said. "He wants to leave pills and vodka in my room. I'm supposed to keep my mouth shut. I told him that I'm sick of it. He's just using me. I'm done with him. He's so popular. It's like I should be glad to keep him from getting in trouble. He only cares about himself. "

This was the type of incremental change that helped change Benjamin's thinking. It also moved him along developmentally, causing him to work on judgment issues. The parents continued to use this type of small-bites reinforcement system for two years. Benjamin was not an easy teen, but he was friendlier and safer. He did show more appropriate behaviors as time moved along.

Charting for success

I often use charts for children who need reinforcement at school. The sample chart below is a typical example. The topics in bold should be individualized for each child. These categories can change over time as children improve in a particular area.

Emma—Success at School

Check for "yes," leave blank for "no"

Answers Teacher Promptly—with Eye Contact and a Friendly voice.

	Mon	Tues	Wed	Thus	Fri
a.m.					
p.m.					

Accepts Teacher's Leadership—Does not find new activities for herself and others while the teacher instructs.

	Mon	Tues	Wed	Thus	Fri
a.m.					
p.m.					

Body in Control—Follows school rules for lining up, transitions, and circle time.

	Mon	Tues	Wed	Thus	Fri
a.m.					
p.m.					

Friendly body and face to others at school.

	Mon	Tues	Wed	Thus	Fri
a.m.					
p.m.					

Person filling out form: a.m. _____

p.m. _____

Comments_____

_____

_____

_____

Please send this form home in the backpack every afternoon. If parents have comments, they will add them and return the form. A new form will be used daily.

This type of form should represent the collaboration among teachers, parents, children, and the therapist. It helps children apply lessons from therapy to all areas of their lives. As mentioned before, many of the children about whom this book was written have difficulties generalizing information from one context to another. They need help remembering what their goals are in context outside of the home and therapy. These forms help them to focus their attention and to get feedback on small, more contained parts of life.

Backtrack after failures, freeze-ups, or tantrums to practice coping with the triggering problem

When children have difficulties, it is helpful to go back to the situation that caused the problem, and then problem-solve how it could have worked better. In going through these activities, parents and teachers can role-play to help children generate and act out the solutions. The following two vignettes portray typical situations and possible resolutions.

Seven-year-old Madison was playing with her brother at a school event, when she saw her mother's van pull out of the parking lot, leaving her behind. Madison panicked and chased the van down a busy highway, running for over a mile. Finally, one of her classmates' parents passed Madison on their way home. They left one parent with Madison for safety, while the other parent went back to the school to find her mother. Madison had been chasing a look-alike van. Her mother was still at school.

In former homes, Madison had been left alone repeatedly by both her birthmother and a birth relative. Her reaction to the van had been a traumatic stress reaction. We talked about who was responsible for her every place she went. This was new information for her. She had never realized that there was a "go-to" person responsible for keeping her safe in every situation. She spent the next several months identifying these people. She also role-played how to go to them for help. She never had another such incident.

Tantrums can be handled in a similar manner.

One boy refused to go swimming at a family outing to the pool, insisting that the whole family return home. His situation was similar to the one above, in that he was responding to a stress trigger. In this case, his unreasonableness, or his stress trigger, was due to his dread of the shower room at the pool, which reminded him of a prior experience of abuse.

We practiced appropriate and private ways for him to share this type of problem. He needed to learn to ask for what he needed without making himself too vulnerable. Just saying, "I am uncomfortable with the locker room," was sufficient. In the future, he simply changed at home, and then stayed in his suit until he got home.

Children lack the abstract skills of adults, and therefore benefit from having words and choices modeled. They can then practice and memorize them.

Emphasize functional learning

Children need to learn how to operate smoothly in society in order to feel confident about themselves; they need to believe that the world has a place for them.

There are usually an overwhelming number of things for children to learn after placement. I like to prioritize and then focus on the routines and methods of communication that will help children function best. I want them to learn how to successfully handle the tasks that will help them to feel confident every day. Then, with this built-in sense of accomplishment, they can work on the more difficult tasks later.

A 12-year-old was learning to divide fractions, with great distress, while at the same time he was unable to get his backpack together or remember to brush his teeth every day. The functional tasks, in this case his morning routine, should gain the first priority—especially for children who have had earlier maltreatment.

Since many previously abused, neglected and traumatized children will have executive functioning difficulties, it is likely that they will have to work harder to accomplish activities such as learning to wash and put away their clothing, developing good homework (and later paperwork) habits, applying basic math so that they can shop on a budget and manage their bank balance, learning how to cook and clean up meals, and so forth. Some readers, in fact, may recognize weaknesses in themselves concerning the activities above. Start teaching and practicing these routines years before they are needed. Compliment children on their mastery.

Rules are memorized and concrete

Some children with prenatal exposure to drugs or alcohol will not go on to develop higher thinking skills, including sound judgment. Some parents describe this problem by saying things like, "But I told her over and over again why it is necessary that she build trust by not keeping secrets," or "be a friend to have a friend," or "be a person of his word." These types of comments are abstract. The messages need to be broken down into concrete directions placed in the context of specific situations.

In order to compensate for the lack of higher thinking skills, parents, teachers, and therapists must teach these children to live their lives like a script. They need to memorize very concrete rules for a variety of settings (Gray, 2012). For example, "The rule is that you cannot ever keep a secret from your parents unless it is about a present for their birthday or a holiday. Even if a friend says that it is OK, it is not OK. Our family rule is NO SECRETS. NO SECRETS at camp, at school, at home, or at someone else's home. NO SECRETS at the playground." This type of specific information is much more likely to stick.

Please look into the Resource List for excellent websites and books that offer more specific help.

Be aware of children's processing loads and daily variability

Some days, children with traumatic stress and/or prenatal sub-stance exposure will not do well. This does not mean that the parents need be more persistent on bad days. Sometimes there is not enough information available to understand the problem. I like parents to keep a notebook, writing down what seemed to happen the day of and the day before the difficult day. Over time, we can use this log to identify known stressors or trauma triggers.

A high school boy was getting surly and disorganized. It was the end of the year, his grades were great, and it was time for him to attend a big family wedding. It was also around the anniversary of his move from his foster home to his parents' home. Additionally, the extra events threw off school routine and placed him in crowded, overwhelming situations. The combination of emotional and environmental stressors was too much. His father wisely took him for a getaway to the mountains before his bad days escalated.

Start deleting activities and expectations on hard days. Over time, children will learn to do this necessary life editing on their own.

Parents must anticipate and help children with any changes in routine

Children who have trouble with coping find any changes in rou-tine to be difficult. More random and spontaneous parents must real-ize that most children recovering from early neglect and trauma will do poorly in a random environment. That does not mean that every-thing needs to be tightly organized, but parents do need to include predictability and ample preparation time for outings.

An exception should be made for children who will not allow themselves to have anything that they perceive to be a reward.

Two brothers, who were very challenging, would inevi-tably escalate prior to lovely experiences. Eventually, their parents were tempted to cancel these events. Instead, they simply stopped telling the boys about future vacation plans.

One sunny morning, the boys were awakened with, "Would you like to go to Disneyland today?" They agreed, and the family went. They did not have time to worry about or ruin the occasion. As they progressed, the family could begin to plan openly so that the boys could share the positive experience of anticipating the fun vacations.

Making plans for each day, as mentioned earlier in this chapter, will help children prepare for changes in their routine. Help children understand how the events are similar to things that they have already done, or notice how much of the day will stay the same, so that they recognize how little of the event is actually new. Simply put, continually break things down.

Children with prenatal exposure to substances will need many repetitions in order to learn. Essentially, they have a brain injury and have learning differences. Do not lecture them when they forget. This will not help children's stress levels or overall performance; it will just shame them. Instead, teach them again, perhaps have children do what you want them to do several times. Then you can compliment them on how well they are doing it.

Use social cues and role-play social situations

Children from abusive or neglectful backgrounds often have a hard time understanding the main point of a social situation. Or, they may not know quite what to do with themselves in such an environment. Tell them the main point prior to the potential situation. Role-play important parts with them, such as greeting people, asking to use the bathroom, interacting with younger or older children, and so forth. This will establish a motor-behavioral pattern that they can follow once in the new situation.

Teach response flexibility

The abilities to compromise and to learn how to accept disappointment constitute important attributes of emotional intelligence. Parents of the children this book describes regularly report that their children get stuck in "But, I want to," or "I don't want to." That is, their desires represent the limits of their reasoning.

An 8-year-old, Natalya, had no friends in her class. When events did not occur according to her mental image, she balked, tantrumed, and pointed at the girl who had disappointed her with a Cassandra effect. She simply could not process an event in life that had happened in a way that was different from what she had in mind.

Teaching response flexibility helps children to develop emotional intelligence. I tell children in advance that we will be intentionally disappointing them at least four times each day. We practice relaxing together and changing their immediate answer of "no" to "yes" or "I'll give it a try."

I helped one child, Jerome, understand how pleased someone else would feel when he compromised. We practiced this by saying, "I like our ideas. We'll do it your way first, then mine second." We actually rehearsed those routines in my sessions and in the home so that he would stop acting like he was being abused when parents said "No."

Parents can utilize their own opportunities to be flexible as a way to model this behavior. By talking out the process while they are calming themselves, they help the child see how to adapt to a stressor with the shift from frustration to calm acceptance.

There are excellent books with exercises for both the home and classroom for parents and teachers to use when teaching these elements of social relatedness. My favorites are *Navigating the Social World* and *Relationship Development Intervention*. Both are listed in the Resource List. While these resources are developed for children who might have autistic spectrum disorder, they clearly teach the components of social/emotional relationships.

Limit controlling body language and comments

Many children with poor caretaking histories will exhibit some controlling features in their relationships with adults. Align with children by understanding and also explaining why they feel the need to control. However, do not allow this pattern of controlling behaviors to flourish. Control prevents them from learning positive patterns of relating to others. For a more complete description of this subject, please see the chapter on "Anxiety and Control—Relaxing Its Grip" in *Attaching in Adoption* (Gray, 2012).

Use cartooning or social stories to assign feelings and teach cause and effect

Adults and children can use the cartoon drawing style to draw out how certain actions cause others to think and feel. They can start by drawing out three or four frames of a situation. They can draw feelings on the faces of the characters as well as thought balloons representing what other children might think and feel. Then they can use the remaining blank frames to see what might happen next. This will help them begin to predict what other children might do next, and how that will affect their relationships. This cartoon style drawing is used in the case of Kate, age 9.

Kate has no friends because she is bossy and dominating. In session, I talk about a problem situation with her. She draws a picture to go along with our discussion. She draws herself pushing ahead to get the game ball first every day at morning recess. Then she draws a picture of two potential friends and their facial expressions and their thoughts. She draws a picture of herself at the lunch table, asking if she can sit with them. She can predict what they might say to her.

In going through this exercise, Kate might look at me, the therapist, for cues. My role is to help lend some affect so that Kate can begin to understand the feelings and thoughts of another person.

Next, I draw Kate, with help with eyes, details, and thought bubbles from her. She is drawn with a bubble in which she wants the game ball but she is thinking, "If I share with them, they will be nicer to me at lunch." Kate says, "You take the ball. I had it yesterday."

Her potential friends say, "Thanks." They think that Kate is friendlier; that she cares about them and not just about herself. In the next frame, they smile at her at lunch. Even if they do not invite her to sit with them, they are not mad at her and Kate thinks in her bubble, "Pretty soon they will notice that I have changed."

As a practical aside, adults should monitor these drawings. Some children will not understand the main point, and will make picture-drawing the main point. Successful social stories include collaboration from the child with careful adult supervision to facilitate the momentum and the social exchange.

While these exercises seem to be describing the obvious, many children need some help understanding the basic motivations behind the mind of another. Their "mindsight," or knowing their own mind and that of another, is undeveloped. Drawing provides an easy way to assign feelings and actions with results in social situations. The Resource List includes a book and website by Carol Gray that elaborates on creating cartoon models for social situations.

Help children find sad and lonely feelings

After maltreatment, children may feel anger to the point of excluding sad or lonely feelings. They may have to experience sad feelings through another's story before they can relate to these feelings in their own lives. Use pictures and storytelling to help them "kindle" with the sad affect, then change the topic to their own story.

I have pictures of lonely, lost children with lost and scared facial expressions. Sometimes I share these pictures with children in session, asking them what they see. They can project some material on another's behalf. I can also help them by telling them stories that cause them to relate to the feelings.

This process of telling a short story and sharing feelings with children is one of "lending" a feeling to another. Because of mirror neurons, when we are working closely with another person, they can feel some of our feelings. These mirror neurons are in the emotional centers of the brain, allowing children to feel some of our feelings when they are tracking with us.

Then, we can move to a similar situation in their lives. Often, they will be able to identify their own and others' feelings for the first time. Remember, the feelings that are lent and suggested are effective only if they are appropriate. This technique is also effective when used with adults.

A man who was seeing me said, "Why did you say that you felt sad and that I got 'hurt,' when I told you that I was sexually molested? I have tried to never think about the abuse, but every time I have, I felt angry or stupid. After you said that, I went home and thought that my sexual abuse was no different than if one of my kids had fallen off of their bikes. They were hurt; I was hurt. I had never felt any sympathy for myself. I cried for myself for the first time.

"I had always felt so angry with anything that stood in my way. Now I'm not angry at any of the little things. But I am extremely sad over my own abuse."

In his sadness, this man could reach out to his wife and a friend, and ask for some extra support. He also found himself behaving in a more sensitive manner towards others.

Make pathology boring

Some parents try to extinguish certain negative behaviors in a dramatic way. Even though some children may find it quite unpleasant to be reminded of their misbehavior, many formerly neglected children are drawn to the attention.

I had parents who were understandably incensed by 8-year-old Jess' lies. Even after they began therapy with me to do attachment work, they still centered their daily life on the lies their child told. The following is a portion of a note that I sent to them in reference to a humdinger of a lie, which was followed by confusing rabbit trails to explain away the lie:

"Make lying very dull. If you are confused, say that you are confused because Jess is being confusing. If something doesn't

make sense, simply say that in a distracted, calm manner.

"Tell her that you are tired because of the extra work she caused by being confusing. Then, tell her that she will have to go to bed ten minutes earlier because you had to use your brain more when she used her brain less. You need to rest yours.

"You can give her one of your chores if you don't want to send her to bed early. Or, you can give her chores if she tells seven lies, and it is too early to send her to bed seventy minutes early. She is feeding off of the drama and attention. Make this a dull as dirt issue from now on."

These parents stopped fueling the lies with attention. They re-directed their attention to exercising as a family, which became the new hobby.

Children who are distractible and constantly seeking out new stimulus tend to veer towards interesting material. Children are more drawn to lying or resistance when adults make this an interesting, vivid contrast to their bland routines. Be certain to put as much emotional energy as is reasonably possible on the positive routines in a child's life. Act distracted, bored, and somewhat indifferent to the problems that the child makes through nasty behaviors. Show animation, energy, and excitement when children are making good choices, playing well, and relating well.

Watch out for bad lighting

Some children with prenatal exposure or migraines do quite poorly in fluorescent lighting. The constant flicker or variation causes an increased processing load that exhausts them, causes irritability, or triggers headaches. Simply paying attention to this can determine whether or not it applies to a particular child or teen.

Practice happy dances, have celebrations, and mark milestones

Even after children have made tremendous progress, they often do not seem to comprehend how well they have done or how far they have come. Be certain that, as therapists, parents, caseworkers, or educators, you are celebrating the discrete changes that children have made.

Having a happy dance because of a good morning or a celebration at dinner because of positive behavioral changes are ways to help children notice their changes. It is important for them to integrate these changes into their sense of self.

An 11-year old boy, Hayden, talked to me about sexual acting out and stealing, topics we had covered two years before. He mentioned, "But that was a long time ago. I don't do that anymore. I don't *want* to do those things anymore." He had noticed the changes in his identity, in part because we made the markers so clear.

One of his milestones was marked by entrusting him to carry his mother's backpack, which contained her wallet, when they came in for sessions or went shopping. The backpack was heavy, so this was beneficial for his mother. Both mother and son were proud of the responsible way in which he helped her.

Children consolidate positive gains into their identities when celebrations mark achievements like telling the truth, being honest, being safe with hands and feet, and so forth.

Developing an internal locus of control over time and exploring options

It bears repeating that children who have been treated poorly tend to believe that they caused the bad things that happened to them, i.e. they were not worth care, not lovable, and so forth. On the flip side, they also feel little shame or responsibility for the events that they can effect.

These children have often experienced earlier situations in which they could tantrum, fuss, or dissociate but nothing really changed for them. They had few options for exercising control over their lives. The difficulty that occurs is that they then do not go on to believe that they have control over their lives through their hard work or their problem-solving skills. They may be depressed, defensive, or aggres-sive when faced with problems, but have the attitude that something or someone else is in charge of their lives. This is called having an *external locus of control*. We want them to move to an *internal locus of control*, one in which they believe that they can exert themselves to change outcomes.

I like to explore options with children for every situation. I teach children to think about and ask the question, "What are my op-tions?" It helps them exercise some appropriate mastery in their own lives. It gives them a sense of responsibility rather than a sense of helplessness.

Even if they don't proceed with the options we have discussed, they change just through the telling of the problem and the search for solutions. The secret, as Daniel Stern describes, is that, in telling the story to another mind, the story has changed (2004). The story-telling process allows the child to utilize the stress regulation and caring support of another, causing her to feel somewhat better about the situation. In addition, the verbal centers of the brain have better stress regulation, so putting things into words helps the teller lower her stress levels (Briere, 2003).

I also like to ask children to practice practical problem-solving in situations. They can do this by writing out or drawing out plans for their days, as described earlier in this chapter. The main point is to change their world view from one where events happen because life is controlled by others to one where people can powerfully affect the quality of their lives. Teach children that even if they did not have this type of power earlier in their lives, they have it now.

This mastery may feel wonderful, but it is also unnerving to chil-dren. Often they have put all of their efforts into their previous de-fenses. They require encouragement and practical exercises in order to feel like they are thinkers, problem-solvers, and planners.

Soothe and teach self-soothing and deep breathing

Children who have been abused and neglected will not naturally gain the capacity to calm down as they age. Some children have told me that they simply do not know how to calm themselves. Teach children to breathe in through their noses and out through their mouths slowly, concentrating on having the diaphragm move out as they take a breath and in as they release breaths. Have them visualize all the things that bother them. Then, tell them to blow those thoughts and feelings out into a big balloon. They will naturally take a deep breath right after that. Then tell them to let the balloon float away and have them blow up another one.

Children may spontaneously imitate parents or therapists who model taking and releasing deep breathes as a way of reducing tension, especially if they narrate what they are doing. I like to practice deep breathing with children and parents, taking and releasing breaths in three sets of three breaths, until they shift into a relaxed state.

Sometimes children do not like feeling calm, since it seems so unfamiliar. Some children have told me that they think that something will sneak up on them when they are calm. Make certain that they can recognize that they are safe before moving into this exercise.

I teach parents to sooth stressed children in ways that they will enjoy. Therapists can try different techniques with parents and children in order to determine the best way to calm each child. These techniques include having parents try the following:

- Stand behind the child, speaking calmly and reassuringly by the child's neck and cheek.
- Pat the child on the back in a circular motion, listening intently.
- Squeeze the shoulder joints gently.
- Ask children to draw a picture of what makes them upset and share it with parents.
- Draw a picture of a solution and share this picture.

The adults should concern themselves both with the logistics of a particular stressful situation and also with the calming processes, so that children feel like they have better self-control. Children have a difficult time starting each day if they are unsure as to whether or not they have the capacities to meet the day's challenges. They also will have a natural stress reaction, or breathe high in the chest. Children feel more confident as they learn calming as part of the skill set to increase coping.

Reach out to withdrawn children in a positive manner

Children need the help of parents, caseworkers, and/or therapists when they have confusing and conflicting feelings. Often children withdraw when they lack previous experiences of adults providing buffering from stress and helping them to organize feelings.

Reach out to withdrawn children, giving examples of how people have helped you emotionally during a difficult time. Relate clear stories of how children will receive support in confusing or upsetting instances. Let children know that you are interested in helping them.

Repair upsets quickly

Do not let hard feelings linger following problems between children and adults. Adults should be actively trying to change children's early scripts. In the early scripts, kids think that they do not matter or that adults cannot effectively help them. When children feel like their former templates fit, as in the case of a conflict, they start to revert back to these old templates. Listen to children's feelings vigilantly, accepting how they feel. Parents or adults do not have to agree with children, but they can understand and accept children's feelings. Empathically describe how a limit is based on safety or fairness, but that adults still care about children's feelings.

Use non-verbal language to show affect and important messages

Very young children are treated to a variety of body cues that help them derive the meaning of day-to-day tasks. Adults usually stop giving these types of cues as children move into the school age. When working with children who have missed this early training, use your hands to show amounts, your face to show more expression, and your body positioning to indicate important concepts. Maintain this over-expressiveness for these children. It will help them understand the significance and the amount or degree of emotions in situations. In other words, decrease the lecturing and turn up the body language.

Use accommodations in school situations

Most children who have experienced neglect or trauma will need an adapted approach in school in order to level the educational playing field.

One father said, "I was not sure that I agreed with this at first. It seemed like an easy out. We used a Section 504 based on my son's ADD and learning disabilities in order to help him get special help at school. Before, he was a D student. I thought that he just would not get to higher education. He'd get a menial job. Now he is a B student.

"Now I see that this is what he needs so that he can learn in the manner that he learns best. He still does the work, which is fair. He knows the material. It has made a believer out of me. I am planning for a post high school training track for him—either college or technical training. He'll be able to make a good living and have an interesting job doing something that he likes."

Good testing that assesses how children move or process information is essential when helping children work around learning issues to achieve up to their potential. Many parents are finding that neuropsychological testing at ages 7 or 8 is tremendously beneficial for determining the best learning approaches at school and at home.

One mother said after testing, "I used to get so mad at him, saying, 'What did I tell you just yesterday?' Now I know that he really doesn't remember. He needs a daily check-off sheet. It isn't a relationship problem. It's just how his brain is wired."

Summary

The processes used in all areas of daily life are intentional in promoting emotional intelligence, confidence, and better emotional and physiological regulation. These processes take time and energy, and require making lifestyle accommodations in order to obtain optimal results for children who have had suboptimal beginnings. Life is better for everyone when children are met where they are actually functioning instead of expecting them to function as if neglect/trauma had not interfered. That being said, the processes in the above sections should be undertaken with the expectation that many, many children will benefit from them and then outgrow the need for these specialized parenting and professional approaches.

CHAPTER 9

The Role of the Child Welfare/ Social Worker

"If I'd only known then what I know now."

—Every Parent

The preceding chapters have demonstrated that today's adoptions need to be supported by sophisticated casework. This chapter discusses specific casework activities, including those involving the homestudy/parent-preparation process, assessing and moving children, and post-placement services. The training process for families should include accurate preparations, so that parents can embrace the reality of parenting, as described in Chapter 8. Essential issues in any training and homestudy process are

- adoption triad issues,
- adoption identity issues over the lifespan,
- grief and loss issues for all triad members,
- transracial adoption issues,
- cross cultural adoption issues,
- infertility issues,
- promoting attachment,
- incorporating a new family member.

Typically, agencies are good at addressing these necessary basics. The challenge today is to incorporate information on neglect, trauma, prenatal exposure to harmful substances, and institutionalization into the homestudy and casework processes.

A family said to me, "Our caseworker pushed us into therapy. We are so grateful for this now. I don't think that we would have disrupted, but we certainly wouldn't have become the healthy family that we are today without that therapy." Their social worker took the time to call me about this case, attended trainings on recognizing trauma symptoms, and set up supports for the family during her post-placement visit. And, she recruited and trained a parent volunteer who mentors other families and assists with foster-adopt trainings. Ultimately, she saved time, as she had far less requests for crisis services. Although I was only in contact with one of her families, I believe that her standard of excellence reaped benefits for all of the families she served.

Good casework prepares parents and children, decreasing the rates of *disruption* and *dissolution*. Disruption refers to situations in which children leave families prior to the finalization of a planned adoption, while dissolution occurs after an adoption finalization. The older the children are at the time of placement, the higher the rates of disruption or dissolution (Bird, Peterson, Miller, 2002). NYU Professor Trudy Festinger's 2005 research indicates that currently 10-25% of domestic adoptions of children over three years of age disrupt.[1] There are no reliable statistics available on disruption rates for international placements. Since many of these children come from institutional settings and few are adopted during the first few months of life, the risk factors that place strains on families are substantial in international adoptions. Increasing family support and putting more time into the casework and placement process helps more families experience successful adoptions.

---

[1] Festinger, T. (2005). "Adoption disruption." In G. Mallon and P. Hess (Eds.) *Child welfare for the twenty-first century: A handbook of practices, policies, and programs* (pp. 452-468). (New York: Columbia University Press)

Use the Homestudy to Identify Challenges and Strengths in Parents

Which parents provide the best emotional rehabilitation for maltreatment? Parents do not have to share the same DNA to shape their children's brains. As discussed previously, parents play a large part in wiring their children's moods and stress regulation. It is imperative that the professional community examine literature on maltreatment and its repairs carefully when assessing parents. Nurturing adoptions to success begins with careful and thorough homestudies. This section describes homestudy and preparation techniques and questions that are meant to help integrate maltreatment, attachment, and neuroscience research into interviews. It goes on to describe ways in which the homestudy can be conducted to reveal attachment-oriented information or the stress regulation capabilities of individual prospective parents.

A homestudy should be an educational opportunity for parents in order to keep them within their capacity for successful parenting. The majority of prospective first-time parents and would-be adoptive parents with healthy biological children have little understanding of traumatic stress as being a chronic condition. They also may not comprehend that prenatal exposure to alcohol might necessitate extra commitments throughout the life cycle, not just for the child and his parents, but for the siblings in a family. Social workers must think of their ethical role as educators during placement. Parents must have all of the information available, so that they can be fully prepared to meet their children's needs.

A social worker's job is to facilitate the formation of close relationships through families. While some families—the ones who want to adopt—are willing to assist the developmental processes of children in need of a family, it is important to continue to view these families as working units. The placement field has suffered after taking a stance that all children can and should be placed in available homes, seeing children as pegs to be placed into family holes. It is more helpful to think in terms of the child's capacity to form thriving relationships in individual families, and also to consider the overall health of the prospective family before and after placement.

Children are placed into families so that they can learn patterns of intimacy that can only be experienced within a family. But those patterns must be kept intact in order for children to benefit. This being the case, social workers need to be asking themselves and potential parents these questions:

- Can this parent form a caregiving relationship with this child?
- Will the relationship simultaneously allow for the necessary activities of daily living to proceed for all members of the family?
- Will an adoption allow for healthy development to occur for the child within this family?

Homestudies are also assessment opportunities. In addition to imparting enough information about adoption to allow parents to be realistic about the road ahead, social workers also need take seriously their role in protecting children's best interests. They must objectively examine the capacity of would-be parents to form secure attachments and teach children self-regulation through these attachments. Homestudies, then, should predict which potential parents are emotionally healthy caregivers with whom children can form secure attachments. It is essential that the homestudy assess whether or not parents value close, emotionally attuned relationships themselves and have the desire and ability to develop them in others. Placements of convenience, or those that seem too good to be true, usually prove with time to be ill-fitting.

There are administrative pressures to increase numbers of placements and to accomplish them more quickly. That must never be done at the risk to children or the families who are caring for them. It is an ethical practice issue to inform and to prepare families for the road ahead—even if such information causes them to determine that they cannot meet the needs of a particular child, or to determine that adoption itself is not for them. Consider the inconvenience and additional emotional pain that disruption will cause an older child before you make a placement based on convenience or administrative pressure.

There are three critical emotional areas that social workers must address in the homestudy:

1. Is this a parent who is sensitive to the needs of others and who meets needs respectfully and accurately?
2. Does this person have well-regulated moods? Or, has she been impacted by unresolved grief and trauma?
3. Does this person have empathy? "An important part of empathy is being able to tap into your own pain. If people deny their past, forget their past, pretend that it did not matter, or that it had a positive effect, then they are shut off to some extent from others' pain. They do not make themselves available for empathic experiences" (Cassidy, 2006).

The balance between points two and three comes from having made peace with the past. A stable person will have resolved and derived meaning from his life struggles. He can use these experiences to respond empathically to others, and does not become disorganized or overly emotional when recalling those struggles or losses. These key domains underlie the potential for success in any placement. They must be assessed by social workers who have been thoroughly trained and as well have the emotional intelligence to understand the core elements of successful family interactions.

Look for consistent, coherent life narratives

The ability to form a consistent narrative, or story line, for our lives is indicative of being capable of understanding ourselves and our pasts. Gaps or difficulties with recalling a storyline indicate that some information is neither integrated nor resolved. Insight into relationships, as revealed by a narrative, is especially significant when anticipating an opportunity to love and be loved and feeling secure in close relationships, an opportunity that prospective parents should be seeking. The life narrative reveals any inconsistencies, as well as resolutions and insights.

Training to use the Adult Attachment Inventory (developed by C. George, N. Kaplan and M. Main, and first discussed in Chapter 7) results in the ability to categorize a parent's or prospective parent's attachment capabilities and their style in terms of secure/autonomous, dismissing, preoccupied, disorganized/unresolved, or "cannot classify." The AAI probes essential questions about whether the person

- values close relationships
- is sensitive to the emotional needs of others
- understands his or her history as it relates to current close relationships
- has explanations for and has processed feelings about frightening or overwhelming events in his past
- has the capacity to grieve, to resolve, to establish safe relationships
- responds to the interview with insight.

Familiarity with the lessons above can help caseworkers avoid some of the more common mistakes that occur in the standard homestudy interview.

An error that social workers make all too often is trying to fill in the blanks themselves or to distract clients who are having difficulty with parts of the homestudy interview. The desire to help clients sometimes occludes obvious and ominous warning signs, as in the vignette below.

> Melinda's toddler son was difficult to soothe and had a shocked "still face" at times. His mother fretted about attachment problems, so she never left him. She had become exhausted from giving constant attention to her son. "I become suicidal when I think of my children leaving me someday," she confided. "If one of my sons preferred my husband to me, I do not think that I could bear it."
>
> The homestudy interview done prior to placement had revealed that Melinda was quite sad over her secondary infertility. At no time, however, did the worker ask about the possibility of additional trauma or grief issues in her past. Melinda's social worker had smoothed over the lapses in Melinda's narrative, and tactfully changed the subject when she became overwhelmed. The social worker had enabled Melinda in hiding her long-term history of mood issues, including instances of suicidal behavior which spanned fifteen years. In fact, Melinda had been diagnosed with *borderline personality disorder* long before her infertility issues caused additional grief. Now, Melinda was frequently sharing her extreme mood states with her infant son, who responded in a confused, disoriented way.

Without having explored the situation with enough depth, the social worker had given a beatific reference that concluded that, with a child, all would be well with Melinda. All was not well. She should not have received an approved homestudy at all.

This social worker should have been leery and cautious of the way she felt as if she were "saving" Melinda. Melinda's tendency to idealize should have caused her social worker to feel further discomfort. Rather than stopping the interview when Melinda seemed overwhelmed, the worker could have asked direct questions about her moods and suicide attempts. Had the social worker looked at the degree of resolution of losses in Melinda's childhood, she would have seen a woman who was unresolved and disorganized. She would have seen that Melinda's husband walked on eggshells to keep his mentally ill wife in some kind of daily balance. She would also have noticed Miranda's lack of friendships. She would have seen a role reversal in Miranda's relationship with the child already in the home. This adoptive placement was definitely not in the best interest of any infant.

Sometimes the issues are not as extreme as a mental illness or a disorganized attachment state of mind. Individuals who have a dismissive state towards attachment can make the homestudy process seem too easy, as suggested by Cheryl's vignette.

Cheryl returned to the agency after a homestudy interview, feeling pleased. She had finished the interview in record time—her first efficiency in a messy week. Talking to her adoption co-worker, Cheryl summarized, "The mom in this family is fine, but I don't know about Dad. Mom had a great childhood with nurturing, wonderful parents!"

Cheryl went on to describe the husband as too sensitive. "He says that his wife finds time for everyone but him. But he said the same thing about his parents. I think that he is a whiner."

The agency put this family's adoption process into rush mode. There was a little girl, Melissa, 4 years old, whose foster parents wanted her moved by Friday. This seemed like perfect timing. Cheryl was caught up in the flurry. She did not notice or question that all of this family's references consisted of casual work friends. Placement went forward.

Later, Cheryl was aghast to witness the mother's dismissive attitude towards both Melissa's and Dad's emotional needs. After a horrible afternoon on the first day of placement, Cheryl groused to her co-worker. "Mom told me that in her family the family always came first. What a joke! Dad called me twenty minutes after I left the home. He was wondering if Melissa and Mom were with me! Mom told him that they were going to the store. Dad was left at home, alone, waiting for them. After Dad's call, I called Mom on her cell phone. She told me she was at work! So, I stopped by her office. Melissa was sitting in the waiting area, rocking back-and-forth, completely alone. When Mom heard me talking to Melissa, she came out and said, 'It took me a few minutes longer than I thought, but she's fine.'"

Cheryl finished bleakly, "I tried to talk to Mom, but she tuned me out. When I asked her why she had not left Melissa with Dad, she said that she wanted Melissa with her. She gave no further explanation. Melissa waited at her office for two hours! Now do I move Melissa again, make the parents take a parenting class, or what?"

In the vignette above, Cheryl responded in a burned-out fashion, joining the prospective adoptive mother in dismissing the father's emotional needs. The placement of convenience might also have seemed just too compelling. It is exciting to get on the bandwagon of an "it was meant to be" placement.

Cheryl should have been looking for evidence that the parents were capable of protecting and comforting Melissa. Melissa needed buffering parents who would help her to organize the confusing new world into which she had just moved. Instead, her arrival was treated like an item from a to-do list: "Get a child. Check."

What did Cheryl miss?

- The mother did not honor attachments.
- Her closest relationship was distant.
- She denigrated her husband for his requests for emotional closeness.

- Her descriptions of her relationships with her parents were devoid of supporting details.
- The father clearly said that he had insensitive parents and an insensitive wife.

Sensitivity in parenting is one of the strongest predictors of the ability to form a secure attachment. This lack of sensitivity, then, should have been treated as very critical information by the caseworker. Just a few more questions would have revealed that the mother's "close" relationship with her parents consisted of two phone calls per year and two brief visits within the last five years. If the caseworker had asked the mother to describe specific instances in which she felt especially close to her parents, the details would not have made sense and/or would have lacked emotional depth. Directing the mother to specific relationship help prior to placement in order to build sensitivity in the marriage and family life would have helped the new family enormously.

Ultimately these "hurry-up" homestudies and placements do not increase the number of stable, permanent placements. They bog down the placement professionals who attempt to change parents after children are already in their care. As in Cheryl's case, the process of working with Melissa and her family took much longer than would have doing the homestudy correctly in the first place.

Assess parents' attachment capabilities and readiness

Homestudies should not be expected to identify only "perfect families." All families have areas of weakness. The homestudy should act as an educational tool that will help families be successful. It is also a screening process that acts to remove families who are markedly unsuitable for parenting children who will need extra help from sensitive parents. The small percentage of prospective families who should not adopt children are also the ones who take inordinate amounts of time away from the child welfare system. Identifying unsuitable families before, not after placement, allows for significantly more time for post-placement training and support for families, completing adoptions, and recruiting more families.

The interview template which follows should only be used in

the form of a face-to-face interview, not in the form of questions soliciting written responses. The template incorporates some of the research and theory behind the Adult Attachment Inventory. This format presents homestudy questions from an attachment point of view. It adapts concepts from attachment research and literature to the homestudy process.

Homestudy Interview Questions

1. Describe the relationship you had with your mother as a child. To your father? List five adjectives that describe your mother, and five for your father.

The social worker should write down these descriptive adjectives, and then ask for examples of situations or events that demonstrate those qualities.[2] Social workers should be looking for a description of parent-child intimacy. They should also be judging the general quality of the description. The narrative should be smooth, coherent and have a firm basis in reality. Words and facial expressions should be consistent. If people cannot remember any examples to support the qualities that they mention, then start tracking the quality of sensitivity in their other relationships.

2. Can you detail some times in which you really needed to depend on your parents? How did they respond? How did this affect you at the time? What do you think of it now? Would you parent in the same way or differently?

The examples should fit the answers to the questions. Any contradictions indicate the presence of something that should be explored further. One big red flag to watch for is the interviewee trying to turn instances where the parents were not there for them into advantages.

3. Can you describe times when you felt lonely or rejected by your family? Were they aware of your feelings? How did you interpret their actions as a child? And now? Would you parent in the same way or differently?

---

[2] Both the concept and the format of this question are credited to the work of Carol George, Nancy Kaplan, and Mary Main (1996).

Ideally, people should be able to describe painful experiences in a way that demonstrates an understanding of their parents' points of view. They should have an idea of why something happened, and also be able to acknowledge the effects of painful experiences on their own development. The person being interviewed should be able to do this without becoming overwhelmed with bitterness or any other emotion.

4. What is your current relationship like with your parents? How often do you see them or talk on the phone? If they are not living, what was it like when they were alive and how did their loss affect you?

Answers to this question should contain information about
- the degree of reciprocity/attunement that they had as children
- descriptions of how painful family situations were acknowledged and repaired versus being ignored
- smoothness and coherency in the descriptions
- insight into how those first relationships shaped their present lives.

5. Were you ever frightened of or hurt by your parents? How was this dealt with in your family? How do you think that this affected your childhood and who you are today?

Parents-to-be who describe bitter memories of abusive, insensitive, or abandoning parents, and who also show little resolution, will need to work these issues out before placement. They will need a referral for therapy. Watch for positive indicators as well. People who experienced childhood abuse may have been buffered by positive attachment figures, like grandparents, who were sensitive and responsive. Descriptions of their alternate caregiver's sensitivity, with a sense of resolution about why their parents were not there for them are good signs. The more people are able to describe the reasons behind parents' actions, with appropriate, regulated emotion and insight, the better. An appropriate answer to this question looks like this.

"My mother would not listen to me when I was upset by my family's sudden move. She ignored my tears and said,

'Pack.' Now I know that she had just had a Caesarean section a week before, was hormonal, in pain, and had to move our whole family, including a new baby. My dad had to choose between flying to the new city within 48 hours and losing his job. We had to follow him. As an adult, I have concluded that we must have been behind on rent. That's one reason why we moved so quickly.

"My mother never apologized, though. I think that I would do things so differently. I would at least try to explain what was happening and let my daughter know that I cared about her feelings. That would have helped a lot. My grandma let me cry at her house and took me to my school and around our neighborhood so that I could say goodbye to my friends and my teacher."

Notice that this sample contains an honest description of pain and a conclusion about her mother's point of view. It also includes a description of a sensitive parent figure, the grandmother, who provided support during an overwhelming situation. She went on to describe how she would do things if she were the parent. The example is relatively brief and easy to follow. It is clear that this person has the ability to use her own life stories as a source of empathy for others.

6. *Give me a ten-minute description of your life, including main events and the major decisions that you have made. Start either at the present and go backwards, or begin at birth and go forwards. What are your earliest memories?*

This type of narrative should demonstrate a person's sense of mastery over most of the events in life, or their ability to take responsibility for personal decisions and actions. Answers to this question will also highlight the contrasting attitude of blaming others. It will show thinking that is shame-based and also reveal whether people view themselves as helpless victims or in a grandiose way. Listen for the inclusion of instances of seeking out support and acknowledging helpers, as these abilities act as important attributes for adoptive parents.

Look for a coherent life narrative. The narrative should be relatively smooth and should not have gaps. Emotions, as conveyed both through facial expressions and with words, should match the person's story. Pay special attention to life narratives that do not make sense! Why is the person lacking integration? If *you, as an adult,* find the person emotionally confusing, a child will certainly have difficulties using this parent as an emotional guide.

7. Tell me about your best friends. How did you meet them? How long have you known them? What do you do together? How often do you get together? How do you work out problems in relationships?

Get a sense of how connected the person is to their community and also the quality of their relationships. Check to see how long-term their relationships are. Loners who cannot work with others are not good choices as adoptive parents. They cannot instruct a child who needs help learning how to resolve problems and become more trusting. When angry, does this person cut people off permanently? Certainly this trait comes back to haunt social workers, in the form of disrupted placements.

Scrutinize people who have the following characteristics, as they are potential child abusers.

- They are charming.
- They are willing to accept an especially needy child.
- They have intense but short-term relationships, and no one knows them well over an extended period of time.
- The person seems too good to be true.

If you observe these traits, look for a hidden price tag. Sexual predators and antisocial personality types gravitate towards the most vulnerable members in our society. They tend to be especially charming throughout the homestudy process. Check these peoples' histories thoroughly. Make certain that they have a clean, well-researched record. Take seriously minor charges, such as fraud, assault, drug or alcohol abuse, and domestic violence, and examine especially carefully all charges that are accompanied by great rationalizations.

Pay attention to red flags in the history that indicate instability: sudden firings, financial irresponsibility, frequent moves, lies, multiple marriages, affairs, and a lack of continuity in relationships. These form the symptom clusters predictive of personality disorders. It is important to remember that a caseworker cannot simply befriend every family. The homestudy process must effectively screen out predatory adults.

8. Do you consider yourself to have been a physically or emotionally abused or neglected child or teen?

Ask about any abuse that may be a part of the person's background. If there is abuse, when did it start? Did it involve the person's nuclear family? How have they come to understand it; what are they doing to resolve their relationships and gain safety? Were there multiple traumas? Does the person have night terrors? Does the person have flashbacks? Are they bothered by loud noises? Would a screaming or aggressive child bring out reminders of the abuse?

Remember that there is a difference between Type I and Type II abuse. Type I abuse is short term and does not result in traumatic stress reactions. It stands out as an unusual and unique experience. Social workers often have optimistic views, taken from accounts of parents who have been successful in spite of abuse and in the absence of counseling. These views are usually based on people with Type I abuse, as they were impacted less.

As described in Part One, Type II abuse involves multiple events or long-standing abuse, with extreme stress. People with Type II abuse who have had no or poor treatment outcomes pose a risk for high-stress children. These parents can easily fall back into a behavior pattern of dissociation, flood with old trauma, and suffer from anxiety and depression. People with Type II abuse tend to incorporate numbing and dissociation, substance abuse, rage, mistrust, interpersonal relationship problems, suicidal ideation, and uncompleted grief into their personalities (Veitch, 1998). Even children with no histories of maltreatment find these personality states alarming. Children tend to form disorganized attachments with these adults. These individuals have often the complex trauma described in Chapter 2. These homes are not healthy enough for adoptive placements.

9. Have you had periods of depression, or do you think that your moods swing more than most people's? Do you think you have anxiety problems?

Please ask these questions in person, not just on a form. It is easy to check "no" on a form. It is much more difficult to lie in person. Many people have experienced periods of anxiety and depression but have responded very well to counseling and medications. These people do quite well with children after placement. They certainly should not be screened out of adoption. Check into the mood issues in a person's history. Are there periods of depression? How have they been handled? What is different now? Did they show resolution over losses from infertility? Are the losses related to infertility being confused with a long-term mood disorder?

Be wary of people with ongoing problems with depression, anger, or anxiety. Depressed parents will have attachment problems with any child, even a healthy newborn. They are simply not capable of doing the difficult emotional work that is required in the placement of a toddler or an older child. People with anger management problems make children feel as if they are still in a hostile environment. This signals them into fight, freeze, or flight mode instead of attachment. Anxious parents cannot help children calm down. They instead reinforce a wary, paranoid outlook on life. Encourage angry, depressed, and anxious applicants to get treatment for these issues first, and then proceed with the adoption process.

10. Are you comfortable letting others help you with this child? Do you mind working with professionals?

Parents need to embrace the team mentality. Children described in this book are best placed as special needs adoptions. Parents should expect that they will need to coordinate a helping team for such children. They will have to develop resources that help their children. Mistrustful, angry, highly anxious, or depressed individuals will not be able to meet these children's needs, as they will not understand their need for advocacy and the use of teamwork within a community.

11. Are you able to accept lots of acting out and controlling behaviors in children as a probable scenario for the beginning of placement? For children who have trauma histories, will you be willing to get therapy, a necessary part of children's medical care?

Many parents naïvely believe that the child they are adopting from foster care or from an orphanage overseas will be a withdrawn, sad child who will be gradually drawn out in their home. Of course this is frequently not the case. Parents need to be informed of the long-term consequences of sexual abuse, physical abuse, trauma, and exposure to domestic violence. In particular, physically and sexually abused children are among the most aggressive children seen in clinical samples. Professional adoption workers must include, as part of the homestudy process, a discussion of the essential trauma-specific therapy that will probably be a part of their child's future. Research clearly shows that children who receive trauma therapy, especially when it includes a cognitive-behavioral approach, do enormously better as compared to children whose parents omit this therapy.

12. Will you be able to provide more structure and nurture for children who need this approach, rather than using the parenting style that most closely fits your own personality?

Successful parents of children who have experienced neglect, prenatal exposure to substances, or maltreatment almost always run highly structured and nurturing homes. While the structure may be gradually relaxed as children develop more internal structure and emotional maturity, success does require that parents use consequences rather than emotional outbursts or lectures.

13. What resources available in your community will help you support a child who has been neglected, abused and/or otherwise traumatized?

This question includes the opportunity for some educational work so that families understand the differences between children adopted later in childhood or after maltreatment as compared to children who have a healthy start. It gives families time to think and talk about these differences in an individualized manner. It also gives them time to ask and answer a variety of questions and do their own homework. For example, does their insurance have mental health coverage for families? If not, could they change their policy to one that does? When is the open enrollment period? Have they located a mental health provider who takes their insurance and could see them with their child? Will the child need occupational therapy to remediate the effects of neglect? What are the monetary and time commitments of these therapies? What will they give up in order to make time and money available?

Parents need either to have a rich assortment of resources already in place, or to be well-connected to their communities so that they can acquire these extra resources. Cover the potential needs of a child similar to one they would like to adopt in a specific manner, detailing the necessary community resources. For example, help them locate respite care in a specific manner during the homestudy process.

Many people assume that their friends, relatives, neighbors, or religious community will help them. This often is not the case, and it is also one of the saddest disappointments for parents adopting children with special needs. Most people have busy lives and do not readily volunteer their time to these commitments—especially long term. Parents need to ask potential supportive people to commit to meeting the prospective child's needs, in specific terms, in advance. I have given several trainings where close friends have come in with the prospective adoptive parents. The parents had asked for support in advance, and, as a result, their friends had time not only to clear their schedules in preparation for the child, but to receive training.

About 30% of adoptive parents are single parents (AFCARS, 2006). Social workers should help single parents work on identifying their future support systems throughout the homestudy process.

14. What resources are available for children with learning issues through the school district?

In a study in the State of Washington, the average foster-adopted child was two full years behind grade level by the 8th grade. Will the school in the parents' district help their child immediately and effectively? Do the parents understand an IEP process?

This information is part of the educational effort of the homestudy. It should include providing or assisting in locating resource numbers and references for the educational services in the parents' school district. Even if the family is lucky enough not to need these services, they will be informed and can support other families who do need them.

15. How will you individualize and meet the needs of this child or children?

Parents need to have enough time and space for each child in the family. Educate parents about the differences and the special needs of children adopted after stressful beginnings. Sometimes one parent has deferred to the other in a decision to adopt such a child. They have a tacit understanding that they will still enjoy eighteen holes of golf weekly after the placement. These issues of entitlement should be recognized and addressed during the homestudy process. It is unrealistic to believe that one parent can plan and implement the entire childcare and community resource plan alone, without coming to resent the other parent.

Sometimes parents are taking on too much. These constitute one common reason behind poor placement outcomes; families accumulate too many stressors and adopt too many children. Ask parents who are already too busy or too financially stretched to make a list of the activities they will drop. Give each parent a sheet of paper, and ask the partner to list what the other should drop. This leads to a healthy discussion about compromising as they barter with the partner's lists. Ask them to begin the "dropping" process before the placement. Single parents do this exercise with a close friend or relative.

Families should be able to individualize the needs of all existing members, and reflect on how they are already meeting those needs, as well as how they will continue to meet everyone's needs after placement. This gives them a sense of the resources that they have. They should then talk about how they will meet a new member's needs, in specific terms.

*16. What type of child's needs do you think you would **not** be able to meet the needs? Can you tell me about this?*

Parents need to explore what they could not see themselves handling. This exercise gives the social workers enough information to help parents avoid these and related situations. Be certain to listen to parents and help them plan for placements that realistically fit their strengths. For example, parents may say that they are planning to have children share rooms and they could not handle sexual acting out behaviors. This should lead to a discussion about placement issues so that the family's wishes are met as closely as possible. It should also lead to a conversation about what to do if acting out did occur.

In conclusion, this section's approach and information is a necessary addition to homestudies in the 21st century, helping families prepare realistically for the parenting ahead for those who adopt traumatized/neglected children being placed today. It should be considered a best practice standard for today's adoptions. Organizations are welcome to scan and to reproduce the 16 questions above for use in their work.

Commitment

Words like *commitment, promise, my word, unconditional,* and *no matter what* are what an experienced social worker wants to hear in an interview, as opposed to emotional phrases like, *what I've always wanted, I need, we feel,* and so forth. Successful families are committed to the child, not just to their own emotional desires. The importance of commitment was made apparent when I asked experienced placement professionals what families adopting older children really need to be successful. Mary Ann Curran, Director of Social Services at WACAP in the Seattle area, responded with the following comments.

"I believe that most professionals working with families would come up with the same list of attributes and characteristics to describe the well qualified family who wishes to adopt an older child. Some of these might include *flexible, committed, strong support system, sense of humor, realistic expectations, resourceful.* No one could argue that these qualities are not vital. However, what is vital is what is meant by these words and what happens when these familial qualities and resources don't seem to impact the child's adjustment.

"Take *flexible.* One family's flexibility is nothing like another's. One family considers themselves flexible when they have to attend a special parent meeting due to their child's difficulties in school; another considers flexibility in education to be when their child has been expelled from two schools already and they must gird their loins to talk the child into a third.

"Or *strong support system*. Some families have systems built on the family being wonderful. Everyone admires them and wants to take care of their delightful children for the afternoon. Another has a support system that provides a friend to drive over at midnight to help them look through the neighborhood for the runaway.

"Or *resourceful*. One family has a list of therapists they got from the internet. The other has found two local families who have adopted similar kids and has met with them and befriended them, exchanging child care and providing mutual support.

"The real meaning of these qualities becomes apparent when the child does not respond to flexible, committed parents who have provided many resources. Their support system is burned out, or the family is too ashamed to ask for more help. They can't laugh anymore and their 'realistic' expectations have been proven to be woefully optimistic. It is at that point that we see things happen that reveal the real nature of the families.

"One is that a timeline becomes apparent. The family could perhaps put up with about anything if the child responded and made progress. Commitment is rationed; expectations are actually trimmed to meet the family's needs; resources are measured; flexibility only stretches so far. And they are done. The idea of commitment has to be stretched to mean a family who remains committed no matter how long it takes for the child to understand what a family is and to accept that he is loved and cherished and can trust. Maybe this will happen at 25, maybe at 30 years of age.

"Another factor that becomes apparent is the pride of families. What often happens is that the family congratulates themselves on their sterling qualities and thinks that the force of their love, their commitment, their nurturing will have such an impact on the child that he will become a trusting, affectionate child, just like their other children or the child of their dreams. When that does not happen, the family becomes angry, feels rejected, feels devalued. They need regular doses of success to feel good about themselves. Really successful families need a large dose of humility.

"Flexibility does not mean bending family rules and timelines to help the child learn family values and traditions and thus eventually fit into a new family. Often families pick up their lives a short time after placement, with a round of activities, family visits and vacations, both parents back at work, and expect the child to fit in his adjustment around the family's routines.

"Real flexibility means having enough humility and acceptance of a lack of control to change the very definition of your family to fit this new child. Flexibility means jettisoning the idea of being a family others admire for its well-behaved, high-achieving children to one that others may point to and say 'They adopted, you know, and it's been tough for them.' Or, 'They have done really well with all their children, but this latest one.' It means becoming not an object of admiration but of pity or of criticism. Redefining your family tradition of academic success to include GEDs earned at some later date. It means giving up the idea of seeing your child successfully compete in sports to redefine successful competition as showing up for practice every day and handing towels to the other players. Redefining emancipation is not the 18-year-old off to college but perhaps sharing an apartment at age 23 with some financial support from parents.

"We all know that successful families also need to be able to detach their own self-esteem from the successes of their children or their children's troubles. Often parents feel like good parents only when their children are succeeding in the eyes of the world, or if they can top everyone's horror story at their support group.

"In my experience, families either get it or they don't. And usually it's hard to tell until the child's difficulties become very great. At that point, families either start talking about themselves, how this is impacting them or their other children, how difficult it is, how much they have done already, how the child ruined their vacation, how much time has passed, and how the child is manipulative and sneaky OR they start talking about the child, how difficult his past has been, how difficult it is for him to trust and love, and how badly they feel abut the child's troubles. It seems to be just a matter of unconditional love. Just!" (Curran, 2006).

Commitment is the loyalty issue that forms the foundation in a family. The concept and importance of commitment needs to be discussed in every placement process.

Decision-making in adoption— discussing risks with parents

Parents who have a basic understanding of neglect, prenatal exposure, and abuse can have social workers explain some of the types of support children will need for each of the symptom clusters at different points of their lives. Neglect and trauma have been covered in some depth in the earlier chapters of the book. The grid brings the common issues down to the daily life level.

For international adoption, I appreciate the clarity of the research done by Dr. Dana Johnson's group at The International Adoption Project at the University of Minnesota Their research indicates that the following factors have significance when determining the level of needs in internationally adopted children:
- prenatal malnutrition,
- alcohol exposure,
- premature birth,
- social neglect,
- physical neglect,
- physical abuse,
- time spent in an orphanage.

The parents in Johnson's studies based their information about these factors on their own observations or records. Of course, the percentages are always determined on a group basis. Individual children are not solely the average of the group. Yet, it is important to look at the research in order to most closely match the resources and expectations of parents to the needs of children they are adopting (Johnson, 2003).

Table 9-1

Risk Factors for Children Adopted Internationally (displayed as percentage of children with certain risks who have been adopted from each region) Dana Johnson M.D. et al., University of Minnesota International Adoption Project			
Region → Risk Factor ↴	Eastern Europe	Caribbean/ South America	Asia
Prenatal Malnutrition	50	41	25
Prenatal Alcohol Exposure	44	15	9
Premature Birth	30	14	28
Social Neglect	57	22	13
Physical Neglect	45	25	12
Physical Abuse	13	5	13
Greater than Six Months Spent in Orphanage	79	17	13

Dana Johnson's group describes a condition called post-institutionalized spectrum disorder (PISD), which includes behavior problems, cognitive deficits and growth failure. The study looks at each of these issues in turn and how endorsing factors on Table 9-1, above increased the risk of some of these issues. In this book, I will be summarizing the issues of behavior problems, attachment, and cognitive delay.

Children score one point for each of the risk factors listed in Table 9-1, i.e. their parents know or strongly suspect that these events have occurred. Of the children who have 6.7 risk factors in the scoring, for example, 38% show internalizing problems (depression, fearfulness, and anxiety) and almost 50% show externalizing problems (aggression and conduct problems [Table 9-1]).

Table 9-2

Condition → Symtoms and Needs →	FASD	TRAUMA	NEGLECT	Family Capacity Required →
Affective Regulation problems (Emotions are unstable)	Yes	By age of four Yes, almost universal when trauma has happened before the placement	Yes	Needs to be skilled in handling their own affect and helping with children's affect
Control Issues	Yes, structure decreases control battles	Yes, predictable, safe homes decrease children's need for control	Variable	Needs structure, skills in defusing control battles, and access to respite care
Specialized Educational Needs	Yes, school will need to accommodate for success	Variable, but needs a safe, predictable environment	Variable	Needs to be able to advocate within school setting
Life Cycle Needs	Needs continued help in adult life	Prognosis for independence is good	Prognosis for independence is good	Resources and parent age a consideration in first category
Child Care Use for Working Parent(s)	Calm setting, consistent child care provider tends to work well. Extra supervision needed as teen	Variable, in calm setting consistent child care provider often works well	Variable, but with careful attention to number of hours, consistent child care provider often works well	Flexible working schedule and access to structured, and nurturing day care
Normal Range of Experiences Causes Overstimulation	Yes	Yes	Yes, with sensory integration problems common	Should be calming and structured

Children who were adopted before the age of six months, and who also had almost no other risk factors, scored the lowest. They actually scored lower than the general population in internalizing and externalizing problems. This is significant, since it demonstrates that we are looking at an issue of maltreatment, not an adoption issue. In fact the adoptive families are showing a better outcome than the general population.

"Children adopted from institutions are at dramatically increased risk for attachment disturbances. But, the majority of children do not demonstrate problems" (O'Conner et al., 2000). According to Table 9-1, of the children with a score of 6.7, 67% of those children demonstrate attachment difficulties. Children with the lowest scores demonstrate only a 3% rate of attachment difficulties.

Educational attainment is also an important factor in measuring the well-being of children. Children who scored at the high end of the scale, 6.7, used special education services at a rate of 57%. Special education use was similar for children with lower scores, with rates of 55% for those who scored 4.5, and 50% for a score of 2.3. These rates correlated to the length of time children spent in an orphanage setting. The rate was almost 30% in children with no other scores, other than spending 24 months in an orphanage.

Carefully presenting and then discussing these statistics helps parents, who are looking at outcomes and resources, make realistic projections about their prospective children's future needs. For example, some of my clients recently told me that they had tapped their son's college fund to pay for tutoring and swimming lessons. "Our son needs successes now, not later. We will be blessed if he can succeed at community college. Why keep money for a four-year college in savings?" they said.

The positive traits of healthy families

Considering family strengths is a positive way to end this section. The connections that parents make with their children, throughout the life cycle, give both children and their parents the satisfaction of lifelong relationships. Parents and their children are presented with the challenge of coming to know and accept each other authentically.

This means that they must put aside their idealistic, wished-for parenting or parents, and love the family members as they are. Healthy families have attributes that enhance this sense of security in relationships. The following list of positive attributes is adapted from the work of Daniel Siegal and Mary Hartzell.

1. Awareness. Be mindful of your own feelings and bodily responses and others' nonverbal signals.
2. Attunement. Allow your own state of mind to align with that of another.
3. Empathy. Open your mind to sense another's experience and point of view.
4. Expression. Communicate your internal response with respect; make the internal external.
5. Joining. Share openly in the give-and-take of communication both verbally and nonverbally.
6. Clarification. Help make sense of the experience of another.
7. Sovereignty. Respect the dignity and separateness of the individual's mind (2003, p.71).

Parents who want a long-term, positive relationship with any family member can use these essentials of human interrelatedness. Families strengthen their relationships to the extent in which they work on these factors.

Set up inexpensive supports during the homestudy or adoption training process

As demonstrated in the preceding sections, the majority of today's adoptive parents will need a variety of services after placement. However, it is also far more difficult for busy new parents to organize these services after placement. Help families arrange some of the necessary services pre-placement. Some of the activities can be done cooperatively in training sessions. Other activities can be incorporated into the homestudy process. Use the training process to implement the following easy supports, which are both low-cost and high-payoff.

Educational services

Parents should call their school districts while they are in the application and preparation stage. They should get an outline, with contact numbers, of the processes that govern identification, testing, and services for children who have learning disabilities or developmental delay. They should also get the necessary forms to begin the processes, if possible. Parents who are adopting children of preschool age or younger should research early intervention program requirements and locations. They should also determine whether intervention services will be done in the home. Parents adopting internationally should inquire about English as a Second Language programs. Classes for the parents-to-be in the language of the child-to-be's homeland are also helpful, and may be available through their district's adult and continuing education program.

Modern-day special education has changed, in that its scope is different. It is not typically a self-contained class for children. It offers remedial services and also the capacity to use accommodations to make children academically successful. Unfortunately, its services can be difficult to access. Many parents are delighted to find that their children qualify for coordinated physical therapy, occupational therapy, speech and language, academic areas, and social development services available through their school district. Other parents find that they have missed out on these services, either because they did not know how to access their special education department, or because they used a "wait and see" approach.

Parents, as a group, are the most instrumental in getting educational opportunities for children with learning disabilities, learning differences, and delays. Parents may have an excellent district that is quite willing to help bring out the best in their children. However, it is equally likely that they will have to know the law and develop strong advocacy skills in order to acquire and protect their children's access to an appropriate education.

When a child is moving, it can be easier to get an appropriate IEP from a school district that knows a child than starting over with new staff. Ask for additional testing and an updated educational plan to carry into the parent's district if children are being adopted from domestic foster care in another district.

Respite care

Parents of children with complex backgrounds will need breaks. Parents will need downtime, and respite is helpful even if it is initially done in the children's own home with the parent present. Parents should identify ways to receive this help before placement. Family members who offer this service in the form of a steady commitment can be ideal. People who are listed as parent references in the home-study may also be excellent prospects for respite. Social workers or parents can easily ask references if they would be willing or able to provide respite.

One family had grandparents watch their children every Friday night for three years. The alternate grandparents took one weekend a month. While the siblings were extremely challenging, the parents not only coped, but actually reported that life remained enjoyable, and even romantic.

Respite is mentioned here as a "break." It is not meant to substitute as the balance for perpetually overextended families. One such family adopted more children than whose needs they could meet. The adults were always calling for therapeutic respite. In effect, they were habitually reducing their family numbers down to the level that they could actually manage. This is not an appropriate use of respite long-term, and the situation reflects placement errors on the part of social work professionals. Some of these errors can be foreseen, some not. Asking a family to experiment by inviting some high needs children over during a busy time of day can help parents determine whether adopting one child or a sibling group is manageable, or whether respite is how they might be tempted to handle day-to-day.

Insurance

Ask parents to check their insurance policies for mental health coverage and other important medical providers. Parents should make sure that their managed care plan includes specialty providers so that, if necessary, they can change plans during open enrollment periods. Or, they can ask if an out-of-network referral is plausible for their plan.

Some children being adopted from foster care do not have mental health access beyond limited sessions. Parents who do have coverage on their plans may be able to be seen with their children under a family therapy code.

Health professionals

Parents regularly assume that their family doctor will provide their child's care. After placement, however, they may find that their family doctor is not specialized enough to meet their needs. Families should be encouraged to research this type of information prior to placement. Families often want the pediatric care for their children done at an adoption medical clinic. These clinics have longer visits and more up-to-date information on specialty topics. Most adoption medical personnel are available pre-placement and can assess the medical records of children referred for placement. While the number of these clinics and practices is growing, they are not yet available in all cities, let alone in rural areas. Many families use them on a consultancy basis, linking them to their local pediatrician or family physician so that they can explore more complex adoption or international medical possibilities.

Recently, I mentioned my concern for a child to his parents. After four years in the country, their child still looked thin and ill. The child had received regular care from a family physician who is kind and capable. After doing more extensive tests, they discovered that he had an undetected intestinal parasite. His parents are kicking themselves for using their family doctor rather than the adoption medical specialist they had used with their daughter. Parents should be informed of these specialty service providers in their training classes.

Parents should also find an adoption- and attachment-literate mental health provider prior to placement. Many specialty providers have long waiting lists. Parents who are forward thinking can do their waiting while they are also waiting for placement.

Support groups, mentors, and adoptive parent associations

Parents should receive assistance locating support groups, including a group for waiting parents, prior to placement. They need to find and arrange to join local groups in advance. That way, they can attend a parent meeting before they need to, to see if the group fits their personalities. Some support groups have childcare available. Parents who join support groups who do not offer this should locate childcare prior to placement. After placement, caseworkers can determine whether they can match the family to a mentor family.

I often find that agency caseworkers are unaware of the excellent resources available to parents—even resources located in their area. Agencies can easily find and distribute sample copies of information and registration forms from local and online groups so that parents can sign up for helpful magazines, newsletters, or on-line support groups. An attendee of an all-day training I gave recently mentioned that her favorite thing about the day was when I gave her a copy of the magazine *Fostering Families Today*. People want to feel connected to others and to excellent information. (Please see the Resource List at the back of this book for some of the options.)

The tickle file

Adoption professionals should organize what needs to be done month-by-month and year-by-year on either the computer or in a card file. Precise information about upcoming tasks is often given to parents during placement. However, this information is hard to remember after placement. Additionally, parents should have their own tickle file. This can be computerized or as simple as a recipe box organized by months and years. The types of tasks that should be recorded are diverse and may include items like writing the birthparents, sibling visits, following up with medical conditions, filing post-placement reports, and assessing development through the school district.

A client of mine was responding to a question that I had in therapy about genetics. She went through the stack of papers that she had received at placement, and in doing so, discovered that she had been given specific instructions about an inheritable condition that affected her daughter. In the tumult of placement this typically well-organized woman had completely forgotten the information. "I wouldn't have believed that they even gave me the medical information or the additional testing instructions, except that I found notes in the margins in my own handwriting," she said. "I was supposed to have this testing done two years ago."

File information

Social workers might suggest that parents bring accordion files to their preparation meetings and classes. They can label the file compartments, and insert any important papers as they receive them. Then they can find or re-file the paperwork later, when they need it. The headings will help them remember the types of information that they have. I often ask parents to revisit old papers to find background information. They regularly find that they have much more information than they remember receiving. Parents easily forget what they have when it is mixed up in a stack. It is important to find those facts when children have specific questions. A simple filing system beats no filing system!

Get ready for placement—Hands-on!

Parents should be encouraged to borrow a couple of children the age of the children they expect to begin raising. They can begin with an afternoon visit, and then work their way up to most of a weekend. Or, they may ask to spend time practicing parenting routines under the partial supervision of a mentor family. New parents often have unrealistic notions of how much they will be able to accomplish when children are awake. Spending time with actual children will help prepare them for reality.

At a recent conference, a parent waiting for placement voiced his belief that an "I mean business" voice would halt a child's misbehavior. The audience grinned and sympathetically whispered about his coming wake-up call. While I applauded him for preparing himself by coming to a workshop, some actual experience with children and a mentor family would strip away his naïve notions.

Recruit target groups during the preparation process

Many people are interested in adoption and foster care in a vague manner, but have never actually followed up on their interest. Use the ripple effect to help reach these people and convince them to follow up. This works especially well in the context of influencing members of a minority group. For example, it would be extremely common for a potential parent to discuss her plans to adopt with friends at church. Ask applicants if they have any friends who would also like to go through the process with them during the preparation phase. Spend some time making phone calls or drop a card in the mail to access these friends. Demographically, people who are interested in foster care and adoption have similarities as a group. Recruitment can also be done through one member of a group reaching out to others in the same group.

Since almost 40% of children waiting to be adopted domestically are African-American, and only 13.5% of adoptive families overall are African-American, it makes sense to ask people to talk to their friends about adoption (NACAC, 2006). These friends are likely to be culturally competent or themselves members of a minority group.

In concluding this section, it should be emphasize that parents have to be able to manage the activities of daily living with the child in the home. In other words, parents need to be able to bring in income, shower, shop, clean, and have fun. Social workers must factor in the extremely taxing work that will occur when parents are monitoring the moods of children who have experienced neglect, trauma or abuse and helping them to regulate their moods and behaviors later in life.

Prepare Siblings for the New Family Member

Parents have the task of talking to the children who are already in the family about the new arrival. Of course, there will need to be a realistic balance of enjoying the new person as well as being realistic that the new brother or sister will have some unique needs. Frequently parents want to be the ones talking to their children about adding to the family, but they may ask questions about what works best in preparation.

I like to have parents think about the developmental age of the child(ren) already in the home. What are the normal needs in the stage their children are in right now? What will they need next? What can be done to be certain that these children continue to get their needs met? A lengthier description of placement of a child with traumatic stress issues is described by a sibling—who tells the story through his point of view—in the book *Attaching in Adoption* (pp.288-92, Gray, 2012). At the risk of redundancy for those who have read the first book, I am including that vignette again here.

> Jim had grown four inches in the last year. At age 11, he was not at the most upbeat stage in his life. He had figured out that his parents were not all that bright. His mother said that he was going through a normal stage of "de-idolizing his parents." That typified her weirdness. Nobody in his school talked like that. The biggest evidence of their failing was in the arrival of his 5-year-old "new sister." They had blown it big time. During the family meeting before Lili came, Mom and Dad had described her "special needs." Even his brother got it.
>
> "Mom, Dad, you've brought home a bad girl!" Joey had exclaimed. His parents had explained things so that Joey started looking happy!
>
> As his parents kept talking, Jim sat in a state of shock. When he tuned back in they were describing possible sexual acting out and hitting. Jim just knew that *he* would never baby-sit. He was amazed when Megan, his sister, said to their parents, "Sure. I can watch her after school on Tuesdays and

Wednesdays while you run the boys to baseball and trumpet. I don't have as much homework on those nights."

Nothing in Jim wanted to help in any way. He felt ashamed of himself and mad at his parents that they had made him feel so selfish. It was just that nobody in his class would ever understand if they heard about Lili. Jim felt crushed by the impending burden of this sister. He blurted, "You just don't realize how much it took out of me to help Joey turn out OK. This time it's just impossible!"

Mom and Dad stared at him when he said this. Megan was so annoying. She laughed and then went to her room. He heard the door close. He had no allies to change his parents' minds.

Lili move in gradually over the next few weeks.

Jim found himself rounded up for a session of family therapy. He didn't see why he had to go since Joey was the one complaining. Lili had been "accidentally" hurting Joey. Jim was curious about that, because Lili actually seemed to like Joey best.

The therapist taught Joey how to put his hand out against Lili's forehead and command, "Back off, Lili!" Lili also had to ask before she touched any of the kids. On the way home in the car, Lili asked Joey if she could hit him. "No!" said Joey, with his rehearsed commanding voice. Jim relaxed. The session with that therapist was funny.

Getting out of the car, Lili climbed over Joey, digging a knee into his stomach. Joey told Mom. Lili had to go to bed fifteen minutes early. Dad spent those fifteen minutes throwing balls to Joey. It seemed fair to Jim.

Later that night, Mom and Dad came into Jim's room. Mom said, "Whether Lili turns out OK is an adult problem. It's not your job. When we adopted Joey, he was a baby. It was easier." Mom said that Jim had to concentrate on baseball, school, and his life. They would be the ones to help Lili. The therapist had asked him in the session what he did not want to have changed in his life. He hadn't known then. He had needed to think about it. Jim had his list now.

"I don't want to be late for baseball practices anymore," he said. "Lili gets into my room, too, and breaks little things. I know it's her! Also, Dad and I haven't gone to the batting cage, and I'm, like, eighth in the batting order now! It's really embarrassing. Last year I was number three! I'm afraid to have my friends over, too. She is always following me." Jim started to cry with big, gulping sounds. He leaned into Mom and Dad and choked out, "I'm afraid that you'll think I'm mean and selfish, and that you won't love me!"

Mom said, "Jim, everybody in the family has needs, not just Lili. We care about you as much as we ever did. We didn't know what it would be like to parent Lili. No one really knew her. Now we are making adjustments in our family so that things can go better for everybody." Dad squeezed Jim, and Mom stroked his hair. Jim cried for a while and his parents stayed right there. He felt a burden move off him—like he could depend on his parents again.

The next day Lili sneaked into his room again. When he told Mom, Lili had to do his job. He and Megan watched out the window from behind the curtains while Lili swept the front porch and walk. She howled and threw the broom. Mom just kept reading the paper and sitting on the porch swing. She said, "You can come in the house for dinner when your job's done." Finally, Lili picked up the broom and started.

When the pizza arrived with Dad, Lili swept into high gear. Mom said, "Great, Lili. Wow. Good choice to get your dinner with the family!"

Before Jim started his homework, Lili came to see him with Dad. "Sorry," she said.

"Sorry for what?" Dad said. "I will believe you're sorry when you look into Jim's eyes and tell him what you are sorry for."

Taking a big breath and looking at her shoes, she started, "Sorry..." She stopped, looked into Jim's face and tried again. "Sorry, Jim, for coming into your room and taking your markers." A look of real regret came over her face.

"I forgive you," Jim said. He did.

Mom told Megan that she was not going to baby-sit on Friday nights anymore. Jim realized that Megan had also made a list of what she needed. It took a month, but when his friends began to come over again, Mom taught Lili to let them alone. She put a "hand holder," which Jim thought looked like a leash, on Lili's wrist to keep her close. Lili got the idea that she could not take over the guests. This was such a relief to Jim.

He had never been able to bring it up to Mom and Dad, but he asked Megan, "What do I do if she pulls down her pants or something when my friends are over."

Megan did not laugh. "That's a parent problem. When my friends are over, Mom or Dad will keep Lili close. Mom told me that I shouldn't have to think about any weird stuff that Lili learned somewhere else. It's not her fault that she learned it, but Mom and Dad handle any gross stuff. We don't have to think about it. She's getting better, anyhow. She hasn't tried to do anything like that since right after she came."

When Jim was 12, he wrote his autobiography for school. He wrote that he had two sisters and a brother. He picked out a picture of his family that looked pretty good. Lili was cute now. He wasn't sure when she got cute. She was glued to his parents these days. Jim played on the trampoline with her sometimes. She'd laugh and laugh when he jumped beside her. When he needed to be picked up at school, Mom and Lili didn't embarrass him now. But he didn't risk talking much. They could really embarrass him in front of his friends!

He noticed that Mom and Dad did not let Megan make excuses for Lili. Megan sometimes tried to save Lili if she got in trouble. "Megan, her life is just plain going to be harder for several years," Dad finally said. "Megan, stop stepping in. She needs to learn the rules like everybody else. When she goes to school next year, there won't be anybody there to save her. Besides, weren't you and Mom supposed to go shopping tonight? Get your homework done so that you are ready."

That got Megan's attention. "Can we pick up Rachel, too?"

Joey still liked to sit and read stories with Lili and Dad.

Joey acted like a baby sometimes when Lili started sitting on Mom's lap. Jim thought that was why Mom started to take Joey out for breakfast. Sometimes she played chase with Joey and Lili, yelling, "Where is my giant old baby?" For some reason Joey really got a kick out of that. Mom would act all shocked when she "found" Joey and claimed that he had grown since that morning.

Joey still sat on Mom's and Dad's laps. He looked huge, but he wasn't ready to give it up. Sometimes Joey acted like a little kid, even though he was not the youngest. Mom and Dad reminded Jim that he had sat in laps until he was ten. Jim realized that Mom and Dad had let him do the same until he moved on by himself. Jim knew that he had turned out well, so he decided that Joey would turn out well.

It was almost two years before Lili stopped crying over missing her birthparents and a foster mother. She got really sad, and she cried two or three times a week. Jim felt awful when Lili cried. He had grown up knowing that Megan and Joey missed their birthparents at certain stages. He got the same feeling that he had had for Megan and Joey. He wished that he could make their sadness go away. He remembered how mad Joey was when he was 7. He had been really mad that Mom and Dad couldn't fix his feelings and he had ranted, "Why wasn't I given a choice?"

"You couldn't talk," Dad said.

Megan was starting to go places with guys now. Once Jim asked Mom if she was afraid that Megan would have a baby too young, like her birthmother. "No," Mom said, "Megan's a good decision-maker. She's been making good decisions and not many mistakes for along time." That was true. Except for being oversensitive and too bossy, Megan was almost perfect!

Lili started school the next year. She was 7 now. Mom had home-schooled her for kindergarten. Jim walked her down to the playground every day for a week before she started school. Jim told her how to act so that other kids would like her. Lili listened hard, slid a hand in his, and whispered, "What about bad guys at school?"

"Lil, don't worry," he said. "Stay by the swings and away from the big kids. They play flyers-up over there." He pointed far from the elementary buildings. "Megan, Joey and I all went to this school and nothing bad ever happened to us." That reassured Lili. She was not very big for her age. She looked and acted more like 6 than 7.

Jim had brought up Lili's size and maturity to Dad as a concern. Dad thought like Jim did, "Lili missed a lot. That's why we are putting her into first grade, not second."

"Just checking," Jim said, and took off. Lili seemed like she was going to do OK. Jim had to make a couple of phone calls to see who else had lunch period with him in eighth grade.

When talking to children, allow them a variation in their feelings.

One woman would ask her sons, ages 10 and 13, "How are you feeling about brothers and sisters today?" They would give a 40% for and 60% against. Other days, it would be 60% for and 40% against. Over the course of a few months they discussed "their number" in the car daily.

It takes time for children to process their questions or to think about how their lives will change. In this case, the family was not suggesting that when the percentages were 100% that they would proceed. In fact, the parents had made the decision and the agency was preparing to place with the family. But they did encourage honest talking and thinking together about the big changes in the family. The boys were ready and affectionate when two scared siblings, ages 2 and 5, arrived through an emergency placement after disruption. They knew that their sister and brother would be worried, in grief, possibly mad, and needy. They had prepared. The boys were among the most tender siblings I have known in their support of the new family members.

Another family used a card file, writing down the responsibilities and increased privileges that their children got year by year. They went through the card file, discussing how these might change with a sibling group, adding new responsibilities and privileges. They added some things that they did not want to have change after the placement. Some of those things included having a birthday sleepover, climbing into parent's bed in the morning on Saturdays, being back on swim team within six months (which would necessitate a car pool instead of the parent taxi service), special one-on-one time every day for fifteen minutes, and a right to declare his bedroom off-limits.

Things that are positive to anticipate are fun to describe as well. Those can be having someone to play with, to teach things to, someone to talk to, and so forth. It is fun to decide how to tell friends that a new brother or sister is coming. And, the reality is that most siblings are intensely loyal to each other.

Discussing the difference between the adjustment period and the long-term is important. In the case of the brothers who were so tender with their new brother and sister, they knew not to personally interpret the children's negative emotional states.

"They got two big disappointments," the older son told me. "First they moved from their birthmothers' and then from their first adoption. We'll help them here. They'll want to stay around Mom and Dad at first. But we'll get them outside and playing pretty soon. Our parents are letting them get used to things first. We saved our baseball mitts for them so that they can use them. Soon we'll use those mitts."

Another family prepared their daughters, ages 6 and 8, for the expected low mood and immaturity of their brother.

They described that he was 4 years old, but had stayed in the orphanage much longer than either of them. Their mother said, "All those things that we taught you about treating each other nicely, sitting at the table, making friends, asking politely, and taking turns...no one has taught him. He is like a little, little boy; more like a 2-year old. In the beginning, tell Poppa or Mama if he grabs, hurts you, or scares you. Then we can teach him the right way." That was exactly what occurred. The little one was coached through the intervention, being shown the positive response when he yelled, grabbed or tried to bite. He was taken out of the situation if he could not respond to the coaching. He was neither scapegoated nor permitted to hurt.

One little girl was initially quite ruthless to her family. She daily hurt others, going after her brothers' eyes or genitals. After about a year in therapy, the brothers lobbied to come in to talk with me. I had seen them for a few family sessions throughout the year, but this insistence intrigued me. "We want you to know that she is doing better now," they said. "No offense, but we don't want to sit in that waiting room any more for her time with you. She's good enough. We just push her back or say 'stop' and she knocks it off. We can handle her now, even if mom's in the bathroom. But our cousin needs help. Could you see him?"

In the examples above, the children were prepared. They had time to process what they needed and to adjust to the changes in the family. All of the children benefited from a simple understanding that their brother or sister was hurting, angry, and immature emotionally. Equally important, they understood that they could get help with problem behavior and that their own development and welfare were important. Lastly, all the children were in the process of incorporating a sibling into their lives in a positive manner. They enjoyed playing with the new sibling. They had a vital relationship, even if they had to delay in getting to the point of enjoying the new sibling.

Families are setting the foundation for siblings so that everyone is respected in the family, and that everyone gets needs met. Boundaries and privacy issues need careful attention. Usually older siblings need to be reassured that they do not need to constantly play with the new brother and sister, or, that they are allowed to shut their doors, play with same-aged friends, or say that they have to get homework done. It is done in the context of teaching the new sibling about how the household works. Parents should be careful not to set things up for maladaptive roles as the *entitled sibling* and the *underdog*. Instead, an atmosphere of respect should be taught.

Some siblings need extra support, especially if the brother or sister continues to have special needs. I have encouraged some time for them in therapy sessions. They will often ask for some time for themselves as needed. *Sibshops* have been a good resource for them, as well. Those are group activities shared and for the benefit of brother and sisters of children with special needs. (Please see Resource List.)

Matching Children and Families— A 20-Question Worksheet

Assessing children usually begins with a history, as provided by a caretaker who knows the child well. Completing an accurate and sensitive appraisal of the child is a challenge when children have been in a series of foster care homes or are coming from an international setting.

Working from a broader perspective, histories can be used to do a current assessment in terms of ten major areas. It is helpful to assess each area on a continuum, ranging from having a strength or good experience, to having a weakness or poor experience. The ten areas are

- physical nurturance
- attachment opportunities
- trauma(s) versus safety
- temperamental endowment
- physical health
- intellectual capacity
- grief and loss versus continuity of relationships
- resources for emotional support
- support for cultural and racial identity formation
- emotional regulation capacity of child and family.

These factors, as related to child development, informed the following list of assessment questions.

1. Were there any attachments? When? To whom? What preceded the break in attachment? What developmental stage was the child at during each break in attachment?

2. How was the child fed? Was the food adequate? Did the feeding involve emotional closeness? Was this child warm enough? Were the physical needs met adequately?

3. Was this child traumatized or abused? Was the child a victim, victimizer, or both? Was the orphanage or home the child came from organized by a dominance hierarchy of big kids over little kids? What was the nature of adult supervision? How did this child attempt to keep safe?

4. What is the baseline for this child developmentally? In a nurturing and stimulating environment, is this child gaining against a normal developmental curve, staying on the curve, or maintaining a slower curve?

5. What does the medical exam indicate about the child? Is there evidence of prenatal exposure to alcohol or drugs or other toxins?

6. What attachment producing cueing is the child open to? Is she open to feeding activities, auditory stimulus, visual cues like eye-to-eye gazing and responsive smiling, tactile stimulation like touch, affective modeling, excited states, play, and movement? Which of these qualities can be more closely associated with the parent, intensified, or paired with an underdeveloped quality?

7. Which of the qualities listed above are in the parent's areas of strength? Are there any qualities that the parent plans to withhold?

8. What is needed, long-term, to gratify the parents as well as the child?

9. How does the parent's attachment history play into her resolve to keep trying with this child?

10. What factors are weakening attachments? Could they be avoided?

11. What is this child doing that might diminish family self-esteem? What can be introduced to help raise family self-esteem?

12. How can the parents find and use support when raising this child?

13. What do the parents hope for the most in their adoption experience? Will this be realized? Can the parents be strengthened to grieve the loss of the wished-for child if this child's

problems represent a permanent loss? Can strategies that the family has used before be adapted to deal with this situation?

14. What temperament does the child seem to have, regardless of circumstances?

15. Were parting instructions given to this child? Was the child told not to tell something or "wait for me?" Could these instructions be interpreted in a way that gives this child the freedom to love new parents?

16. What felt like "winning" for this child in the past? How was this child shamed in the past? How can this information be used to the family's advantage?

17. Was this child emotionally closest to other children? Can an older sibling give this child permission to accept the parents?

18. How is the family perceived in their community culturally and ethnically? How is the child's sense of self as an ethnic/cultural minority member being strengthened?

19. How do the parents regulate their own emotions? How have the child's mood states been altered by neglect or abuse? Who has worked with the child's stress system before, i.e. teaching comfort, calming, and soothing?

20. What areas of mastery will the parents bring into parenting? What are areas of mastery in children? These areas are predictive of long-term successes, with the chance of success increasing as they come into practice more. Take advantage of them. For example, a parent who has been a skillful older sibling or a coach will have strengths in joining with and motivating youth. Children may have a singing strength that makes them feel joyous and competent.

This form can be brought into placement meetings. Families and caseworkers can fill it out together. It helps families concentrate on the areas that will be the most meaningful long-term. And as in the homestudy section, permission is granted to scan and to reproduce these questions.

Move Children with Emotional Preparation and Respect

Why do children need to be moved so carefully? Hasty and insensitive moves have terrible repercussions, including:

- Children lose the people to whom they are attached. They decide not to risk other attachments.
- Children learn that people are replaceable.
- Children are afraid all of the time. They believe that their worlds can be changed at any moment.
- Children learn that their feelings don't matter. No one really cares how they feel about leaving the home and people they love. They are not worth much.
- Children decide that adults do not have children's best interests in mind. They will control adults as much as possible.
- Children decide that they need to either be in charge all of the time or just give up.
- Children lose a sense of who they are. Their identity formation is interrupted. They are easily manipulated by others. They struggle to choose life patterns that fit well, careers, and life partners because they do not have enough sense of self to make these choices.

A respectful move shows children that

- There is some predictability in their worlds. The move takes place for a reason that, with help, they can understand and process.
- The people they value also value them. Their new parents care about the pain of moving and will comfort them when they grieve.
- Adoptive parents are willing to get to know them. They are not asking the child to simply change to meet their expectations.
- They will not be moved abruptly and without warning. They can relax instead of guarding themselves.
- Adults who know them well will be there and help them grieve. They can receive comfort and help during these and other hard times.

- Their feelings matter. *They* matter.
- They are important enough that people will arrange their life events around them.
- They do not have to control everything or use learned helplessness as defenses.

Children who are allowed time to spend processing the move, and the meaning of the move to their identities, do not have a shocked reaction.

One agency was particular about avoiding a move in December. The caseworker argued that she did not want the brothers to associate the move with the holidays. While her concern showed that she was well-meaning, she designed a move after Christmas that was too fast and therefore extremely shocking to the boys.

She told the boys that they were moving in the morning, and arranged the first visit with the prospective adoptive parents in the therapist's office that evening. The prospective adoptive father complained, "What a way to guarantee that they won't like us! Couldn't we just slow this down?"

But the decision about transfer had already been given to the foster parents. They did not like one boy very well, and liked the other quite well. In their confusion over their feelings of how to say goodbye to both, they came up with this schedule. The foster parents also felt that they could enjoy an out-of-town trip. They wanted to do the transfer because it gave them a nice car trip with some expenses paid for, with time to talk to their children about the changes in their family. The foster parents felt that it would help their own children to see these two children in a new family. They were good people, but made the decision based on their understanding of their own family circumstances.

The caseworkers saw the decision as a stress-free and quick transfer of two difficult children. On the side they mentioned that they did not want to give the foster-adopt parents enough time to change their minds. They agreed that they had other children to place. Let the adoption unit in another area supervise this placement.

The move schedule was accomplished within three visits, including the transfer, none within the foster home. This schedule was rigid and insensitive not only to the attachment needs of the children moving, but also for the children in the foster and adoptive homes. The next six months were hellacious for the adoptive family. The move was traumatic, and caused traumatic stress triggers. The trauma had nothing to do with the holiday itself, but rather the schedule. The case worker simply substituted New Year's as the new trigger.

Children who are moved gradually do not have traumatic stress triggers of the move like the holiday symbols. Instead, they gradually work through the grief process.

A recent study by Harvard University and the Casey Family Programs reported that over half of the children in foster care leave with an anxiety disorder. They have twice the rate of traumatic stress as compared to Vietnam veterans (2006). Obviously, treating children with more sensitivity, predictability, and respect during moves can be phenomenally beneficial. In therapy, children reference sudden moves as among their most difficult problems when working through grief and shock. Children describe sudden moves as equally or even more traumatizing than being sexually abused. Moves that are done abruptly, and especially those that include trauma, lead to pathological or complicated grief.

Pathological grief

Complicated grief, or trauma-contaminated grief, is a byproduct of sudden moves. Some of these traumatic, quick moves are unavoidable, as in the case of removing a child from a dangerous situation. However, there are many, many more moves than those justified by true crises in foster care.

Pathological grief versus normal grief

One of the hallmarks of a grief reaction that has gone awry is a refusal to accept the reality of the loss, or to process information about the loss. The child avoids the loss, or acts completely overwhelmed when faced with an unavoidable reminder. Children often display rigid denial. They will typically insist that they are going back to former homes, or that they do not care about people lost in moves. The following guide, informed by the work of Mardi Horowitz, details the typical stages of the grief process as compared to atypical stages that are predictive of complicated or pathological grief (Horowitz, 1993).

Normally, the first stage of the grief process is outcry or a vigorous "no!" An abnormal beginning response is panic or dissociation. Children who either dissociate or become panic stricken with the loss of the parent are marked as high-risk.

Children who are mute during the separation often report internal screaming. They may later fantasize about having said, "No!" and somehow preventing the separation. Sometimes they seem to be saying "No!" incessantly as if to make up for the missing "No!" Children will often say that they were scared silent.

Denial is the typical second stage of grief. In pathological grief, the child/teen will instead report feeling dead or numb. Teenagers may use drugs or promiscuity to escape the feeling of "being dead." Younger children may look frenzied and run around in a state of frenetic over-activity. They seem like they have attention deficit disorder with hyperactivity. Then they may swing into looking completely detached and shut-down.

This numb state's uniquely uncomfortable feeling should not be underemphasized. It is one of the leading symptoms for which people request help and relief for posttraumatic stress disorder pharmacologically (Friedman, 1997).

Intrusive and emotion-evoking feelings are common in the third stage of grief. In normal grieving the individual does not flood with negative images, however, in pathological grief they do (Horowitz, 1993).

Children report that the last view of the parent prior to removal is the image that floods into their minds. The last traumatic moment is the evoked image, which is not comforting (Pynoos, 1997). The last image is often one in which the parent or caregiver is angry, crying, getting arrested by police, etc. Children cannot seem to think of the parent, or hold onto the parent emotionally, without encountering the emotionally overwhelming last image.

In typical grieving, the individual gradually works through the information about the loss and its significance to their identity. In pathological grief, children integrate the loss into their sense of self. They are enraged, guilty, and feel responsible. They feel shame for being helpless during the separation, shame for being left and asked to go on alone, and the shame of rejection. "I was not worth enough for her to make the choices that would have prevented the separation," they think. These choices may have been successful treatment for drug and alcohol abuse, leaving an abusive relationship, and so forth.

Typical grief stages include the completion of mourning. Reminiscing about the loss is not overwhelming, but rather an enjoyable way of holding onto the memory of the lost parent. In pathological grief, there is no completion and children continually mourn. They remain highly reactive to reminders of their loss. Their negative emotions remain intense rather than decreasing over time. They cannot enjoy reminiscing, since they become so overwhelmed by the feelings evoked by the lost parent. Adults and children say things like, "It was years ago, but it feels just as awful, like it happened today."

This is an ominous and accurate list, and stages of pathological grief explain why children do poorly after undergoing placements done by workers who are poorly trained or looking for convenience. Children stop processing the feelings and information about the move. They cannot take advantage of the emotional support of adults, since the adults are all strangers. Children move into a shock stage which leaves them with diminished abilities to attach to new people or to grieve the loss of loved ones.

There are alternatives to accumulating successive damages from moving. The simplest and most effective technique involves asking adults, who are competent enough to support children's grieving and processing, to devote time and compassion to the child. Adults who know and relate to children in a caring manner act as adjuncts to children's stress regulation systems. Children who have close contact with an adult can "borrow from" or regulate to that caring adult in order to organize facts and feelings about the moves—and about themselves. The relationships between caring adults and children requires time and planning. But, drastically improved outcomes can be as simple as spending three more weeks with a foster parent, or an extra month while children remain with their familiar therapist. Caseworkers need to coordinate with the important adults in a child's life.

Move children in a healthy fashion—time frames and essential risks

This section is written as a model of the best practices social workers and parents can aspire to, moving children with as little damage as possible. Those who have read or heard Vera Fahlberg, M.D. speak will recognize her insights in this section.

Everyone working with foster and adoptive families has horror stories about the shocking moves that children have endured. These moves were accomplished by well-meaning people who used their best judgment. Unfortunately, sometimes they used judgment that was devoid of accurate information on child development and loss.

Carefully defining the essential needs for children, *tailored to each development level*, is a crucial part of successful moves. Focusing on accomplishing the essentials when moving children means paying careful attention to the following tasks:

- Maintaining children's identities and areas of mastery.
- Transferring attachments from one caregiver to another as much as possible.
- Maintaining attachments to family members, and especially siblings.
- Moving children with as little shock and trauma as possible.
- Helping them calm down and achieve predictability in their new homes as quickly as possible.

In order to accomplish the objectives above, all moves should abide by these standards:

1. Allow children enough time to actually process the information about the move.

    A key concept in moving children lies in understanding that the move usually means that the child will lose their attachment figures, or psychological parents. Children require time to process the reality of the loss and then assimilate the facts and concepts around the loss into their life story. This processing explains why children always need time to process the loss, regardless of how carefully the "why" behind the move is explained.

2. With the exception of an extreme emergency, do not move children 2 years of age and over with less than a two-week transitioning period. Allow for three or four weeks of transitioning time for children who are in the elementary years and up. (Infant time frames are listed separately in the following schedules.)

Often children are moved so quickly that they go into a shocked phase. If they are not given time to process the move, they will be in such a shock state that they will not understand or process facts or concepts about the move. And, it is not possible for children who are in shock and denial to form a smooth attachment to a new psychological parent, or attachment figure. They do not even have the facts straight, so they cannot understand what is happening and what it means to them.

Children who are moved correctly actually feel their grief when they move—but they do not feel overwhelmingly anxious, shocked, or frightened. They can use the emotional connections made with their adoptive parents during the transitioning process to reduce their stress, fear, and grief if they are moved with even a minimal two-week transition period.

Discuss the move with children

Explaining moves to children in an accurate and sensitive manner is a critical task for caseworkers. Sometimes the task can be taken on or shared by a therapist who has a relationship with the child.

For children ages 3 through 11, I like to create booklets about the move tailored specifically to the child's needs. Caseworkers can take photographs for the booklet or draw pictures with the child. Children are encouraged to draw and write in the booklet with their therapist or caseworker. I let children help dictate words, and then I read the booklet back to them. The words are written down so that the children can keep track of the ideas that we are discussing. They have a sense of the dignity about the process of moving when we record what we are discussing.

A typical booklet for a move into a foster-adopt or adoptive home is formatted like this:

Page 1: The child's picture is on page one, with a caption like: Emma says, "goodbye" and "hello" to families.

Page 2: The second page has a picture of the home she has been in and the people there. This might be the foster home or the kinship home. The caseworker says that she has done a great job loving those people, but that it is an in-between home. They love her and it would be great if they could adopt her. Often a child will ask, "Why don't they?" Simply put the answer into realistic terms, explaining the age of parents, families who see themselves as short-term, and so forth. Explain that this is not a permanent family.

Let the child express and feel the pain of moving away from her family. Console her, and do not move away from the child's grief too quickly. Write the child's feelings down.

Page 3: On page three, write in things that the child has loved about the family and will miss.

Page 4: Put a picture of the adoptive family on page four. Express that, while we understand that she may not want to move, this family is not a short-term family. This family is the one who wants to adopt her. Help her express some of the things in a family that are important to her. List things with her that she would like to tell the family or let them know about her. Those might be: I like to collect bugs. I am a great soccer player. I know all of my math facts and got a prize. I don't like to wear belts. I like to get a nice snuggle in the mornings before breakfast.

Page 5: Write down her concerns about the new family on page five. Be certain to cover concrete essentials like: When do they eat? Who takes care of you when you are sick or scared in the night? What happens to you when you get into trouble? What do these people know about me? What happens if you have a toileting accident?

Tell the child who has been abused that the parents know that some sad and scary things have happened to her. They are sorry that those things have happened, but they are excited about adopting her.

Be certain to include that this child also has some positive relationships that she may want to remember.

Page 6: Make a calendar of the days left until the child moves on page six. Write down things that will happen before and during the transition plan. Be certain to write down things such as:

- saying goodbye to his teacher or coach
- going swimming one more time with his friends
- introducing his new parents at his Sunday School class
- taking pictures of his room, special outdoor place, playing with friends, foster brothers and sisters and cousins
- getting addresses to send prints of the pictures
- setting up times for next visits with important people in his life
- deciding where his possessions will go in his new room and home.

When this booklet is completed, the child and caseworker can share it with the foster and adoptive parents. As the caseworker is sharing, the child will tend to want to add to the story, or tell a little more of what she was thinking about. In this way, the parents can easily come alongside their child emotionally. The lifebook is a tool that builds toward a sensitive start.

Some of these pictures and descriptors make great additions to the child's lifebook. The lifebook is an interactive piece of work, as the interactions assist children in processing their thoughts and feelings. It helps them feel more in-control in a positive manner. It builds and shares his identity with others as well as helps him to understand himself. It encourages self-reflection and expression of his feelings and thoughts.

Another template that is helpful in discussing moves with children is the Life EcoMap by Vera Fahlberg (*A Child's Journey though Placement*, 2012). This helps them discuss where they are in their lives and determine and discuss the events that are causative. Some older children, especially 10 and up, do well with the guided book, *Filling in the Blanks* (Gabel, 1988). This book helps children process the reasons why they need a family and how a family functions. More visually oriented children may enjoy using the relevant pages from *Here I Am: A Lifebook Kit for Children with Developmental Disabilities*

(Shroen, 1985). This book has good pictures, particularly those cap-tioned "When I had to leave, When I was born... who was there?" All these materials assist children with the tasks of processing the parts of their lives, with feelings, into a coherent life narrative.

There are particular issues concerning a move that are specific to each developmental level. Children may lack the abilities to discuss some of these issues at the age of their move. However, they will undoubtedly emerge, and should be discussed, when children have more support and cognitive ability. An example is the case of Wil-liam, who is 8 years old.

> William came into therapy with oppositional issues and attachment problems. He was moved six times between the ages of 2 years and 4½ years. After eight months of success-ful work, William was much more agreeable, and frequently relaxed beside or turned to his fathers for reassurance or to share his emotions. When I asked William if there were was anything that he wanted to talk about that day—anything that bothered him—he said vehemently, "Yes. Mothers! Why did they treat me so mean and keep giving me away?" Wil-liam was letting me know that he needed to work on a critical issue common to children moved during the preschool years.

Supporting adults will often have to circle back to work on the damaging issues in moves after children develop the cognition and opportunity to remediate them later in childhood.

Important concepts during any move include reassuring the child with messages such as the following.

- We will keep you safe and will meet your needs for food, comfort, mastery, and companionship.
- Your feelings of grief over losing homes are normal feelings and matter to us.
- You have ties to people who were in your family before this family. Those connections are treasured.
- Your achievements matter.
- Your grief will cause you to feel hopeless sometimes. Families can understand that loss of hope and can support you.
- Your parents loved you. They were not able to meet your needs. (Be specific as to what those needs were, i.e. supervision for

the child wandering in parking lots, food for the child who was failure to thrive, safety for the child who was in domestic violence situations.) The plan made by adults is that you should have a family that can meet your needs. You will always care about your birth family but you have permission to care about and be a member of this family. This family will meet your needs and will love you authentically.

Changes in self-concept with sudden moves

There are specific damages to the emerging personality when children lose their homes and their attachment figures. Those stages are summarized by developmental stages, as follows:

Phase I: Birth through seven months of life

Infant's needs at this stage include the following elements.
1. Parent(s) who are socially responsive—wiring the baby for social and emotional interactions.
2. A buffered, or protective, setting. When the baby's hunger, loneliness, fear, tiredness/overstimulation, or pains are met with effective parent, this helps to reduce these problems.
3. The baby feels that she is safe and that her parents are as well.
4. The baby learns to be curious and playful, by having parents who are able to be engaged and responsive.
5. The baby has parents who can increasingly move the little one into a settled routine over the first few months of life.

Phase I moves done abruptly cause children to

- lose their physiological regulation, since they are still getting much of their regulation from their primary caregiver
- lose joy and social responsiveness
- lose progress towards emotional connection and attunement
- lose attachment-in-the-making, emotional development, and even motor and verbal achievements
- feel unsafe, anxious, and wary. Their protection is through relationship at this age. Too much is new, not just in the home, but in the caregiver.

Phase II: 7 to 18 months

This is typically the stage in which an exclusive attachment to a parent is seen. In a safe environment that has continuous care from nurturing caregivers, children feel safe and insulated from danger. By this stage, normally developing babies form a sense of attunement, or a feeling of being "in-synch" between themselves and family members. They can easily share the same feelings, or affects. In nurturing contexts infants effectively use parents to help get back into balance.

Babies at this stage need these things:

- a consistent and nurturing parent who is emotionally available to the little one. Separations of more than a day should be avoided unless they are emergencies
- a parent who can be patient with the baby's need for proximity during this stage
- a safe home with parents who are neither frightened nor frightening
- parents who can celebrate the baby's movement into more mastery—standing, crawling, and speaking
- parents who are "in synch" at least 30% of the time—the definition of the "good enough" parent. That is the percentage that the parents need to aim for when creating an emotionally healthy environment (Fosha, 2004)
- parents who can stimulate language by speaking with and responding to their babies
- parents who continue to provide buffering and soothing, as well as play and social experiences.

Phase II moves done abruptly cause children to

- lose their attachments. Moves cause a vulnerability to life-long fears around attachments, dreading abandonment and feeling anxiety
- lose a sense of attunement, or the ability to get on the same wavelength emotionally with others

- lose developmental milestones in motor achievements, language development, and exploration of their world
- become less socially oriented
- feel and look stressed and anxious. Their emerging abilities to handle stress are already taxed.

Phase III: 18 months to between 30 and 36 months

This is the stage in which most children begin to explore their worlds, moving out with curiosity. They are developing autonomy and a beginning sense of their own identities. They say "no" quite a bit, and love asserting their preferences. In nurturing settings they can use parents as a secure base from which to explore. They continue to need their parents to help organize their feelings and provide nurturing.

Toddlers think of themselves as good or bad by the end of this stage. Needs for children at this stage are for

- close nurturing relationships with parents in order to support increasing exploration
- rules, so that children begin the process of learning limits and staying safe
- limits and expansion of empathy so that children learn to care and contain aggression
- new experiences that enhance mastery in play, speech, and social interactions with peers
- shared enjoyable activities between parents and children
- assistance from adults in building a positive gender, and self identity as "good" and also as a valuable member of family
- opportunities to make choices or to say "no"
- ability to retreat to parents or trusted adults when life feels overwhelming.

Phase III moves done abruptly cause children to

- think that they lost people they loved or homes because they were bad
- think that perhaps they said "no" too much, giving a basis in learned helplessness. Or, they may—
- think that they should have said "no" more. They get locked into oppositional, obstinate behavior. "I don't want to" becomes the sum of their arguments…even years later

- grieve without knowing anyone well enough to support their grieving. They have pathological grief reactions
- refuse to attach deeply again
- decide that there is something wrong with their gender
- lose developmental milestones in all areas.
- experience anxiety
- lose social abilities, may become withdrawn or aggressive.

Phase IV: 30-36 months through 48-54 months

By this stage children have formed their beginning sense of self, and most are ready to enter the social world. Compliance usually works well for children who feel that they are in a safe place with caring people.

Children of this age are egocentric. Their world view is "Everything that happens is because of me!" Therefore, they tend to incorporate any trauma into their identities. "I made this happen. I am the kind of person that things like this happen to."

Gender identity further develops during this stage. Moved children may feel that being a boy or girl is "bad." Children think in terms of *big* and *little*. Children's needs at this stage include

- nurturing and sensitive parents who can help foster a positive self-identity
- a simple "what's different" for traumas that occurred. For example: Scary people are not allowed in our house. We don't let them in. It's our rule. Your birth family did not have that rule. I'm sorry that you were scared there.

Support children's exploration in the following ways:
- Follow their lead in play
- Set rules and structure so that children continue the process of learning limits and staying safe
- Expand empathy so that children learn to care, compromise, and contain aggression
- Give them experiences that enhance mastery in play, speech, social interactions with peers
- Share enjoyable activities between parents and children
- Offer assistance from adults in building a positive gender, and self identity as "good" and valuable member of family.

- Create opportunities to make choices or to say "no"
- Nurture the ability to retreat to parents or trusted adults when life feels overwhelming.

Phase IV moves done abruptly cause children to

- lose their attachments. They will grieve but have no one to support their grieving
- lose developmental milestones at a time that is especially noticeable with other peers. She feels behind peers socially and cognitively already
- feel responsible for the choices that were made. "I must have done something wrong"
- lose a sense of predictability in life. "I don't know the rules, the structure, or the rituals"
- feel that big people don't care, and are not to be trusted "This happened because I was small and helpless. Therefore I should control and grow up fast"
- lose the capacities to join ideas and emotions. The basis for attunement and shared activities has been fractured
- feel that their choices, feelings, and attachments do not matter. "No one cares and I cannot make a difference in my own life. Nothing works out"
- feel that adults will not buffer to help him. "I'm on my own."

Phase V: 4½ through 6½ to 7 years of age

Children in Phase V increase in identity formation. Typically they are mastering language, play themes, and are eager for social relationships. They may hope to have a romantic relationship with a parent. Children of this age need a life story that has a "why" in it, but their life stories are quite concrete. They may want to know more about the events that happened pre-adoption in a search for what explains their feelings.

Children at this age need

- support for speech and learning skills as they enter an academic setting
- continuation of a nurturing, sensitive relationship with parents

- safety
- the ability to retreat to parents or trusted adults when life feels overwhelming
- a simple "why" for the events that have shaped their lives. For example, "Your birthmother did not have enough money or any food for herself or for you. She knew that we were all ready for a child. That is why she and the judge decided that you should come be our boy. She wanted you to have a family with lots of good food, love, and a warm house"
- therapy for trauma that they experienced
- help in handling their feeling extremes (Please see Chapters 8 and 10 for practical suggestions)
- buffering and soothing help when they need to retreat to their parents for a cuddle, comfort, props, or ideas
- social experiences that help them to develop peer relationships. These experiences may need to be coached for success
- basic chores so that they contribute to the family
- structure in going to bed, brushing teeth, etc., along with consequences to maintain this structure
- positive statement about their gender, their accomplishments, and their value to the family
- help in organizing their life story, social contexts, and increasingly complex worlds.

Phase V moves done abruptly cause children to

- lose their attachments. They will grieve but have no one to support their grieving.
- feel that their contributions to the family were inadequate, or perhaps their family did not like their gender. "I failed. I am a failure."
- be grandiose and dramatic in the telling and understanding of their life story.
- lose developmental milestones and lose the sense of mastery that is key at this stage.
- feel responsible for the choices that were made. "I must have done something wrong. I am not like my peers. My peers are better."
- lose a sense of predictability in life. "I am not someone whose efforts pay off."

- feel that big people don't care, and are not to be trusted. This interferes with relationships with authority figures in school.
- lose the capacities to join ideas and emotions. The basis for attunement and shared activities has been fractured. Their social relationships will suffer.
- feel that their choices, feelings, and attachments do not matter. "No one cares and I cannot make a difference in my own life. Nothing works out."
- feel that adults have let him down. "Don't trust others."

Phase VI: Ages 6½ to 8: How am I the same and different as other children? Ages 8-10: Joining in and finding my place

Children entering these stages of development are rigid in defining what is normal and what standards they use for group inclusion. This development causes children to compare their lives to the lives of others. In their rigid self-assessment they realize that they are different having had to change families. Unless they have had sensitive adults as compassionate helpers in their lives, they may avoid any talk about trauma or other painful topics.

This is an age of mastery and social development: finding one's place, cooperating with groups, and accomplishing tasks. Needs at these stages are for

- safe, nurturing homes and parents
- experience-rich lives that help them to develop a sense of mastery
- academic successes, either with or without accommodations and school support
- social successes giving them friends and a fit with their same-aged peers. Social support in the way of social skills groups and/or counseling may need to be given to assist in this development
- a life story that helps them cope with adoption issues and trauma/neglect issues. It should both give facts and correct any distortions
- therapy that helps them to process and de-sensitize to trauma and shame
- building of moral, spiritual development, and empathy

- structure and discipline in order to move smoothly through the cycle of the day and necessary chores
- help in handling feeling or behavioral extremes. Consequences are given to help enforce limits.

Phase V moves done abruptly cause children to

- lose their attachments. They have no one to support their grieving. They do not want to attach again. It is too painful.
- feel that they did not meet their family's needs. "I am a reject."
- be ashamed of their life history, about avoid talking about it. "I don't fit in. Where is my place?"
- lose developmental milestones and lose mastery and accomplishment.
- feel responsible for the choices that were made. "I must have done something wrong. I am not like my peers. My peers are better."
- lose a sense of predictability in life. "I am not someone whose efforts pay off."
- feel that no one cares. "Don't trust." This interferes with relationships with adults at school and home.
- lose attunement and intimacy not just with adults, but with friends. Their social relationships will suffer.
- feel that their choices, feelings, and attachments do not matter. "No one cares and I cannot make a difference in my own life. Why bother?"
- feel angry much of the time.

In summary, children moved abruptly without careful transition may think that they were moved because

- they were bad
- they were angry with people who retaliated
- they were rejected or were not liked by their parents,
- they were rejected in favor of another person
- they were too much trouble
- they did not protest the move
- they were someone's sexual partner and were later banished
- they misbehaved to the extent that no one could stand to live with them

- they told a secret that caused the parent to get into trouble
- they did not take good enough care of a parent or sibling
- they are the kind of person who brings trouble to families.

Sometimes they have made the correct assumption, but have not placed it into a healthy context. For example, they were moved because they told a secret, but it was a secret that should have been told! The problem was not the secret, but the illegal activity. Sometimes they are simply looking at life events through the lens of childhood and the scope of their own developmental stage.

> One 8-year-old said, "My aunt told them that she was sick of me calling her mean names, fighting her, and the screaming in the night. She was done. She told them that she was leaving me with a worker that day. And she did. I cried and cried but she did not change her mind. She told me that it was my own fault. She was not taking me with her. I was not her boy."

> Interestingly, he was just 4 years old at the time, but he remembered his aunt's words and his feelings clearly. It took a long time before he had the increased mental abilities and wanted to work through this information.

Placement discussion should include the following explanations:
- You are valuable.
- It is against the law for people to mistreat children. When this occurs, society values children enough that the judge has to make a decision to keep you safer. This did not happen to you as a punishment. You are not being rejected just because a family did not meet your needs.
- Your parents loved you and wanted to raise you. They could not, so this plan has been made for you.
- It is painful to lose people in your life. We will help you with care and support during this sad period.
- Children act out when they are scared and angry. That is a result of the maltreatment, not who you are.

Some of these reasons cannot be worked through right away. Children must become older and capable of working on issues in therapy and at home. Specific, factual information helps children

determine the accurate reasons why things occurred. Equally importantly, as time goes on, they develop reasons that are more complex.
This is a typical example from a child in late elementary school.

"I think that my birthmother just can't stay away from
drugs. She did not want a bad life for me and she did love
me. She has tried to stop the drugs five times. She keeps going back to all that drug stuff. I feel sorry for her. I know that
she has missed out on my life. None of her children live with
her. But I just can't wait around for her, like, 'I wonder if she's
going to take me back or not?' I needed a family that treated
me like I was worth something! Like my parents treat me.
I'm a regular kid. I wonder what happened to her to get her
started on drugs?"

Listed in the Appendix are aids for professionals and parents who
are assisting children with their grieving process. It includes assistance for parents' whose grief may be triggered, as well.

Healthy moving schedules for infants

An infant moving schedule is short, but not so abrupt that they
experience high levels of stress. There is evidence that moving infants
abruptly causes a massive disequilibrium in neuroendocrine regulation, with potential for partial long-term effects (Dozier, 2006).

Spend at least seven to ten days moving babies. That way, babies
and parents have time to become comfortable with one another. Babies can learn to anticipate that the parents will react in a somewhat
familiar way. The following schedules are laid out in a way that guides
the move in a developmentally sound fashion.

Infants 1-4 months, transition time: 6 days (for a domestic place-ment or an international placement with a flexible program)

Day 1 and Day 2—Parents meet the baby in familiar surroundings. The primary caregiver or institutional worker is present and
caring for the infant. The parents spend time giving basic care for the
baby under the caregiver's direction. They do not introduce anything
new, unless it is a colorful rattle or similar toy. They do not take the
baby into unfamiliar areas. They visit for three to eight hours. Then
they go home or back to their hotel.

Day 3 and Day 4—Parents return to the familiar setting, this time to visit all day. They take over the feeding, holding, and so forth. They become comfortable with the baby's care. They get feedback from the caregiver, who can reinstate care when the baby gets upset on Day 3, but not on Day 4.

Day 5 and Day 6—The parents take the baby away from the familiar setting. Babies are almost exclusively sensory learners, so take great pains to use the same or familiar foods, styles of feeding, textures, smells, and schedule as in the caregiving environment. The baby goes back to the familiar setting at night on Day 5, but the parents keep the baby overnight on Day 6. The parents continue to use the familiar bedding, clothing, formula, and schedule.

Day 7—The parents and the baby return to the former home to visit. Pictures are taken, and the last items for childcare are exchanged. The former caregiver gives quotes that are recorded in the lifebook.

Notice that this move also honors the first caregivers. Caring about everybody is the right thing to do, and also in the best interest of the infant. Caregivers who are asked to participate with an abrupt move will often be overwhelmed with sad feelings preceding the move. The baby, then, sees facial expressions of either stoic self-control or uncontrolled weeping, putting them into a state of stressed wariness. Taking the time to honor relationships helps mitigate these negative reactions.

If there is a pressing need, not just a desire, to move faster, this schedule can be condensed into three to four days by skipping the even-numbered days, or Day 4 and Day 6.

Infants 5-10 months, transition time: ten days

The tasks for these infants are essentially the same as in younger babies. The supposition is that some babies will begin moving into an exclusive attachment relationship, if a caregiver is available, by month seven and almost all will by month ten. Babies will also have learned an attachment pattern by this age: secure, insecure, or disorganized.

The parents will use the same format as the one above, but some extra tasks are included for the caregiver. As the caregiver transfers care, she will also be symbolically transferring her attachment to the new caregiver.

Day 1—Parents meet the baby in familiar surroundings, with the primary caregiver or institutional worker present and caring for the child. The parents spend time talking to the caregiver while the caregiver holds and cares for the baby. They visit for about three or four hours.

If the baby is playful, curious, and reaching out, then the parents can hold the baby. If not, they will wait until the next day. The parents bring a small, personal gift for the caregiver(s). These are hospitality gifts, like chocolates, lotions, a fruit and cheese basket, etc. They ask to learn from the former caregiver. They indicate that they appreciate the sacrifice that she is making by providing care and love, and then having to say goodbye to the baby.

In a family setting, pay attention to the other adults or children, so that their feelings and thoughts are honored. If there are other children in the home, small hospitality gifts are brought for them as well by the next day. Ask the caregiver for permission and advice about these small gifts for siblings.

Notice that the parents are indicating their gratitude to the caregiver. They are approaching her on a conscious level and honoring her for going through the emotionally ambivalent process of transitioning a baby. Of course, the caregiver wants a permanent home for the child, but she also has a bond with the child that will cause her pain during the move.

Often this step, recognizing the mixed emotions of the foster or kinship caregiver, is skipped when babies are moved. The caregiver, then, will conclude that these are the "wrong" parents. She indicates this in a variety of non-verbal ways to the baby, who squirms, resists and avoids the new parents. As a result, a placement schedule is commonly accelerated in order to avoid conflict. The baby, parents, and caregivers all lose.

Day 2—Parents bring small-scale, interesting toys to their visit. They sit with the caregiver to play a little. This allows the caregiver to indicate to the baby that she can enjoy these new people without being separated from her caregiver. The prospective parents do not take the baby into unfamiliar areas. They visit for three to eight hours. They go home or back to their hotel.

Day 3 and Day 4—The parents participate in basic care for the baby, under the caregiver's loose direction. They visit all day in the home. They take on the feeding, holding and so forth. They become comfortable with the baby's care. They get feedback from the caregiver, who sometimes takes the care back if the baby gets too upset. The caregiver stays relatively close by, and gives reassuring feedback to the baby and the parents that things are going well.

Day 5—The parents take over the basic care, even if the baby gets upset. The caregiver leaves the baby for a couple of hours. The caregiver is offered some support from the social worker for her own grief and conflict. To assuage the pressures on the home's schedule, arrange for take-out or easily prepared food for the next few days.

Day 6—The parents take the baby away from her familiar setting for a few hours. They use the familiar foods, styles of feeding, textures, smells, and schedule of the caregiving environment. They stay with her in the caregiver's home either before or after the out-of-home visit.

Notice that the baby is at about the half-way point in splitting time between the caregiver and parents. From this point on, the care will move more towards the new parents, who now know the baby.

Day 7—The baby stays with the adoptive parents for the day, only returning to the home at night to sleep. (She will nap with the adoptive parents.) The baby may be fussy and cranky, showing the effects of moving attachment figures. However, the baby does not look panicked and the adoptive parents feel that they know a lot about this baby and her care.

Day 8—The baby's bed, car seat, and other items are moved to the new parent's home or hotel room. They buy the baby's crib if it is a domestic adoption and this is feasible, allowing the parents to use the familiar bedding, clothing, formula, and schedule. On this day the baby will be moving to the new parent's care for the night.

Day 9—Parents return, with the baby, to the former home to visit. Pictures are taken and last items for childcare are exchanged. The former caregiver gives quotes for the lifebook and siblings have a chance to say good-bye.

This is a ten day move. One day has been left out for use as a time margin, since there is often a day or two in which people get sick or have a conflict in schedule and do not have the chance to spend time together.

Infants 11-24 months, transition time: ten to fourteen days

Infants of this age have not only formed an exclusive attachment with their primary caregiver, if they are in a home setting, but have also done a great deal of learning about how their worlds work. (For a more complete description of emotional development at various ages please see Chapter 8 of *Attaching in Adoption*, 2012.) It is important to spend a couple more days visiting in order to learn about the child's routines and developmental milestones. This helps the parents learn the familiar phrases that cue a child. It also helps them to understand some of the little one's emotional attachments to other adults and siblings in the home. It helps new parents not to personalize the, "No, Me, Mine" stage children naturally go through by the second half of the second year of life when they can see it in context. Children moved too abruptly at this stage can get locked into this protest "No" stage; or they may feel reluctant to attach again.

Typically, the social worker should try not to move children who are in a six-month window of attachment, which is an exclusive stage between about nine and fifteen months of age. There is some normal variation of a couple of months because of children's individuality. This assumes that the baby is in a safe, nurturing, and securely attached relationship with the caregiver. Leaving children in a situation of neglect is, of course, not ever a solution. Moving neglected children into permanent homes prior to that window is optimal. To determine whether the baby is in that exclusive window, social workers can note whether the baby usually cries or fusses when the caregiver walks out of the room or has progressed to the stage in which he knows that the caregiver will come back.

The days break down in the same way as the previous section. However, the move includes a little more time in which to make the transition so the baby does not lose as much of her communication language, routines, and social skills in the move.

It takes time for the parents and baby to learn to do those things together. By 12 months of age, for example, babies whose mothers have used active distraction instead of just, "No" will show better delayed gratification skills. By 3 years of age these babies are more socially competent (LeCuyer, 2006). This subtle type of developmental communication can be lost so easily in an abrupt move.

Parents should take time to note how the baby gets attention positively, expresses delight, shows off, shares delight, calms down, organizes himself, handles frustration, and deals with limits. The baby or toddler may regress for a while after placement. Understanding and identifying the typical interactions for the little one helps the parents approach their child in ways that make him delighted, calmed, better organized emotionally, less frustrated, and so forth. Parents need to pick up the language, or the dance, of the infant so that they can continue it and then modify it to fit their personalities. Spending time getting to know the baby/toddler first helps them read the baby after placement.

As in the section above, bring a small gift to the caregiver, and honor her for her care for the child. Please see the section above for more explanation of the reason for the gift.

Preschoolers, 24 months to 5 years, transition time: fourteen to twenty-one days

This type of move is more painful for all parties because children grieve so openly when they are given the support and emotional permission to do so. It is always painful to watch children's grief work. There is a sense that the move should be sped up to "get it over with." Those speedy transitions meet the adults' needs, not children's needs. While moves can be sped up to transition children from a grief to a shock state, there are long-term costs to that strategy.

Attaching in Adoption gives detailed information on losses that are part of moves, and attachment, and the subsequent developmental impacts. *Nurturing Adoptions* will not repeat this information, but it will stress the major areas that need to be addressed in a move, especially as children become more verbal during these stages.

Very young children are not able to hold time frames in their minds. Sequencing, and phrases like "the day after tomorrow" and "the day before yesterday" are difficult for them. Because of this, we do not prepare them weeks in advance. This preparation is too anxiety-provoking. If toddlers and most 3- and 4-year-olds ask whether they are going to stay with their parents, the parents say, "For lots and lots of days," until they are actually close to a move.

Explain more to 5-year-olds. "Right now, you are living with me. I will take good care of you. You will someday have other parents who will also take wonderful care of you and love you. I will let you know when that time comes. They will not be strangers or mean, but will be nice and friendly. That time is not right now, though." (Caseworkers can simply substitute the name of the foster parents and add that the judge and adults who care about children, like her, will look for a great home for him at the right time.)

The glitches that snarl moves are common and to be expected. Children who are in a careful schedule, as suggested here, do not experience the agony of being told they are moving, then having it cancelled, and then back on again, or maybe not.

In this move schedule, the caseworker can tell children that they are moving part-way through the visit schedule. Before that, if the preschooler asks, "Are these my new parents?" the appropriate answer is, "I don't know yet. The adults are still deciding. Will you tell me what you think or how you feel?" That allows children to share how they are reacting to a potential move and to leaving and becoming part of a new family. If things do not result in a move, children can be told that the adults decided that it was not the right fit. If it is because the potential parents determined that they could not take care of the needs of a child, *some* of this can be shared with a child.

The caseworker might say, "Moving to be part of this family will not work. Some of the reasons are hard for kids to understand. One reason that you can understand is that one parent in this family travels too much. He thinks that he needs to change jobs before they can adopt a child. And, they live far away from the school, the doctors, and therapy. They did not realize how many times kids need to go there. They need to make some changes before any child comes to live with them."

In her book *A Child's Journey through Placement*, Dr. Fahlberg recommends putting causation into terms of *needs and responsibilities* (p.151, 2012). This prevents a blaming and shaming way of looking at placement. Instead, as in the example above, the explanation states that children need many trips to schools, doctors, and so forth. The family could not meet these needs until they reduced their driving time.

Sometimes the move stumbles because of disagreements over continuing contact agreements or the levels of adoption support in the placement. These agreements need to be finalized before children are too far into the move schedule. By day 4 or 5 of the move schedule, described in the upcoming paragraphs, these issues should be resolved. That way, the child is not destabilized if there are difficulties.

It is not uncommon to encounter problems that put the adoption in question, that are resolved within a week. In this move scenario, the schedule would simply stop and resume after the issues are resolved. If the lag is more than a week, back up a couple of days and resume the schedule.

If the move does not occur because the prospective parents simply do not like the child, do not share this with the child. Simply say that the adults could tell that it was not going to work out. If children do not like the prospective adoptive family, it is extremely helpful to find out why.

One child I knew complained that the prospective parents were angry and that they scared her. When questioned, the prospective parents admitted that they were embattled and the child had overheard their heated arguments. The placement did not occur.

This child, who was almost 5, did move to a more resolved family within the next month. The first family had a couple of visits with the caseworker and then concluded that they should adopt a child they had formerly fostered, who had been placed with the birthparent and was now available for adoption. That had been the source of their arguments. One parent thought that they should proceed with the placement, and the other parent wanted to back up to adopt the child they had fostered.

The example above illustrates that caseworkers should not get too enraptured with the drama around a particular placement. Sometimes their plans for a family need to collapse to meet the pragmatics of a situation. Ultimately, changing course was a better plan for everyone.

Children ages 2 through 5, transition time: sixteen days

Day 1—The child meets the parents in his home. The parents relate much more to the caregiver than to the child. The child is <u>not</u> told that he or she is moving to these parents. However, if the child asks, the child is told that these are parents who would like to adopt a child. The child might say, "Me?"

"I do not know that answer yet," is a good response. If questioned further, the caseworker might say, "The adults haven't finished making their decision."

Reticence in offering explanations is suggested because many adoptive families do not adopt a child they visit for reasons that are either personal or logistical. Equally important, the child should not feel pressured or think that she makes the placement decisions.

Day 2—The parents come back to the child's home. They spend time playing with the child as well as the other children in the home. They spend more time with the child, however. They do not overwhelm the child, but do spend some special time enjoying what the child enjoys.

Day 3—The parents spend about five hours with the child, including playing, feeding or eating with the child, and helping with toileting/dressing under the supervision of the caregiver. Notice that the child begins to form a relationship without feeling the stress of separation from her caregivers.

Day 4—The parents take the child out of the home to a playground or a similar activity where they can get to know the child and his likes, dislikes, personality, and so forth. The child is out for two to five hours, depending on the child's age and nap schedule. The parents will have an opportunity to set limits, structure the day, and so forth.

Day 5—The caseworker talks with all parties to find out how they all think things are going. She spends some time with the child in order to find out how the child is feeling about the family. If the feelings are positive on all fronts, then the placement schedule proceeds.

Day 6—The child is told that she will be moving to live with the adoptive family. The caseworker goes through the information contained in the next section of this book, "Discussing moving with a child." The caseworker also spends some time with the other children and adults in the family from which the child will be leaving. A discussion about their feelings and wishes occurs. Sensitive plans are made to honor everyone in the transition as much as possible.

Day 7—The parents visit a longer time with their child outside of the home. They share pictures of their home. If the home is within a convenient driving distance, they make a plan to visit the home. They leave a toy so that the child may play with it with them the next day. They also take pictures of their family to leave with the child so that he can share it or just look at them.

The child may act out with the adoptive parents at this time. This gives the parents time to try giving limits and consequences, and affirm that they are not looking to adopt a perfect child. They may find that their attempts at limit-setting are failures. Fortunately, they can ask for assistance from the current home, dig out their pre-adoption training materials, or consult with a caseworker to problem-solve and try again before they are responsible full-time.

Attention is given to the other adults or children in a family setting so that their feelings and thoughts are honored. If there are other children in the home, small hospitality gifts are brought for them as well by the next day. Ask the caregiver for permission and advice as to their nature.

Day 8—The parents bring their child to their home for the whole day if it is nearby. They talk about where the child's belongings will go and introduce the child to their new home. The child will probably show some signs of distress by now. Parents can help him when he is frustrated, sad, or angry when transitioning between homes. They can help him name and organize his feelings, with empathy and comfort.

Day 9—The parents have the child for the whole day again. They may take the child to preschool or kindergarten to meet friends and the teacher. By this time, the child will probably be having some grief reactions to the move. The caregivers who are saying "goodbye" will begin to think that this is a very hard process and probably that it is too long. Everyone becomes aware of the true cost of the move. However, they are able to meet the child's needs and to provide comfort and reassurance as this child moves her attachment.

Somewhere between Days 7 and 11 everyone takes a day or two off from the schedule. It is typical that people end up tired and everyday tasks that require attention build up.

Days 11 and 12—The parents pick up the child and some of his belongings to take to the new house. This time, the parents take their child with the intention of an overnight visit. They take the bed and bedding with them, if possible.

Day 13—The child returns to spend the day with the caregiving family. He plays, gets cuddles, visits favorite places, and has a chance to relax after experiencing so much "new." The adoptive parent(s) may want to use this time to go out to dinner one last time without having to arrange for childcare. The parents can pick him up for the night or leave him there, depending on logistics.

Day 14—The child's belongings are loaded and moved to the new home. Please pack this child's items in luggage or boxes, and treat her possessions with respect. Do not use garbage bags or she may feel like garbage. The child officially moves to the new home.

Day 16—The child returns to say "goodbye" officially. She takes pictures, shares, gives affection to the new and the old caregivers, and reminisces.

If a child is having more difficulty, this schedule can be lengthened to allow for more time to process feelings and the reality of the move.

Long distance domestic placements

Sometimes families will need to fly or drive long distances to visit and move the child. In these cases, the prospective adoptive parents should travel to the child's home city over a three or four day long weekend. They must decide whether they want to proceed with the placement after that time. If the decision is to proceed, the parents travel again, following the template in the section above. The time away from the caregiver is spent at the place the parents are temporarily staying. They will stay three to four days on the second visit as well, with the child going back-and-forth between the hotel and the home.

At the end of the 4th day of the second visit, they bring the child and some of his belongings to their actual home. After two days there, they return to the child's first home for goodbyes and to packing his belongings. That visit usually lasts one day. Then they fly home with the child and all of his possessions.

Sometimes the first family will offer to bring the child to the new home or deliver the possessions. While this is a nice offer, it is not as sensitive to the child. It is important for the child to say some goodbyes and see the home that he is leaving.

Children who have been through these careful processes tell me later that they understood what was happening and that they enjoyed seeing the home one last time. They will often keep in touch with these earlier parent figures. Children who have been moved quickly think that people and homes disappear. They frequently demonstrate bitterness and a sense of helplessness about losing important people from their lives.

Comments like, "He won't remember this," or "She doesn't really understand what's happening, so let's get it over with," are excuses for short-cuts. In fact, children provide compelling descriptions of the pain slack casework and abrupt moves have caused in their lives. And, the DSM IV-TR describes foster care moves as one of the causative factors for reactive attachment disorder. Young children, who cannot speak out for themselves, need special care from our society when they must move between families.

Children 6 to 12 years, transition time: twenty-two days

Children are increasingly aware of the concepts of family and their permanence at these ages. Children who are legally free for adoption should be told that their caseworker will be looking for an adoptive placement. The meaning of adoption should be discussed. Certainly the grief issues from the loss of the opportunity to live with the birthfamily should be addressed by a therapist or a caseworker in counseling before the caseworker can talk about being adopted by a particular family.

While the stages used in these sections are chronological ages, children develop and will need different concepts at different times. Some children will need to discuss permanence and families even when they are 4 years old. Some children who are 6 years old still have trouble sequencing. They cannot grasp leaving the current home and going to a permanent home until they meet the people involved and can begin to experience time frames with them. The work needs to be adjusted according to emotional/developmental needs as dictated by what gives children the most predictability and stability in their lives—while still being honest.

Day 1—The child meets the parents in his home or in a neutral setting. The child is told that these are parents who would like to adopt a child. The child might say, "Me? I don't want to move!" Or he might say, "They're nice! Do you think that they will be my new parents? What kind of cool stuff do they have? Can I move now?"

The emphasis in the first few days should be on getting to know each other. Helpful responses are, "We do not know yet. We have to figure out whether this family will be able to meet your needs. (This leads to a discussion of what needs they have.) We should know if you like each other. Why don't you get to know each other and have some fun." When questioned further, the caseworker may respond, "The adults haven't finished making their decision. It will take them a while. You are too important to do this too fast. We don't want to do a move—and then say, 'Whoops!' We want to do a move—and then say, 'Yes!'"

Again, I emphasize that one compelling reason for the conservative beginnings stems from the reality that many adoptive families do not go on to adopt for personal or resource reasons. A second compelling reason is that we do not want the child to think that she makes the placement decision alone. It is too much pressure on her, especially when she may have loyalty issues over wanting a new home instead of remaining in mourning over her birthparents.

When adopting siblings, discuss how normal it is for one child to want to be adopted more than the other child does. Lobbying between siblings should be discouraged. Instead, adults should give children the freedom to feel their own feelings.

Day 2—The parents come back to the child's or children's home. They spend time playing with the child as well as other children in the home. They, however, spend more time with the child or siblings that they are interested in adopting. They do not overwhelm the child/children, but do spend special time enjoying what the child enjoys and sharing their special activities. Suggest bringing something to the next day's visit that parents and children can enjoy together. Limit video games. This type of activity is fun but does not build relationships.

Day 3—The parents spend about five hours with the child, or siblings, including playing, feeding or eating with the child, and helping with toileting/dressing under the supervision of the caregiver. This time they spend almost all of the time with the children whom they may adopt. Notice that, with this schedule, children begin to form relationships without the stress of separation from their caregivers and home. Secure attachment patterns are best developed when children are not stressed and are instead playful, relaxed, and available for relationship building. The caregiver is still there as a secure base for the child.

Day 4—The parents take children out of the home to a playground or activity in which they can get to know something about his likes, dislikes, and personality. (Vera Fahlberg, M.D. cautions that if you want to find out if children like French fries, take them to McDonalds. If you want to find out more about this child, select other activities.)

Children stay away from the home for about six to eight hours, depending on the child's tolerance for time away. The parents will have an opportunity to see the children experience some mood changes, talk at some length. Parents will set limits, structure the day, and experience some positives and negatives with them.

Day 5—The caseworker talks with all parties to find out how they all think things are going. She spends some time with the child in order to find out how the child is feeling about the family. If the feelings are positive on all fronts, then the placement proceeds.

In sibling situations, it is not unusual for one child to be negative about a family and others to be positive. It is not uncommon for parents to have doubts as to whether their relationship with one child will progress further than with another. This point in placement is a great time for the social worker to discuss these realities. Rather than proceeding with a placement in which parents may not be able to meet the needs of a sibling, it is better to stop the process at this point. Caseworkers may have to discuss whether placement together means that one sibling is going to end up in disruption, or whether any available family can meet the needs of the sibling group as a whole.

Day 6 and 7—Children are asked what they think about the potential placement. There is an informal poll taken. Children, parents and caseworkers all need to feel positively about the move in order to continue. Some children are candid in saying that they do not want to move from the foster home.

A 9-year-old was talking to me about moving. She wanted most to be able to live with her birthmother and youngest two siblings, although she said that prospect scared her. Secondly, she felt that she would like to live with a former placement. That was not a possibility due to sexual acting out that had occurred with that sibling. Thirdly, she did agree that she would be glad to be adopted by the visiting family. She did need to double check the finality of the losses of former homes before she could agree to join the new family.

If all parties feel that the placement seems to meet children's needs and that the family is able to take on the responsibilities, then children are told that they are going to live with the adoptive family. The foster family is certainly part of the decision-making. Their assistance in discussing this with the other children and bearing the emotional costs of the move schedule should be openly acknowledged.

The caseworker should cover the information in the next section of this book, "Discussing moving with a child." The caseworker also spends some time with the other children and adults in the family which the child will be leaving. Discuss their feelings and wishes. Sensitive plans are made to honor everyone in the transition as much as possible.

Paperwork should be completed at this time, committing parties to responsibilities. In cases in which parental rights will be relinquished through a voluntary placement and adoption, the legal work should be complete at this stage. It does not make sense to put children through the next part of the move if there are going to be problems that make adoption impossible.

Day 9—The parents visit with the children outside of the home for a longer period of time. They share pictures of their home. If the home is within a convenient driving distance, they make plans to visit the home. They take pictures of children and parents together to leave with their child so that he can share them or just look at them. Some parents may have wanted children already in the family to be introduced before this, some do not. This is a decision that is influenced by the age, temperament, and style of the family. If the children have not met, now is a good time to arrange this meeting.

Children may act out with the adoptive parents at this time, which gives the parents time to try giving limits and consequences, and affirm that they are not expecting to adopt a perfect child. They may find that their attempts at setting limits are merely attempts. Fortunately, they can ask for assistance from the current home, consult their pre-adoption training materials, see a therapist, attend a workshop, or consult with a caseworker, problem-solving before they are responsible full-time. (This is a great model in getting help in the future. The organization of resources described in training and homestudy processes pays off now!)

Attention is given to the other adults or children in a family setting so that their feelings and thoughts are honored. If there are other children in the home, small gifts are brought for them. Again, ask the caregiver for permission and advice as to their nature.

The adoptive parents should contact the school in their area about a transfer. By this time, they can arrange to talk to the school in a more knowledgeable manner about classroom placement and any learning needs. If there is an IEP, parents should schedule an IEP meeting with the new school. Some parents wish to home school the child. This can be a great option for extending the amount of time spent together for attachment purposes. Even if parents are home schooling, it is still helpful to talk with the school staff about academic attainment, testing, academic support for home schooling, and the child's learning process.

Day 10—The parents bring children to their home for the whole day. They talk about where the children's belongings will go and introduce children to their new home.

Children will probably show some signs of distress by now. Often they get frenetic and then move into crying or arguing. It is a way for them to show how hard the process is for them. Giving children permission to talk about how overwhelming big changes are helps children learn to converse about core issues with parents. Rather than treating upsets during this time as just a discipline issue, parents can ask about stresses that their child is feeling. It helps children learn that they are expected to feel a mixture of joy, confusion, fear, and sadness during a move.

Parents can help a child who is frustrated and at the end of his coping by expressing compassion. They can assist him in describing and organizing his feelings, supplying comfort.

Day 11—Day off. Sometimes everyone needs a day without a placement task.

Day 12—The parents again have the children for the whole day. They may take children to their home, or to school to meet friends and the teacher. By this time, children will probably be having some grief reactions to the move. Everyone becomes aware of the true cost of the move. However, parents are able to meet the children's needs and to provide comfort and reassurance as children move their attachments.

Day 13 and 14—The parents pick up the child and some of his belongs to take to the new house. This time, the parents take their child with the intention of an overnight visit. They take the bed and bedding with them, if possible. If not possible, at least take his pillow and a favorite blanket.

Friends are quite important, especially for children towards the end of this age range. A farewell occasion for children to say goodbye to friends and foster family is helpful.

During this period children can see the school that they will attend and the homes of other children with whom they will make friendships. They may or may not want to actually meet other children or visit the school.

> An 18-year-old girl stopped to see me in my office. I had seen her briefly when she was 7 years old. She particularly remembered the party that her 1st grade teacher arranged for her as she said "goodbye" to her class, which was something that I had asked for on her behalf. She felt valued and liked by her classmates. It was one of the few positive memories that she had from a several year period.

Day 15—The child returns to spend the day with the caregiving family. He plays, gets hugs, talks about his new home and community, visits favorite places, and has a chance to tell others about the changes in his life. The discussion helps him integrate the changes that are happening in his life in the presence of people who care. Often this is a day in which the child has a chance to say "goodbye" to people who were not available before.

Sometimes people the child hardly knows will want to visit at this juncture. Particularly in kinship placements, there are relatives who want to see children before placement. Or a birthparent may ask if her new boyfriend can meet the child before placement. This is not the time to introduce unfamiliar people to a child who is already experiencing high adjustment demands. These requests test the parents' abilities to set boundaries, and their capacity to say "No" to things that are not in their children's best interests. These boundaries should be encouraged and supported by the caseworker.

Day 16-21—The child's belongings are packed in luggage or boxes, never garbage bags. The child officially moves to the new home. He is welcomed by his family, who take some time off to just enjoy each other. The next five days is a holiday time. The parents reduce outside stimulation and demands. The family enjoys each other, plays games, does enjoyable activities, and eats good food.

Day 22—The child returns to say "goodbye" officially. She takes pictures, shares, gives affection to the new and the old caregivers, and reminisces. Notice the contrast between these supported psychological tasks and the impacts of pathological grief. We are also able to conclude this move schedule with "reminiscing is enjoyable."

Long distance domestic moves

As described in the section above, sometimes families will need to fly or drive long distances. While the steady daily schedule above does not fit, it is imperative that family travels at least three separate times. Notice that this amount of time allows for people to begin knowing each other.

Initially, adoptive parents travel to the child's home for at least a five day period, laid out like the section above. A decision to proceed with the placement occurs after that time.

If the decision is to proceed, the parents travel again, following the suggestions in the section above, but bringing the child to the place that they are staying during their scheduled time away from the caregiver. They stay five days, with the child going back-and-forth and spending the night with them for the last two nights. They share pictures of their home and usually bring siblings on this trip.

They bring the child to their actual home at the end of the fifth day with some of his belongings. After four or five days, they return to the child's first home for goodbyes and packing of belongings. That visit is one or two days, depending on the number of places that their child needs to say "goodbye" to and then they fly or drive home with the child and all of his possessions. If the possessions don't easily fit, then they can be boxed and shipped. Children lose so much identity through a move that they need to have all of their possessions sent with them. Having their "stuff" helps them to keep track of their associated memories.

The return of the child to the previous home and community in order to say "goodbye" is an important part of the grieving process and helps bring closure. Many children this age think that they can easily move again. In part, it is a perception that has been taught by caseworkers who gave few facts and little processing time in earlier moves. Or, even if they were capable and willing to give time or facts, emergencies may have dictated a sudden move. Giving children a chance to see their former home/family, and to process the facts and feelings about moving homes/families, helps them to integrate the enormity of this life change.

Children who have been through these careful processes tell me later that they understood what was happening and that they enjoyed seeing the home one last time. They will often keep in touch with these earlier parent figures.

Children who have been moved quickly think that people and homes disappear. In times of distress, they quickly suggest a move of homes/families. They reference this casually, as their move was casual. They frequently demonstrate bitterness and a sense of helplessness about losing important people from their lives.

Teens 13 to 17 years, transition time: three weeks to three months

Teens can have the same yearning for a family as younger children. If they have a realistic caseworker, they are aware that it is harder to find an adoptive family at their age. It is critical to describe what a family is looking for when talking to teens about adoption—a real teen to love, not to idealize. Teens' feelings and opinions tend to be very hot and cold. The teen who "just knows this is *the* family for me" will reverse this decision on a dime. Carefully review the normal variations in moods that they will have towards their families.

One girl said that her parents had described her in such overrated terms that she felt like a fraud. She felt incredible pressure to live up to this ideal. When she did not, her parents would relate all of her failings to learning the lessons of her birthmother. After some melodramatic screaming matches, everyone came to a realization that they were not cast in a romanticized drama. They were real people, yearning for authentic acceptance and love as they became a family.

In a session with me she said, "We all figured out that it drives me crazy when they compare me to my birthmother. She is actually a nice person. She just can't keep away from booze more than a year at a time. I don't want to go there with them. I did so badly for a while because I couldn't stand the pressure of trying to be their wonder teen. They had to understand that, of course I had a life before I met them. My old life wasn't completely bad! I don't want to forget it just because they weren't part of it."

This girl summarized many of the realities of teen adoption. A lot of the personality is formed by the teenage years. Parents must like the teen they are adopting. This teen is not going to be a façade of a person, easily remade into the parent's image. In fact, the teen is looking for love and acceptance without changing very much. The parents are looking for the same thing. As Vera Fahlberg, M.D. wisely observed, both will end up making huge changes (1995).

The schedule for teens should be no less than three weeks and may need to extend to up to three months. Caseworkers can use the template from the section above, with an understanding that teens will have more abstract thought. They can space out visits, giving the teenagers time to think about where they are going. The transition time may take a number of weeks. Caseworkers must recognize that teens will have a great deal of transitioning to do. Placements need to include continuing contact with friends, siblings, and the community.

Even if teens move rather abruptly and the connections do not seem critical or important to teens at the time, do not be surprised if this is just a reaction. Over time, teenagers often want to revisit and integrate old connections. Any placement should include the expectation and resources for teens so that they can reconnect with important people from their pasts in the years following placement.

Teens often have a rigid and superficial idea of what their families will be like. This is typical of the age. It seems counterintuitive that teens will have so little concept of the number of daily problems that must be negotiated. Emphasize this as part of the human condition, normal for everyone, throughout the transition process. Negotiation skills tend to be weak in children who have been abused, neglected or traumatized. Working on those skills within an accepting environment is necessary. Teens tend to be easily discouraged and especially sensitive to negative comments made towards them.

Parents should expect that they will need to teach their teens a lot about family commitment, to deal with high levels of anxiety, help identity strengths, deal with emotional immaturity, stop arguing marathons and/or prolonged sulks, and define their own limits of tolerance. Finding and meeting with a good therapist weekly will help reduce stress in families. Finding this person during the moving process is helpful—while things are still relatively rosy.

Friends are particularly important to teens. Parents can be proactive about meeting this need in placement. Identifying structured friend-promoting groups is a critical task during placement. Supportive church youth groups, sports teams, and finding schools with a history of inclusion are all great places to start. When teens are moving into a new community, they naturally gravitate towards the other teens who lack friendships. These available teens are often available because they have been unsuccessful in forming relationships with others. Arrange for teens in the community who are part of an established group to reach out to the teen. This can make the difference between teens struggling or thriving. This takes some planning, but is well worth the effort.

There are initiatives that promote teen adoption and give ample practical support for these adoptions. Please see the Resource List for additional information.

Moving siblings

Whenever possible, place together siblings who know and have lived with each other before. Those who work with this population have observed that siblings who cannot rely on parents often develop much closer ties to each other. These connections should be preserved in placement because they are significant attachments. Additionally, sibling relationships provide children with a great deal of information about their own identities. A brother or sister gives them daily clues about their identity. Children feel that they still know who they are, even after placement, when they have someone who remembers part of their stories and experiences.

It is equally important to determine if the sibling group will accept parenting or new family rules. Discuss this significant topic with older siblings before placement. They will naturally want to adhere to the family structure most familiar to them. New parents should recognize that they are adopting a family system, and that there will be a subculture within the newly expanded family. To the extent that this is healthy, it can be encouraged. The unhealthy aspects, however, necessitate strategic interventions in the home and therapy.

Clearly discuss the developmental aspects of each child and the need for spending time with each child separately with parents. Parents should avoid making a "group" approach to children their predominant pattern. Individual attachments must be made with each child. The more people in the home, the more complex the relationship needs will be.

Sometimes the siblings are so challenging that they cannot be placed together (Gray, 2012, pp. 301-305). Rather than expose children to post-placement bail-outs, caseworkers must work harder to learn how to assess whether families can realistically meet the special needs of siblings. Sometimes this is not in the children's best interest, and caseworkers can instead design continuing contacts between two adoptive families or look at proximal placement locations.

The more damaging the birthfamily system was to children in terms of trauma, sexual and physical abuse, domestic violence, prenatal exposure, and neglect, the more careful caseworkers will need to be with sibling group placements. Children can re-traumatize each other. Sexual and physical abuse can continue between older and younger children even after placement. While certainly no one wants to cause further harm to young children by moving them away from their siblings, that concern is vastly outweighed by the need for all children to feel a sense of safety and capacity for attachment in their homes.

A 10-year-old boy described his feelings for a sibling placed in a different adoptive home, "I am afraid of my brother. He says that he misses me, but he tackled me and choked me in our visits last year and this year. He says that he wants to come and stay a week. I was thinking like, maybe in about four years when I am bigger. I used to get hurt by my older sister who lives with me, too. But we got that stopped. I don't think that my parents could stop either of my older brothers if we all lived together. My dad was right there when my brother put his hands around my neck. Dad pulled him off of me. What would happen if Dad couldn't watch him all of the time?"

Interestingly, at an earlier age, this boy claimed he was fine with either brother living with his family. He was so traumatized and dissociative that he was not able to give an accurate report of his feelings. He dissociated during his brothers' physical bullying. Fortunately, a caseworker saw the extent of his brothers' acting out behavior and placed the children with continuing contact, but with separate families who were appropriate for safety and healing. In fact, the parents were hard-pressed to stop the violence between the sibling pair that they adopted.

Sometimes the patterns of violence are so fixed in an existing sibling family system that parents do best with continuing contact. Always interview carefully to find out what the patterns are between children, interviewing them individually about safety issues. I like to tell children that there are some promises to keep secrets that you can make because someone scares you or because you feel sorry for them when they say that they will get into trouble. Or, sometimes you believe them that you will get into trouble. Those are promises that you don't have to keep. We give examples and then interview, looking for any instances of coercion by adults or between siblings. In homes where lots of drug-using adults have moved in and out, the rate of child victimization is especially high, as is the rate of physical aggression and sexual acting out between siblings.

In orphanages the situation varies between settings. Some orphanages have serious problems with sexual and physical acting out, others have better supervision. The families who have drug and alcohol problems, domestic violence, and physical and sexual abuse issues domestically are similar to the ones in other countries. If children were removed from birth homes in Russia, for example, the children's issues will be similar to those in domestic adoption only with additional stresses from a cross-cultural move and institutional placement. Sibling placement issues will be similar.

When to delay discussing adoptive placement

Sometimes children are free for adoption, but adoptive families are not forthcoming. Telling children that they are safe where they are, and that if a better permanent home is found, then they will move, is an honest explanation. Help children enumerate who the people are in their lives which are most significant to them. Make certain that these people know how significant they are so that they can take particular care of their relationship with this child.

One caseworker was anxious to tell a child that he would be looking for an adoptive home. When I asked him what his chance of success might be, he answered, "I don't know. That is up to the adoption unit. I prepare him. They find the family." The child was 11 years old and had been, until recently, in a residential treatment unit. He was now in a therapeutic foster home that was willing to be a permanent home. He had settled and was finally thriving. He had assumed that he was home.

His foster family did not feel that they had the resources to adopt. They were older and worked at lower paying jobs. A proposed adoption support subsidy did not cover the items that were critical to this child's welfare. In this case "preparing" this boy would have been de-stabilizing. After a discussion about the statistical probabilities of finding an adoptive home, the caseworker agreed to talk about moving to an adoptive placement only after a family evidenced itself.

This does not mean that caseworkers should ever give children the idea that they are *unadoptable*. But, talking about placement in an overly optimistic manner leaves kids feeling like something is wrong with them if they are not "chosen." It is important to talk to older children about adoption's limitations, due to the supply of families, in a realistic manner. Often people mistakenly try to avoid these discussions; it is so painful to face children who have spent years going in and out of placements and are now without families. The average age of children adopted from the foster care system is 6. 7 years, with the median being 5.6 years. The average age of children waiting to be adopted is 8.6 years old and median age of 8.4 years old (AFCARS # 13, 2006). Children may be older when coming into foster care for the first time, so this is not always a problem with foster care drift.

International moves

International moves add a level of complexity to the task of understanding and meeting the needs of children. These needs are often filtered through a variety of reporters and cross-cultural differences. However, children and families anywhere are the same, in that, children have attachments, and they should be transferred slowly and deliberately, if possible. Additionally, children should be moved in a way that helps them experience as little shock as possible. And, after a transition, parents should help children to calm as quickly as possible.

The gradual transitions listed in this book are recommended for children who have formed attachments to fostering families. The adoption policies of many countries, however, make that gradual process impossible. Arrange to have an interpreter present when moving toddlers and verbal children. The interpreter can help explain what is happening and also help children understand the steps detailing what will happen next. Bring pictures of the airplane, the house, and the parents to assist the interpreter. Basically, the parents should use the interpreter to go through the booklet for moving children as described in the earlier section.

Some parents can arrange to provide care for their child within the orphanage every day during the transition. Families who are not permitted this access can often negotiate for a series of visits, during which they can provide care. To the extent that the parents can do this, they should. While they may miss out on some of the sight-seeing opportunities in the country, they will reap the benefits of getting to know and comfort their children before the move.

Many times parents have described returning to their hotel room after placement, feeling panicked and thinking, "What have I done?" The child will act wild and the parents have no a clue as to how to calm them or explain their circumstances.

> One woman described her daughter's reaction to the move. She wanted to walk around under the mother's dress, while the mother was wearing it. "My husband thought that it was funny. I wasn't laughing and I worried that it was a sign of sexual abuse. The more it bothered me, the more she wanted to do it. I found her bathroom habits lewd and weird. It was so hard to warm up to her."

Other parents have described their difficult beginning being soothed by the fact that their children already recognized them, the feeding routines, the schedule, their clothes, and their own acquisition of some basic language. One woman said that the most helpful thing for her was that someone from the agency came and assisted her in the hotel.

This discussion does not seek to advise what items to bring on international visitations, or any of the intricacies of cross-cultural adoption. A discussion of preparing for cross-cultural adoption is included in *Attaching in Adoption* (Gray, 2012). This book does, however, promote the importance of spending time getting to know children in familiar settings, and then transitioning them into settings outside of the home or orphanage. Sometimes parents have few options about the transition timing, which can be abrupt. Duplicating any familiar and reassuring behaviors or settings during the first period of placement can help children calm more quickly.

When moves are made too abruptly

> Carrie had expected a call about placement about three months before the day came. A single parent, she had decided that her family-building first choice would be sibling pair. Finally the call came while she was on a camping trip. She called her boss declaring herself to be on family leave and

called her parents, letting them know her good news. She was too excited to drive and to talk any more.

Scooting back to her home, she still had her camping clothes on when her new daughters arrived. Tammy was 4 and Allie was 6. They arrived from an emergency receiving home. Their mother had signed voluntary relinquishment papers. She refused service beyond the counseling series that the agency insisted upon. The children had been staying with friends. The mother was staying with someone else. These friends had given notice that they were done—and the mother owed them money for child care. So the children were picked up from angry people, saw their mother, said goodbye to their mother, and then were placed into receiving care while the papers were being filed and their father was contacted. He was "done" as well.

The girls both began to shriek when they saw that Carrie was not with their birthmother. Somehow in the confusion the children thought that they were going to live with the birthmother's latest friends, not a permanency planning home. They had not integrated the meaning of the "goodbye visit." They thought that the pictures taken at the goodbye visit were a type of photo opportunity, or just the latest charade to get a place to live. It was all so shocking to them. They were still in denial.

Carrie tried out her first advocacy skills on behalf of her daughters. She calmly asked the caseworker to stay, moving her next appointment. "I think that your colleague failed to convey to the girls all the information that they need to know," Carrie said. "Would you please use your professional skills to explain this move to them?" Carrie was pleased to note that the "mother bear" impulse seemed to come so naturally to her.

The caseworker agreed to spend the time necessary to help the girls. She used pencil and paper, drawing and describing that the birthmother would live in one home, they in another. This was met with hitting and wailing by Tammy. Allie just stared. Carrie and the caseworker got out Tammy's blanket and Allie's toy bunny. Carrie held Tammy and the blanket. Tammy stopped hitting and just cried for a long time. The caseworker sat next to Allie, stroking her hair. Allie held her bunny while the caseworker said, "This is so sad. I know. So sad." Allie started to cry a little then, rocking back and forth. The adults allowed them to feel those feelings, which moved like a wave over the girls.

Then the caseworker said, "You are going to feel sad a lot over the next days. She held up both hands, showing ten fingers. Even after that you will feel sad sometimes. I will come talk to you about this big sad feeling so that you feel better. Carrie will help, too."

The caseworker continued, "It is not a choice to be with Mommy. Your mommy made a choice that you needed a different mother. Mommy could not find you safe places to live. She could not get enough money. She wanted a home where you could have enough to eat, enough clothes, go to school, and have rooms of your own, not the couch. She said that you were good kids. She wanted you to have nice things like other kids. She was your first mommy. She will not be taking care of you any more. It is her choice. She knows where you are and wants you here."

The girls were listening and crying. Allie became more engaged on an emotional level. Allie was remembering the kindergartens that she had attended, left, and missed.

They all took a little break, getting some juice and stretching. After a little break, which allowed the girls' brains to assimilate some of the information, the social worker went on.

She offered the simplest descriptions of how things worked in Carrie's house. The social worker asked the girls for their terms for the bathroom and when they had to go, who wore pull ups at night, whether Tammy needed bathroom help, when people ate, how to get help, and which rooms and spaces were open or private. They also talked about trouble. The caseworker said that if the girls got too hard to handle they would not go back to the birthmother, instead they might have to go take a nap or sit in the time-out chair.

Carrie handled the more positive things. She asked Allie

and Carrie what they ate. Did the girls like to sleep together? Did they like a night light? Did they have their toys with them? What were their special things?

Carrie said, "I know that you are sad right now, and scared. Any child would be. I am glad that you are here so that I can take care of you. I like taking care of children with brown eyes."

The caseworker left the picture of the birthmother's home and their home, which was drawn during the discussion. Carrie taped it on the kitchen wall by the table. Carrie also drew a simple schedule for the rest of the day in picture form, with six basic pictures. She taped that up, as well.

Carrie called her father, who arrived with groceries that included foods that the girls were familiar with. He was instructed about and sensitive to the fragile state of the girls. His visit was to be short. When he delivered the groceries, he was introduced as PapPap. He took some unobtrusive pictures of the girls, impulsively picked Carrie up and twirled her, yelled "Yahoo!" in the driveway, and went home. (Pap-Pap's pictures were printed and in circulation in record time!)

The grocery bags contained a number of wonderful surprises from PapPap. Both girls showed a break in their mood to enjoy the surprises. But Carrie noticed that they did not stay with their new toys very long. Allie put her head down on the table, looking lost. Carrie patted Allie's hair in a comforting manner, but Allie seemed beaten down. She did not respond.

Allie would not brush her teeth that night. Carried remembered that the most important thing for the girls was to help them to calm down as quickly as possible. "It seems like you need to say no to something Allie," Carrie said. "What a sad and mad feeling you are having. You can tell me that you are mad and don't want to be here. I understand."

Allie declared, "I don't like anybody and I am going to be mad forever."

Dropping her voice to a comforting level Carrie said, "Thank you for telling me how you feel."

That night the girls were restless and afraid to sleep in

their new rooms. Carrie, Allie, and Tammy made a big bed in front of the fireplace and slept in the living room. Carrie said, "My job is to keep you safe. Right now, while you get used to our home, you can look over at me and see that you are safe." Carrie did not bring the children into her bed because of foster care regulations, and the fact that she did not know the children's histories as to sexual abuse. Carried locked the doors at night from the inside, as well as the outside, so that Tammy or Allie did not try to leave.

Over the next several days Carrie continued the pattern of a daily schedule in picture form. The girls cried for "Mommy" and asked where she was. They drew some pictures for her and continued to move through the reality of the move. Carrie spent some time rocking and bottle feeding Tammy for bonding purposes. Tammy began to lean into her. Carrie noticed that she had to make a special point to engage Allie, who was showing periods of dissociation several times a day. Allie would masturbate after dissociation. Carrie would bring Allie back to the present, helping her to re-engage with an activity.

Getting out her phone numbers from training class, Carrie called a therapist to see her daughter. She also scheduled physicals with the foster care and adoption clinic medical provider, who was able to screen for sexual abuse.

Carrie did not bathe the girls for two days. They acted terrified by the notion of a bath. She simply wiped their hands and faces. Carrie's mother, Nonny to the girls, brought the girls new swim suits with fish and flowers on them on day three. The girls were beginning to understand that Nonny and PapPap appeared with nice things. (Nonny and PapPap were celebrating that the "grandparent project," their term, was off to such a fine start.) Carrie let them wear the suits into the bathtub together. She promised to let them play in the Jacuzzi tub at Nonny and PapPap's house the next day. The girls wore swimsuits to bathe for over a month. They soaked off dirt rather than scrubbing. They were "clean enough," which was the standard for a while.

Both Allie and Tammy hit Carrie or tried to throw things when angry. Carrie would stand in front of them, hold their hands, and say, "No hurting anyone. This is a no-hurting house." Then, Carrie would take them back through the situation so that they could learn a more appropriate way. One day Allie threatened to beat Tammy with a toy when Tammy would not give it up. Carrie sat on the floor with the girls, demonstrating how to wait or trade. She had Allie choose which she wanted, trying things the friendly way or the time-out chair. Allie chose the time-out chair. "Maybe some other time you can try the other way," Carrie said.

Tammy said, "I'm going to try the other way." She made eye contact for approval. Carrie said, "Great. But I like that kid in the time-out chair, too!"

At that point, Allie got off the chair and started rolling around the floor, waving her feet in Carrie's face. Carrie took Tammy into the next room, playing there. Carrie said to Allie through the doorway, "This is a safe home. You need to sit down." Allie came into the room, ready for a fight. Carrie took Tammy into her bedroom and closed the door behind her.

Allie began to kick the door, yelling, "I want in now!"

Carrie opened the door saying, "You need to finish in the time-out chair. This is a safe house." She closed the door again as Allie screamed and kicked the door. Carrie continued to speak reassuringly to her, and after about fifteen minutes, Allie's crying changed in intensity.

Carrie opened the door and said, "Let's sit in that chair together." Carrie led her to the chair and sat in the time-out chair with Allie, holding her in her lap. Then she announced, "Done. Two minutes in the chair is done. Thank you, Allie." She gave Allie a smile. "Now let's get a drink and go outside to swing."

She noticed that Allie wanted to connect with her through confrontation. She watched that she did not set the pattern of the good versus the bad kid. The children were already showing that they had a pattern developed in former home settings of one preferred and one less preferred child. Carrie became skillful in connecting with Allie in positive ways before Allie had the chance to act out for attention.

This is a vignette that describes proceeding when children are moved in shock. Carrie used support and asked for what she needed. The caseworker would have left much more abruptly had Carrie not asked for assistance. Because of loyalty issues it was better for the caseworker to discuss the finality of the birthmother's decision. Carrie was active in setting up the caseworker's next visits before the caseworker left. She had a competent but busy caseworker.

Carrie helped the girls move into a sensitive relationship with her. She accepted the sad and angry feelings that were natural. Carrie used foods that the girls were familiar with. She also helped them to get comforting rituals established with the blanket, bunny, rocking, and sleeping with access to her. She recognized the avoidance around baths and bedtime and dissociation that indicated trauma in Allie, and possibly Tammy as well. She got mental health care immediately for assessment and treatment.

Carrie kept things low-key and predictable in the home. Notice that she got her relatives to help her get food and swimsuits soon after the girls arrived. She did not have enough knowledge or behavioral control to take them out to stores yet. She waited until she knew her daughters a little more. She tried to keep their stimulation level, and hers, within a tolerable level.

Emergency moves

Sometimes there are extreme circumstances which necessitate a jolting move. Caseworkers should be aware that, no matter what their age, children in these circumstances may not be processing what is happening in their lives. Children will exhibit the parallel manner of processing that was described in earlier chapters on trauma. As a result, they will sometimes operate on an "automatic pilot" that belies how deeply they have been affected.

Watch for children who look as if they are simply proceeding with life, as this almost always indicates a delayed grief reaction. Spend time with such a child, processing what is happening to them and the facts that necessitated the rapid move. If possible, find someone the child knows well, and have them help comfort and speak to the child compassionately.

Children do not grieve with strangers and cannot do their grief work without facts and access to the emotional strength of others (Gray, 2012). Former foster parents, respite workers, former therapists, preschool teachers, school teachers or counselors are all helpful people who can be brought into a situation in order to give children a sense of consistency and identity.

Do not be surprised if the careful explanations given about what has happened are soon forgotten or twisted. The more shock children are in, the less they integrate. That is why it is such a good idea to work with interactive booklets, which can be reviewed. Booklets give children the ability to go over things more than one time.

Post-placement Visits and Services

Post-placement resources for families

Thankfully, the federal mandates written to help place children into adoptive families in the U.S. have been successful. Additionally, agencies are beginning to successfully meet new Hague standards for intentional adoption. However, the drawback is that the development of support systems for families post-placement is still a work-in-progress, with some areas of the country far ahead of others.

The current position of the North American Council on Adoptable Children (NACAC) in regard to the need for post-placement services for adoptive families is as follows.

Necessary Post-Adoption Services

Post-adoption services must be available to families—including all members of the adoptive family and the birthparents—whenever they are needed. Each state and province should develop a system for ensuring that all families who adopt children with special needs—especially children adopted from the foster care system—have access to the services described below.

Services should be provided by people and organizations that are adoption-competent, and should include (but not be limited to) the following:

- information and referral from a single entry point (including a toll-free number answered 24 hours a day/7 days a week)
- support groups for adoptive parents, birthparents, and adoptees
- support for connections with birthparents and other birth-family members and former foster families, whenever possible
- training on special needs and adoptive parenting
- educational and information services
- therapeutic counseling
- respite care
- full disclosure of all background information
- case management services
- advocacy and support for school-related problems
- adoption assistance payments (subsidy for children adopted from foster care)
- other financial assistance when needed
- crisis intervention
- mental health services, both in-home and residential.

The sources for these services may include

- states, provinces, and territories
- counties
- placing agencies or professionals
- parent support groups
- resource and referral services
- child advocates/ombudsmen
- medical insurance companies/health care providers.

Post-placement visit assessments

The caseworker arriving at the home post-placement should have re-read the family's homestudy report and the information gathered about the child in pre-placement visits. Each worker should arrive at the home with a clear idea of what is typical for a child of that age, behaviorally and developmentally. Certainly the worker can adjust that depending on the child's experiences, or lack of them, but they need to know what is and what is not typical for a particular age. Placement agencies should have developmental schedules for children on-hand.

Caseworkers should also have lists of referral organizations for their families, and phone numbers and websites that are up-to-date. Depending on the community, some of these numbers will be for supportive services that will coordinate care for parents. These numbers may also be for referrals for specific service providers.

Post-placement visits with healthy infants should include playing with the baby and making certain that pictures and letters are going to birthparents if this was a prior agreement, or that the post-placement reports required by foreign countries are up-to-date. Caseworkers must also suggest adoption-related books and periodicals and groups to support adoptive parents and guide families through "adoption ages and stages."

Modern post-placement visits contain casework activities that may include referrals for many specialty services. This does not mean that caseworkers should not celebrate with families. However, they should also not limit the post-placement visit to merely checking to see that things are generally fine. The post-placement visits should be used to deliver specific casework services, with resources and recommendations for evaluations and specialized parenting approaches.

Red flags to watch for in post-placement visits

Parents expect behavior not typical of normal childhood

When parents lose sight of normal childhood development, expecting much more than developmental progress allows, there is trouble ahead. The set-up for the child is that the parents will always be disappointed and displeased. The child can never feel like a wanted and accepted child.

"She is so self-centered," parents complained. "Everything is about her." Their child was not yet 3 years old.

When they read a child development section with me

on children at their daughter's age, they realized that their daughter was actually about on-track. I discussed with parents what their expectations were: a cuddly, curious, companionable, social, eager family member able to occupy herself for periods of time, wait during important phone calls and during times when parents got ready for work—about 45-60 minutes. I told them that the family member who usually was expected to have such traits was called a *dog.*

Neither parent was quite up to the compromises necessary in parenting. I had no easy solutions for them, since it was a stand-off as to who would make the sacrifices necessary to prioritize the child.

We approached this situation by my talking about my sadness. I told the parents that I was sad that they were so pressured by their work and hobbies that they would be missing their daughter's early years. I was sad for their daughter that she was unable to be anything other than a small child, and that she got messages that she was not acceptable.

The parents came to grips with the concept that their current lifestyle did not support parenting. They began a conversation about needed changes in their expectations and commitments.

Parents treat the child as an emotional peer

"I look at it as a divorce," a mother said. Her attitude was that she had done her share in the relationship, and her young son had failed to do his. As she went on to describe the relationship, her frame of reference showed just how much she expected from her child emotionally. "I need to move out of this destructive relationship. This is just like the one with my first husband. I will never let anyone ever take me for granted again."

In this situation disruption was around the bend. The parent did some counseling, but she had come into the adoption with an attitude that the child was responsible for meeting her emotional needs and showing his appreciation through rapid molding to her ideals.

She said, "I have always been called controlling and rigid. I do not think that I am cut out for this type of parenting. I doubt that I can change."

The best that could be saved from this situation was time to find another placement and process with this 6-year old boy why he had to move. It turned out that he had been threatened with disruption from the first week of placement.

When parents are treating children as emotional peers, it is helpful to talk to them about how they would have felt as a child with that type of pressure. Often they are simply passing the pattern on. If they can remember their own childhood feelings, they may be willing to work on changes in counseling, but this is a difficult pattern to change. Children in such homes tend to do poorly. Sometimes the alternate parent in a two-parent family can help meet the child's needs more intentionally in these situations.

Parents enjoy their children's distress

Parents who are developing antipathy towards their children are sadistically pleased when their children are harmed. Sometimes this is wrapped into the guise of some type of natural consequence. While it is normal for parents to want their children to learn a lesson from a natural consequence, this is distinct from parents who enjoy watching children feel shame or pain.

Normally, parents feel a sense of pain and sadness when their children suffer from the consequences of dubious behaviors. Parents who are empathetic have to resist the urge to intervene so that their children can learn from mistakes. They focus on the lessons that can be learned from childhood errors, instead of the reaction, "Serves him right!" When parents have more of an attitude of, "Ha, ha, ha, look who is miserable now," it is an ominous sign.

Some of these parents are in great need of respite and self-care. They will be more empathic if they can get some sleep and time to themselves. Sometimes they need more help in handling specific problem behaviors so that they are not so frustrated. Sometimes the child is quite difficult and needs more effective individual and family therapy.

The key is to determine whether this is a stress reaction or part of the parent's character. The character attributes of a parent will be resistant to change. Some parents admit to enjoying their child's distress and are upset that they enjoy it. These people are much more workable as they and their caseworker or therapists talk through their reactions. Other people are fixed in a sadistic pattern. Disruption is better than having a sadistic parent.

Parents equate their child with their own former abusers

Parents can experience powerful feelings of being out-of-control when children are difficult. Sometimes parents have had similar feelings when someone abused them emotionally or physically in the past. This was the case with one parent, who said in a session, as she began to cry, "She seems a lot like my first husband when he became so angry and rejecting towards me."

Usually, immediate counseling and support can help these parents work through old issues. However, sometimes a parent has adopted a child so that they can master their abuse situation through a re-enactment. These cases constitute dangerous situations for the child. Disruption should be considered if the pattern cannot be interrupted. In two-parent families, the alternate parent can be asked to provide the day-to-day parenting until the parent with unresolved issues can work through them and move on to a healthier way of relating to the child.

A man approached me in a straight-forward manner when we worked on his son's anger in the family: "My son is reminding me of a bully, notably my father. I react randomly. Sometimes I fold and sometimes I yell. How about a referral for some counseling for me?"

This was a sensible and productive course. His parenting steadied.

Parents scapegoat the child

In describing a family history, relatives depicted the mother as someone who always feared that her son would become a menacing alcoholic. She was suspect of his character, even though he had been placed at birth with no prenatal exposure to dangerous substances. She predicted large problems before he was even 2 years old. He was the reason that her life was going to be ruined. By age 14, he was using drugs and alcohol and threatening her.

During the post-placement visits a plan could have been made in time to intervene on behalf of this family. Scapegoat patterns take a while to work through, but the family mentioned above had the time. Simply asking the family what their hopes were and what they most hoped would not happen would have opened a necessary conversation.

I have had good luck talking to families about the tendency to use a scapegoating pattern (especially if parents themselves were raised in a scapegoating family) and have offered them ways to avoid being a family that blames, accuses, and fights. Family therapy to change these patterns can help support the changes in the family. Most families want to steer away from such family patterns at all costs!

A preteen girl made great progress in therapy. After the parents acknowledged how much better she was doing, their marriage problems became extreme. They had notable conflict. Within two weeks, they were back into the office talking solely about how impossible their daughter was.

I met with the girl, whose response to the marital crisis was escalating symptoms again. "I'd rather be the problem than to have my parents divorce," she said. "I hate to look out into the driveway and to see my Dad's car gone. Mom will be on the streets if Dad goes."

The last message was one that she had heard during a shouting match between parents and taken seriously. "I feel bad that I am the problem, but Mom says that she can't handle me on her own." Her clarity was remarkable. Of course, she also took on the shame of her behavior.

In cases like this, both parents need to grapple with their marital issues and how children are paying the price. The parents in the scenario above agreed that talking to her about their problems was long overdue. They told her that they had had long-term marital conflict, but could both commit to parenting her. They told her that whether she acted out or not would not affect their marriage in the long-run. They went into marriage counseling, working on their issues rather than talking about her misbehaviors.

Parents threaten to kick the child out of the family

Parents destabilize children massively when they give them a sense that their place in the family is conditional. Building a sense of security and safety is fundamental in any family. When parents lose their tempers and threaten things like, "Well, I'm fed up too. You want a new home, then here's the phone and the number. Call the agency!" there is an immediate need for repair. Threats of removal from the family cannot become a way to force children to behave.

There can be situations in which children's behaviors are beyond what families can live with. When this becomes the reason for a potential disruption, I describe to children that, while their family does love them, the behaviors are too extreme to accept. We have used therapeutic respite care or short-term hospitalizations to help children gain better behavioral control. However, in those cases we emphasized that they still had their family and their home while they were away. Children who have pushed and pushed their parents to test limits, especially after failed placements, often get the message after respite care.

> "I hate having to go to the respite provider to work on how to follow rules," one boy said. "I think that I'd rather work on following rules at home."
>
> His parents said, "Exactly what we want, too! We'd rather have you at home."

This is a healthy message for extreme behaviors. The message that predicts disruption is one where the parents have the ultimate disciplinary weapon—kick the child out of the house.

Divorce threats

Some parents find that the stress of a special needs child on the relationship is more than they can handle.

> A woman said to me, "I'm hardened by too much stress. When my husband wants some attention, I tell him to get in line. I know that's not right, but I'm too tired to listen to anybody else by the end of the day."

There is a much higher rate of divorce among parents with special needs children, whether those children are born to the family or adopted by their families. Since many of the children being placed today will be considered to have special needs, families need extra protection for their relationships. Gottman weekends are great resources for couples who need to increase closeness and cooperation in a hurry. The Resource List of this book includes the website for this resource.

Depression in parents

It can be extremely hard on the parent's regulation to parent dysregulated children. The parent is constantly using his own stress regulation to bring children into a regulated state. The attachment process to a little one who is sad and scared can induce the same feelings in the caregiver.

As a result, there is a high rate of clinical depression, both with and without anxiety, in adoptive parents of children with special needs. Unfortunately, depressed parents have a hard time with attachment, sleep patterns, organization, energy, and problem-solving—at the time that they most need competence in these areas. Professionals should recommend and support parents getting enough sleep, exercise, good food, access to supportive friends, and positive activities in order to best protect themselves from depression. However, some of the shifts in the parent's emotional states are more complex than explanations of self-care. Counseling and a consult for medication should be pursued promptly when depressive symptoms present. Many parents use an antidepressant to help them to sustain a positive mood. An antidepressant also can help with feelings of guilt, which are unwarranted.

> One woman said, "I love this antidepressant. I can organize my time better, making decisions quickly about how to handle my son. I feel like I have been in a fog for about a year. I now have the energy to exercise every day, too. I don't think that I'm going to be in any hurry to get off this medication."
>
> Her husband said, "I have been telling her to get help for a long time. She changed slowly enough that she could not see the difference in herself. She's able to manage her life now."

Some parents have gotten depressed and then describe feeling as if they are weak when not handling the challenges of normal parenting. In fact, some of the parenting that is being undertaken with the children on which this book centers is high stress! And, the parents aren't able to leave the stress at the end of the day. It is full-time. The work of Dr. Elinor Ames includes looking at the stress levels of adults parenting children from orphanages in Eastern Europe. The stress levels are extremely high in parents (Ames, 1996). My experience is that the wear and tear on parents in domestic adoptions can be quite high, as well.

Any parenting is essentially an in-home rehabilitation program after a child's early neglect and trauma. Parents need to be warned about depression so that they can take prevention seriously and obtain treatment early.

Disruption and Dissolution

When families cannot or will not go on

Sometimes families are giving all of the signs of being too worn out to go on. Some of those signs were discussed in the above section. Parents who are at the end of their rope think in terms of "It's him or me."

Parents who start to think in terms of one of them prevailing and surviving, and the other not, are in the danger zone. Parents expressing that sentiment need an emergency intervention. If not, a crisis will follow to force a resolution. There is high risk for physical or psychological harm in the family when parents are expressing these thoughts.

Putting in emergency support works well. Many counties have wrap-around services that prevent further out-of-home placements or hospitalization. While these programs vary, they commonly include in-home therapy and a behavioral specialist or parent aide who intervenes on a daily basis. Usually there is emergency access on a 24-hour basis. Often prompt medication consultations are available. The Homebuilder Model is a successful one-month intensive model to bring family functioning up rapidly. Families can ask to be enrolled in crisis services but may need to wade through several numbers to find the route for access. If families know that they are in a tough placement, finding out about access before it is needed is a prudent course.

Sometimes caseworkers or therapists can pull in extended family members for help. The parents may simply be too worn out to think and plan for help. Other family members can often step in, giving support.

Caseworkers should always discuss these cases with other people on staff. Others may see even more danger than the primary caseworker sees, or others may know of another approach to take in terms of resources or mentoring that will make a difference. Parents may need a mentor and/or some individual and intensive psychological help. Making a plan that includes help for parents can ensure not just the placement, but the family well-being.

In one case the child stayed with one parent while the other parent went into an intensive program to help with traumatic stress. He was the primary caregiver and was gone for three weeks. He was still quite fragile when he left the residential program. With careful rebuilding, the family ended up doing reasonably well. It took a great deal of attention to stress levels and extra nurturing parenting on the part of the other parent, as well as a commitment to try any reasonable approach to make things better.

When is it better now than later?

Sometimes children have parents who do not like them and who do not want to like them. Some children have parents who are scripting them for roles in the family's existing dysfunctional drama. Disruption or dissolution must be an option for these children.

All children deserve homes in which they will be fundamentally respected. Unless parents can realistically anticipate that transition, caseworkers should plan a dissolution and placement into another family. This is an extremely painful decision, so it should be allotted ample time and processing.

Sometimes, when parents are working on issues but are too tired on every level to go on and so give up, something shifts. They find that they move past the crisis point and want to continue parenting after all. Proceeding slowly means that children are not moved before the parents decide that they have made a mistake and can indeed meet the child's needs and the needs of others in the family after all.

Some traumatized children, especially older children, are unlikely to be adopted again after a disruption or dissolution. An out-of-home placement in which they can become prepared for the future should not necessarily be avoided.

> In therapy, a man told me about being used as a scapegoat by alcoholic parents and his exposure to sexual abuse by the extended family. Due to his acting out behaviors, he was placed in a group care situation that he stayed in for four years. In that situation, he met role models who helped him grow up to be a man with values. Years later, he reconciled with his adoptive parents, gaining insight and a sense of connection. He clearly understood that he could not have grown up in the family and probably would have self-destructed. However, he felt that some reconciliation with parents was in his best interests. "I know that I can get by without them," he said. "I did that for years. I like to talk to them, though. I know that they love me and my wife to the degree that they are able."

In situations where dissolution is being considered, insert a time frame into the decision-making process.

> One family decided that they would work as hard as they could for six months. If, within that time, their daughter could make progress to the degree that she was no longer a safety risk to a younger sibling, then they would proceed as a family. If not, they would disrupt.

Other families have come in to consult with me, agonized. They could not keep a member of the family safe. Sometimes the treatment with a therapist has not been successful. I have seen parents whose other children were developing symptoms of traumatic stress. When other children in the family are being sexually assaulted or are witnessing assault of the parents, and no plan for treatment has been successful, out-of-home placement or dissolution may be the best option.

Sometimes children cannot resist the impulse to hurt younger, vulnerable children. Placement into another family may be necessary. When the family resources, emotionally and physically, are so depleted that the family cannot raise the child, looking for another adoptive family makes sense.

> A 5-year-old girl who had developmental delays and traumatic stress was initially placed into a family with three siblings under the age of 8. She became the family scapegoat. After a year of escalating rejection and, finally, repeated episodes of face-slapping by the mother, she was placed again into an experienced adoptive family.
>
> "Yes, she's hard," the new family explained. "We thought she would be. But we have the ability to supervise her. When it gets too rough she goes over to Grandma's house for a while. She's learning to play with her sister. She's not very likeable yet, but we do love her. With time and counseling, the rest will come along." It did.

Occasionally, parents do not like a particular child or the child does not like the parents. Sometimes, people just do not like each other and are not able to become close. Again, this is rare, but it does occur. Usually, these placements have occurred very quickly, with little time for parents and child to come to know one another, and the child's problems were initially described as "adjustment problems," though, indeed they were more complex. Looking for another placement makes sense in such cases.

Situations can be especially complicated when siblings are placed together, since the parents may be bonding to one child, and not to the other. Or, the child may have an attachment to her sibling, but not to the parents. There is no generic formula for how to help these types of problems. They need consideration on a case-by-case basis. It is important, though, to try to isolate a "why" the parents and child are having the problem.

It may be that parents have felt coerced into bring another child into the family. Their lack of commitment becomes evident early.

Persuading parents to take a sibling by saying that they come as a pair tends to be a poor long-term strategy on the part of social workers. While these placements can work, usually they require revisiting and processing the reasons why the family had originally restricted themselves. For example, if the "why" is a lack of time and energy, usually providing more resources will make the placement viable.

Some parents have a difficulty with children's autonomy. Be certain to ask not only about a child's needs for nurture, but the process of autonomy when interviewing parents. Guiding a discussion that focuses on the teen years can help reveal these parents who, as one woman described herself, "just don't like bratty teens."

> One woman described a young child like this, "We feel that we can always turn her over to the State when she gets to be a teen. Then it will be their problem to find someone else for her."

These types of adopting parents are rare. Most would-be adopting parents are committed and will give a brief summary of the expected challenges and resources when asked about the teen years.

Dissolution sooner provides younger children with a better chance of being adopted by another family. In the case mentioned above, it was better for the child to enter a healthier family system early.

Working with children to understand disruption

When children are going to have to move, I help them understand that a combination of things is not fitting. I have told children things like, "This family thought that they were the adoptive family, but it turned out that they were really only ready to be an in-between family."

> I had a girl put on my shoe and try to walk around in it. Of course, she tripped and had a hard time. "What's wrong with the shoe?" I said.
>
> "It doesn't fit!" she said.
>
> "That's the way that your family was with you. It just didn't fit. You couldn't get far without having troubles." We reviewed the problems: a father who worked long hours, a

mother who was a perfectionist, constant fighting over details, the lack of contact with any other children, and so forth.

She observed, "I think they wanted a perfect 'girly girl;' someone who could make them look good. I couldn't do that. They were always saying, 'It's our way or the highway.' In kindergarten, I was thinking, 'What highway?' I did not get what they meant. Now I wish that I had one more chance, but it's too late. Now I get what they meant." She wiped away tears.

We were able to talk about how much she did care for her family and how she never wanted to go through a dissolution again. She and I discussed the need for a family who was not a "my way or the highway family." It was new information to her that most families do not threaten this. I put on her shoe and told her that families that require that are like shoes that are too small. They are always pinching.

We were able to discuss and list all of the things that she did learn in her family and talk about what new skills she could take into the next family. We discussed her pushing-away behaviors honestly, and how they made things hard for others. We talked about alternatives that she would want to practice when she felt like pushing people away. We also prepared her next family. I let them know that she did not want to move, even if she said or acted as if she did.

While a disruption or dissolution is always heartbreaking, it is important to process the meaning behind it in order to salvage some lessons and share some blame. In the example above, I shared that the adoptive parents' expectations should have been questioned in the homestudy. With careful processing, this child went on to have a rocky beginning but ultimately a successful adoption experience.

Committees can help prevention disruption

In looking at factors that prevented disruption, Hilde Price-Levine found that the use of committees who made written placement plans was effective in preventing future disruption (2004). The committee was able to correct for a caseworker's possible bias or blind spot. The adherence to a written plan that all parties signed made certain that the placement process occurred as planned. When used in conjunction with careful screening and training, the committee's efforts improved placement success.

Kudos and Quotes

This chapter must finish with some of the positives that I frequently hear from families and professionals.

Recently a family described their relationship with their agency. "We were very well prepared. They were thorough, gave us practical support, and have been there every step of the way for us. They have handled some complicated issues with our boys' birthparents, who have drug problems, letting us correspond with them safely. They helped us to contact the birthparents for some medical information. They took a lot of time transitioning our sons to us, so we had a chance to get to know the boys."

The parents went on to describe the agency contacts with therapists and how they coordinated therapy and placement processes.

This example illustrated the excellence of casework. The family felt prepared. They needed and obtained sound information. The family had access to caseworker time. They were dealt with promptly. The family had the ability to receive some post-placement services, so that they could continue to get help with some continuing contact issues. The caseworker coordinated the children's therapy and placement issues, smoothing a rocky start.

In another situation a family said,

"We love how our agency helped us form connections with other families. Not only do they have a great summer camp, but they told us about a research study that helped us deal with our son's medical condition. They have specialized information. They told us about The Center for Adoption Medicine, who referred us to you. You helped us, and also referred us to a neuropsychologist. Our agency's staff know which doors open other doors. We know that we can call them if we have a problem."

This organization excelled in aiding the formation of the family's positive identity as an adoptive transracial family. They were given organized ways to spend time with families similar to theirs. The family did not need the agency to know every resource, but they did need referral to key resources that could refer, in turn, to other specialized services. The agency was a source of ongoing support.

Another parent said, "I thought that I must be doing a lousy job. My daughter acted disgusted with me even six months after placement!

"My caseworker said, 'There's good news and bad news. The good news is that your parenting is pretty good. That's also the bad news. Let's find out why your daughter is not attaching as she should. We'll get you some help. Let's find out some answers so that she can start bonding with you.'

"That was so reassuring. I was afraid that nothing could be done or that I was flawed. I thought that they would suggest moving my daughter. Our caseworker gave us three numbers for help—and all of them worked! Now it seems impossible to believe that my daughter and I ever struggled with attachment. She spends time with me, talks to me all of the time. She is not fearful. Her biggest issue is getting off the phone to get her homework done."

This typifies a successful casework intervention. The caseworker assessed the problem, supplied hope and support, and accurately referred. The resources were current. The interventions were effective.

Another family said recently, "Our adoption support program manager, Aaron Washington, has been so helpful. He helps us to provide the resources that we need for our sons. I feel like we are old friends after all of these years. He's friendly and professional. He calls back! What a pleasure to have a person to call and a system that works!"

Individuals make such a difference in these interactions. Even though this worker is only one part of a larger community, his part makes a big difference to the families with whom he works. The words *accessible, effective*, and *resource-rich* come to mind as great casework attributes.

Yet another family described the process that their caseworker went through in assessing and preparing their daughter.

> "Sandra, the caseworker, knew so much about our daughter from visiting her in the foster home. I was amazed at how many things she could tell us. It helped us enormously in getting the educational piece set up as well as a daily structure. By the time we had visits in our home, we felt like we could be successful. We took our time, but our daughter was ready to be adopted. She went through her lifebook with us and told us about herself. She and her caseworker told us how to make her adjustment easier and what her dreams were. I listened and thought. 'Hey, we can do all of that! Welcome home.'"

Summary

The issues that caseworkers deal with in their practice are certainly daunting. Breaking these issues down into steps helps caseworkers successfully guide prepared families into well-fitting placements that include the necessary resources. The entire child welfare field should be commended on the increased rate of adoption in older children both domestically and internationally. Following-up on these placements with the necessary supports for families, however, is currently a work in progress. The tools that are described in the sections above will help caseworkers acquaint families with the realistic nature of parenting, the tasks that are most critical, and the services that parents and their children will find the most helpful in forming thriving families.

CHAPTER 10

The Role of the Mental Health Worker

"I used to be afraid all of the time, mad all of the time. Now I know that I have a family to keep me safe and to take care of me. I worked on hard abuse stuff so its not on my mind."   –Jamie, aged 12

Working with children and families who are requesting relief from emotional dysregulation, traumatic stress, and loss is not for the faint-hearted therapist. This section is written not just as a guide to essential therapeutic tasks, but as an encouragement to those who are undertaking this challenging work.

This chapter uses examples to describe classic cases. A common thread in all cases is the ability of the therapist to care for and respect children in the context of their families. The therapist sees children and families, in all their authenticity, and joins with them as they work toward daily patterns of emotional balance. The therapist envisions and helps create warm and resonant family interactions. These balanced patterns and qualities in a therapist are what all families hope for when they seek counseling.

Necessary Accommodations in Therapeutic Approach

Therapies will have to include necessary accommodations in order to effectively treat this specialized population of children. Some of these areas of accommodation were described in a general manner in earlier chapters. This section provides specific information necessary to complete successful therapeutic plans for children who have been subjected to abuse, neglect and/or trauma.

Stress regulation capabilities

One fundamental difference in working with children with the backgrounds described in this book is in their underdeveloped stress regulation systems. Not only do these children need to learn some skills to calm themselves, but they must open themselves to the support and the better regulated brains of the therapist and parents. They will not be able to work on trauma and loss unless they feel connection and safety with an adult. This connection permits some "borrowing" from the adult's stress regulation abilities. A therapeutic goal is to teach children to view both the therapist and the adoptive parents as safe adults,

As mentioned in earlier chapters, stress regulation systems tend to be taught through early attachment systems. Most therapies presuppose that children already have some resources for dealing with stress, and that they view adults as agents who help with problem-solving. The children that most therapists will see coming out of the foster care system or from international orphanages do not have this background. Children coming from orphanages may never have had even one attachment. Other children of neglect or abuse may have been so affected by the home atmosphere of drugs or alcohol that their deprivation is profound. Not only do these children lack the foundation for stress regulation, they also do not have a conceptual map for healthy family roles.

Teach and Practice Family Roles in Real Time

The most efficient way to foster attachments with these children is through direct interventions between children and their parents. The therapist can invite the dyad to do the initial work on attachment together, rather than separating the parent in the waiting room.

In the tradition of Selma Fraiberg and Daniel Stern, the therapist changes the children's and parents' representational models through direct contact (Fraiberg, 1977; Stern, 1985, 2004.) This direct contact begins the process of neural imbedding between parents and children, to permit the building of a stress regulation system in the child.

Traditional modalities like sand tray, puppets, or drawings are less effective in changing these children's views of their parents. These play therapies do not give children the guidance they need to work on forming attachments. (They remain helpful resources for other therapeutic issues.)

Often the children on which this book focuses simply have no idea what the role of parents might be. Or, they may sense the love and comfort that might come from closeness with the parents but feel desperately afraid of wanting this. They have learned that love comes at a high price, costs like loss, abuse, or rejection. Sometimes they have never experienced love at all. Their solution to this dilemma is to control their parent's actions and their degree of closeness. Parents temporarily accept this control during the initial adjustment after adoption, with the anticipation of a gradual relaxation of controlling behaviors over time. However, this control may not diminish; trauma and neglect continue to act as anxiety heightening agents long after the actual instances of trauma and neglect have ceased.

Therapists may fall into a similar pattern of allowing children to control. Allowing these controlling behaviors results in a failure to give children the foundational help in forming attachment, learning to calm, or learning how to get help. Giving children intentional support in calming and attachment allows them to open up to the necessary work on trauma and grief.

One of the most avoidant children I worked with told his mother, "I have something that I need to talk to Deborah about. When do I see her?" After she told him when the appointment was, he went on to say, "I like to see her. I feel better after." His mother was in the room for the therapy sessions, at his preference, but he correctly used the therapy room to process sexual abuse issues.

When I had first seen him in therapy, this child was quite controlling and found surfacing these sexual issues to be too painful. I structured the sessions to give him a skill set for relaxation and helped him improve the quality of attachment, which allowed him to decrease control. This boy's therapy will be in discussed again in a section called "Chris' Therapy" later in the chapter.

Organizing Memories Meaningfully

Typical children's therapies assume that children will organize their memories—with support and in a play therapy medium. Some of the effects of neglect mentioned earlier in this book demonstrate that many children cannot organize memories effectively. Help children move through the tasks of therapy by initially forming a plan for the therapy with them and then organizing an approach with them each session.

The child-therapist alliance must be flexible enough for children to reflect, share, and sometimes lead. It must also be structured to the extent that children feel security through predictability in the sessions. This balance aids pacing and anxiety issues so that children do not re-experience trauma and hyper-arousal in session; the degree of emotional arousal needs to remain within a child's working tolerance.

Use pictures, lists, and self-made booklets that describe and summarize the work that has just been done to help children retain more information in their working memories. Use tools like these when reviewing how topics just addressed fit into the "big picture." In session, I usually draw a picture at the end of each session summarizing what we did, even if just we role-played and talked.

Visual references also help children with executive dysfunction. However, adapt therapy for children with executive dysfunction. These adaptations should help children make meaning of their lives, not just through the tasks chosen, but through the methods chosen.

Prenatal Exposure to Substance: Using Strong Modalities

Children with prenatal exposure to drugs and alcohol, in particular, can be helped through role-play and visual work. These children may or may not generalize from one part of the brain to another. Sand tray and play therapy techniques simply may not lead to changes in substance-exposed children's mental schemas or their behaviors.

One difficulty which occurs with FASD is that affected children tend to behave as if they are understanding much more than they actually are understanding. The therapist should ask the child to repeat what is being talked about or worked on in his own words. The reflected message is often astonishingly far afield. Children with FASD regularly demonstrate that they have taken a few of the words discussed in session and added a completely different meaning, or that they have missed the main point. Make certain that you are using feedback loops throughout sessions with children with FASD.

Treatment Limitations

Therapists who have the internal capacities, the skills, and the support to work through trauma with their clients will work best with the variety of cases discussed in this book. Some therapists feel out of their depth with these clients and may want to move children on to another therapist when these children begin to move into trauma issues. These therapists should clearly state to their families, from the beginning, their actual availability and capacity to treat all aspects of the child's needs. Traumatized children need as few changes as possible in therapists. Children should be warned if there are going to be limits on how much work is accomplished.

Children who have just entered families represent a special need for initial adjustment work. This is a great area for specialization; it provides a niche for therapists who enjoy short-term work. Therapists who are planning for upcoming job changes or family leave might want to consider taking on either these initial adjustment cases or those of anxious children without trauma, as described later in this section.

Alternatively, if children are only coming in for a couple of sessions, it is important to limit the scope of the work.

> For example, in one case, I agreed to meet for two sessions with Christina, a 9-year-old in a short term foster home who was dissociative and aggressive. I told her at the beginning that we were only going to meet twice, and that we were not going to talk about her whole life story.
>
> In the first session we worked on what specifically was keeping her so angry. In talking, it was clear that she missed her father, who was in another state. Rather than sharing her loneliness with anyone, she became angry and resistant. We set up a plan so that she could signal when she was missing her father. Then she could get a hug from her foster mother.
>
> In the second session, she went on to write to her father, including a picture for him. This helped her to get some comfort and a means of expression for her pain. We did not delve into the untreated sexual abuse or emotional abuse issues. This longer-term work was delayed until she relocated geographically.

Assessments

Medical assessments

Be certain that children have been seen by their pediatricians or family physicians before they begin treatment. Check for health problems that may be causes or contributing factors for emotional problems. In my practice, I have encountered many medical problems masquerading as behavioral difficulties, including ear infections and hearing issues, information processing issues, juvenile diabetes, thyroid imbalances, herbal remedies incorrectly used in conjunction with medications, infections and parasites, and asthma medications. Certainly ADD is both a source of and a contribution to behavioral difficulties.

One pediatrician told me, "I have been practicing for so long that I can tell what is going on with families about five minutes after they come into the room." She was right. Even though the process of change was in my hands, it was certainly helpful to ask for her observations. Getting a summary from the physician speeds the progress of overall care.

Many children will need extra time during medical appointments. Adoption and foster care medical clinics and practices offer this extra time, pay special attention to referrals, and have access to additional resources. While still not available in every state, let alone every city, such clinics are becoming more numerous and therefore more generally accessible, acting as sources of specialized information and referral services to treat the complex needs of children who are moving from domestic foster care into adoption or who are coming into the country through international placement.

In my area of the country, The Center for Adoption Medicine through the University of Washington has a particularly helpful website with developmental information, especially suited to adopted children. Julia Bledsoe and Julian Davies, the pediatricians at the clinic, have made excellent information on ADHD, regulation, prenatal exposure to substance, and other issues available though this public resource. (Several similar clinics across the country have similar sites. Please see Resource List.)

Educational assessments

The education system has its own language and culture. Educators do not speak the language of the DSM, adoption, or even effects of maltreatment on development. They have their own way of defining the certain handicapping conditions that they will accommodate. Their assessments, then, only look for these conditions. Boris Gindis, a developmental psychologist and expert on children adopted from international orphanages, points out that schools are mandated to assess children if parents request an assessment. But, the request for assessment has to use terms that reflect the school's mandate. For example, one might say, "I am concerned that my child may have an educationally handicapping condition that may interfere with education and learning. I would like an assessment."

Parents should request this assessment in writing. The school is federally mandated to do an assessment as a response to a written request from parents, and then follow up with recommendations for services, if children qualify. Ideally, try to arrange that the learning assessment for a child arriving internationally be done by a professional who speaks their language. If a professional who speaks the language is not available, find an interpreter who is trained in medical interpretation (Gindis, 2005). This topic is continued later in this chapter, in the Speech and Language Assessment section.

Neuropsychological assessments

An evaluation by a pediatric neuropsychologist, or a psychologist with a specialty in neuropsychological assessments, can be invaluable in understanding how children approach their world. This type of assessment investigates the brain's process as it understands tasks, whether the brain plans, how long or accurately it stores information, how much information it handles before it gets tired, how it solves problems and applies solutions to new situations, how it arrives at conclusions, whether it speeds or slows in task accomplishment, how much detail or generalization it uses, and how parts of the brain work together when tasks become more complex. The assessment gives great information not only about how children learn and the best ways to teach them, but also about what is not effective and why.

Neuropsychology assessments are helpful when working with the school as well as in the home. In my own office, I change my methods based on these evaluations, catering them to each child's individual issues, such as processing loads and processing speed.

One girl could barely bridge concepts from one topic to the next either in my office or in school. Yet, the school testing did not reveal ADD. Their testing was too simplistic. This child, in fact, had the hallmark hyperfocus capacity, so she looked fine in a short-term setting without distractions, as was the case in the brief assessment setting. The real world, however, provided few such settings. A neuropsychological assessment diagnosed the ADD, and also revealed new, more effective ways to educate her.

The test results led to successes that helped this girl's self-confidence enormously. Success at school included not just being able to connect the ideas in academics, but also to connect through friendships. Achieving academically allowed her to feel far less anxious in the school setting.

Her school assessment had placed her IQ in the low 80s. The more complex neuropsychological exam, however, revealed some learning disabilities, as well as some areas in which she was normal and above average. The testing changed the way the school saw her academic potential, and it gave them approaches that would help her reach this potential.

Therapists are in a good position to make referrals for neuropsychological assessments. They are working closely enough with children to observe their unique needs when approaching and breaking down information. Optimally, these referrals should be made at ages 7 or 8, again at about 5th grade, and again at the beginning of high school.

Speech and language assessments

Language development tends to parallel the amount of nurturing stimulation that children have received in their early years. While there are exceptions, overall, language development is impeded in children coming from home or orphanage environments of social neglect.

This group needs extra attention to support their language development. Often these children can communicate in a concrete way without difficulty. Their ability to function in day-to-day communication can be good, as long as they can read body language, gestures, or can get assistance in language from others. Academic language does not contain these nonverbal clues, however, so this type of language can be much harder for children. They cannot rely on a gesture or a contextual clue when they are reading a book or trying to write a paragraph. Higher academic skills are difficult to attain when the fundamentals are underdeveloped.

Parents may not realize that their children are not processing complex language ideas, dismissing their difficulties as boredom or opposition. Parents might miss their children's frustration with their inability to follow directions, sequence, or use the cognitive language functions involved in forming sentences, decoding a story problem, and summarizing information from a book into an essay or a report. Instead, these families experience homework wars.

It is estimated that over half of internationally adopted children require special assessments and remediation in speech and language areas. This is not simply an English as a Second Language issue. It is, instead, a representation of their lack of early opportunity for learning the fundamentals of language and communication.

According to Dr. Boris Gindis, children 5 years and above should be evaluated within the first three months of arriving in the country, and within the first month if they are below 5 years of age. They should be evaluated in their native language by a person qualified to do such an evaluation. This evaluation will help to determine whether or not they need special services (Gindis, 2005). Try not to miss this window, as doing so will make it difficult to demonstrate that the issue is related to speech and language, rather than to second language acquisition, and the next opportunity will not occur for two years. Unlike other bilingual children, whose first language is supported in the home, internationally adopted children lose their native language about seven months after their arrival, if not quite a bit faster. Young children may lose it by about a month of age. Their primary language becomes English, since they actually only have one language within a short period of time (Gindis, 2005).

The amount of instructional time has a significant impact on how children respond to remediation efforts for speech and language issues. Two of the most successful programs, the Wilson and the Lindamood Bell methods, are effective not just because of their theoretical basis, but because of the large amounts of time that children spend in intense instruction (Gindis, 2005).

Boris Gindis has many excellent articles on speech and language and other learning issues on his website. He has co-authored a program that parents can use with their 3- to 8-year-olds that teaches attachment skills and speech and language simultaneously. This helpful program may be ordered through his website. (Please see the Resource List.)

Be sure to read through speech and language assessments carefully, as they often contain information on the best ways to communicate in therapy. Certainly children who are having difficulty expressing themselves or understanding their social contexts will be more likely to act out or oppose. A good evaluation will inform parents and professionals as to whether speech and language issues contribute to children's problems, and will identify the strength areas that can be utilized to help solve problems.

Psychopharmacology

Many of the children with high anxiety and attention problems will benefit from medication. Some children have depression, anxiety, or attention problems that interfere to the extent that they cannot make progress in therapy or school without medication. Usually, therapists allot time for getting to know children before referring for medication, so that they can wait to see if improvements can be made without the use of medication.

One girl, age 10, began to have anxiety attacks at school. While her pediatrician was willing to use medication, I asked first to spend a couple of weeks trying some relaxation techniques as part of cognitive behavioral therapy. I included some home phone calls before and after school to support the therapy. She calmed without the use of medication and became free of anxiety attacks.

Typically, therapists will work with a child psychiatrist when children have suspected mood disorders, PTSD, or need multiple medications. Pediatricians are excellent at working with ADD and stimulant medications. Many family physicians are experienced and comfortable with prescribing antidepressant or anxiety medications and/or a stimulant for ADD. Neurologists are especially helpful handling situations like static encephalopathy, autistic spectrum disorder, brain injury complications, and sensory integration dysfunction. Some nurse practitioners or physician's assistants also have specialized training and will help track and prescribe medications.

Medications and therapy work best when used in conjunction. However, even after therapy is successfully underway or has concluded, children/teens may need medication in order to maintain mood or to decrease anxiety. Teens have said to me, "I wonder if this is what my birthparents went through—they didn't have anybody like you to help and were without any antidepressants. No wonder they drank! I can't see myself going off of antidepressants."

Children who have suffered from neglect and deprivation experience a high rate of ADD in addition to executive dysfunction. Children who have prenatal exposure to alcohol are estimated to have a 60-80% rate of ADD. Parents often report the positive effects of treatment by stimulant medications, in terms of their efficacy in helping such children to inhibit impulsivity and stay on-task.

A 9-year-old boy said, "That pill makes me smart! Now I know what we are working on in class. I am going to tell Dr. Fleming, 'Thanks!'"

Another child said, "No more nightmares. No more guys-with-a-mask dreams. I take that pill and sleep."

These children's reactions illustrate the correct usage of medication. Medication is prescribed to increase coping and to decrease suffering.

Occupational therapy

"Sensory integration is the process by which the brain receives, organizes, and interprets information from the environment. The information is received by sensory receptors, such as the eyes, nose, ears, fingers, mouth, and skin... The information that is received from the environment is then sent to the corresponding regions of the brain where it is interpreted and organized. This process is what gives us our perception of the world. In children, it provides a crucial foundation for later, more complex learning and behaviors. Proper sensory integration helps us to maintain attention and build positive relationships with others. All of these things contribute to positive self esteem as well as the ability to learn and concentrate. In children, it provides a crucial foundation for later, more complex learning and behavior" (Chasnoff, 2006, pp.54-55).

For many children, the world seems too loud, too tippy, too rough, too bright and too chaotic. Neglect deprives children of the early activities that help their brains develop a normal tolerance for stimulation. Occupational therapists help children to stay physically regulated while living in an overstimulating world. Children can also learn calming approaches in occupational therapy that will help them in emotional situations.

Occupational therapy is not a solution or substitution for trauma treatment. Sensory issues tend to comprise a piece of the puzzle, or part of the difficulty that children are having, rather than being the source problem. Sometimes children will be seeing an occupational therapist for problems with overstimulation when they actually need trauma work. This issue can be confusing for the therapist, as well. Sometimes children who look dissociative when they actually have sensory integration dysfunction.[1] Many children have both chronic trauma _and_ sensory integration dysfunction as a result of experiencing prenatal exposure, neglect, and trauma before placement.

Certainly, some children need occupational therapy even in the absence of a history of maltreatment or neglect. Sometimes therapists are looking for an emotional reason for behavioral issues when

---

[1] Sensory processing dysfunction describes the difficulty that people have in taking information through their senses and using this information in a meaningful manner. Sometimes the sensory information may be perceived as too intense, not meaningful, or not integrated with other sensory stimulation. Some others may be sensory seeking, needing firmer touch, more noise, and bright lights. Children on either end of the continuum feel out-of-sync even in typically stimulating surroundings. It is hard for children with sensory processing disorders to move into complex learning when they are struggling with sensory issues.

children are actually distressed due to sensory issues. One boy I was treating needed less of me and more sensory integration work in order to succeed. His sister needed the reverse. It was a lesson in humility for me, as the parents were the ones who recognized that an adjustment needed to be made.

Diagnosing

Almost all of the children described in this book will have emotional dysregulation issues. In addition, they tend to exhibit more immature behaviors, more challenges with attachment, and higher levels of anxiety, attentional problems, and social problems, all of which make compromise, attunement, and empathy difficult.

These children have survived situations that would cause *anyone* to feel dysregulated. Lack of human affection and proper caregiving shapes the brain. Our goal as therapists, caseworkers, and parents is to provide new, positive experiences that will also shape the brain— and the beliefs children have about themselves and their worlds.

But all of these complexities make diagnosis tricky. When selecting a treatment plan, it is important to use an approach based on the primary needs of the child while simultaneously considering the approaches that will give them the resources and support to work on issues. A typical approach is as follows.

A 10-year-old boy had been in his home for five years before we began our work. We worked on attachment first, even though he also had ADHD symptoms and high anxiety. He began to crave hugs and parental attention. At first, he forgot to initiate hugs, but he did enjoy affection when it was offered. After he felt better connected, he told me about two situations of sexual molestation by an adult and long-term bullying by older children in his prior homes.

This child still had speech and language issues, and, after I gave a referral to a neurologist, he was diagnosed with static encephalopathy. The treatment plan, then, began with attachment work and then proceeded with trauma work. The boy was initially anxious all of the time, but responded with a sharp drop in anxiety after successful treatment. He began an ADHD medication after the diagnosis of static encephalopathy. This helped him to feel more successful in school and social situations.

In spite of the complexities of the diagnoses, we proceeded to work in a logical order. First, he improved the quality of attachment, which made him feel safer and secured his placement. Second, we focused on trauma, which was timely since he was sexually acting out. The trust that he had formed in attachment helped him with the trauma work. Empathy and attunement, which improved with the attachment work, were also useful during the trauma phase. He had a slow, but successful, course of therapy. This is typical for children with static encephalopathy, which is a common condition in children have been prenatally exposed to substance.

It is helpful to form working impressions about what is happening in children's lives prior to beginning treatment, i.e. how are they functioning? Why does it make sense for them to operate this way in their worlds? What needs to be different for them to behave and believe differently? This functional approach provides a practical view of changes in the environment and ways of approaching children and families.

Diagnose anxiety and trauma quickly, and make treatment plans for these areas. Patterns of attachment are altered in response to direct work with children in their families. Diagnoses like reactive attachment disorder should only be made after working with a child over an extended period of time. Note that this is a controversial diagnosis. In most children, the attachment problem is actually more closely associated with PTSD or grief than an attachment disorder. Even though I will start with treatment-focused on attachment, to help with regulation and attunement, I see attachment problems as secondary to the regulation issues: chronic trauma with emotional numbing, and/or grief in children.

Sometimes parents themselves have already "diagnosed" their children prior to meeting with me. They have decided that they have a "RADish" or "RAD" kid. I realize that they are looking for support and solutions, but I discourage this way of labeling a child. The label can lead to a dehumanization of children, allowing parental frustrations to slide into the realm of insensitivity, maltreatment, and cruelty. Phrases like "He's an attachment kid," or "She's RAD," are a misuse of the diagnostic purpose. People who lack resolution of their own pain may slip into the use of these labels to justify ugly ways of treating children, acting out retaliation as related to their own issues, towards children.

One father, after working on his relationship with his son, commented, "While my skin crawled last May at the thought of a summer with Jack, this year it didn't. Before treatment, the most beautiful sound in the world was the sound of the diesel engine as the bus pulled away from the house—and I could not hear that sound all summer. Now I like summer with Jack. It is so—relaxing. This is what my partner and I thought that parenting children would be like. And it's gone on all summer."

While their son did initially meet the criteria for reactive attachment disorder, we conceptualized in terms of building better patterns of relating. The son practiced talking to his father, feeling close, hearing about his father's feelings and talking about his own. We drew out, acted, and talked about the pain of losing so many homes. We did have to work on his defenses, what purpose they served, how he might be consequenced if he hurt others, and what more helpful responses than opposition and control might be. We modified our methods for prenatal exposure to alcohol. Our functional approach helped much more than acquainting his parents with a controversial diagnostic category. Children like Jack tend to advance and regress and then advance again. When parents hear reactive attachment disorder they become particularly wary of the regressions and may lose hope.

Often children's neglect issues will look like oppositional defiant disorder, because these children cannot handle very much stimulation. It can be difficult to tell the difference, initially, between neglect and an autistic spectrum disorder. The chart on the next pages shows the similarities. I will typically see strong progress after working with children over a series of sessions on their feelings, the feelings of others, and emotional regulation. If I am not seeing strong progress,

I will either refer children back to their pediatrician for further assessment, or directly refer them to a child psychiatrist or an autism clinic to assess for autistic spectrum disorder (ASD).

Children who qualify for the ASD diagnosis will find the diagnosis an advantage in obtaining services. Even though some extremely deprived children may eventually outgrow the diagnosis, it is still enormously beneficial when convincing schools and insurance companies to recognize a real need and to help accommodate and finance that need.

Paul Wang, M.D., has looked at post-institutionalized children and the extent to which they "outgrow" ASD (2003). This group of children is clearly moving out of the diagnosis much more often as compared to the group of children born in North America. The significant issue, however, is not how they picked up the spectrum of autism issues. The required resources for these children are very much the same, whether they outgrow the diagnosis or not. Assess and obtain the diagnosis so that the child can benefit from the array of specialized social skills groups, peer playmates, and parent techniques.

The following chart compares approaches across diagnostic categories.

Table 10-1

Diagnosis → Issue ↓	Asperger's Syndrome[2]	Autistic Spectrum Disorder	Neglect	Family and School Needs⊠
Affective Regulation (mood) Issues	Yes. Anxiety and anger due to predictability problems, sadness due to social rejection	Not unless the child is pushed into a difficult situation. Anxiety and anger result	Variable, with improvement in many children over time.	Needs to be skilled in handling their own affect and helping with children's affect
Control Issues	Yes. Cannot read body or social cues, Control instead of cope	Yes. Particularly when overwhelmed	Variable	All will need structure and adults able to teach social skills

Table 10-1 (Continued)

Diagnosis → Issue ↴	Asperger's Syndrome[2]	Autistic Spectrum Disorder	Neglect	Family and School Needs
Specialized Educational Needs	Needs predictable and structured classroom.	Variable, but needs a safe, predictable environment	Variable, depending on severity and length of time of neglect.	School must use placement preference, accommodations, and social skills groups.
Developmental Delays Lifelong	No	Probably	Probably not, but higher rate of learning disabilities.	Excellent assessments with defined future goals.
Capacity for Emotional Connection	Impacted, with improvement later into the life cycle. Improves with specialized help.	Variable. Attachment often delayed but does occur. Reciprocity is difficult.	Usually good given social and emotional help for children who lack empathy or self-reflection.	Home and school must promote emotional exchange within context and in real time.
Normal Experiences Overstimulate.	Yes	Yes	Initially, yes. Over time not usually.	Calm, predictable, interesting, and structured.

[2] Asperger's Syndrome is part of Autistic Spectrum Disorder but is broken out for clarity.

The chart above clearly illustrates that the techniques and accommodations used in most contexts for ASD are the same as those used for neglect. This is why a functional outlook is so important. It is enormously helpful for parents to know that there is a "why" for children's behavior so that they do not take it personally. It helps parents to come alongside children, recognizing their neurological differences instead of feeling defeated or as if their children do not care about them. Children with ASD require an intentional approach to skill-building.

Children commonly exhibit extreme moods at the beginning of therapy. Sometimes we already know the history, so we know that there is trauma work to be done. Sometimes the symptoms of traumatic stress are present in the absence of a known trauma history. It can be difficult initially to determine whether the child has traumatic stress or has FASD, which will require some accommodations. The chart below shows that many of the things done for traumatized children also work well for children who have been neglected or who have FASD.

Table 10-2

Diagnosis→ Issue ↓	FASD	Trauma	Neglect	Family Capacity Required
Affective Regulation problems (Emotions are unstable)	Yes	Yes, almost universal when trauma has happened before the age of four	Yes	Needs to be skilled in handling their own affect and helping with children's affect
Control	Yes Structure decreases control battles	Yes Predictable, safe homes decrease need for control	Variable	Need structure, skills in defusing control battles, and access to respite care
Specialized Educational needs	Yes, school will need to accommodate for success	Variable, but needs a safe, predictable environment	Variable	Needs to be able to advocate within school setting
Life Cycle Needs	Needs continued help in adult life	Prognosis for independence is good	Prognosis for independence is good	Resources and parent age a consideration with FASD.

Table 10-2 (Continued)

Diagnosis → Issue ↓	FASD	Trauma	Neglect	Family Capacity Required
Child Care Use for Working Parent(s)	In calm setting consistent child care provider tends to work well	Variable, In calm setting consistent child care provider often works well	Variable, but with careful attention to number of hours, consistent child care provider often works well	Flexible working schedule and access to structured, and nurturing day care
Normal Range of Experiences Causes Over-stimulation	Yes	Yes	Yes, with sensory integration problems common	Should be calming and structured

Many children who have experienced early trauma do not remember the trauma—but they have feelings related to the trauma. We can use a timeline to show children what their care may have been like as a baby, but I do not tell anything beyond what we can reasonably know.

For example, we worked on the history of one boy when he voiced his feelings of dislike for mothers. This boy had been a failure-to-thrive infant who gained weight quickly after placement, lost it again when he lived back with his birthmother, and gained it back when placed with a foster parent as a toddler. I told him, using his timeline, that he was not getting enough to eat back then. We drew a hungry, fussy baby. He said, "I just don't think that mothers like me."

I told him that we were not sure why he was not eating in the home with his birthparent, but since she was on drugs, it could be that she was not able to see his needs. This time he looked at his timeline and the six placements after that and said, "I should have gone from here," pointing to his picture of birth, "to here," pointing to placement with his father. "I'd be nicer if I didn't have all those mothers giving me away."

His choice of words was telling. It gave us the opportunity to talk about short-term foster care, rather than "mothers giving me away." Using the timeline, we could make sense of his feelings and the meaning of his life's events.

Children stop reacting explosively to trauma and loss after they have improved attachment, define a "why" for what happened, are given support to express their feelings, and learn de-sensitization techniques for trauma. If we do not start to see this progress, we further diagnose, considering a mood issue, or receiving more help with FASD. Sometimes, when children have made strong progress and then begin to have major problems, we have to look at further diagnosis. Is stress causing more traumatic stress symptoms? Sometimes the current environment is too complex for children with executive dysfunction and/or FASD to handle. Other times, they are developing a mood disorder.

Table 10-3 below compares and contrasts some issues, in functional terms, across diagnoses.

Table 10-3

Diagnosis→ Issue↓	Traumatic Stress	Mood Disorder	Reactive Attachment Disorder	Family and School Needs⊠
Affective Regulation (mood) Issues	Yes. Improves with nurturing home, secure base and specialized therapy	Yes	Yes, but in social contexts more pronounced	Needs to be skilled in handling their own affect and helping with children's affect
Control Issues	Variable	Usually when children with bipolar become overaroused they get controlling.	Yes	Needs structure skills in defining control issues.

Table 10-3 (Continued)

Diagnosis → Issue ↓	Traumatic Stress	Mood Disorder	Reactive Attachment Disorder	Family and School Needs
Specialized Educational Needs	Needs predictable and structured classroom	Bipolar will need attention to arousal levels	May need help with behavioral issues	Assessment, accommodations
Developmental Delays Lifelong	No	No	No	Excellent assessments with defined future goals
Impacts on Attachment	Most common reason for attachment issues	Yes, Especially at each end of the mood spectrum	By definition. May show indiscriminate affection	Family is nurturing, predictable, and working with therapist closely
Normal Experiences Over-stimulate	Variable	Variable. Responds well to medication	No	Calm, predictable, interesting, and structured

It makes sense to begin teaching a skill set of attachment and attunement, rather than immediately diagnosing a mood disorder in children coming into therapy with dysregulated moods, poor attachment, and backgrounds that have included ample incidents of trauma and neglect. Certainly, keep those possibilities open, but functionally, it makes sense to first teach children the skills necessary to attach, calm, and relate to others on an emotional level.

After completing attachment, calming and connection work is a much easier time to assess where children are having trouble functioning. It is easier to distinguish the reasons behind reactive and over-sensitized behaviors as being caused by overstimulation in a manner typical of FASD or autism, a reaction to trauma, or a mood disorder that does not yet show a particular pattern. The contribution of ADD or ADHD in behavioral problems also becomes clearer as the therapist gets to know the child. Referrals and the use of medications, when appropriate, help children to function better.

Children who appear to be severely impacted by drugs and alcohol exposure may show surprising improvements after attachment and trauma work. The damage caused by prenatal exposure is permanent, but some children may be presumed to be more damaged if they have never learned any skills of attachment or had any relief from trauma.

Recently, 11-year-old Annie completed testing, with the presumption that her prenatal exposure would reveal more learning issues. Surprisingly, her test results showed that she was above age level in many academic areas. Annie's early school progress had been complicated by aggression and social problems. She made strong progress in therapy and home, and it turned out that she was far less affected by her prenatal exposure to substance than it had been thought. "I have been *flexible* with friends, too," Annie confided to me in a soft voice. "I've been trying hard on all of the things that we talked about. I get picked for groups." Annie's principal, who had been kicked in the shins a few years earlier, was particularly pleased with her progress.

I conclude this section on diagnosis with the suggestion that therapy be started in a practical manner. Get as much information as possible at the beginning, help children learn patterns of attachment and social behavior through methods that are in their strength areas, give referrals for specialized assessments for medication and diagnoses of mood disorders, autism, or learning issues as you learn more about the child and can identify the issues that need attention.

Parent and Therapist Collaborations

Co-regulation with the therapist

The therapist will need to enter the session with the child and family with the capacity to join with their clients emotionally. In a remarkable study by Mary Dozier and colleagues, the therapist's state of mind towards attachment was measured through the use of the Adult Attachment Inventory. The progress in clients whose caseworkers and therapists themselves had a secure state of mind towards attachment was significantly better as compared to the progress of clients whose caseworkers/therapist did not, as long as the client wanted a connection (Dozier, Cue, Barnett, 1994).

The explanation behind this study is that the therapists most comfortable with joining with their clients, through their secure state of attachment, can help parents regulate better. This emotional regulation is a fundamental quality in moving through anxiousness and grief in therapy. Additionally, people with a secure state of mind towards attachment tend to have better stress regulation capacities. The therapist, by making herself emotionally available, supplements her client's capabilities.

This is typical in relationships that include parent-child, close friends, and couples. We all "borrow" a little balance from people who really care for us, dealing better with life stressors as a result.

It is essential, then, to enter sessions with the capacity for co-regulation. Therapists can easily find themselves becoming disoriented, dysregulated, or distant, unless they are supported in their work and refreshed emotionally and spiritually. Joy should be a regular by-product of therapeutic work done in a balanced state. Families can get a significant lift from the therapist. It recharges their batteries so that they can complete their difficult emotional tasks throughout the week.

Typically, I tell parents that I care about how the entire family is doing, not just the member who is getting the treatment. Identifying opportunities to make the families' lives more pleasurable, interesting, and balanced is an ongoing activity for the therapist.

I use the twelve-hour-a-week rule for parents who are tired, burnt out, or worn. I suggest that the adult spend twelve hours a week, either in three four-hour chunks, or four three-hour chunks, doing nothing but what is pleasurable for them. They may use one of those chunks to do something with another adult, but the rest must be spent outside of the family. Within a month, and usually within two weeks, the parents experience an increased vitality. Parents report spending their time walking in the park, sitting in a hot tub, eating dinner alone, reading a book, crying, screaming, going to a museum, and sitting in a stupor in front of a television. They do not experience any pressure to do anything during their time. They get back in touch with themselves as an individual person rather than as a person in a parent role.

Not only should therapists pay attention to the parents in the home, but they need to ask about the siblings in the family. Siblings already in place when the troubled child arrived may be being over-looked, bullied, or frightened. For the overlooked siblings, I help parents find time to individualize children. I have often taught my clients to be in their rooms alone so that their sibling could get some individual time. Grandparents are great resources to take difficult children once a week so that a sibling can get some time with parents. I like to find out what is most important to siblings and then make certain that they have their parent's attention during that time.

On the way to a fencing tournament, a difficult child de-cided that she did not want to go to watch her brother's activ-ity. She began to tantrum. The parent and I both agreed that she should call a respite worker. She dropped the girl off, and then went on to the tournament, really focusing on her son. The girl said, "I just thought that if I gave Mom a hard time that I wouldn't have to go." She needed to learn that other children in the family were a priority as well.

Sometimes I will meet with a sibling to make certain that we have a game plan for physical or sexual misbehaviors on the part of the troubled sibling. They are taught some way to tell and to gain justice.

One boy used to touch his sister's thighs in order to get immediate parental attention. At first she was scared silent and would finally tell in a whispery voice. I told her in a ses-sion with me that she could push her brother away and then tell on him. She would never get in trouble. She role-played in session with her mother. (The mother did not touch, but just gestured. The mother showed exaggerated affect from her powerful girl.)

One day her mother asked her if she had ever gotten touched again, since the girl had not told on him. "No," she said. "He tried to touch one more time and I slugged him. I remembered that Deborah Gray said that I could push him. I thought slugging was better."

It is important that all of the children in the family stay healthy. When a child is dominating another, I like to come up with a system of justice.

One child, Julian, used to shout cuss words at his brother, Sammie, loudly. When Julian swore the next time, Sammie was allowed to go with a parent to the doorway of Julian's room, and pick any toy or item to play with for the next three days. The parent walked into the room, giving the toy to Sammie.

Sammie not only got one toy, but a second and third as Julian erupted after seeing the toys emerge. Finally Julian practiced some self-control. Later Sammie said, "I like the toys. But I'd rather have my brother be nice. That helped him stop all that swearing." Of course, it took Julian more than one event, but it did not take long, and when he slid back, the same remedy had a positive effect.

Even though I want a system for fairness in the family, it is important not to get into an "angel kid, devil kid" split. I like to coach things in terms of some kids having learned some things that other kids in the family are still learning. Or, I tell kids that their brother or sister got their hearts hurt, and it will take a while for us to help them with all of the mad and sad.

Therapeutic Protocol for Attachment, Trauma, and Loss

Children who have been traumatized pose a special challenge in attachment work, as trauma impairs their response to their parents' attachment invitations. Some children have experienced specific traumatic events that numb and emotionally flood them, making them unable to respond to their parent figures. The main difficulty encountered when working with young, traumatized children with attachment issues, however, is that their traumatic responses are triggered by exposure to their caregivers, not just by traumatic events. Having and recognizing safe parents who have the abilities to calm, protect, and buffer children is essential to the process of recovery from trauma. Unfortunately, these required caregivers paradoxically elicit conditioned emotional responses caused by experiences with the former caregivers who were traumatizing (Briere, 2002a).

Children who are showing traumatic responses to parents, not simply to events, must have a detailed home and therapy plan. They may benefit from a de-sensitization to caregivers program at the beginning of treatment. This de-sensitization constitutes the beginning of attachment work for children who have traumatic responses to their caregivers. Begin the treatment plan with attachment work in cases of trauma that lack this conditioned traumatic response to the caregiver as well. The children in the latter category usually respond to the highly nurturing attachment exercises with less resistance.

Attachment work is not as simple as "Put a caramel in his mouth and rock him," which was the summary of attachment work by a naïve mental health worker. Attachment work is complicated and difficult. Remember that when parents attempt typical parenting tasks, these children will access memories and fight, freeze, or dissociate as if their lives depend upon it.

As mentioned before, many of these traumatic memories are stored in implicit memory systems, rather than in the explicit memory systems. That being the case, children are not even aware of the learning that informs their reactions. Children can repeat, "I have a great parent and I love having him as a foster (or adoptive) parent." This belief becomes part of their explicit memory system. They believe it and they know this to be true. When they go through their normal day, however, their implicit memory system is triggered by the frequent need to depend upon and yield to this parent. They begin to react in a traumatized fashion as a result of the "other" belief system that, while subconscious, is fully operational. This "other" belief system, the implicit memory system, may result in actions such as the child elbowing or kneeing their approaching parent. Or, they may spit and arch their backs while sitting on their parent's lap. These children's traumatic memories were laid down in the earliest phases of childhood, and are not verbal or narrative. When questioned, "Why are you doing this?" these children will have no answer. Instead, they express anger, shame, and sometimes fear.

Usually, maltreated children have a combination of two types of traumatic issues. The first type will be their conditioned emotional responses to the caregiver, as described above. The second type will be a reaction to the actual traumatic events in their lives. Of course, there is an interplay between these two issues during trauma work. Be sure to explain these two types of traumas to adults.

Attachment helps children with basic regulation and safety, so forge ahead in forming some attachment with children in spite of the trauma history. As in the invasion of Normandy, we begin to establish the beachhead of attachment so that children can experience some emotional relief. This gives them a place in which to retreat when they feel overwhelmed. It becomes the safe beginning in the process of emotional regulation.

It is on the lap of their parent, or sitting beside their parent, that traumatized children can first begin reporting what is happening within them. This gives them the first experience of actually talking about their feelings, without the intense and overwhelming sense of re-experiencing the trauma and being back within it. And, with the help of the safe person, kids begin to experience affective regulation. Someone, the parent, is there to help them breathe out and feel a little better. This begins their process of being able to talk about, draw, or role-play their feelings rather than feeling as if they are in the throes of them. While they may still be avoidant about their therapeutic work, they will begin to experience a fundamental change—that adults supply comfort and emotional and problem-solving resources. This experience encourages them to continue forward. It forms a template for seeking and receiving help when they feel overwhelmed.

Untreated grief and trauma constantly intrude upon children's lives. It silently shapes everyday experiences. The children who have not worked on trauma maintain trauma-contaminated core beliefs that distort their developmental perspectives of themselves and others. They either do not develop, or they lose confidence in the protective function of adults or of rules governing other areas of their lives. Beginning therapy with attachment work reasserts the healthy developmental perspective. It shows children that they will not have to face life's challenges alone.

The disturbing beliefs and images caused by trauma can gain momentum, rather than recede, as the years pass. Researchers note a "sleeper effect" in psychological damage resulting from sexual abuse. As time goes on, children with untreated sexual abuse issues have more marked impairment in social relationships, exhibit disruptive behavior, have concentration problems, and show poor tolerance for frustration (Putnam, 1999). These children's brains are constantly preparing for quick responses to a perceived dangerous world; the brain either fails to develop or it loses its ability to adapt and function in a safe world.

Prior to beginning the treatment, therapists should determine the emotional health of the parents, as well as obtain as much history as possible on the child. Often it is necessary to do some work on stabilizing parents and home situations before undergoing specific therapeutic tasks with the child. Develop a basic home program with some strategies for self-care for the parents and behavior management for the most difficult child behaviors. It may take several weeks to accomplish this initial pre-work. Therapists should provide support and help improve or maintain the parents' and also other family members' emotional well being throughout the entire course of treatment.

While the phases in this protocol are described as three points for cognitive clarity, they will blur into each other in actual practice.

Attachment-specific work/stabilization

As explained above, the first phase of treatment should be attachment-focused. Attaching to safe adults helps children begin to feel safe and protected. Until children have some sense of safety and connection of helping adults, they do not have the emotional resources to deal with trauma. They must use a combination of trauma-ready emotional defenses. These defenses include avoidance, dissociation, fighting, controlling parents, and so forth. Until children begin to accept safety, they cannot leave behind the artillery and armor necessary for their unsafe world.

For children who have just experienced trauma and who are in a new placement, our goal is to help them to calm down and feel safe in any manner that seems reasonable. This is a critical time frame in terms of the prevention or acceleration of the onset of PTSD.

In spite of the circumstances of the original trauma, maintain an environment that seems as familiar and normal feeling to the child as possible. If there is any possibility of keeping the child in a familiar surrounding, great efforts should be made to enable it. Even if the child is in a new, emergency placement, at the very least see that the child brings belongings and is offered familiar foods. If children are moved to new parents, avoid the trauma work until they show some beginning attachment. It may be necessary to address it in order to give crises relief, swinging back, then, to connection and attachment work.

Attachment will not develop optimally until the trauma and grief work are done. However, children will need some emotional support through attachment to even begin that work. I look for ways to buffer children from stress, even within the family. If children begin to regress and to look needy, meet those needs, encouraging the child to depend on the parents. For example, a child who begins to speak "baby talk" should not be told, "Stop talking like that; you are not a baby." Instead, notice the regression, ignore the baby talk as a topic, and add extra acts of comfort and security to the day. Try to maintain consistency and predictability in the child's care, as this will soothe the overstimulated or dissociative child.

Use markedly nurturing techniques with children during the attachment-producing phase. Encourage them to depend on and trust in parents. Some children who have been traumatized, neglected, and moved, but who are not specifically afraid of their caregivers, will respond to attachment-producing techniques by looking still, flat, shut down, or out-of-sync rather than resistant. In these cases, parents and children should practice ways of being close. Give homework for in between the sessions so that parents can give their children a nurturing home program with closeness exercises every day. These children tend to move into closeness with dependence upon and reciprocity with their parents with less resistance as compared to children who have conditioned emotional responses to their caregivers.

Children who have been physically or sexually abused by their earlier caregivers may arch, spit, kick, and pull away from new care-givers. The way they hold their bodies or what they say will often make it painfully obvious how they have been physically or sexually abused. The therapist does not delve into that abuse at this time, but instead helps provide safety by using reassurances. While this is a type of trauma work, its desensitization techniques are aimed to-wards the goal of encouraging some beginning attachment. Work at this time should not be oriented towards the goal of desensitizing the traumatic events or in the creation of a narrative. Rather, this work should be skill-based and present-focused. Children will often, but not always, look forward to these sessions.

The therapist should gauge the amount of emotional resources that the child has, working near the limit of the child's therapeutic potential. For example, a child might be encouraged to count up to ten while sitting in a parent's lap. If she becomes arching and fear-ful at the count of five, the therapist can encourage her, pointing out that she is safe. The therapist can point out that the child can see the parent's hands or that she may get up and then try again in a minute, and other specific reassurances. The vocal tones of the therapist and parents should be reassuring and gentle, but at the same time upbeat in order to positively challenge children.

One preschooler got quiet and stiff, shaking her head to show me that she was too afraid to sit with her father. "Maybe next week, then," I said.

The next week she said, "I'm ready now!" She eventually became her father's shadow. When later describing an inci-dent of abuse by a father figure, it was especially helpful to have given her the chance to have her feelings valued in the first situation.

More specific nurturing techniques to promote attachment are age-dependent, and are well-described in *Attaching in Adoption* (Gray, 2012). I like to approach the attachment work as a skill set: "learning to be close to parents." I like to take children's pictures with an instant camera throughout their attachment work. Children can review the pictures and also the great feeling of closeness with their parents. The pictures help anchor the safe feelings. Children who begin to breathe out with an audible exhale and drop their eyelids a little while sitting on a parent's lap, or lean into the parent with a delicious little giggle and grin are showing the ability to "down-regulate," or reduce emotional intensity. This skill is a pre-requisite for trauma and grief work.

Trauma and traumatic grief-focused therapy

Move into trauma-focused work after children have some attachment and some basic family stability. The goals of treatment now are twofold: correct distorted and self-toxic beliefs, and desensitize the child to trauma-related memories. Help children develop a narrative of their lives that makes sense of their lives' events. In the order of the tasks of therapy, concentrate on attachment first, trauma second, and grief last. Young children who have not clearly separated their identities from former parents will flip the last two tasks. They will work on attachment, then work on grief, accomplishing some clarity from the identities of the former parents, then move into trauma work, and then move back once again to finish their grief work. Continue to focus on and build attachment throughout the grief and trauma work, regardless of the order.

In these sessions, the therapist must constantly assess children's abilities to process memories. The therapist uses her skills to expose children to material in a manner that neither overwhelms them nor undershoots the therapeutic window.

The sessions are divided into three parts and vary in length from fifty-five minutes to two hours, depending on the needs of the child and the commuting distance for the family. In the first part of the session, the therapist talks with the parent while the child waits outside of the room. The therapist gets a report on the past week. This report usually helps the therapist gauge the amount and degree of traumatic memory the child is experiencing. The therapist also supports the parents as they continue therapeutic parenting at home. This support helps the parents maintain their sense of stability or regulation. The therapist co-regulates with the anxious, shocked, or worn parent so that he can calm and the child can enter into a regulating environment. One parent said, "I feel like I just got a massage. It is so calm here after you have talked to me. Even though you are working with my daughter, I get to sit back and give the job to someone else for a while."

In the second part of the session, the therapist makes an alliance with a child to work on a certain amount of the traumatic material. Usually this material is tied to whatever is bothering children. Parents may either overexpose or want to protect children from working on trauma. The therapist takes on the responsibility of calibrating the amount of material covered in the session. While I choose to have the parents present in many sessions, I control the pacing and the amount of work attempted in the session.

Work on de-sensitization, the impact of the trauma, and the meaning of the trauma during the second part. There are a variety of therapeutic techniques that can be used; choose the most appropriate one, depending on the age of the child, learning style, and presence or absence of prenatal exposure to substance. When in doubt as to how much trauma work to attempt, I attempt less, rather than more. For example, if a child comes in looking more dissociative than usual, the parent has a cold, and I have a headache, I back up into stabilization and surface little trauma.

Therapists should have inquiring minds, and encourage parents to have inquiring minds as well, in response to episodes of acting out behavior.

> A child was quite difficult to manage after his mother went on a short trip and did not improve after she came home. He finally revealed that a woman he thought of as his mother in a former setting would leave, calling a sexual predator, who masqueraded as a volunteer, to come spend time with him, i.e. abuse him. He had forgotten his anger at this woman and the similarities she had to his mother. He could not calm until we processed the abuse, his feelings of betrayal, and worked on de-sensitization through phone conversations. This is a typical pattern when trauma memories surface in very traumatized children.

In the last part of the session, we work on affective regulation, to making certain that the child is able to calm and cope after the session. Attending to this segment is critically important. In fact, the goal is not to speed through the trauma work, but to help the child to cope with life. The parents are regularly used to help the child modulate affect, comforting and calming their child.

The third segment of the session is also the time that the therapist works with the child and parent to make a plan for the coming week. The plan includes times in the week that the child can access comfort and support from parents, and plans for coping with daily challenges, for example, the school bus, an overnight visit from relatives, or an out-of-town trip by a parent. For fragile children, the plan includes check-ins with the therapist by phone and the possibility of an extra session.

In the first and last segment, especially, I talk to children about their progress, how much I appreciate the chance to work with them, and we celebrate their advances. When they tell me about good things that have happened in their lives, I am excited with them. Following Diane Fosha's sound advice, I want to spend as much time processing the positives as the negatives so that the positives are integrated into their life narrative (2004).

Grief

The sessions that are focused more on grief are set up similarly to the trauma sessions. Meet with the parents first, work specifically on grief second, and do affective regulation and plans for coping third in the sessions. Usually the grief work and trauma work are inter-mingled to some degree, since most children's losses have traumatic features.

In the grief segment of the work, the child not only mourns for the people that she lost, but for the loss of the life that she once lived. Children do not have the emotional resources to grieve alone, so most children will not have progressed through the grieving process until they are attached to their parent. The child needs to have a consistent adult who can support her through her grief in order to get through the grief staging. In most cases, this adult is the parent. Occasionally, children will use the therapist instead. I will take on this role if children do not have a parent who can do this grief work.

During this phase, whether it comes largely before or after the trauma work, children will need

- factual information about the loss; what really occurred and who was there.
- assistance in reality testing. Most children want to deny certain things. They need help with talking about their feelings. Most maltreated children report anger when they are feeling anger, sadness, or fear.
- help determining their part in the loss. Almost all children place themselves as central to both trauma and loss.
- the ability to share their feelings about the lost person.

Encouraging children to share feelings about the lost person can manifest an especially tough dilemma in therapy.

One boy who was nearly lethally neglected as well as sexually abused by his birthmother still missed her. Before he worked on trauma, he successfully dissociated from the trauma and felt only his desire to be close to her. It took patience and a firm grip on theory for his parents to hear and to support his grief work. Because of his age, it was necessary that he grieve and separate from his birthmother before moving into his trauma work.[2] In this case example, I supported the parents as they supported their child as he grieved. After completing his grief and trauma work, this same child concluded that his birthmother should be incarcerated due to her ongoing threat to the community.

It can be trying for parents to hear the loss their children feel towards the same people who harmed them. Alternately, sometimes the parents want their children to feel something less intense.

One teen said, "My mother wants a normal child and says, 'See, it worked out for the best.'

"But what's best about having traumatic stress? My birthmother was an idiot! I wouldn't treat an animal the way she treated me. My mother just doesn't want something like that to be part of my adoption story."

---

[2] This child was, in addition, psychologically unprepared to integrate his birthmother's malevolent intent with his sense of self. That would have been too devastating to present during this stage of therapy.

Parents—in or out of the therapy room?

Obviously, parents should be in the room during attachment work so that therapists can use the most effective model for attachment work. During the trauma and grief stages, however, the decision concerning whether parents stay in or out is individualized to what works best for a particular family. (Sometimes two parents are in the room for sessions. Often that feels like too many adults to children, so one adult is in the room at a time.)

I do the first part of the session, as described above, with the parents in the room during almost all sessions with children under 12 years old. For the grief and trauma work, I will often work with children separately. I tend to finish the sessions with the parents and their children together again. Typically, children want their parents to know what they worked on and want to get support for their work.

Some parents cannot contain their own grief and trauma when they hear what happened to their children, or this information can re-activate the parents' own past grief and trauma issues. Some children are too humiliated to talk about the worst of the worst experiences in the presence of their parents. In all of these cases, I work with the children separately, and then tell parents what we worked on, in a global way, later.

I will often say to children, "It doesn't matter to me whether your parent(s) are here or not for this part. What do you want? How will you work best today?" Parents will agree with this, giving children the ability to assess what is best for them. Some children will say, "Mom, are you sure you don't mind?" or, "Dad, will you come back in at the end?"

By this time I have enough history with parents that they are comfortable. Sometimes children will specifically ask for parents to be with them. Usually this is because they are still using their parents a lot for comfort and support as we go through trauma work. Sometimes we need parents part-way through the session, because we have a question or because children need a hug. So parents usually do not go far.

Finally, as children mature into teens, I typically work with them alone. They are being prepared for self-sufficiency. The parents, the teens, or the therapist may ask for some time working altogether as a family, however.

Overlapping themes in grief and trauma

There are overlapping themes in grief and trauma. These overlaps cause confusion and make it difficult to determine which needs the child is presenting. In order to best help the child by using an appropriate treatment approach, it is important to make attempts to determine what the need is.

> Recently, a boy came into session after showing minor concentration symptoms all week. As he sat on his mother's lap and we sorted out the feelings, he said. "Deborah, I am sad all the time about being abused." He went on to say that he was thinking about what he would have been like if he had had a better start in life. He was grieving for himself and the meaning of these losses in terms of his identity. Working on his sad losses was exactly what he needed help in verbalizing. Working, in error, on traumatic de-sensitization, would not have been helpful.

What are some of the overlapping issues?

Hypervigilance is present in both grief and trauma. The search for the lost person is notable in grief, and especially pathological grief. Hypervigilance in trauma takes the form of children looking for former abusers, signals of upcoming violence, and searching for individuals who might be unsafe.

For children who have been traumatized by a parent, there is a true convergence of these themes. They may be searching for the lost parent, as well as terrified that they will see the parent. In therapy, we sort out the longing for the parent who terrifies.

Avoidance of Loss is a major theme in both traumatic stress and pathological grief. Due to traumatic stress, children are emotionally constricted when making new attachments. Children who have lost attachments remain past-focused, denying the reality of their loss and limiting their availability to the new parents for a new attachment. They are afraid to think of their losses.

Anger and Guilt. Children believe that it is their fault that the people they love left them. When children ponder the alternative to the loss and trauma being their fault, they alternatively believe that there is something so dangerous and overwhelming about the world that there is no shield or no social protection for them.

I ask questions carefully so that I can approach these themes correctly. I can ask some questions like, "I am not sure about something. I can't tell whether you are looking, looking, looking, because you <u>want</u> to see someone, or because you <u>don't want</u> to see somebody. Can you tell me more about this?" Sometimes children will describe both.

Disconnection from Trauma and Grief, Reconnection with the Present

At the end of therapy, children are able to be more fully in the here and now. Their life narrative is developed to a large degree. They are dealing with the residue of trauma in a manner in which it interferes with their lives to the least possible extent. They have developed strategies to deal with scary reminders of the past, i.e. traumatic triggers or reminders.

Therapists must continue to watch for any trauma re-enactment themes. We help children who are doing this find ways of coping that are less dangerous. We work actively on developing healthy coping skills in place of arguing, fighting, withdrawing, or self-punishing. We help children make safe choices. Neglected children are particularly helped by discussions that point out the people there to help them in every part of their daily lives, and how to get help. Much of each session is spent reviewing progress and helping them develop a sense of mastery and self-esteem. This replaces helplessness, avoidance, and shame as core issues.

Recall

A pulsed therapy approach works well for children with attachment, trauma, and grief issues. Families will work hard with me for about seventy hours, in weekly 55-90 minute sessions or twice monthly 90-120 minutes sessions, and then move into a rotating schedule of every other week, then once a month, or take a break of a few months and then come back to check-in. They have a list, developed for them individually, that indicates when to come back in. Sometimes trauma and grief issues build in intensity. Other times, behavioral issues become compelling. Life's stressful situations may necessitate coming back in for extra help.

Children also return to therapy when their developmental issues change. Children who have done work in the early elementary school years will want to review their work as they become more abstract thinkers at age 11 or 12. Some issues they will approach differently at this later time since they now have the mental equipment to think about things that were too complex for them before. For example, they will understand status, social class, and sexual stigma at this stage in a new way. Understanding how society sees sexual abuse for a preteen who was sexually abused is a typical type of issue at this stage. Most children are ready and interested in talking about the complex issues of neglect, abuse, or being raised by parents who are not biologically similar. They need facts and emotional support during this stage. They are making meaning out of the events that shaped their lives.

At ages 13 and 14, teens will need to think about how they are the same as their birthparents and different than their birthparents, and how they are the same and different from adoptive parents, as part of forming their identities. I like to spend time with them at the 11-12 year stage in getting facts and concepts straight about their birthparents. That insures that they have the facts in order to sort these issues out at 13-14 years old.

Some teens need extra help with romantic relationships or as they prepare to move away from their parents. They need to do more work because the meaning of the trauma or loss to their identities is different at different ages. Sexual abuse is an example of a type of trauma that needs additional treatment at different stages of the developing identity. Children and teens usually understand the positive effects of therapy, and will request appointments with me as needed.

Sometimes children will need another type of therapist in the teen years. They are either ready for another approach or think of me as the childhood therapist and feel that they have outgrown me. We discuss their needs and I refer them, without giving them the sense that they have burned any bridges. They are welcome to come back if they wish.

Teens genetically at-risk for mood disorders may show some of these signs as they get older. Recall helps differentiate diagnoses, i.e. determine whether their problem is re-activated traumatic stress or a mood disorder. Seeing a familiar therapist is comforting for teens, even if they just want a referral for medication.

At recall, teens do their work without their parents most of the time. They have already internalized the attachment and emotional modulation during earlier work, so that they are more independent in their process. At times, teens will request their parents in the sessions, as they feel the need for extra help with emotional modulation. Other times, I request the parents if I feel that family work is helpful, or if I feel that attachment is slipping. In all sessions, I continue to reinforce attachment, even when the parent is out of the room.

Types of Cases

This section describes classic types of cases for therapists specializing in work with children who suffer abuse or neglect and trauma before moving to adoptive families. The treatment process will be covered in depth for each case, so that readers can see an integrated, practical application of the theory and methods described earlier in this book. This section is meant to be a practical guide for therapists, giving them outlines of classic cases with processes and concepts. Therapists who do not have a specialty practice can use these cases as a template. Therapists who have a specialty practice should still find the cases helpful, as we are always learning from each other, but specialists may also enjoy additional reading from the resource and reference sections.

Therapists without much specialized training in adoption, attachment, and trauma may find themselves treating children simply because they are the best local mental health provider available to the family. This section should assist them as they develop treatment plans and move through therapeutic tasks for this specialized population.

In the first case we will meet Chris and his family. Chris not only suffered from trauma and neglect, but also from prenatal exposure to substance. The work with Chris fits the description of the protocol described in the sections above. Then we will meet Leilani and her family. Leilani's case will highlight the treatment of anxiety after an early grief experience. Last, we will meet Madison, a child with significant neglect and multiple moves in the earliest years, who was adopted through a kinship placement.

Chris' Treatment: therapy for a boy with attachment, traumatic stress, and grief issues

Chris was 6 years old and his sister, Jasmine, was 5 when their caseworker approached me after a workshop on trauma, asking if I could treat Chris. "The family isn't at the end of their rope, yet," she said. "But I don't know how long they can go on. I came to this workshop because I needed to know the signs to look for in treating trauma. All I could think about during the workshop was Chris. He's the poster child for un-treated trauma in adoption."

I agreed to treat Chris, on the condition that I would re-ceive all of these records first: copies of the placement history, developmental/health records, visitation notes, case notes, police reports, CPS complaints, and the homestudy of the foster-adopt parents.

Savvy therapists know to ask for any helpful records up-front. Acquire these materials before the first session, as part of the prepara-tion process, whenever possible. These records become more difficult to obtain once treatment has begun, as the caseworker's interest has already turned to the next emergency. The parent's homestudy, how-ever outdated, will help the therapist get an impression of how the parent has changed over time. I also typically ask for copies of the post-placement report, any evaluations, information about academic progress, and a brief description of the issues the parent believes we should address in therapy. Get copies of police and CPS records when treating trauma. These give the therapist precise, specific instances of trauma, which are much easier to understand during treatment.

Intake session

I asked Chris's parents to come in without the children first, so that they could provide a history and help with the treatment planning process.

Chris' parents, Sally and Ed, were first-time parents. They had waited to parent and enjoyed a wide circle of friends. They had had some short-term fostering experience. After the placement, it was clear to both parents that a determined and united parenting approach was necessary.

Ed narrated the placement story, "We decided to adopt siblings because we knew that any placement was going to shock us. We've been together without children for eighteen years, enjoying reading, playing music, and our hobbies. We wanted two children. We were afraid that we would never have the guts to do the second adoption. So we plunged in and asked for siblings.

"'How bad could it be to get two at once,' we thought?" Sally and Ed glanced at each other and laughed. "Now we know! Really bad! We are exhausted and Chris is just getting warmed up. Now he's got my number and he baits me. 'You hate me, you know you hate me. You want to kill me. Hit me, go ahead and hit me.' He accuses me of things that I would never do, and then gets as furious and violent as if I had."

Ed continued, "Jasmine is settling in. But Chris! Whew! He's angry, scared, and doesn't listen to anything we say. He walks like a gang banger and tries to threaten me and his mother. He puts the moves on Sally. I know that we should be sorry for him, and sometimes I am. Other times I just about lose it when he pokes Sal's rear end and says, 'Come here, bitch.' It's been six months and we aren't even making a dent. We have to watch him or he grabs Jasmine's crotch. She looks glazed over and lets him. He has nightmares most nights that he can't wake up from. They can go on for two hours, sometimes up to three. I can only imagine what he's gone through."

Sally tried to point out some progress, and mentioned that Chris seemed so sorry after he acted out. As she spoke,

Eddie looked away, shaking his head. "I'm not going to give up," he said. "But I'm not going to put a good face on this. We have a wife batterer in training. He acts sweet and charming right after he's punched or kicked you. I don't think that you could call that progress."

Sally and Ed then described their need for help dealing with the way Chris interrupted his sister's positive development. Jasmine had begun to try to please her parents. She would sit next to her parents, relax, and cooperate. Chris would react to this by clearly breaking a family rule. When the parents tried to intervene, Chris would yell, "Help, help, they're killing me." Jasmine would either join Chris or dissociate.

Ed and Sal gave me some interesting information when asked about grief issues. Their caseworker said that Jasmine and Chris had never lived together. Ed and Sal discovered, however, that the children had had much more early contact than the official record showed. Both children said that Chris frequently joined Jasmine in their birthparents' home. Jasmine had been placed intermittently with her grandparent until the grandparent's death. She was returned to her birthparents quickly and frequently, always more so than Chris. I noticed that, according to the police records and the case records, Jasmine was placed into foster care after one of the birthparents' drug-related arrests. Chris was inexplicably present during this arrest. He was then placed in emergency care for several weeks before returning to his aunt's home.

Chris' placement record was important, in terms of his developmental history and his early lessons about safety, his identity and his caretakers. He had tested positive for methamphetamine at birth, so he was placed with his aunt. His birthmother went to rehab and his aunt took over his care. He kept getting picked up over and over again during domestic violence instances at the aunt's home. The birthparents were either present or were the perpetrators during these instances. He was placed with his grandmother once, after spending three months in foster care. She became too sick to care for him, so he went back to his aunt.

If this placement schedule seems jumpy and hard to follow, it is because the placements were just that. I had to carefully trace out the police and CPS records to work out a chronology.

Chris had spent almost a year, in total, in various short-term foster homes. The exact amount of time spent with his birthparents was unknown. He had spent a few months with his grandmother, and the rest of the time with his aunt. He was never in any home for more than six consecutive months. His foster home placements were never longer than three to four months. He constantly cycled between short-term foster care and being placed back in a home with domestic violence. It was questionable as to whether he had developed exclusive attachments with any parent figure. He had every reason to believe that he would lose any safe home.

Finally, with Chris' birthparents facing longer prison sentences, his aunt had said that she could no longer keep him. She had other children and intended to move away and leave no forwarding address—far from the violence and drug use of the birthparents and her own boyfriend. So Chris moved from the aunt's home into a receiving home, stayed for a few days, and then moved on to Sally and Ed's home.

With the aunt no longer a resource, the birthparents decided that it was best for Chris, Jasmine, and their two other children who were in relative placements, to relinquish parental rights.

Jasmine had been in another foster home since age 3½. She had settled in that home, sharing affection not only with the foster parents, but with the other children in the home. She seemed startled at seeing Chris, and at first thought he was a different, older brother. She asked whether her other brothers would be joining them at Sal and Ed's. Ed reported that she was afraid of them.

The parents described the sibling problems as being compounded by siblings with similar issues and exposure being placed together. Chris and Jasmine took turns scaring each other. At times Jasmine beat on Ed when he attempted to restrain or talk sternly to Chris. When Jasmine threw tantrums, Chris would approach her and would get hit or kicked. Warned to stay away, Chris still got close and then yelped, screamed, and sometimes fought when he got hurt. It was hard to have one child acting out without having the other join the fracas.

Sally had been working with both children on having fun, learning routines, and feeling safe. Ed was making a point to play with both children. They continued to plan positive activities with the children in spite of parental exhaustion. The children melted down almost every night at bedtime. Jasmine had the hardest time going to bed, so more effort was put into helping her settle. Chris fell asleep after the usual tussle, but woke up every night, screaming.

Chris had been 5 when he moved into his home. He had come in without a transition. His sister, Jasmine, had come into the home a few days before Chris, after a two-week transition from her foster home. Chris met his parents for the first time at the doorstep of his new home.

Treatment planning

As I concluded the intake session with the parents, we agreed that both children needed therapy. We decided to begin with Chris and with some family work, since our schedules precluded starting both children at once. Additionally, Jasmine's speech issues were so severe that she was difficult to understand. Earlier psychotherapy had halted, as the therapist could not understand her. We hoped to include her in therapy as her speech therapy progressed.

(Jasmine's therapy is not covered in this casestudy, except as it applies to Chris. Due to the children's similar and intertwined issues, it was necessary and helpful to coordinate the cases. It was best for both children to be seen by the same therapist.)

The records clearly indicated that Chris' aunt's and birthparents' homes had both been reported multiple times for neglect. He had been referred for services for developmental delay. The police reports detailed domestic violence, drug deals, and weapons on two occasions when Chris and Jasmine were picked up. There were also reports of sexualized activity, which indicated that inappropriate exposure had occurred, and that sexual abuse was also possible.

The parents and I agreed on a therapeutic plan, as based on the case history and current behaviors. They wanted help with specialized parenting techniques that would give them a better return on their time and energy investment. The parents and I agreed that we would begin work with better behavioral management, which included managing sexual acting out. We would help Chris form an attachment with both parents. We would then help him with trauma and grief issues.

We knew that Chris would need other referrals, as well, and would be obtaining more services over the next few months. We staggered the referrals to help maintain the energy level of the family. The children were especially out-of-control in the car, screaming and trying to hit each other or to lob objects at the parents while driving. They hoped that we could make enough progress in therapy to reduce some of these transport problems.

I talked openly with both parents about the range of outcomes in therapy. We talked about some of the limitations of therapy for children who are prenatally exposed to drugs and alcohol. We also talked about the treatment time frame. I told them that I expected that we would be meeting almost weekly for a year and a half to two years. It is impossible to predict the precise length of treatment for a particular child, but most parents will want a range of possibilities so that they can plan accordingly.

I gave Sally and Ed psychoeducational information on attachment, grief, and trauma during the intake. Both parents identified signs of trauma and grief in Jasmine and Chris. Once they saw the symptom clusters, they were able to give me details about the trauma reactions. This highlighted the areas where the children were suffering the most, informing my treatment plan. This conversation continued during the treatment.

We talked about ways to order the home so that the level of stress decreased—for everyone. Sally encouraged Dad to get a twenty-four-hour getaway every two weeks, so that he could sleep in and get time alone. Sally said that she did not need a break and felt comfortable beginning the nurturing techniques right away. Parents frequently become so tired that I worry as to whether they will be able to do some of the techniques unless they get a rest. I shared this with them, letting them know that I was interested in everyone in their family doing well, not just the children.

Eddie mentioned that his own childhood had been marked by vicious verbal attacks between his parents—and occasionally towards him. He thought that he had overcome his past until the placement. "I'm not over it like I thought I was," he said. "The yelling really gets to me." I believed him, and immediately recommended steps that would give him recuperation time. The family functioning was approached pragmatically. The issue was not one of entitlement, but rather of determining stressors and strengths to keep each parent working within their limits.

During that first session, Sal and Eddie concluded, "The way that you describe a traumatic trigger and response is just how Chris gets in the car."

"'Don't, please don't make me go,' Chris starts to beg. 'I'll be good. Please! Please!'" Ed mimed the voice.

"And we are just taking to him to the grocery store. He goes into a wild man mode. Of course, Jasmine only holds on for about a minute before she joins in," Ed continued.

The parents and I agreed that we would work on behavioral issues, not only from "outside" rewards and consequences, but from the "inside," that is, what was happening in the hearts, minds, and memories of their children.

In summary, the first, long intake session with Eddie and Sally accomplished the following: assessed the parents' functioning, gave them some strategies for immediate aid, gave them psychoeducational information that helped them understand their children better, outlined a treatment plan and approach that everyone agreed upon, and gave them some beginning understanding of information outlined in Chapter 8.

Treatment planning with Chris

Chris began therapy one week after the intake session. He was 7 years old and in kindergarten. At my request he brought in things that he liked to share and something that gave him a sense of mastery. He shared some amazing robotic guys. Then, with a big grin, he demonstrated his big achievement. He stood on his head. I cheered.

I began working with Chris while he sipped on apple juice. I drew the discussion out on paper, because this technique helped me control the pacing of the session, it helped him organize thoughts, and it was visual—which I presupposed would be a stronger modality for him. (Verbal memory tends to be impacted by neglect/trauma.) First, I drew a big heart with a crack down the middle. He picked out a purple crayon and colored the heart with me. I told him that I worked with kids who had had their hearts broken a long time ago.

"Do you know what breaks kids' hearts?" I asked him. He shook his head and I continued. "Being really, really scared. Like so scared that you can't even make any noise. Or, losing a mom, or someone who you thought was your mom." Chris was feeling pretty big feelings, but still tracking me emotionally. He started to wiggle off the couch, looked at my face instead, was reassured by a kind smile, and used that to steady himself. He nodded.

"The kind of work that I do with kids is to help them with their hearts." I shared as I looped circles to close the heart and then put a band-aid on it. Chris was pulled in.

"Do you know why we do this?" I asked. Chris was engaged, and looked at me. I continued. "So that your heart can hold more love. With this big crack it can't hold much love. We drew some little hearts within the bigger heart. We drew some falling out. I also said, since he was captivated, "And if you don't have much love in here, then lots of mad and grouchy feelings fill up the space. Plus, there's all that mad and scared that we talked about a minute ago. That's why we work on getting more good feelings in there.

"Do you think that you have gotten as much love as other kids?"

"No!" Chris agreed emphatically. Finally, someone was agreeing that things weren't fair. I was talking his language!

"Well." I said, "I have some ideas for how to get you the love that you missed. It's not too late."

Within a couple of minutes, Chris agreed that he would like to try this by having some cuddly time with his mother. He climbed into her lap, let me arrange her arms around him, and then looked into her eyes. I showed him how to relax with her and then asked if he would like some apple juice in the bottle. He agreed, and then grabbed the bottle, heading for the corner. I said, "It seems like that was what you got when you were little, the bottle and no mamma love. Let's try it with mamma love." I took the bottle back. He tried again, this time sitting on his mother's lap as she held the bottle, and looking into her eyes. He began a true emotional exchange. Sally dripped a few tears and smiled.

"Why is she crying?" I asked. "Let's ask."

Sally said, "I'm crying because I love you so much and I have waited so long to be your mother." Chris wiggled a little, but let the tender feelings continue for a few more seconds. Then he pushed himself up, elbowing her sharply in her breast.

My assessment was that his disorganized attachment schema had been activated and that he needed to interrupt intimacy. My response was to ask Chris to do a repeat, so that he could get up without hurting her. "You don't have to," I said. "You have already done so much in just this first session that I am happy. But you could really amaze us if you could put another ending on this."

Chris paused in his rapid retreat from the intimacy. "Let's keep the part that you are proud of and try again without the hurting part," I suggested. I pointed to one hand for the proud part, the other hand for the hurting part. "Which part did you like?" He was at a developmental stage such that he loved to choose. He chose the proud hand. "Great. This time just say you're done."

Chris tried the process of getting up again. "Mom, I'm done," he said. Then he jumped off—this time grazing her feet with his, hurting her just a little.

"Almost. You did only a little bit of hurting. Do you think that you are strong enough to get down without any hurt?" He tried again, this time thinking about her body and being careful. I cheered for him as he got off of her lap in a caring way. He basked in the praise and the happy moment.

Chris and I talked about how sometimes, when kids have been hurt, they want to show their parents that kids are in charge—hurting them just a little bit. I asked Chris if he ever got the "ha-ha-ha on you" feeling. I role-played, showing the face and the body language of getting pleasure at the other's expense. Chris agreed that he did—nodding somberly. I talked with him about how that feels bad at the same time. Chris interrupted, "Because she is a good mom. She takes care of me and gets up in the night. But I do the 'ha-ha-on-you' thing, too." We agreed to work on stopping that. I told Chris that he had a good heart, and that it had just been hurt. We needed to help him let his good heart show through.

The lap work, role-playing, and discussion took about forty minutes. It gave us time to assign homework. Chris was to practice rocking with a parent for fifteen minutes every day. He was also to get special time alone with Mom or Dad, without Jasmine, for another fifteen minutes a day.

Chris came in the next week with the homework largely completed. He showed me how he was getting close to Mom. We agreed that the next week his father, Ed, would come in so that they could work together.

During the second session, Chris and I completed a treatment plan. It was done like a patchwork quilt. Chris and I drew the topics on squares: getting close to Mom and Dad, arguing, having more fun, not being so scared all of the time, learning to calm down, missing his aunt, and scary stuff. We used simple pictures to designate the topics because he was not yet reading. He used his favorite colors and designs to fit the picture. Picking out colors and coloring helped pace the work.

With some children, I would have been a little more detailed about the scary stuff, mentioning something like the person who used the gun, etc. In Chris' case, however, this would have overwhelmed him.

I told Chris we would fill in the scary stuff later. Chris was pleased with his work, holding it up to show Ed. Then Chris and Ed did some lap sitting that was similar to the work with Sally. Ed was very gentle in approach, but finished the lap sitting with some mild rowdiness. It was great because we could talk about that being a way that Chris could learn to get excited and then calm down. It helped him to learn to use his brakes.

Focus treatment on attachment and regulation first

Over the next six sessions, Chris and I worked on attachment and attunement. Chris began to look at his parents' faces, coached by me in the sessions, noticing what they were feeling and talking to them about their feelings and thoughts and his feelings and thoughts. He continued daily rocking and cuddle times. He came in and reported the number of hugs he got every day.

Chris began to be spontaneous. "You look sad, Dad," he said one day. "Did someone hurt you?" It was the first time that Chris had reflected on feelings.

Ed said, "Thanks, Chris. Someone hurt my feelings at work when I made a mistake. It made me feel bad."

Chris closed a circle of emotional communication and said, "Ahhh, too bad."

Previously, Chris had acted frantic or chaotic when he noticed sadness or tension in adults. This time, he was positive and responsive. Ed thought this was a breakthrough. I saw it as a life skill that was acquired as Chris became a gratifying and caring person.

I talked to both Chris and Jasmine about their car behavior in a family session. I told them that I did not know why they got so wild in the car, and I did not need to know right then, but I hoped that some day they would figure this out with me. Chris sat by me and his dad during this talk and Jasmine sat by Sally. (Otherwise they probably would have been so emotionally activated that they would have run around the room.) I told them that I was afraid that someone would get really hurt while they were behaving this way in the car. If they could not keep safe car behavior, then they could ride with their coats on backwards, zippered in the back, and with arms inside. I also made certain that positive car behavior included some rewards for both of them.

I had Mom and Dad promise the children that they would not be driving the children anywhere dangerous or to a new home. Both parents said that, of course they were not planning anything like that.

The ride home was tranquil. Later that week, Chris did act out in the car. First, Mom pulled the car over and read a book that Jasmine liked. Jasmine was also offered rewards for not falling into the misbehavior—as discussed in session.

"I'm rich! I'm rich!" Jasmine exclaimed gleefully. "I get a nickel every minute that I don't lose it with you, Chris." It irked Chris that his sister was getting more money the longer he acted out. Still, it took twenty minutes of sitting beside the road until he calmed enough to be safe in the car. Jasmine had not participated in the fracas with Chris, so the time frame was shorter than normal. But, Chris became louder and wilder when Jasmine changed her behavior.

Chris had not only yelled but he had thrown his shoes at Mom's head. Chris was informed that the next ride in the car would be with his coat zipped backwards with his arms inside. Chris also had to take his shoes off prior to getting into the car. I suggested to the parents that I give Chris the news in session.

Chris said, "But I don't like that. Can't you just give me another chance? That's what we always do! How about a warning?"

"You know the rules," I said. "No more warnings. The warnings have not worked and it would not be fair to you if we kept doing something that was not working. I want your family to feel safe for everyone." I gave this information in a kind, but firm voice. "I know that you don't want your coat this way. I don't either. But I can't think of another way for your head to get the message to your arms and legs."

Chris rode home from my office with his coat on backwards. Over the course of treatment, this only had to be repeated two more times.

At home Chris moaned, "No more warnings, Jas. No more three chances. Now we just have to do it the first time."

I told Chris that not following the rules had made him tense. I told him that I had noticed that he looked tighter and more worried as he was waiting for a parent to intervene. We role-played this. I told Chris that I did not want him or his parents to be so tense. Parents, then, would respond more quickly with actions instead of using warnings and threats.

By the seventh session, Chris was steady enough in the sessions to wait to be greeted. He could wait in the waiting room while I talked to the parents and helped them with co-regulation, behavior strategies, and listened to their description of the week. I spent ten minutes doing this with the parents, about forty minutes with Chris and the parents, said goodbye to Chris, and spent five minutes closing with the parents, addressing any issues that had come up during my time with Chris and the parents together. I used this format for the next year. We scheduled extra sessions for parents, as needed, to provide more information exchange or behavioral help. Family sessions were also scheduled in order to work on some issues that Jasmine and Chris needed to do together.

Chris and I spent the next six sessions working on increasing attachment and behavioral patterns. Chris saw his friend acting out at a picnic and said, "Eric sure needs to see Deborah Gray!"

On another occasion, he mimicked Mom to me saying, "You just learned that from Deborah? Do you do everything she says?"

More positively, he mentioned good behaviors before sessions, "Do you think that she'll be happy when she hears that I helped you pick up the living room?" Or, "I haven't hit anyone in the car all week, have I, Dad? Will you tell Deborah Gray that?"

My interventions diluted his intense negativity towards parent figures. The transference helped him to work out some things with me. Chris reached out to his parents more, but began to use me as another person with whom to get angry or from whom to receive praise. This took some of the pressure off the parents.

After three months and twelve sessions of therapy, Chris had learned some calming strategies. He used them spontaneously or when cued. He approached his parents for hugs and affection more often. He accepted the notion of making strategies to repair major upsets that he had caused. He was trying to prevent upsets in the future. He was developing emotional alliances with his parents and with me.

I spent another three hours with both parents, working on behavioral systems in the home, elaborating more on alleviating stresses, and designing ways to focus attention on reinforcing desired behavior. The positives experiences occurred much more regularly in the family. The nightmares had diminished, but were still twice-a-week events. Chris wanted to come in for sessions, although he asked parents not to tell me about certain misadventures, especially sexual acting out.

I spent two sessions with Chris and Jasmine, working on boundaries, including sexual ones. We measured out personal space with outstretched arms and with seating. We drew outlines of feet on plastic shelf lining, flopping them where they should stand—or not. Jasmine role-played pushing Chris away and saying "Stop" if he loomed too close.

Chris role-played the same activity with me. He put a hand-drawn mask of a pig (his choice) in front of my face.

"Stop! Get your...er...paws...hoofs out of my personal space... my privates," he commanded. He showed anger and humor, and ended up giggling. (Of course, I did not put my hands forward at all toward Chris, as this would not only have been inappropriate, but overwhelming.)

Jasmine, in the role-play, teased Chris to come too close, moving automatically into their pattern. Role-playing revealed their actual dynamic. Chris practiced ignoring Jasmine's part of the sexual acting out.

Jasmine rehearsed moving away from Chris during his tantrums. Chris did the same. Sally and Ed hid nickels and gum throughout the house. When Chris began to rant, Sally would say, "Jasmine, you can be part of this tantrum or go look at a story in your bedroom. There's gum under your pillow."

Jasmine took off for her room. Chris was so curious about the gum that he could not focus on his tantrum.

These types of interventions helped Jasmine and Chris transition into friendlier patterns, ones that no longer triggered each other's traumas.

I used body postures to help Chris regulate to me at the beginning of each session. He stood in front of me while I was seated, with his hands on top of mine, looking into my face. This helped me to mirror him, as well as to keep him in regulation. I smiled frequently and expressed concern appropriately. Then he sat beside me and we drew and talked, or we role-played. When he needed comfort or ideas, I would suggest a hug or some coaching from Mom or Dad. In this way, Chris learned how to use parents not only for regulation and nurture, but in organizing his memories, his emotions, or in getting helpful ideas. Chris was less avoidant, more interested in problem-solving, and liked sharing his successes.

Trauma-Focused Treatment

Chris also began sharing some traumatic material after the first three months of therapy, saying that he saw people looking at him through windows and that he could remember his bad dreams.

We reviewed Chris' treatment plan. He agreed that he had made a lot of progress in many areas, including getting closer to Mom and Dad, reducing arguing, having more fun, and learning to calm down. We filled those squares up with designs to about half-way, a little more or less, depending on his thoughts. We pointed out that he was about half "done."

We had not worked on missing his aunt or scary stuff. I asked him to pick the one that was bothering him the most. He said, "Scary stuff." We decided to work on that next.

We filled out the column that was not labeled anything but "scary stuff." We broke it into three areas: getting taken to different homes, weapons and scary guys, and sexual stuff. I drew a picture of a car for the move section, a guy and a scruffy guy for the second, but simply wrote "sexual stuff" for the third. We decided to start with what he was dreaming about, since it was giving him the most trouble.

Notice that, by this point, Chris had formed an alliance with me. He actively decided what we should work on together in the session, even though he was just 7 years old.

We still had a parent in the room during sessions. I took control of the pacing of the session, but they helped with word choices, details, and especially with hugs and care. Sometimes they coached Chris when there was confusion. "Are you trying to tell Deborah about such and such?" or, "I think that you are trying to describe X." Those clarifications were welcome, since the parents knew Chris so well.

I referred Chris to a child psychiatrist I trusted, who prescribed medication. Chris was making progress in therapy, but had shown levels of reactivity such that both the psychiatrist and I worried about beginning the trauma section of his work. Usually that work temporarily causes some decline in mood and an increase in reactivity. Chris had unreachable periods of time during his tantrums. He sometimes showed hopelessness as we talked about his life.

The psychiatrist suggested Remeron*, since some sleuthing showed that his biological sibling had responded excellently to that medication, but poorly to Zoloft* and another SSRI. Chris liked the psychiatrist and decided that trying medication was a good idea.

Chris began the medication and described feeling "not so grouchy." He still reported having intrusive thoughts, being afraid lots of the time, and sometimes feeling like he couldn't stop arguing, like he could not feel his parents' love, and being afraid that something bad was going to happen to him or to his family soon. The medication helped assuage Chris' extreme reactivity. His parents said that he was less volatile and more social. His thinking seemed clearer. In other words, he had a good response to the medication, but still needed trauma treatment.

At this point, the working diagnosis was traumatic stress disorder. While Chris had met the criteria for reactive attachment disorder at the beginning of treatment, he was developing a secure base attachment pattern with his parents.

Chris began telling me about a dream where he was removed from a place where he was playing and taken somewhere terrifying. First, we drew a picture of what he wanted in real life—his mother and father always keeping him safe. In the picture we drew Chris and Jasmine, with Sally saying, "It's okay now. I'm here." His dad's arms were around the family.

I asked him if his dream might be his mind checking to see if he really was safe. He thought it was. I asked whether there might have been another time or times that he was feeling safe and something had happened. Chris got up, and said, "Yes! I was playing, and then my birthmother came and took me in the car." Chris needed to move around. We both sat on the floor as we drew out the picture and discussed who was there, and how big each of his feelings was, and he told me about being taken away while his cousins were left safely at home with his aunt.

Rather than getting more descriptors and flooding Chris with emotion, we stopped and helped him work on the trauma he had just released. We drew cut-outs of his aunt and his birthmother. He spoke to the cut-out of his aunt saying, "No. It's not okay you butthead. Don't you know anything you f——- bitch? A mother is supposed to take care of you!" He described how his aunt smiled when she handed him over.

We carefully spaced the sessions so that Chris could express some traumatic material, but would also have at least twenty minutes to calm and be comforted for the rest of the session. I told Chris that my job was to try to make sure that we could stop the scary talk so that he could calm down and feel better as he came out of the session. We had lots of time for calming.

Over the next sessions, Chris stapled his aunt's picture inside an envelope with instructions to her. "Don't let bad guys in the house. Don't let my birthmother take me!"

He and I talked about how he had done the best job that he could of loving his aunt—but that he was so mad at her. Chris hid his head in his mother's lap and cried for his aunt for the first time. He was comforted. His mom carried him to the car after this session. They went to a nearby park where she let him run off his energy from all of the fight and flight energy entering his system.

Chris established a pattern for the next few months of sessions. He would tell me some of his memories and then decide what he wanted to do with his energy. One of his favorite activities was to dress in armor. We drew the face of the person who had abused Chris onto a piece of paper and taped it on a four-foot-long monkey puppet. Chris whacked the puppet and yelled out what he was angry about and what the miscreant should have done. As he was able to express these motor gestures that had been inhibited, he would come to the end of a wave of emotion. "There," he would say. "I'm done."

It is important to give traumatized people a chance to express these inhibited motor desires. Because of the threat involved, Chris could not fight back or express what his body wanted to express. Not only do people need to express their feelings as part of the integration after trauma, but they need to express what their body wanted to do. It is best expressed through the motions that they would have liked to have made—kicking punching, gesturing. This is not done for anger release, but as true integration of mind-body.

Chris disclosed sexual abuse after about eight sessions of trauma work. During that session and the sessions after that, Chris had his mother leave the room. At the end of the sessions, he wanted her to know what had happened, but had to let me tell her. He would nod and get consolation from her. Chris preferred that his mother bring him to sessions during this time.

I got out anatomically correct dolls for Chris to help him disclose sexual abuse. He had been threatened, and so he was afraid to talk about what had happened to him. I told him that he could show me, though. First, I explained to him that the dolls had their private parts. Then I let him show me, in two different sessions, what had occurred with the man doll and the boy doll, and the woman doll and boy doll. He did not have anything to show me with the girl doll. He did not need to use the dolls again after two sessions. However, I spent time straightening and dressing the boy doll carefully, putting him into a different drawer than the adult dolls. This pleased Chris. He saw me pat the boy doll carefully and he smiled.

Chris used a play jail and play figures dressed as cowboys, villains, sheriffs, and boys and girls playing basketball during the trauma phase of therapy. He also used a police car and weapons. He spent time jailing his birthparents and some of their more violent friends. He enjoyed the process of justice. He occasionally joined with the violent team, making them stronger. I did intervene, suggesting that the "good guys" could send for reinforcements. For the reinforcements, he used some larger figures, a tank and spider, which were high on top of my shelves.

I use these figures for children whose toxic memories overwhelm their play. I have a tank and other big stuff for the good guys if children choose to use them. I also mention to kids that sometimes they must feel like they have to join the bad guys to win. Its nice to know that they can send out for help. With some children I would not have been so direct. With prenatally exposed children, direct is best.

During this time, Chris told me that violent guys used to get taken to jail, but would just come out again. We talked about bail and jail sentences. Chris had believed that the violent people in his life had "beaten" the police. The play allowed Chris to show me things that he could not form into words or concepts.

At another time, I set up a play basketball hoop. I suggested that maybe the kids would like to just play ball. Maybe they would like to let the police take care of these guys, teach them how to behave, and let them keep the kids safe. Chris played ball with the figures and said, "We are ignoring you. We are so done with you. You never played any games, like baseball, basketball, or wallball. You are borrrrr--iiiing."

I scheduled some extra sessions for both parents in order to help steady them through the grief and anger they felt over what had happened to Chris and Jasmine. Jasmine appeared in some of Chris' descriptions of trauma. Her therapy was separate, but the events were corroborated by the other almost all of the time. I asked them not to discuss therapy with each other. They respected that boundary because we related it to the relief that they each felt that their therapy was private. Of course, I was also working constantly on establishing good boundaries.

Chris described being brought to a house for sexual abuse purposes and watching money change hands. He used a playhouse in my office, figures, money, and vehicles to show me what happened. This had been his ultimate betrayal. Throughout the sessions Chris and I focused on what the meaning of the abuse had been for him. He needed to share this horror with someone, and, to the best of a 7-year-old's ability, he also had to figure out why it happened.

We spent time making sense out of what had happened and why. It gave us a chance to talk about addiction and sexual abuse as opposed to healthy sexuality. I gave Chris much more explicit sexual information than would be typical for his age, simply because he needed to know what was healthy as a contrast to sexual abuse. I told Chris specifically that he would never have to have anyone put a penis in his anus again. (His parents preferred that I give this information since it included contrasts with sexual abuse. Their pain prevented them from talking to Chris in an even manner.)

Chris was terribly afraid that he would run into someone who had previously abused him. This fear was addressed with some role-play, with each parent acting out how they would leave with him. Chris laughed with relief as he practiced being whisked out of restaurants or stores. He concluded that he was safer telling people in authority about his abuse, rather than keeping the secret. He was interested in my report to CPS and the whereabouts of his birthparents. He wrote them both letters, dictating his anger at them. After dictating the letters, he told his mother during the week that he needed an extra session.

During that session he described not just the physical abuse by his birthfather, but sexual abuse as well. He pulled out my play jail, the police cars, and the weapons. He pointed a gun to the head of his birthfather. "Now it's your turn to be scared. Don't you know that you don't aim a gun at your own son's head? You f--asshole. You told me that you would shoot me if I cried. I hate you. You are a...asshole. And no one will ever give you a birthday party, or invite you over to their birthday party. You will be all alone in jail with beans and with other bad guys like you. You will never get out!" Chris smiled a little as the intensity passed and said, "I liked that."

We also worked on de-sensitization during this time. His adoptive mother's curly, black hair was a trigger for Chris. It reminded him of an abuser. Being silly, she cut a small piece of the dog's red tail hair and taped it on her head. Another day she wore a blond wig. Chris finally said, "You don't have to do that anymore. I'm not going to act mad at you because of your hair."

As part of the de-sensitization to trauma triggers, Chris' mother made and stuffed a life-sized man who wore all black clothes. She used batting from a fabric store. Chris was terrified of black clothes, as his abuser wore them during the most horrific abuse. We put a face on the guy and Chris kicked, hit, and lectured it. Then we had a party, put it in the corner of my office, and ignored it. "You're over," he said over his shoulder. We kept this figure behind my office desk for a year.

At this point, we had been working for about a year. Chris moved into more grief about his life, the abuse that had occurred to him, and how sad he had been over losing his aunt. "I really did like her," he said. He revealed that she had told the caseworker that he never slept, he screamed at night, and that she was sick of it. "She took her other kids and not me," he grieved. He also remembered how her birth children had gotten gifts at Christmas—and he had gotten nothing. This came out first as a taunt to Jasmine that she would get nothing for Christmas. He was the favorite. He apologized to Jasmine and then worked on his feelings in therapy.

Chris was showing more typical empathy as he developed a life narrative that showed the effects of comfort on his painful memories. He looked more relaxed. His dose of medication was reduced, but not discontinued, because he showed an increase in irritable and irrational behavior when it was stopped.

Chris and I worked on strategies for dealing with sexual acting out. At times, he was at especially high-risk. For example, he was at high-risk when he was angry and his mother or father was preoccupied or when he and Jasmine were in their swimsuits. Chris was able to tell when the feelings were coming and then would get close to an adult, or leave the room. He began to tell his mother or father when he got the touching feeling, but he did not touch. He also drew out and wrote plans with me, as well as role-played his plans. His sexual reactivity decreased markedly.

When a visiting child mooned Chris and invited him to play doctor, Chris showed a number of angry symptoms, but did not respond with sexualized play. Instead, he told his mother that he was angry with his friend. After the friend went home he described what had occurred during hide and seek. The parents and Chris were encouraged that he was changing.

Over the next six months, Chris alternated between coming in every other week during some months and every week in others. The parents and I determined that he needed two hours of therapy per month to maintain his progress. His social skills showed spontaneous improvement. We worked specifically on bullying behavior. We built empathy, talking specifically about other children's feelings and how he felt when people bullied him. He needed practice and repetition to prevent bullying. He tended to see stressful social relationships in the polar terms of victim or bully, rather than seeing the third choice of strong and empathic. We drew pictures, role-played, and helped him to elicit empathic responses at home and in therapy, in real time.

Chris came in for more work following a visit with a biological sibling. He remembered having been choked and mistreated by this sibling. He worked through this part of his story, and was able to stop "passing on", the phrase that we used to describe the behavior, the brutal, bullying behavior.

Chris, at 9 years old, completed his treatment plan. His parents still kept a connection for when things came up that Chris wanted to discuss in therapy. He came in once a month for minor "tune ups," the family phrase for this maintenance.

Recall was at 11 years old. At that stage, he was beginning abstract thought and wanted to go over his life story. He had many "why" questions. We discussed sexual issues again. Chris did not have the vivid traumatic stress reactions that had accompanied his earlier treatment. He did choose not to stay in class during the human development section, because he worried that he might experience intrusive images.

Chris came in periodically over the next several years, about six hours per year, usually following a family event. For example, he returned after the death of his grandparent, a parent's surgery, and after he received information about a birth relative. At these times, he wanted emotional support and assistance with processing. Sometimes he saw ways the events in his early life had shaped his life. In the 8th grade, he was able to stay in his health class during the human development section without difficulty.

Chris also did four to six family sessions per year to help with negotiation, cooperation, and family respect.

At the end of treatment, Chris was 16 years old, succeeding in school with a Section 504 for a learning disability, had two good friends, and had only mild and intermittent symptoms of traumatic stress. There were no dissociative episodes. He felt free to come back into treatment as needed. He enjoyed activities with his family and had had a few short-term romantic relationships. Chris felt good about his future.

This treatment plan took longer than the original estimate. The parents were so integrated into the process that they were not surprised. In fact, they assured me that they had expected the extra time and were grateful that they had gotten help for Chris early.

When Chris was 12, Sally had remarked, "He still had a childhood. I would have hated to have him bottle up this stuff inside. He would have missed so much. He is a happy guy most of the time now. We work on things like table manners, homework…normal stuff. Kids are inviting him over. Chris and his dad help some of the older people in our church. They make a contribution."

Leilani's Case: therapy for anxious children after early neglect

Parents regularly request therapy citing moderate worries about their children, who arrive in the home at late infancy or early childhood. Parents typically report histories that include children being left alone for long periods of time. Or, they describe caregivers who changed according to a rotating, institutional schedule. These children are anxious and worried even after they attach to their new parents. Their brains seem to have been shaped by their earliest experiences of neglect. We presume that they may have inherited the genetics for anxiety that have combined with their experiences to result in high anxiety.[3]

Parents describe their children's wearing, constant need for help to soothe anxieties. This anxiety makes parents anxious themselves, as they anticipate the energy it takes to deal with their children. It makes them tense and weary.

It is easy to think that, if the parent relaxed, then the child would follow. In fact, while it is necessary to help the parents return to their more relaxed state, it is typical for parents to act calm around one child and tense with the anxious child. Or, they are calm in all of the other areas of their lives that exclude the anxious child.

The children will need to learn a skill set for calming and soothing themselves. The therapist also needs to figure out what they are worried about, and to help them to learn and master problem-solving skills. Many times, children control their parents. They may do this as their anxiety increases. Or they blame parents when they get distressed. Leilani's case, below, describes a child who became anxious and controlling, as well as the therapy that helped her calm down.

Intake session

As in Chris' case, I asked for pre-treatment information before meeting with Leilani's parents. I asked to read their last homestudy. This gave me an assessment of them individually and as a couple. The assessments showed a couple with a long-standing positive friendship with each other and strong ties to one side of the family. I also asked for developmental information on Leilani, including a recent cognitive assessment and a Child Achenbach test, and for medical information. The Achenbach showed high levels of anxiety for Leilani, mostly turned inward, and a tendency to manifest this anxiety as physical distress.

I met with the parents for a two-hour intake session. I wanted to hear how they talked about their lives, without Leilani hearing their anxieties and frustrations.

---

[3] This is a typical beginning for anxiety disorders. Someone with a genetic predisposition also experiences life stress (usually mild stress is a powerful enough activator). This is distinct from experience-related stress, which is directly related to life events. Genetic anxiety/depression, etc., in contrast, is an exaggerated or unprovoked response as compared to life events.

Leilani's parents came in with concerns about their daughter's anxiety level. Leilani was intellectually advanced, but, by age 6, her anxiety was already interfering and limiting her in school. She had insisted on missing kindergarten many days, and was already ruminating about the expected rigors of first grade. In daily life, she often became distressed to the point of hitting her parents. She would shriek in the car en route to any events that she had worries about. She refused to be left with her father, but wept when he went out-of-town.

Leilani's sister, Mei Mei, was 2 years old. Leilani had to wait for her parents when they attended to her sister. She had begun to retaliate for being told to wait. She would unbuckle Mei Mei's car seat or trip her later. On the other hand, Leilani was also kind to Mei Mei. She often played with her, sought her out, and hugged her in a tender manner.

Since Leilani's placement, the parents had not had a night out together due to her behaviors. She had made them promise never to leave her again. The parents had settled on a wedding anniversary "brunch" while Leilani was at kindergarten.

"What's wrong with her?" her parent's said. "She seems attached. We don't really think that she is a psychopath. Our parents say that we should spank her. We really don't think that will solve the problem. But we did tell her we would spank her if we ever caught her unbuckling the seatbelt again. Last night she was crying in the night saying, 'They are going to spank me, spank me!'"

"I know that this sounds ridiculous," her mother said, "but she really is suffering."

Leilani had been found near a police station in China when she was about 4 months old. She had a heart murmur, but was otherwise healthy. She went into an orphanage and then to a foster home. She was placed with her parents by 10 months of age. After screaming for about two days, she grabbed tightly onto her mother—and did not willingly let go for most of the next six years.

Leilani had had an allergy-related medical emergency at 18 months. She was hospitalized for it twice. These incidents seemed particularly hard for her mother to forget.

She observed, "I think that my anxiety has been part of the problem. I think that I will need to learn some ways to calm down, too."

Even as the rest of her developmental milestones marched along, Leilani continued to over-respond to the normal stresses of life. She lacked any desire to self-soothe. Her worst fear was that her mother would be killed in a car accident. In order to best prevent this from happening, she specialized in calling out the speed that the car was going—continuously— while her mother drove.

The parents' daily activities were dictated by their daughter's anxieties. As she got older and others expected her to be able to handle more, she began to act out because she could not meet the challenges. The family was worried about the other relationships in the family, as well as about Leilani's development.

Meanwhile, Mei Mei was learning a passive and co-dependent pattern. Everyone knew that her sister's needs came first. She automatically waited until Leilani interrupted. She had even learned to roll her eyes as she waited. (Neither parent wanted even to think about where that had been modeled.) The parents were concerned that Mei Mei was learning that her own needs did not matter.

With school coming up again in three months, the family wanted desperately to start therapy. Leilani resisted going to school, and in a creative touch, asked her grandmother to inform her parents that she had decided not to go to back to school. She had nightmares every night. A hardball approach backfired. She seemed to get more anxious with punishment, her parents observed.

The parents had been part of an adoptive parenting group. They felt that their problems were unwelcome in the group, since their daughter seemed to defy the premise of the group. The group believed that, with unrestricted access to sensitive parents, their daughter would reduce her anxiety and use her parents for a secure base, leaving and returning smoothly. Instead, their daughter seemed to be an outsider in the group.

The mother said, "We've used this approach faithful-
ly. Mei Mei has done great with it. She's already surpassed
Leilani. We were down to the wire with school starting, and
the group facilitator told us, 'Maybe your daughter needs another type of approach. Have you considered family therapy?'

"Our doctors gave your name to us. So here we are."

Treatment planning

These parents had tried to fill their daughter's needs for security
by being with her constantly. This had not worked. Instead, they had
as anxious a child as ever, who was now also used to being indulged.
Leilani set the rules for the family.

The parents enjoyed coming together and forming a
plan they could both support. The process of parenting had
strained their own relationship, which had been filled with
enjoyable camaraderie, mutual support, and good humor
over a 15-year period of childlessness. Now, the father often
felt shamed and like he was doing things wrong. His feeling
was not-so-subtly promoted by Leilani's shrill, "I want Mom.
You do it wrong." Mei Mei would lisp the same refrain. "Yeth,
Papa. You do it wong."

He explained, "I have four big brown eyes accusing me.
Then, my wife walks in and makes it six." She looks at me
like, "Can't I even take a shower or make a call without everything falling apart?"

Before she had been diagnosed with allergies, Leilani's
father had given her a peanut butter cracker, and she had
ended up in the hospital. Part of Mom's anxiety and over-
response was a reaction to Leilani's medical emergency. She
had never taken time to process the incident. She questioned
Dad's judgment largely based on this one incident. In the
session, Mom agreed that his judgment was typically sound.

"I know that you are getting set up," the wife said.

I suggested that when the children called for her, that she
should say, "Papa is a great dad." She should kiss him and
leave again. As time went on, she should ignore the girls and
just not arrive.

In the initial session, I spent time with Mom, reminding her of some of the things that she enjoyed. She loved parenting, but she also missed spending time with her husband and with her friends. Both parents had long-term friendships and great social skills.

Dad was spending his adult leisure time alone. He had adjusted to spending his adult "buddy time" without his wife. We talked openly about remedying this pattern over the next several months.

We also individualized Mei Mei's needs. Leilani interrupted individual attention to Mei Mei. The parents agreed to take Mei Mei into their bedroom to finish what they were doing if they had to. They decided to close their door and let Leilani wait. They would explain the strategy to Leilani in terms of being fair to Mei Mei. If Leilani retaliated, then Mei Mei would get a half-hour alone with the parents while Leilani went to bed early.

Note that we discussed the whole family in the planning session, not just Leilani. The treatment process that we agreed upon was
- to help Leilani learn relaxation techniques
- to help Leilani use relaxation techniques while anxious
- to help Leilani with cognitive behavior therapy in sessions, i.e. using helpful thoughts to guide her behaviors instead of unhelpful thoughts with maladaptive behaviors
- to help the mother to maintain her regulation in the face of Leilani's anxiety—initially with me and then without me
- to help Leilani with some insight-oriented work around early experiences and adoption
- to help the family with some family skills, including rewards and consequences that helped reinforce Leilani's coping
- to strengthen a marriage that was going through a difficult adjustment to parenting.

The approach that I used with the parents was to suggest that Leilani needed to learn a skill set to deal with anxiety. She needed to work on being a girl with courage in order to become a strong and capable woman. She also needed a supportive milieu that encouraged an incremental use of relaxation and coping skills.

The mother volunteered that she did not want Leilani to turn out like her own mother, whose anxiety was a bane to the family. She observed that she was probably accommodating Leilani much like she had learned to accommodate to her own mother. (This insight was met by a bulgy-eyed, lip-compressed facial contortion by Dad. To his credit, he kept his mouth shut so as not to un-do the progress just made.)

I nodded as she discussed her mother. I told her that I would help her stay on track as she made some changes. She could talk to me each week when they came in for help. At this juncture, the mom turned to Dad, "OK, OK, you can stop holding your breath now. I know what you are thinking about my mother." They both laughed a little and held hands.

"This is helping already," Mom said. "I feel as if things are more manageable and we haven't even started therapy." In fact, the initial session was designed to be practical <u>and</u> therapeutic.

The father particularly liked the concept of helping Leilani develop more courage and to see herself as a strong girl. Both parents valued emotional intelligence, and saw it as essential to career success and friendships. The father wanted more of a relationship with Leilani. The mother liked the notion of having more time as a couple. "I don't like how Leilani's moods determine what I do every day. I feel like our house is ruled by a 6-year-old. This is going to stop."

The first session with the parents is critical to success. Come up with an understanding of the problem and an approach to treat the problem. This provides a strong foundation for the upcoming work. This session also gave me the future ability to speak to either parent about Leilani and to have both or either in the sessions.

In the first session with Leilani, I started out by brightening the emotional tone before describing the work on anxiety. I asked her parents to have her bring things that she was particularly fond of or had mastered into the session. It gave me a chance to see some of Leilani's successes and interests. She brought her soccer trophy, a picture that she had drawn, her bear, her favorite book, and a panda costume. We discussed all of those items as she shared her identity with me. She relaxed with me in the session, laughed, and looked confident. I kept her mother in the office with us so that Leilani would feel more comfortable.

I told Leilani we would talk about our work and draw up a plan in the next session. I promised her that it was my job to make certain that I gave her tools so that her scared feelings did not get too big. I would teach her how to use those tools. I asked her whether she was good at learning. Of course, she beamed and described herself as smart and fun. I asked her to think about the colors we should use to draw the plan next week.

Children who worry want to know what is coming next. They also worry that they will not know how to do something—before they have even had a chance to learn it! I like to give them something positive and specific to think about. It guides their brains into preparation in a positive manner. In the first session, I exaggerated the positive affects and was a bit dramatic. Leilani wanted to come back. I used this approach not only because it was a kind way of proceeding, but because the family stress was such that I did not want the parents to have to drag a reluctant Leilani into therapy.

Treatment planning with Leilani

In the next session, Leilani described the color scheme she wanted and we made a treatment plan that looked like a patchwork quilt. We used the following squares: losing Mom forever, anger at parents or her sister, fear when she was away from Mom at school, being embarrassed by her disagreeable behaviors, Dad's traveling, and being afraid to go to friends' homes. I asked her about adoption issues, but she did not endorse that those were anxiety-producing, either verbally or through body language. In summarizing those sections, I was careful not to get the feelings too intense. We got up to take a little walk around the room or I distracted her positively with talk about the colors of the plan when she began to get pale, stiff, or to lose verbal fluency.

Leilani colored and decorated the treatment plan with me, which helped modulate the pacing. She nearly forgot her mother, who got bored, cleaned out her purse, and then stepped out to the waiting room for a magazine. "I guess that I can relax," she said, as she watched us.

In the first sessions, I took over some of the job as the emotional regulator for the dyad. In the process of the first two sessions, I told Leilani that my job was to help her to "be strong—be a woman" and to feel much better inside. In the next sessions we would work on those activities. Leilani loved the exuberant facial expressions that came with "be a woman." She laughed a lot in the sessions. Because I was taking over the affect in a positive manner, Leilani began to attune to me positively.

I demonstrated deep breathing and the body language of relaxing before I even taught it to her. The mother began to pick up the skill set of relaxation just by having it modeled. "My mother was always so tense," she volunteered. "You make being with children a lot more enjoyable." The mother supported me as I worked, which was typical of her generous attitude towards others.

In the next session, as we worked on relaxation techniques, I took Leilani's picture with my Polaroid® and pasted it to a page entitled "Leilani has courage."

We joked around, with me saying, "Leilani, you must chill. Have courage! Be a Woman." Leilani mimed and laughed and said, "But I'm a girl."

"Oh, all right. Be a Girl!" I said with the same strong emphasis.

Leilani and I worked on where she felt anxiety in her body. Notice that we were improving the mind-body connection. She liked being able to feel a little and then to relax herself. For homework, Leilani was asked to set the timer for once an hour and relax whenever the timer went off. I asked her to call my voice mail and leave a message every time she started to get the feelings of anxiety and then relaxed instead. She called twice during the third week. She said that she actually relaxed more, but she wanted to call twice.

By the fourth session, Leilani was ready for some challenges. We had built enough anxiety regulation that we moved to some exposure to normally stressful situations. For Leilani, this meant separating from parents.

We moved to a structure that we continued using for the rest of the treatment. First, I got a report on the week from the parents. I asked Leilani to sit in the waiting room for ten minutes, giving her my watch so that she could come in "when the big hand was on the 2." Her parents were surprised that she was able wait. This time was used helping parents with their co-regulation and parent skills, like appropriate expectations, if-then, if-when statements, and reward systems.

Secondly, I met with Leilani to propose a schedule and topics for the session. Leilani brought in topics that she felt we should address: hitting her sister, having to travel by plane, her father's trip, etc. This section gave her predictability and helped her to join with me emotionally. She also practiced thinking about a problem without becoming flooded by the emotions of a problem. This helped her to see challenges from a problem-solving perspective

We spent time making booklets that detailed our plans for problems. We wrote down our ideas and plans. Leilani was an early reader, so we used words and pictures. In this way, she could see the end results of successful interactions, including the feelings of mastery. For example, she could predict the great feeling of relaxing, riding on the plane, and then seeing her aunt and uncle. We included a parent in the room if Leilani requested this.

Thirdly, we worked on anxiety and relaxation in real time. At the last part of the session, we reviewed the positive aspects of her accomplishments and talked about ways to expand the progress into the coming week. This helped Leilani integrate her changes into her sense of self.

In the fifth session, Leilani and I left the office to take a walk as part of our plan. The plan was to help Leilani use relaxation techniques in real time, by having her deal with anxiety when separated from her mother. The goal was to walk up to the count of 100. (This was an impressive number for Leilani, who also wanted to show me that she could count that high.) This was an exposure technique, designed so that she could begin to use her skills while experiencing the anxiety of separating from her mother.

We went out of the office, allowing her to feel some anxiety and to bring it down. I made use of the ripe blackberries up the street, suggesting picking some as a destination. Leilani not only did well, but she agreed to leave the office two more times during that session. Her homework was to do the same exercises at home, while Mom went outside or upstairs, for the count of 100. I find it helpful to elaborate on a goal, helping children to visualize something like the blackberries. It gives them something else to think about rather than just thinking about separation.

By the next session, Leilani was forgetting to count and was able to tolerate several minutes of separation. We expanded the time and began to think of goals that Leilani might want. Those included going somewhere alone with her father and seeing something interesting in her friend's home. She was able to use the same template as she was using in the sessions, which included making a goal and then working with her body to keep herself in a regulated state.

Leilani worked with me on her fears over the next six to eight sessions. This work included self-talk or images to help deal with those fears. We wondered together whether she might have some memory of being left as a baby, but she added, "But it isn't happening now. I could, you know, move on."

Leilani wanted to talk about her adoption. She said that she was concerned that she had gotten lost from her birthmother. As Leilani and I talked about her adoption story, Leilani said that she did not miss her birthfamily but she was a little sad about China's one child policy. She concluded, "I think that Mei Mei and I belong here, with my mom and dad. I would feel funny being part of another family when I don't even know those people. I'm glad I know why I came here from China. I didn't really understand it. I'm glad that no one is looking for me. I don't want to go back." Leilani had needed a concrete explanation that emphasized the finality of her family placement.

We began to work on Leilani's dreams in the eighth session. Leilani had dreams that included separation from her parents and getting hurt with no parents to help her. We were able to talk about this fear in terms of her life story and how it must have been so difficult for her to be separated from a birthparent and then a foster parent. Leilani's mother verified that Leilani had cried for almost twenty-four hours after placement.

We included the reality that Leilani had become affectionate very quickly with her parents, but had never quite settled into believing that they were permanent. In discussions with Leilani, I wondered if she could begin to teach herself that her separations were in the past. It seemed that her brain was questioning whether or not separations might still be happening.

She wrote a poster for herself for nighttimes. It said, "My parents are here for always." When she had a bad dream or worry, I asked her to fix her dreams with her parents appearing and saying, "Here we are!" We acted this out in the office with Leilani and her mother. Leilani's mother began to use a babysitter, without major protests from Leilani, by the fourteenth session.

During this time frame Leilani did have a big issue over the time Mom spent with Mei Mei. Her mother took Mei Mei into the parents' bedroom, closed the door, and told Leilani through the door to quiet down, calm down, and then they would come out. Right now, it was Mei Mei's special time. Leilani yelled for a little while, and then calmed herself and even apologized.

The parents moved into a steady, rather than tentative, pattern. Much of the change came from the parents' feeling like they were using an approach that was good for their children. They projected a steady assurance to Leilani and her sister.

Mei Mei noticed that the tide had turned. As she turned 3, she tried to tell some transparent lies in order to get Leilani into trouble and get herself some extra attention. The parents saw this as a normal rebalancing of the family. Leilani no longer did painful paybacks, although the girls occasionally argued.

A couple of times, when Leilani was interrupting herself, Mei Mei told her, "Stop. You're erupting me." Leilani saw the humor in this and seemed to settle into a more balanced relationship. Mei Mei also told on her sister or hit back now. Leilani noted that her sister seemed to have picked up the hitting from Leilani. She felt that it was important that she stop teaching her sister this behavior.

As school approached, Leilani practiced the process of being dropped off at school and the ritual of saying "Goodbye" several times. Over the first few weeks of school, she cried for ten to twenty minutes almost every day. Her teacher was supportive, but not doting. The mother was instructed to leave after a short goodbye. Leilani actually preferred this, and told her mother that it just took her a little while to stop crying.

Beginning at session sixteen, we worked on the feelings that Leilani had towards her father. "I just don't trust him," she said. "When I need him he might be on a trip or at work."

We worked on some concepts and practical methods of holding onto his love even when he was not home. These included looking at pictures of them both on the computer, making a videotape of him saying good night to her and then watching it at night, and discussing the practicalities of money and what they bought through him working. It turned out that she was angry at him for causing her anxiety as he left. After two sessions, she said, "I'm not mad any more. Somebody has to make money for our family. It is silly to be mad at him for something he has to do."

We took pictures of the two of them together that showed her as being relaxed and enjoying his presence. Her plan was to review these pictures when he was gone and then write a couple of things that she would share with him after he came home. They began to go places together both with and without Mei Mei.

We talked about the feelings that Dad had when Leilani accused him of doing things wrong. He told Leilani his feelings, eye-to-eye. Leilani hugged him and said that she was sorry for hurting his feelings. This understanding of the state of mind of another person was a great success for Leilani. Not only did she understand her father's feelings, but she repaired the relationship with coaching. I guided her through this interaction, since she otherwise would either have ignored him or focused on how she felt when he expressed himself. With help, she completed a cycle of repair. More and more she was able to emotionally attune and complete age-appropriate repair.

Leilani turned 7 years old. We moved the sessions to every other week and then monthly. She developed skills in calming and problem-solving with awareness of self and others. When Leilani had something that promoted anxiety, a parent responded with, "What's your plan?" She drew or wrote a plan for how she would cope. She was able to ask for help. She gave herself powerful self-talk and began to coach herself.

Leilani experienced a big downturn and said that she was sick three days in a row. This occurred the week after she was home from school with a bad cold. We simply went back to earlier work and reapplied some of the same techniques. We talked about her jealousy of Mei Mei, who was home with Mom, and her fears of being ill. "I was really sick once," she said. "I'm not now, but I get afraid that I might die."

We worked on helpful thoughts, listed them, acted them out, and then drew them in cartooning fashion, placing the helpful thoughts and good feelings in bubbles above the characters. She felt and saw the transition from being very afraid to calming down.

I gave Leilani five stay-home passes for the next three months. With no questions asked, those could be used for sickness or otherwise. That way she did not pull the family into anxious morning discussions (arguments) over the level of illness required to stay home. (This was beginning to occur.) I did not want Leilani to learn to either suffer more or become a better liar. Leilani used two passes right away, but saved the rest. "What will happen if I use them all up?" she asked me.

"I guess you'll have to be careful." I said. "You are a smart girl. You can tell whether you are just a little ill or whether you need to stay home in bed."

Leilani responded; "I have to watch it so that I don't have to go to school really, really sick because I wasted my passes playing with Mei Mei." She still had two passes left at the end of the three-month period.

Over the next six months, Leilani came in as needed. This was weekly for a few weeks over a particular issue, such as the family looking for a new home. Then she would not come in for several weeks.

At about month seven, the mother asked for a few sessions to talk about her own childhood and the demands still placed on her by her mother. We worked on establishing healthy limits and responses to meet her mother's needs and also on her pain and anger. She described loving her mother but feeling guilty over resenting and avoiding her. She decided to live out being compassionate while having limits.

"I felt as if I had to harden myself to my mother or she'd take me over completely," she described. "Working with Leilani helped me to see that my life is important. And it's good for Leilani to care about other people's needs. It's not just one person who gets to have what they want. The adoption parenting class made me feel as if I owed my children everything because of their adoption loss. Or, maybe it was just me. I could have interpreted things that way because of my childhood."

The family moved to a new home during month eight. The family planned to leave the trundle bed in Leilani's room behind. Previously, when Leilani woke up with nightmares, her Mom would come in to calm her and then sleep in Leilani's room the rest of the night. I suggested giving the trundle bed away before the move, since the move itself could be anxiety-producing. The new solution was to keep a sleeping bag under her parents' bed. That way, if Leilani woke up with a bad dream, she could still come in for reassurance. She could either go back to her own bed or pull out the sleeping bag, remaining beside her parents for the rest of the night.

Since she knew that the trundle arrangement was not going to be available any longer, Leilani negotiated for a purple room with stars and princess netting over her bed for the new house. "I'd rather have my mom, but she says that she is getting too many dark circles under her eyes," Leilani confided. "So I made a good deal on my new furniture."

The parents began to go out occasionally in the evenings. Leilani's parents showed a more positive marriage adjustment to parenting. They joked more, socialized more, handled the children separately and together, and slept together. The family was done with regular therapy sessions by the one-year mark.

This approach worked so efficiently because it gave Leilani and her family the skills they needed to reduce anxiety and increase emotional reciprocity. It provided emotional support for the family while they established a new pattern. The treatment approach was direct and used her strengths, but it did not pressure Leilani to leave her defenses of arguing and controlling behind before she had developed her new abilities.

The therapy also made good use of the parents' strengths. While it was easy to see their short-comings, it was much more productive to focus on spending time building new patterns. The mother's desire to talk about her past came naturally and was helpful for her, but, by itself, this narrative work does not easily segue into learning a new pattern. The direct work, however, did. This direct course of therapy took about thirty-five sessions.

Madison's Story—therapy for an explosive child in a kinship adoption after neglect and frequent moves

Madison, at age 11, was difficult to get to know. Her answer to questions concerning her choices, tastes, and feelings were, "I don't know," or "I don't care," or "What do you think?" Like many children who have experienced neglect and been moved between caregivers, she lacked self-regulation and self-reflection. This casestudy tells the story of her treatment and her work on developing mindfulness and a sense of her own personal strength. Madison was placed through a kinship adoption. Her family is African-American, as is her birthfather. Madison's birthmother is Caucasian.

Initial session and treatment planning

Madison's parents were referred to me through their pastoral staff, who knew of me through the church's involvement in supporting adoption. Madison's parents, Curtis and Marsha, were worried about her future. In an earlier chapter we met Madison's father, who was anxious about whether she would be taken advantage of since she was so compliant to gain acceptance. She would do her brother's chores to get his attention saying, "But I don't mind!"

Madison's parents reported that she had little tolerance for frustration. She would give up on hard assignments at school, complain about her chores, and physically block her mother to prevent her from leaving the room at nighttime or during homework, piano practice, or arguments.

Their need for therapeutic help was becoming immediate. Madison was increasingly explosive as the social and academic demands in her life increased. She screamed at her mother at least twice a day. In the week before our first session, she tripped her mother and shoved her hard. Later, during her apology, Madison wept and cried. "But it was all about her," Marsha said. "It was completely about her restrictions and begging to be forgiven of the consequences.

"It's a good thing that I'm a strong woman. I've always been an athlete, so I hold my ground when she gets physical. But this is ridiculous! I'm embarrassed to tell people how wild she gets. She acts shy, sweet, cooperative, and withdrawn at church and school. Everybody says, 'We just think that your daughter is so sweet.' They ought to try to do a State Capitol project with her! It's a nightmare."

Curtis said, "We are a close family. We are supportive of each other and put a lot of emphasis on helping one another. Madison is more than competent in sports, even fearless. Even though she has her trials in schoolwork, Madison has good values. But sometimes she can't seem to think. Her brother and sister were not perfect, but we never had these struggles.

"Madison goes past the point of no return. I don't think she can stop herself when she gets to a certain point. And I think that is why she keeps herself a little apart from other kids. I think that she is worried about what they'd think if they saw her so out of control. She whines that she doesn't have friends, but she won't invite kids over."

Prior to the first session, the parents sent me Madison's background information, including her medical history, sketchy placement history, and school testing. Madison had been a premature baby, born to birthparents who were not yet sure about their plan for parenting. The birthmother had severe postpartum depression.

Madison left the hospital with a maternal relative. This relative used a strict feeding schedule and Madison did not gain weight and developed ear infections and respiratory issues. Her health problems were such a concern to her doctors that they suggested a medical foster care placement. So at seven months of age, she went into a skilled foster home and stayed there for four months. Then, she moved to another relative placement for the next year. During that year, Madison's care was shared by her birthparents and the birthmother's sisters. The birthparents were in an on and off relationship.

When Madison was 2 years old, her maternal grandmother asked the birthmother and Madison to live with her. Madison was left more or less alone, and she would sleep, wander around or cry until her birthmother picked her up—or not. The birthmother never recovered from her initial depression. Madison became quieter and less demanding. CPS stepped in when Madison's weight dropped and her ears did not heal. The birthparents finally made an adoption plan when Madison was 2½ years old, placing Madison with paternal relatives, Marsha and Curtis.

The family fell in love with Madison immediately. She quickly reciprocated with Mom, but kept her dad at a distance. She refused to allow her mother to leave her much.

Marsha and Curtis recognized Madison's developmental delays at placement. They saw the effects of the neglect and hearing loss and quickly accessed early intervention services through their school district.

This kinship placement had included much less preparation and support as compared to the placement process in cases such as Chris's. Marsha and Curtis knew little about adoption, special needs, or post-placement support. "Our qualifications were assessed this way—we were warm and biologically related!" Curtis said. "Our nephew had asked if we'd be interested earlier. We told him that we would not take her unless it was permanent. Now I regret that I placed this condition. We can never get back her hearing. Sometimes, when she's struggling with her hearing aids, I feel a huge weight in my chest. We could have prevented some of this." Marsha became tearful and Curtis dropped his head.

"I wonder if you thought that you were protecting your family?" I asked.

"That was exactly it," Curtis said. "I did not want my kids to have a sister, and my wife to fall in love with this little girl, and then have the other side of the family ask for her back. I knew that they'd been doing that nonsense for two years."

"It sounds like you made the best decision that you could with the information that you had," I said.

"That's exactly what I told him," Marsha said. "We just have to go on from here."

Curtis' feeling of regret is common in a kinship placement. Relatives often feel responsible for moving in too slowly, even though, in this case, it is not clear that it would have made any difference.

The parents concluded, "We thought that she'd grow out of this clinginess. After all, we know that she had a rough start. But, it has been almost nine years. We're hoping that you can give us some tools. We are open to learning."

Madison's parents, unlike the parents in Chris' case, did not receive adoption support. They did not have a caseworker to describe post-placement services or partially or fully subsidized support for these services through State and Federal monies. Instead, Madison's parents had to find an attorney to finalize their adoption, all at their own expense. They also paid out of pocket for any of Madison's medical and physical expenses not covered by their insurance or provided by the school. This is not atypical for the 25-35% of adoptions from foster care that are kinship placements. And, in this case, their church community provided the primary support network for their adoption.

I did not outline a specific treatment plan with Madison's parents. I wanted to suggest a treatment plan after I met her. I needed to meet with her first in order to get a better idea of the approaches that would work best.

Madison's parents supplied testing information on academics, an update on her social skills class at school, and also her speech and language assessments and progress. Madison's testing indicated that she learned best through templates and examples. Academically, she was about eighteen months behind in the language-based materials. She was generally liked by the school staff, but she sat alone at lunch unless someone initiated a gesture of friendship. She did not seek out friends, but did respond to others' advances in a pleasant, but superficial manner.

Madison came into the first session smiling, squirming, and acting uncomfortable. She wanted her parents to come into the session. She had also marshaled the support of her sister who sat it the waiting room. She was hard to connect with, turning her face away and intentionally facing the ear with the greatest hearing loss next to me.

I matched some of her resistance by using an expansive, but playful approach. I mentioned her positive qualities, and then attuned to her resistance, "You do all of those nice things and they still can't forgive a little tripping your mother down the stairs. Go figure. The next thing you know you are in therapy instead of eating ice cream and watching cartoons after school." She brightened, joined with me emotionally, and said hopefully, "Yeah. Just what I was thinking. So, are we done?"

"No," I replied, "but nice try." She and her parents laughed a little, but by matching we did join with her emotionally, and I got better connection.

Treatment planning with Madison

I made a basic treatment plan with Madison so that she could predict, in general, what was coming next. Madison wanted to stop putting out any effort as soon as she noticed that I seemed pleased. Her attention would shift. I talked to her about being a strong girl.

"Be strong Madison," I urged. "Be a Woman." I physically demonstrated this with a strong stance and bicep bulge. This notion tickled her. It gave me a sense of what pulled her in, which, in her case, was the kinesthetic modality. This matched her fearlessness in sports.

Throughout the next session, we completed the treatment plan, which was to include six sections. For each section, we took a Polaroid© picture of Madison doing something positive for herself, and an alternate, a negative response. Madison modeled those positive pictures by posing with me. She was a little reluctant and guarded, but she did cooperate. We went for a five minute long brisk walk after she tried to ooze down the sofa in a dramatic feign of sleepiness. I used a bright affect with a lot of physical modeling to keep her attention. This affect was exaggerated to the extent that both parents remarked that watching me work with Madison made them tired.

The sections comprising the treatment plan were these:
- Learning to calm herself. The emblem was a confident Madison. The crossed out version was Madison with her shoulders up and a frozen expression.
- Thinking helpful thoughts instead of ones that put her down. The emblem was Madison kicking a ball with a mental bubble of, "Give it your best." The alternate that

she crossed out was her throwing her books and saying, "But I don't like homework!"

- Separating from mom confidently. The emblem was Madison with a heart filled with little hearts drawn on her chest. The alternate was Madison with a broken heart with little hearts leaking out. We talked about how her baby brain remembered all of those separations. "So that's why I get so mad" she concluded. We did not cross out the alternative picture in this case, but did draw an arrow from the earlier way to the confident picture.

- Anger was the next area. We drew a picture of Madison saying, "I don't like it, but I can handle this situation." The picture of Madison included her biceps popping out, using this as a metaphor for emotional strength. The alternate was her being embarrassed about her anger. We talked about how she hoped that no one would ever find out that she screamed and pushed. I drew the alternate picture of her looking weak and embarrassed. Notice that strength was reframed here. Strength was defined as self-control, not physical acting out.

- Sharing feelings with others was next. She complained that she had felt nothing when her cat died. She also did not really feel much when others got hurt. She felt weird. We drew just one picture here, which was Madison with a balloon saying, "I want to feel normal." We decided that we would come back to this frame later.

- The last picture was of more confidence with friends. She drew herself asking someone over for a sleepover. The alternative picture was her sitting alone and saying, "I don't care." Madison contributed, "I act like I don't care, but I do." Again, we drew arrows from the earlier part of the frame to the positive other.

The treatment planning exercise offered the opportunity to practice pacing. We accessed a small part of her emotion, without it overwhelming her. She got practical experience in not being expected to work on some parts until she had learned a pre-requisite skill set.

Madison had barely developed the ability to think about her life or her feelings. We began the process of learning how to think about her life during the treatment planning. Madison fully intended to let me take her through the therapy process, contributing only a passive approach for her part. I told her directly that I could help her, but that I was a great therapist and what made me great was that I knew that the children did the hard work to be successful. I could help her, but she would have to do the work and come to believe in herself.

Madison liked this approach. Her family's strengths begin to emerge. "I do believe in myself some of the time," she said. "Just not always." We talked about the fact that no person believes in herself all of the time, but our families encourage us. We also have to encourage ourselves with self-talk. We have to try hard most of the time; we cannot surrender and become helpless.

I drew a life timeline with Madison, showing her the times that she would have needed to shut down and give up early in childhood. "Giving up worked right then," I said. "You were a baby and it was the only way that you could live through so much hunger, ear pain, and boredom. It just does not work now." This timeline helped Madison conceptualize a clear before and after. In other words, she had needed the defenses before, when her life was overwhelmingly frustrating, but she did not need them now, after her frustrations became tolerable.

In working with Madison and her feelings, we had to start with basics. Neglect had caused her to shut herself off from her body. We started by asking where she felt pleasure, frustrations, anger, and so forth. We drew her body on large sheets of paper, and she picked out colors for feelings, felt the feelings, and then drew where she felt her positive feelings on her body picture. We also wrote down examples of those feelings.

When we got to feelings of anger, sadness, or frustrations, she squirmed, pulled her fingers backwards, dislodged her hearing aid, and attempted to avoid any of those feelings. I showed her how to feel a little of the feeling, and then do deep breathing to relax the feelings. She needed to feel some of the feelings and learn to regulate them, rather continuing to use her strategy of avoiding, avoiding, avoiding and then feeling very anxious. "Or I explode like a volcano," Madison volunteered.

"Smart thinking!" I replied. I wanted to reinforce her actually staying with the process long enough to think.

I told Madison some stories that contained some frustration, sadness, or pain. As she followed the stories, she felt some of the feelings. At first, she still tried to stop these feelings from emerging. I would point out how she was pulling at her fingers, pinching herself, changing the subject, going to the restroom, or trying self-hypnosis by staring out my window at the cars on the freeway outside. I was sympathetic, but firm, as I helped her stop these defenses. I told her that I would make certain that the feelings did not get too big for her.

Madison was actually quite afraid of experiencing the feelings in the same, overwhelming way that she had as a toddler. We made sense of this fear through her timeline. We listed off all of the things that she could do to calm these feelings, such as deep breathing, putting a nice fragrance on her wrist and smelling it, self-talk about how small the frustration or irritant really was, and so forth.

By the fourth session, Madison was able to feel anxiety and frustration and then calm down afterwards. She practiced deep breathing in real time and using positive self-talk when prompted, and sometimes spontaneously. She still occasionally needed to be prompted to put her shoulders down and breathe. The parents successfully used non-verbal cues, or modeled the behavior, most of the time.

By session number five, Madison could make a plan in session with me, including what was frustrating or embarrassing her and why, and how she planned to handle it. Homework, one of her main sources of frustration, was defined as a specific fifty minute time period each day. This turned it into a definable, finite concept, with a beginning and an end. Her parents were available for her to use as resources during this time.

If Madison did not finish her homework during that time, the parents wrote a note to school, letting them know that Madison had either tried and had not finished, or had not worked on it. Madison missed recess a few times as a school consequence. If she did not work on her homework, her parents would not extend the time, but rather Madison would be restricted from any television or computer time for the rest of the evening.

Madison worked on separating from her mother in a calm, normal way next. She claimed not to know the feelings that accompanied her anxiety. I showed her a picture of a toddler girl, lost and alone. "I don't like that picture!" she said. She looked frozen at first, and then said, "Okay I do feel like that!" We practiced calming with soothing self-talk. Her mother said things like, "I'll always come back. I love you."

Madison and I looked at her life timeline. She pondered the feelings and their connection to her life story. She counted moves between caregivers, the months that she was there, and asked questions. This process helped her connect her feelings with the events in her life.

Madison's moods were brittle, so she acted frightened and then broke into laughter when she exceeded the threshold of her tolerance. This happened at home whenever her parents spoke in a serious manner. Her parents became more supportive once they understood that her laughter represented the underdeveloped state of her moods. After several more weeks of work, Madison stopped breaking into laughter during sad, angry, or anxious conversations.

Madison asked many questions about her care and wondered if her birthparents did not like her because of her hearing loss. "I thought that I was too much trouble for them. Or that they wanted a perfect, popular girl. Did I cost too much money because of my hearing aids?" Marsha assured her that it was not the case, but talked realistically about her birthmother's depression and her birthfather's military service as factors that informed her adoption. I asked her if she ever thought that her race had anything to do with her placement. Madison said that she did not.

Over the next few sessions, Madison talked about her life story. Her mother, Marsha, would become emotional. Madison would sometimes start to look sad, and then become fixated on her mother's feelings. Madison was frightened by Marsha's tears. Marsha reassured Madison that she was just fine, and that she could feel sad but still be capable and strong.

Marsha described some of her feelings and thoughts to Madison. For example, she described wishing that Madison had come to their home sooner, and her sadness over Madison's early neglect. Madison followed her template for processing strong feelings, with some of my help in processing, when Marsha described her emotions. She said, "I get it now. You feel bad when you think of me feeling hungry and scared. I was always worried that you were going to, like, fall apart when you cried like that." Marsha assured Madison that she would not.

We could have gone on to talk about mother figures who could not cope at this point, but we stayed with the treatment plan. I did make a note to get more information about how Madison's birthmother expressed her depression. We could always return to this topic to integrate her history with better information after Madison developed more competencies.

Soon after this session, we began to plan separations between Madison and Marsha, with intentional helping strategies. We gave Madison cue cards that she could carry in her pocket. These cards listed words and body commands that said things like: breathe; shoulders down; she'll be back, she promised; put on one of her shirts if you miss her; play a game; write a note to her; distract yourself with soccer in the backyard.

Madison started to talk about "feeling bad," her phrase for sad. She described an injury at school, and reported that she felt the appropriate feelings for the first time. Madison told me, "I helped that girl go to the nurse; she said that she could tell that I cared. 'You're a good friend, Madison,' she said. I felt really bad for her." Madison said.

Madison worked on her anger. We used her timeline to

talk about why she used anger and control to get adults' attention. "It seems that your baby brain is still expecting that no one will come!" I said. "Or is it that you think that you aren't worth the trouble?"

"A little of both," Madison replied. We talked about how normal it is for babies and toddlers to get angry when they have to wait. Madison said quietly, "I get mad at my parents because I think that they treat me like garbage. I say to myself that they don't care, even though they say that they do. I tell myself that they are selfish and that they deserve to be yelled at."

By talking about these issues, we could identify the trigger thoughts for her anger. Then, we could describe more helpful thoughts like, "They are just a little busy right now. I can wait a minute." We role-played self-talk in session, with Madison playing the mother first, and then being herself second. Madison also created some consequences for herself for losing her temper. Some were too harsh, and her parents would not consider them. Finally, she came up with a proper consequence that involved using a series of chores as restitution.

I did warn Madison that her parents could not tolerate any more physical violence. They would call the police if she attempted to trip her mother again. Madison mentioned this as being an effective deterrent several times. I did not want to use this boundary, but I was worried about the increased risk to her family due to Madison's age and her size and strength.

Over the next two months, we reviewed anger management in every session and talked about feelings in real time. We made plans for each week. Madison also began to develop friendships spontaneously using the tools of attunement that she had developed and practiced in her family. We talked about the things that friends shared: feelings, interests, ideas, and activities. Madison and I looked at pages from *Navigating the Social World* for ideas on how to start and to maintain a conversation (McAfee, 2002). She also got clues from her sister and brother. They were encouraged to respond to appropriate social skills from Madison. Madison's sister used to give in to her wheedling for time and attention, even when she was too busy. She started to tell Madison to call a friend. Since Madison was making friends, she could. Madison's brother found that she would no longer do his chores. "Do your own," she said.

Madison's sister, Ivy, had to be encouraged to tell Madison to back off. Madison liked to fit cross-legged outside of her sister's door—just waiting for time. This bugged Ivy—and pulled at her heartstrings. We spent time with both of them. "Do you really want your sister to feel like she has to feel guilty all of the time when she does not want to be with you?"

"Yes and no." replied Madison. "It works."

Ivy said, "Madison, I like you. I'll spend time with you just because I love you. You don't have to worry about that. I don't want you trying to be in charge of my life. It makes me feel like you are trapping me."

We agreed that Madison would not bug her sister for attention for two weeks, seeing what happened. Madison said, "I don't like having to worry about when she has time. But the good thing is that she does find time with me. She does like me."

Ivy said, "I'm not going to change back, Madison. This is it. You have to accept that I have choices, too."

This was important in normalizing the family relationships. The older brother did not really want to come in. He was respectful, but said that he would come in if we thought that it was critical. He pointed out that he was leaving home soon. At this point in his development this seemed appropriate.

Madison's treatment took about nine months and about thirty hours of therapy. She did not want to do further work on adoption issues, but instead wanted more time with activities and friends. We agreed that she could come back in, as needed.

She began to show very angry behavior almost a year later. Madison came to work with me for a long afternoon. I spent a session with her, but she was quite closed to joining with me. She stayed on into the afternoon, during which she made long lists. I checked on her between sessions and then added another session at the end of the afternoon. She had to write out thirty things that she was angry at her mother about, sad about in life, frustrated over, and jealous about. I asked her to make lists so that she would not return home with very little resolved.

Writing out her lists helped Madison discover that she was very angry about her learning issues, that her sister had such an easier life, her pending ear surgery, and that her mother no longer allowed her to sleep in the parents' bedroom. She and I discussed these issues; she shared her feelings with both parents, made plans for support, and went home. The surgery frightened her. There was also an additional pile-up of other issues. Madison felt much better about all of these issues after she discussed them.

About six months later, Madison came in for three sessions on adoption issues. At that point, we talked about her birthmother's depression and how this had impacted Madison. She was angry about being left in limbo so long. She also could not understand how anyone could have let that happen. "I don't think that anyone really noticed me," she said. "They probably just didn't know that I needed help until the doctor told them. It still makes me mad at my birthparents. I know my birthmother would like to see me. I don't want to though. Maybe when I'm about 18. I don't know if she could help it, but I'm still mad at her. But I'm also sorry for her. It's fine if my mother writes to her. I kind of like knowing what's happening in her life, but not too much. Like, I want to be sure she's okay and everything."

I asked her about race and her relationship with her birthmother. "Well, it would be easier if she weren't white," she said.

"I wonder if you ever think about what your life would be like if I were your birthmother?" I asked.

"How did you know?" she said.

"Well, lots of kids do," I said. This does occur frequently due to transference issues.

Madison said, "I have thought about it. When I first had

to come see you I told my mom that I wished that you were African-American. My mom said, 'Well, she's not. It won't hurt for you to get comfortable with a white woman. After all, you are a light-skinned girl and your birthmother is white.' I feel like I can talk to you about lots of things, so it doesn't seem so strange having a white birthmother now. I'm not prejudiced or anything. I just don't know what it would be like to have a white mother. Then I got to know you. It seems fine now."

I asked Madison how race affected her family. She said, "I was with my sister when her friend said, 'Do you two have different fathers or something?' My sister said, 'I'll forgive you for being nosy if you just stop right now.' I wish that people would not comment on our skin differences. My sister boldly answers people and defends me. She's smart and good. I am more shy, but I'm glad that she stands up for me. I think that it is easier since I look like my family."

"We get cards and pictures from my birthfather. He's my cousin, you know. I'm glad I know who he is. His kids are my cousins, too. We'll see them again this summer. He doesn't treat me like a dad, so it's hard to think of him like one. Like, my dad's my dad. He's my soccer coach, takes me skiing, and tells me to do stuff."

At this point Madison described herself as having a small, loyal group of friends. "We aren't the popular group, but we don't really want to be. We sit together every day at lunch and we go to movies together."

I will see Madison again at any other sticky points in her development. In this case, after Madison developed better regulated feeling states, many other processes like attunement and friendship skills also developed, with only a little assistance. Her parents are now much more comfortable with their parenting skills and Madison's increasingly sturdy sense of self.

Re-enactments

People are inherently driven to master situations and to solve the problems that have previously threatened them. Overcoming that which has harmed us in the past helps all people feel safer in their world. Children have an inherent desire to avoid re-experiencing the feelings and thoughts about the situations that harmed them, especially if these experiences occurred before they formed secure attachments with sensitive caregivers. They routinely try to solve this contradiction in imperatives through re-enactment. Re-enacting past traumas creates situations like the one described in the vignette below.

> Benjamin had been used in child pornography. His former abuser knew where he lived and had actually come to the home shortly after Benjamin's placement in the foster family. Benjamin did not disclose his abuse for three years. However, he would often approach a new man at his church, avoiding his parents' eyes and their facial cues. Though 10 years old, Benjamin insisted that the man pick him up.
>
> Benjamin's parents reflected wryly that this man had notably poor boundaries. In spite of receiving specific instructions to avoid this man, Benjamin made a beeline for him the next Sunday, asking loudly "May Mr. Smith come home for lunch with us?" Benjamin leaned back against Mr. Smith, pressing his full torso against the man's body. It almost took a crane to separate Benjamin from the man. Later, in therapy, Benjamin mentioned that the man frightened him. He felt that he had to approach and control this man. This gave him the opportunity to attempt mastery of the new situation through re-enacting. "I thought that if he liked me, he maybe wouldn't hurt me." Benjamin said. I asked Benjamin about sexual feelings. "Yes, I did feel those feelings," Benjamin said. "I didn't like the feelings. They are scary, but I still feel like I should go towards that guy. But I don't want to be abused again. I don't want him to touch me."

Children will take on what they believe to be a manageable risk in order to try to master situations on their own. However, they are incapable of assessing the risks. Regularly, children I see will race out of sight, following individuals who resemble former abusers.

I take a strong position with the children I see in therapy. They may not re-enact old traumas, as this thereby re-endangers them. I recommend having an explicit discussion with children with a mental age of 6 years and older about re-enactment whenever working with traumatized children. Children who have younger mental ages are simply given specific rules on re-enactment.

Safety Plans for Sexualized and Aggressive Behaviors

As indicated through the vignette above, it is going to be a process to curb children's impulses once they are acting out their feelings. Simply discussing boundaries will not suffice. Children who are sexually or physically aggressive require a frank discussion that specifically explores when they feel like hurting others, intimidating others, touching others, and have sexual feelings. We make specific plans and update those plans for children during treatment. An initial plan for Chris, shown in the first casestudy, included the elements below.

- He would put his hands in his pockets whenever he felt like touching inappropriately.
- He would stand close to his dad when he felt like touching his mom's breasts or buttocks. If Dad was not home, he would tell Mom that he was having the "bad touching" feeling. She would remind him of all of the fun activities he could do instead, in a friendly way.
- He would try to figure out what gave him the touching feeling. In the early part of treatment, we found that he was having flashbacks sometimes. Sometimes his feeling was part of a memory. For example, for a moment, Mom's hair would look like the woman who abused him sexually. His response was part of an old sexualized pattern.
- Chris would never be alone with his sister. Chris was considered at-risk then. They used to sexually act out when they

were bored or lonely. They were still locked into that pattern. Not being alone with his sister was part of Chris' safety plan.

- The bathroom door was always shut and locked when anyone used it. This made Chris feel better about his safety and more in control of impulses.
- Chris used a private bathroom at school.
- Chris changed at home when his family went swimming and did not walk through the men's locker room. This was too scary and overstimulating for him.
- Chris was not allowed to spend the night with any friends for the first two years of treatment.
- Chris would immediately tell his parents if he and his sister sexually acted out. If he responded to an invitation, he could tell and not get into trouble of any kind.
- Chris would not be left under the supervision of any adult he did not know. During the first year of treatment, he stayed at home when there was a teaching substitute at school. This rule was relaxed during the second year.
- Chris was helped to identify his high-risk times which were anniversaries of his abuse, the presence of strange adults, and whenever he felt lonely or bored. We made a list of alternate things to do during these times and posted the list on the back of his bedroom door.

Eventually, Chris no longer felt like sexually acting out. He might get an impulse or a thought, but he did not respond with any behaviors. This result required a long period of supervision. Chris was encouraged to report and discuss any feelings of wanting to act out with his parents and with me. He got helpful ideas of other things to do instead, like getting a nice hug, playing go-fish, riding his bike, kicking the soccer ball with Mom or Dad and so forth. In this way, Chris learned how to resolve the issue with adult support instead of being sneaky and feeling shame.

Individualized plans for aggressive behaviors are formed in the same way. Children who have been treated aggressively often want to master their experiences. For example, if they felt helpless and weak, then they want to master the situation becoming powerful, or becoming the aggressor. Discuss this in therapy through words, drawings, or play. A plan for Mackenzie, age 10, who was previously intimidated and bullied, included the elements below.

- Mackenzie will spend time every day thinking about the people closest to her and remembering her positive feelings for them.
- She will put her hands in her pockets whenever she feels angry.
- She will stay outside of people's personal space. (Her personal space was measured off as three feet.) She will not make any sudden moves towards others' faces with her arms or hands, or toward their legs with her feet. (Mackenzie would suddenly poke her head or hands close to people, causing them to flinch.)
- Mackenzie will only play with younger children under close supervision and may not play with nonverbal children.
- She will stay within eyesight of her parents when in the yards of other children. She may not go into their backyards or inside their homes.
- She will do restitution for making faces to scare her brothers, or hurting her brothers, cousins, or other friends. This restitution was an earlier bedtime, doing the brother's or sister's chores, a monetary fine, giving the offended child the use of anything in her room for three days or her dessert after dinner.
- Mackenzie knows that competitive games are an anger trigger for her. She will play those games in front of adults for the time being.
- Mackenzie knows that being tricky feels like she is winning. When she feels like being mean and tricky, she should stand beside either parent. If she whispers what she is feeling, they will hug her and help her with other choices.
- Bigger kids scare Mackenzie. She will stay close to parents and other adults when they are around. She will not try to act tough, but will instead stay safe and tender-hearted.

These particular lists of plans are longer than average. Plans can be simplified for younger children. Notice that these plans are specific. They are not abstractions like *respect others*. The plan must be specific and practical in order to work effectively.

School Supports

Some children will need extra support from school, some will not. I prefer not to provide the school with specific abuse information. I limit their information to conveying the child's needs, not their background. This approach assures that first, the schools are spared from confidentiality problems involving potent information, and second, it assures that I can keep children's issues private. I do share that children are easily frightened because of past events in their lives. That suffices to convey information except in a few specialized cases.

Some IEP or 504 plans include social skills goals, as carried out in social skills groups. There is a natural place for children to apply the friendship skills they are taught in therapy. Some children can receive weekly individual time working through guided curriculum with a school counselor. The school counselor can also spend another session during the week coaching them at lunch, recess, or during a group time. This extra school support usually has excellent results.

Many children's school teachers will teach specific social skills within their curriculum, integrating the Relationship Development Intervention (Gutstein, Sheely, 2002) into their classroom. The therapist and the teacher should collaborate in these instances, so that they can use the same words and concepts with children.

I like to give children who are receiving trauma treatment ways to signal for more help. Signals comprise things like calling home, asking the teacher for help, or going to the counselor or nurse's office for a calm-down time. This prevents meltdowns at school.

While I will not repeat the information in Chapter 8 here, I would remind educators that they certainly should use that material. Preferential placement is a valuable accommodation for children. The best placements for children include attributes like the following:

- structured, predictable classrooms
- warm, nurturing, but not gushing, teachers
- visual and hands-on learning
- clear organization of space. All children know where they belong in the classroom
- calm teachers who give lots of positive feedback
- teachers who are low-key about problems, with an emphasis on repair, not punishment
- teachers who do not try to "make-up" to children for their pasts, allowing for slack work, but rather bring them up to standard
- teachers who refer for and use testing information. No "wait and see" approaches
- teachers who collaborate with parents, but handle school problems at school
- teachers who are aware of issues like processing loads and overstimulation. They work within these limitations
- teachers who use accommodations for issues like ADD, Learning Disabilities, Bipolar Disorder, FASD, and PTSD.

Summary

This detailed chapter described the specifics of assessment and treatment and treatment planning in three of the classic types of cases seen in a practice which specializes in the treatment of children with a background of abuse, neglect and/or trauma. In all of the cases there was a combination of individual and family work. The cognitive behavioral approach was employed for the anger and anxiety-related symptoms. At the same time, the negative developmental impacts on identity were addressed so that children could experience healthier views of themselves and others. Adoption issues were included in the treatment plan, but the issues that most affected these children were treated first. Throughout treatment the well-being of siblings was monitored and enhanced.

CHAPTER 11

Structuring Careers and Practices

"Creating the world we want is a much more subtle but more powerful mode of operation than destroying the one we don't want."
                                        –Marianne Williamson

ractices that include the specialties listed in this book are quite rewarding and interesting. They are so interesting, in fact, that professionals need to remind themselves not to overwork. They must insert intentional supports and self-care for themselves into their schedules. It is not as important what the self-care strategy is as it is to have a self-care strategy in place!

Post-graduate certificate programs in adoption therapy have listed such practical, personal self-care strategies as going for a walk in a beautiful setting, quilting, praying, having lunch with friends, reading a great book, writing poetry, playing basketball on a recreational team, painting, woodworking, canoeing, and taking long baths. Anyone doing casework or therapy should be writing these types of personally enjoyable activities into their calendars every week. These break times should be scheduled first, not just after all other work is complete. They are foundational and necessary for good therapy and casework.

Additionally, practitioners owe it to themselves and to their clients to make professional development plans and to set personal boundaries that keep every case worker or therapist at the top of his or her "professional game" while at the same time enjoying a rich personal life. This chapter offers some insights for making those plans.

Availability

In today's world, traditional nine-to-five with-Saturdays-and Sundays-off businesses and professional practices are uncommon. Many professionals and many agencies have established non-traditional hours—seeing clients or holding workshops regularly on some evenings, taking a day off in midweek rather than on Saturday in order to make themselves more accessible to clients. Problematically, the time that is made available to clients tends to be "high value" time for families. The time that professionals may be taking off as comp time may be "low value." The professional position you accept or the way in which you structure a private practice must hold your personal and family needs in high priority. Make certain that you take "high value" time out for your family if you use it in your practice. If you know that you will be away some Saturdays, when your family is home, then be certain to take off more days of family vacation or other hours or days when family members are also home and ready for fun and leisure.

Professionals must set aside time for unavailability to anyone outside of themselves and their families. We can certainly handle emergencies and work off-hours at times, but we should not follow an "on-call" lifestyle. Allowing ourselves to do so will result in burn-out at work or impoverishment in our personal lives. Let clients know clearly when, and how you are available.

- Be certain that clients know your office hours and understand that you are unable to take calls while seeing clients.
- Give them your message policy: Do you use an administrative assistant, an answering service or a voice mail system? What should the client's expectations be about how soon to expect a return contact and how long after that deadline is it reasonable for them to "try again?"
- Are you available by email? If so, under what circumstances should email be the method of contact? Let your clients know

if your email address is for appointments only, or also for personal communication. Is it confidential?

- What happens on weekends, scheduled days off, and when you are on vacation?
- What plan does your practice have for defining emergencies and making emergency contact? Will you be interrupted? Is there an alternate number? Do colleagues take rotating turns taking these calls?

I suggest that professionals do nothing professional or "productive" on at least one day a week. This devotes a day to enjoying relationships—spiritual, family, and friends. It is a day of recreation, in the literal sense, a true Sabbath.

In high-risk situations, try to get help for the case from someone besides yourself. For example, ask for help from a child psychiatrist with an on-call schedule, a crisis number, a friend of the parents, another therapist, a caseworker, and so forth. Help the family to arrange support systems beyond the immediate family and therapist for harder cases. For example, this family may need respite care, a day treatment program, a case aide in the home for some hours during the week, and so forth.

It is difficult to avoid processing harder cases while trying at the same time to parent younger children. It may be better for the professional with small children not to take, or to refer on, some crisis-type cases until later in their own family's life cycle. That way, children are actually able to have their parent's undivided attention, as well as their hearts and minds, at predictable times devoted exclusively to family.

Sometimes client loads become unexpectedly difficult and heavy while vacation time is still far off. In such a pinch, a crisis solution is to take a Monday off in one week, Tuesday the next, Wednesday the next, and so forth. In that way, the professional can get a breather, rescheduling anyone who *must* be seen into the remaining days. This schedule helps to lessen the pressure when work gets out of balance. This allows the person to use the restorative "3/4/12" described in the last chapter. That is, three hours, four times a week or four hours, three times a week, doing nothing but positive and relaxing activities in order to recuperate from overload. Any time caseworkers or therapists take out of their physical and psychological reserves, they must pay back. Otherwise, they will need to use a strategy of care like the 3/4/12 for about a month. (This is the deferred maintenance catch-up plan.)

Volunteering versus personal time

Some of the teams formed to support professionals can become personnel sinkholes. Before joining practices or working groups, assess whether these activities and the other participants will respect your personal time or deplete it. I have been surprised to find myself being called at home about non-emergency work by professionals who chose on-call lifestyles for themselves. They had access to my home number through my volunteer work and used it inappropriately, assuming that I, too, had an on-call lifestyle.

Most professionals will enjoy working on committees or team projects that further child welfare causes. While this is commendable, be certain to allot mostly professional time, rather than personal time, for these causes. Before taking on such a volunteer task or position related to your profession, sleep on it and think about what must be dropped to make time for the new activity. (Asking family members for their opinions tends to drop a plumb line of reality.) It is a good idea to accept such commitments with clear beginning and ending dates in mind. Also make very clear to other participants how, in what manner, and when (at home or work, on a cell phone, via an email address devoted specifically to your volunteer work, on weekends or evenings or not) you are willing to be contacted outside of scheduled project meetings

Many professionals in high stress fields such as ours make it a point to severely limit the amount of time they are willing to invest in volunteering within their professional fields. They prefer, and find themselves renewed by, volunteer projects that have nothing to do with their degrees and credentials: projects such as teaching classes at their house of worship, working at their children's schools, or volunteering in special areas of personal interest as diverse as politics, or the environment, or sports-related groups, or docenting at a museum or zoo.

The Mental Health of the Mental Health Provider and Caseworker

Staying mentally healthy is a challenge. After all, we are using our personalities as a tool to help clients regain regulation. Our "tool" can become blunted! The impact of trauma on the professional and parent includes solemn pressures and responsibilities.

- We become witnesses to the child's overwhelming grief, shame, terror, guilt, and confusion.
- We become responsible for the emotional support that will sustain the child through grieving.
- We become intimately aware of egregious realities, like abandonment of children, injury of children, and death of parents.
- We are asked to provide answers to life's unsolvable problems (Friedman, 1997).
- We cannot communicate the issues with which we work to our loved ones.
- We can experience confusion, disorientation, hyperarousal, and hypervigilance as we deal with trauma/loss themes (Friedman, 1997).
- We can experience "compassion strain."
- We can become numb, distant, angry, and insensitive if we are not supported in our work.
- We can become more interested in our client's or child's life than our own.
- We can require others to try to make up the injustices of life to the child, and to us.
- We can become unstable as our own processed memories of grief and trauma can become activated.
- We can feel compelled to change something when overly stressed—including jobs, relationships, homes, or religions—further destabilizing ourselves.

The therapist or caseworker can neglect taking care of herself even as she is fulfilling her role in taking care of others. Everyone in the field needs a mixture of help and accountability. Some people find that this is supplied by the organization in which they work. However, this is actually uncommon. Usually people have to create at least part, if not all, of their own support systems. These next suggestions require little organization and energy, but pay high dividends.

Consult groups

Individuals can create a stable group to help them with difficult situations by regularly meeting and sharing cases with other professionals. Client confidentiality must be maintained, of course. The casing group can suggest strategies or approaches. They can also alert professionals to their own blind spots. These groups usually share articles, conference announcements, new books, and fresh ideas.

Consult group members support one another when things go badly for a client. During a session a professional usually cannot express how personally grieved she is by a client's misfortune, abuse, illness, or their losses by death. Expressing this in a supportive consult group is a welcome relief.

When a client died, I cried in my consult group as I cased the case—in a way that I could not weep with the client family. It brought up areas of grief in my own life. A member gave me a helpful way to think of this death and sent me a good article; friends in the group supported me. It was restorative.

When working with angry people, professionals may become angry in return. A consult group provides an arena for processing some of that anger in a healthy manner. It helps to describe a reaction to the group in order to get a read on the appropriateness of this anger.

For example, I was angry at an 11-year-old girl. She had lied to me throughout a full session, describing a concerning, but believable, felony that she had not really committed. I told her that I was angry with her. She thought that it was because she had wasted my time. I told her that the waste of time was irritating, but, I told her, I wasted my own time regularly, so her contribution was not such a big deal. What was the big deal, and why I was angry, had to do with her not using the time for herself. She did not respect our work together when she did that, and she gave up on herself.

My consult group included the child's psychiatrist. They gave me feedback, concluding that I had been ethical and appropriate in the way I shared my anger with her. In certain cases, members of a consult group share frustrations that are not appropriate to share with clients. This is a great place to gain some insight as to why the case was so frustrating and how best to channel these feelings. These situations allow professionals to make ourselves vulnerable, and thus get receive help and guidance for us and for our clients.

Sometimes we are just stuck for a new approach. A consult group can give several new ideas or break a log-jam when we are using an approach that simply is not working. If the child's psychiatrist is part of the consult group, it helps immensely in the quality of care, since the psychiatrist and therapist can best combine the treatment and medication plan.

Consult partners

In addition to a group, a consult partner is also helpful. This should be a person who is similarly experienced, so that there is a mutually beneficial exchange. Partners get together and go over difficult cases. I have an excellent consult partner who is experienced and who has some skills in the same area, as well as some in areas that I do not. We spend an hour on each case, which gives both of us enough time to discuss complex cases in-depth. We are able to speak about our subjective experiences in the cases, getting and giving help. We remember details about each other's cases so that we do not have to start from scratch in describing the cases.

While forming a consult group may seem daunting, getting a consult partner may be far easier for therapists. In time, therapists who are more isolated may add additional members to form a consult group.

Consultation

Children can present unusual and specialized problems. Professionals should put aside extra money for professional consultation, if it is not part of agency funding. Presenting a case to an expert in the relevant specialty area can make a huge difference in both case quality and peace of mind.

Sometimes parents are willing to pay or a State agency is willing to pay for a consultant to a case, since the caseworker or therapist in their area is the best bet for their child geographically. When working outside of your limitations, do tell the parents or the State worker that you are being asked to do just that. Ask for consultation assistance. Regularly people have spoken to me as a consultant with the understanding that parents and professionals will cover or split the financial costs. The costs tend to be minor compared to the cost of time wasted that can occur when people are trying to reinvent the wheel.

Supervision

Good supervision gives social workers an opportunity to share their load. A talented supervisor has an opinion of you not solely in terms of your job performance, but as a growing professional. He or she should be protecting and nurturing your development, while at the same time enhancing your work. Look for a creative supervisor who can also give ideas on your cases.

Sometimes the supervisor assigned to workers is disappointing in the above qualities. In that type of situation do consider moving jobs or departments. After all, you were looking for a job when you found this one. If that is not immediately possible, network to determine whether there might be someone else who could supervise from an educational/practice point of view. For example, I have supervised particularly difficult cases or supervised internships without other direct supervisory responsibilities. You are looking for someone who will prevent burn-out and keep your learning and zeal alive.

Mentoring is a variant on this theme. Sometimes a professional organization or colleague will assist in helping to find mentoring relationships that sustains professional growth. These relationships respond not simply to your performance, but to how you are developing resources to cope with job stress.

Personal therapy

Professional therapeutic support may be episodic or regularly scheduled. All therapists should identify someone who can help them with their own emotional regulation. Caseworkers or therapists should schedule therapeutic support any time emotionally laden events happen in their own lives or are triggered by a client. Professionals simply cannot lose their grip with all their clients depending on them. Avoid grandiose denial when working in a difficult practice area or difficult personal situation. Humbly get help.

Sometimes people do not have the money for therapy and support when they need it the most. The National Association for Social Workers has peer therapy exchanges in some areas. Check to see if your professional agency is willing to match you to a peer. These tend to be volunteer-driven services to help increase the support and reduce the burn-out rate for workers. (Worn professionals are not expected to give back until they are further down the path of recovery.)

Inside the Practice

Schedule time to think about your clients and how you do your work

This may mean looking at your schedule and thinking about how you are allotting your time. Is your schedule running you or are you running your schedule? What could change to make the schedule more professionally productive or more personally pleasing?

For example, I like to schedule longer lunch breaks so that I can go for a swim or a walk during the day. This means scheduling the time to do that and working later into the day. But unless the time is scheduled, those self-care necessities will not occur.

I also like to spend time thinking about particular clients. This can be casual, while I am puttering around the office, watering plants, and so forth. Sometimes it is much more intentional. I will look at notes, check developmental schedules or reference materials, and write notes to myself. Again, I put time in my schedule in order to focus on this essential process. Sometimes this entails a call to the client in the middle of the week, checking in. Recently I called a client, letting her know that I wanted to change approaches with her daughter. We talked through the change by phone so that she had a chance to think about it before the next session.

By being intentional about your scheduling you can give yourself a sense of integrity in your work. You have been true to your clients, giving them your best ideas, and true to your self, balancing your work load.

Celebrate successes and lighten up

Enjoy successes with gusto. Often after completing something difficult, we hardly notice prior to beginning the next difficult case. Take time to process the positive events in work life. This could mean buying flowers or going to lunch to celebrate.

> One person, new to an office, was asked about her first day on a new job. She mentioned that she had been taken out to lunch by several people. "Oh," said her husband. "Usually they just do that on your last day."
>
> "That's the reason I left that job," she said. "I felt like a drone. These people are actually interested in whether I like it here."

Take time to enjoy the people around you and to value yourself, not just upon leaving. Similarly, have customs to celebrate birthdays and appreciate the lighter things in life. Spend time in common areas of offices, during breaks, talking about pleasant things, not simply your cases. It is as important to think about other things as to think about your work.

> In speaking with a friend who had worked twenty years in one setting, she said, "I spoke and trained State-wide and

worked so hard for kids and families. I've left that job, and after all those years I have maybe two people with whom I get together at all. Everyone still calls me if they have a problem, but I never formed any real relationships. I was too busy! The more skills I got, the busier I got."

Learn something new. Meet someone new.

Keep a fresh perspective by including new information, approaches, and contacts. This means connecting with people from other agencies or disciplines. It certainly means conference attendance. At times it can be difficult to afford conferences in time or money. Volunteering to work on registration can make the conference affordable. Or, sometimes submitting a proposal to speak on a subject area in your skill area will defer the cost of the conference in part. If the personal or financial costs are still too high, make a point of ordering conference tapes or CDs to listen to in the car while commuting. Some organizations have library copies of these tapes. Or, several people can get together, trading favorite books or resources. Sometimes agencies can send alternating people to a variety of trainings, each of whom later gives an in-service on the material.

Develop and cultivate collegial contacts in the field. These people help to prevent the stagnation that occurs when organizations are too insular. Colleagues will share their unique knowledge about other resources, approaches, and techniques that will help you both grow. Pooling this shared information promotes better advocacy for clients. And, by sharing with others, partnerships are forged so that more complex issues that will take group efforts can be undertaken.

Adoption agencies in particular have a history of being protective of their turf, insular with their staff. Fortunately, that is breaking down. However, do not be surprised if there is some subtle disapproval as you leave for lunch with colleagues from other agencies or you join advocacy groups. Your career and service are more important than pleasing everybody.

Professional Development

Set learning goals

At least once a year set learning goals for yourself. Typically I suggest doing this just after a vacation. There is a sense of distance from the day-to-day after a break that allows people to think more creatively about their work. These goals have action steps that may mean planning to take a post-graduate certificate program in adoption therapy, for example. Or, it might mean visiting a clinic that specializes in FASD. Some people want to write, or start a group, or do trainings. These are the achievable goals that help us to contribute to our own development and to our field.

In one such exercise of setting learning goals, an Adoption Certificate program class asked if we could begin a structured consultation group. Not only did we do so, but we structured it with goals and objectives so that people could earn some of their continuing education credits through Northwest Adoption Resource Exchange's Cascadia Training. Two consultation groups are ongoing in Portland and Seattle, simply because people set learning goals and planned for what they wanted.

When setting these learning goals, put in action steps and time into your schedule to work on attaining these goals. That way they are likely to be realized.

Develop a think tank

Recently some people got together at my office for a think tank day. It was a time in which we considered some training needs of the community, what we could take on as a group, and what our next steps would be. Many of the members were already involved in a number of other groups, but we got together to conceptualize about the gaps and how we could meet some needs. Someone asked me later, "Who sponsored this?" Actually, we all sponsored it. Our time together was planned so that we talk, go for a walk, plan, eat, walk again, and finish our plans. It is long enough that we can move into an action plan by the end of the four or five-hour period. Many trainings have occurred as a result, as well as intentional coordination with other organizations. The group has been small, productive, and friendly. The cost to everyone is simply the time involved.

Multidisciplinary efforts

Part of the action plan for one think tank day was teaming with the adoption and foster care medical clinics for mutual information exchange. This resulted in ideas for trainings. Together we approached the various disciplines for a training which included physicians, nurses, social workers, speech and language therapists, parent advocates, and trainees. These trainings are excellent for professionals so that we can see children and what helps them and their families through the eyes of other disciplines. It helps parents "one-stop shop" so to speak, as they attend a day's training. Already the "round two" conference is being planned, including occupational therapists, sexual abuse trauma experts, neuropsychologists, neurological experts, FASD experts, and educators.

My gifts are more as a networker, trainer, and seed planter. Others have a "mover and shaker" gift package. For example, Pat Johnston, my publisher, wrote the following advice:

"In Indiana, I have for many years been involved in pulling together a coalition of adoption-related professionals including public and private placement agencies, attorneys, and support groups to provide periodic two day training events featuring an inservice training for professionals on a Friday and a full day, multi-session and multi-speaker conference for consumers on Saturday.

"Over the years a number of important benefits have come out of this coalition. Attending one another's sessions allows us to identify professionals who have an especially fresh take on a subject, the result being that agencies involved are inclined to invite the clients of other agencies to join them for special topic events, and those clients are likely to come! Like-minded members consult with one another more frequently, and the cross pollination of ideas has resulted in mutual support for legislative change on behalf of children and families.

"An outgrowth of this educational partnership was that after Deborah Gray was the in-service trainer in a recent year and described her own interdisciplinary practice network, the coalition recognized the need for an even more interdisciplinary partnership in our own city and has now reached out to physicians and therapists in an effort to create a Perfect Adoption Team of referral resources in a variety of disciplines. We meet for a sixty to ninety minute (max) lunch quarterly, moving from team-member office to team-member office. This moving around allows for a site tour and description of that team member's practice."

Efforts such as these take a series of lunches to plan. It is exciting to get together with like minded people, sharing the latest and the greatest and how to use that information to benefit children and their families. It is always a pleasure to realize how diversely talented people are—down to the details. For example, the brochure design and wording are happily handled by people gifted in those areas, someone with the right connections takes on the job of finding donated food for coffee breaks, a software-literate person steps forward to handle registration, a coalition member's board member handles finances—one each from several organizations rather than stretching the resources of a single entity.

These collaborative efforts take intentional planning, but the planning is fun and not particularly time-consuming, since the group is focused on a functional exchange of information and practical outcome.

Therapists and Caseworkers—Have Fun!

While the cases and the therapeutic tasks described in this book are complex, it is exciting to be able to blend together many challenging therapeutic activities. Some of the activities in casework and therapy are a lot of fun. In working with a 10-year-old child, she said, grinning, "You sure laugh a lot. <u>We</u> laugh a lot!"

It would be a mistake not to mention that many of the things done in the office result in release, relief, and just plain fun. I generally do not use games as a way to form relationships with children, but, I have regularly incorporated fun things as part of therapy. As Diane Fosha has taught us, it is just as important to process and store the positives as part of therapy, as it is to process the negatives (Fosha, 2004). Seven-year-old Garrett's sessions describes this.

> Garrett had been neglected, physically and sexually abused, and moved from one foster home to another, over and over again. After a rough four months of therapy, he came into the office reporting one full week without one incident of sexual acting out or aggression. Full of hope and pride, I clapped for him and enjoyed the best week he had ever had in his life with him and his mother.

> To celebrate, we got out the stamps and stamp pad. He wanted an eagle for his arm. But, it was hard to choose just one stamp. So, we stamped a raccoon on his other arm, and a squirrel on his knee. Getting caught up in the activity, we moved on to stamp his forehead with an elk, forearms and shins with bears, and, finally, his toes with butterflies. His mother was in the room, a little giddy herself. She and Garrett were laughing with full resonance. It felt safe and fun. Garrett still describes the lightness of that session. That joy is shared with as much emphasis as the trauma work.

I enjoy children's successes. I experience a daily pleasure in working with children like Garrett. These are moments in which children are connecting and free to share life with zest! Make certain that as professionals we are allowing ourselves time to celebrate these successes. Our clients do need these positives; we need them too.

Summary

The professionals who work in the child welfare field tend to be creative, hardworking, and chronically behind due to the crisis nature of the field. There is always something more to be done that beckons. Recognizing that running faster on the hamster wheel will not get us much further, it is important to approach tasks differently. This is a great area for creative thought and collaboration. Self-care is a necessity if people are to work long-term in a successful manner in the field. But, beyond necessity, people are encouraged to recognize their intrinsic worth. They are more than their work, and have the option of a positive and balanced life even while working in a difficult practice area.

CHAPTER 12

Creating Resilience in Children and Their Families

"Never doubt that a small group of thoughtful, committed citizens can change the world; indeed, it's the only thing that ever has."   –Margaret Mead

C hildren who have been through suffering bring it with them as they enter families. The adversity they face is part of the human condition. But meeting and overcoming adversity with resilience should not have to be just a "bounce back;" it can become a "bounce forward" according to an expert on family resilience, Froma Walsh (2006). I love her expression, since through adversity we learn how to have courage, to learn from mistakes, to deepen our belief in one another, ourselves, and our God. Resiliency is the process of that bouncing forward; it is requisite for success for children and families after trauma and neglect.

Sometimes after hearing of the educational and emotional challenges that are part of today's adoptions, people relate to the winner of the Pulitzer Prize in journalism for his work on adoption issues, Adam Pertman. He joked at the 2005 FRUA conference, "Is there anything all right?" He was referring to the list of specialty areas covered in that extraordinary conference's agenda. He went on giving the excellent news that includes the progress that children are making and the family strengths that are so laudable in today's adoptive families.

This concluding chapter discusses the process of developing family strengths of resilience. Professionals in casework and therapy should encourage their development. Families reading this book should be aware of these areas. While the earlier chapters have discussed specific areas of resilience in reparative terms, this chapter describes beliefs and activities that professionals should encourage, teach and support in the daily lives of their clients. I have seen these beliefs and practices inspire courage and transcend struggles in families. Professionals should be practicing these positive traits in their own lives, as well.

Build Positive, Optimistic Outlooks

Suffering is part of life, but its meaning is transformed as people begin to discuss ways in which they will focus on the future, reshaping their dreams.

> Ruthie's mother was not hugged for almost five years. Ruthie instead treated her mother with anger and disgust. After treatment, which had good results, I asked the mother what had given her the power to keep trying. She said, "I always wanted a daughter. I just would not give up on her. I looked ahead, thinking that if I just kept looking and trying things, sooner or later I would see results. That kept me looking ahead and hoping. My husband and I agreed that we would not give up even if one thing or another did not work."

Rallying around a positive outcome helps families to stay mobilized and to continue trying. It also models that optimism for their children, keeping the children, as well, open to the possibilities of change and help. This is not to diminish the reality of pain. But, all too often people forget that pain itself can be transformed into advocacy, social change, and compassion.

Parents came in describing the academic mismatch of their boys, ages 6 and 9, in a school that used a poorly fitting curriculum. Both boys were failing. In a family session I asked the parents what their dreams were for the future. The family described their dreams: children who could live on their own, make a living, and make a contribution to the world. As we talked, we agreed that this seemed like it should be attainable.

We broke this down in sessions, discussing what steps they would have to take to get an education for their sons so that they had an educational foundation that would allow them to function in good jobs. This discussion helped the family focus on what needed to change to move towards their dreams. They stopped focusing on their school. They gained momentum over the next weeks, looking for a school that would better educate their children. They recognized that education was their next step towards their dream for their children. They advocated to move their children and gained entrance to a great public school that was using a sequential, but multimodal, teaching approach.

In the sessions above, I helped the family to break down the obstacles into manageable pieces. We used a step-wise fashion to move towards the goal. The professional coaching provided some scaffolding for the family's developmental progress.

Strengths can come from inside the family, not just from outside resources. Family stories that are intergenerational form sources of strength. I ask families about these stories.

Roger was angry over his earlier abuse and getting into difficulties from his anger. His father revealed his own mother's abuse of him as he talked to his son about anger. "I hated her," he told Roger, "but I decided that I would use that experience to learn from. My mother slapped and kicked me. I never laid a hand on you. You had already been abused. I know what that's like, son, believe me. I was too. But you can change your path, just like I did. Sure I get angry, but I have practiced getting out of the situation if I can't take it. You can do this, too."

These are shared stories that give powerful identity information and normalize reactions to life pain. Positive stories are the Rosetta stone for unique family sources of strength. Notice that the story above did not minimize the pain—or the potential for a good outcome. Both examples—examples which I as the mental health archeologist "dug out" of their own histories and polished in the therapy setting for the families to use—were touchstones for initiative and perseverance—qualities of resilience. Professionals should ask families to share ways that they have overcome difficult situations, asking if there are traits or attitudes that people see that will help them with the present circumstances. Parents should describe these relevant stories to their children.

Encourage Learned Optimism

Aaron Beck discusses at length how necessary learning the skill of optimism is in creating a positive future (1987). This is related to the area above, but is distinct, as it reflects the development of the intentional habit of looking for positive outcomes, solutions, lessons and so forth.

> Casey, whose birthparents had both died, and who had physical challenges, told me. "I am stronger and more focused because of what I have been through. I am living in the country that my birthparents hoped that I could get to. It's the best place in the world. I know that I will never give up, no matter what. I talked to my older brother and he said that he is proud of what I have overcome. I know that my parents are here for me and my birthparents would be proud of me."

This is not denial. In fact, I had worked with this boy and his painful grief issues earlier. Instead it is courage and learned optimism—traits modeled by his family daily.

Parents appreciate learning positive self-talk and understanding "learned optimism." Professionals should describe what learned optimism sounds like. It can range from simple comments like, "That felt good to get that accomplished," to "I know that this is a worthwhile project. I am going to start it and see how far I can get. I think I'll find answers and help along the way." Parents have discussed with me the lift that they feel to have positivism modeled by their therapists and to begin to use these attitudes themselves.

Some people predict worst case scenarios, apparently so that they will not feel so bad if terrible things happen. Actually, they waste energy and momentum that could be used to solve problems. I have asked families to use their resources in a positive way rather than wearying themselves with gloomy predictions.

Help Families Avoid Pile-Ups

When families are first adjusting to problems, they let some things slide. Compartmentalizing allows people to focus on a challenge, temporarily screening out other things. Checking accounts may not be balanced, the taxes may be delayed and delayed again, and other children in the family may be parented too casually. This approach may be temporarily advantageous, as it helps families divert attention to more pressing problems. Over time, however, it can turn into a big problem.

Compartmentalization does not work when people use it to the extent that a big problem or several problems pile up. The style that worked short-term, as a way to get through a crisis, now threatens the family by creating more crises.

Therapists and caseworkers should warn families and help them to avoid these pile-ups. Professionals are in an objective position to notice such trends. I have suggested practical solutions within the sessions. For example, I suggest stopping to get the windshield wipers fixed on the way home from therapy, arranging child care for a day to pay taxes and bills or to go to the bank to straighten a snarled checked account.

Health issues are often overlooked. Families arrive at my office out of medication, with illnesses that require a physician's care, and evidences of chaos—having not yet eaten at 4:00 in the afternoon, for example. These physical problems require the same careful attention as any psychological issue. Without being negative, help families to come up with practical and orderly solutions.

Janine came into session angry and overwhelmed. She and her husband were home schooling their two children, since that was their best, but not first-choice, option. (Their daughter had been kicked out of the private school they first chose. The public school in their district was inadequate.) To top it off, the family was remodeling, doing most of the work themselves. Every room in the house was under construction.

We worked together on the chaos. We made a rule that one room needed to be neat, completed, and could not have any tools in it. They spent the next two weeks making that room orderly. Janine had to remind her husband that he could not start or drag new projects into that room. She could sit in the room every evening and organize herself, the homeschool plans, and their resources. "Now I finally feel like I can think and relax," she said. "My eyeballs don't bulge with frustration when I see my husband with project materials. I called my friend and we talked! I scrapbooked! My husband comes in here in the evening and just talks with me. It's so peaceful. My bedroom gets this treatment next."

This is the type of practical intervention that keeps people from becoming human snowballs rolling down hill.

Help to Re-establish Family Rhythms and Routines

Family routines steady every member. Adding a new member to the family rocks the routines and knocks the rhythms off-kilter. Help families to re-establish them in an intentional way. This will help everyone feel better regulated. If the former routines do not work, they will need to re-establish new ones. For example, re-establish cozy talking time with siblings in the mornings, rather than at the former evening time.

Some families have groceries delivered to help them get back into healthy cooking and eating schedules. Other families ask a teenage neighbor to come in for child care, playing with some siblings so that parents can spend time with the others. One single parent had a neighbor come put locks on several cupboards and doors so one child could not ransack the house while she was dealing with the other. All of these suggestions were brought up in therapy. Parents can get so distracted that it is hard for them to think of practical solutions. They need to hear that it is normal to need regular help from outside community members.

Educate families in advance that these problems may arise after placement, and when you see this begin, bring the issues to the family's attention. For example

> Sometimes the house work piles up. Since many children cannot classify or organize well, their items tend to get strewn underfoot and then trampled. Suggest organizational strategies so that precious family time is not wasted searching for items or living in chaos. Teach them to teach children how to organize by using methods that do not require a lot of mental classification. "First we make the bed. Then we put all the clothes in the laundry or hang them up. Then we put books and papers away. Then we put toys away. Then we take out the garbage. When you are done, I'll look at your room. I'll bring up the clean laundry and watch you put it away." This beats, "Clean your room."

Here are some strategies you might suggest:
- Box up extraneous items.
- Pare down the children's possessions.
- Use labeled plastic bins.
- Have fifteen-minute clean-ups daily so that everyone cleans up for fifteen minutes.
- Pay children twenty-five cents for every lonely sock they find a mate for, etc.

One woman hired a neighbor to get the laundry done and put it in the drawers twice a week, as well as to take her garbage can out to the street. "That is self-care to me," she said. "The best sound in the world is the sound of the garbage bag hitting the bottom of an empty can the day after pick-up."

Keep the family machine running.

Teach Clear Communication and Teamwork in the Family

The families who are able to convey their feelings and needs clearly are the ones who can best mobilize to form a team. One of the changes facing families who parent children who have suffered from neglect and abuse is the need to become flexible, taking on new tasks and reorganizing time quickly and efficiently. Family members who can clearly describe facts, feelings, and needs do the best job of moving into their adaptive phase.

A family described the upcoming tasks necessary in order to successfully move both sons to a private school and also structure an in-home program for the son diagnosed with autism. They were able to reorganize the jobs in the family through a discussion that shared facts about the issues that lay ahead. One parent, who had never cooked, picked up that job. He felt that family dinners and good nutrition were important, and he volunteered to take those tasks on so that his wife could do "floor time" with their son.

If families can communicate in a respectful, clear manner about the specifics of the challenges, their feelings about the needs of all family members, and the resources necessary, they can adapt much better. This is a pathway to success for challenged families.

Caseworkers and therapists can facilitate these discussions by helping families to become specific about their goal setting: what steps or jobs must be taken to reach the goals, and who is in the best position to do those jobs. Actually putting hours that the jobs will take on a timetable or schedule can help families to see what will work and what will not. Creative solutions often result.

Marsha took a part-time job with great benefits because the family needed a variety of therapies for their child. Her husband, who was self-employed, began to do the children's morning routine. "I work for benefits," Marsha said. "It's great for the family, since we receive about $1,000 in insurance payments for medical needs and therapy every month for just one child. Our portion is $100. I can't get the kids off to school, but that's okay. We're paying our bills and meeting the children's needs."

Model the Use of Clear Communication

It is best to help client families establish and follow some simple rules about communication as soon as they are feeling conflict and are under stress. One rule is that each family member should state and defend his own opinion and his own point of view, all the while listening respectfully and openly to the other family members' points of view. Each person must stand up for himself or his point of view without becoming defensive, blaming, accusing, arguing, or threatening (Walsh, 2006). This is hard to do, but becomes a source of power for people who learn to communicate in this manner. When social workers and therapists use this model in their own communication styles with families, they model this strength for them. Families should be instructed on the basics. They are easy to learn, positive to use.

Demonstrate that when people under stress need to take a break, they should do so. Come back later to the issue when emotions are cooler. Thank people for sharing their points of view, even when you do not agree with them. At least you have a way of understanding them better. It never hurts to say, "I would like to think over what you have said. I will come back to you later after I've had a chance to process what you have said. Thank you for talking to me."

Work hard to clear up the debris after any break in communication (that being a nice way of saying that people lost it and had a nasty snit). There are situations in which everyone got hurt. Therefore, everyone feels entitled to an apology. Teach clients to start by apologizing for their own part of the problem and to take care of the others' feelings, if even they get no reciprocal care. When there is a fracture in relationships for any of us, at least we can do our part in taking responsibility and offering an apology.

In high-stress situations, even normally caring people do not operate very well. It can take a while for some of them to return to full functioning level. Family members need to know, however, that they do not have to function poorly to match them. I like to talk to family members about the impact of grief on everyone's functioning in the family. People who are aware of their own lapses are more forgiving when others are operating poorly. Sometimes I suggest to parents that they need to build up some positive feelings before they even approach some of their more difficult problems. They need a couple of weeks of supportive comments and care within the family before trying to go back to analyze and repair a problem situation.

When working on problems in sessions, approach the problems like templates for the future. The families can use the piece-by-piece analysis to understand not only what went wrong, but the process to avoid the pitfall the next time. The specific instance can be used as an example of successful conflict avoidance in the future.

Teach families to seek help if communication requires a third person to re-establish good communication. Certainly professionals should be getting help themselves. While it is not appropriate to share specifics of your situation with families, it is fine to share that you, too, get help as needed. Sometimes the issues are so potent that they cloud people's opinions. But, over time, people can learn to listen respectfully, and with heart, to understand why another holds a particular stance. Usually they are standing up for an important piece of the family or an individual's functioning. Even if you do not agree, it is important to hear their perspective in order to work toward a compromise.

Caseworkers must be talking to families about the importance of family patterns of unity and support as being ultimately more important than getting the precise degree of fairness determined. Don't play the blame game with the family instead of helping families to work toward better functioning. One of the great things about working on this with families is that professionals get to remind themselves of these communication basics!

Team Up with Others to Solve Problems

Many of the issues shared in the adoption community are too large to tackle alone. People often have strengths and resources that they can share in a group, saving everyone time and energy.

Recently a parent emailed me about her son's homework assignment. He was to make a timeline with dates for the "first smile, first steps, first words" etc. The entire class was to post these timelines on the classroom wall. This 1st grader had long passed these milestones by the time he was placed in a home.

Rather than having to deal alone with this issue, the mom gave the teacher links to several adoption advocacy groups and tools including *Adoptive Families* magazine, which is listed in the Resource List. Additionally, I was able to refer her to a local group that had developed stock replacements for these assignments. (Please see ARIS in the Resource List.)

When professionals make it their best practice to keep themselves informed about available resources both locally and nationally, they enable parents to connect with peers for some problem-solving directed at sharing resources for issues that are described in this book. Certainly I have been invited to speak by many parent-led groups, who invite me to present information on needs that they all share. This type of approach spreads the load and speeds progress.

One parent support group needed resources for ADD. A parent member not only compiled a summary of resources, but also all of the IEP and Section 504 processes, best testing professionals, and internal resource people in the surrounding schools. She would have researched this information for her child anyway, but broadened the scope to the extent that everyone benefited.

While some parents will move into these group processes by themselves, others need encouragement to call others and to reach out. The members who need a little more encouragement are typically just as competent in groups. They are often private people who have less experience with team projects. Introducing people by email, phone calls, or at conferences is a great way to help people with similar concerns to get together.

Form or Support a Community

Sometimes there is no community that has been formed. In these days of overloaded family schedules, local peer-to-peer support groups for adoptive families are not available in all cities—even the larger ones. Some families find comparable support through internet-based support groups in the form of discussion groups and email lists. Still, because it can be especially helpful to know and interact face-to-face with other families in similar circumstances, it behooves professionals to do their part in establishing and/or supporting local adoptive parent support groups in whatever ways they can—for example providing meeting space and drinks, printing newsletters, helping to coordinate speakers, etc. This type of support can be especially successful when several agencies and counseling professionals share these supportive responsibilities for as long as it takes for the group to become, and remain, self sufficient.

This does not have to be done with bells and whistles.

> Some parents of teens I saw in a group began to meet at Taco Bell during the time I met with their children. I noticed that they seemed to be carrying a lot of paper to these meetings. Later I came to find that they had accomplished a successful lobbying effort to change State Child Welfare practice in regards to pre-existing conditions and releasing their children's records.

I have asked a colleague to start three social skills groups for children. In all of the cases we were able to use a method of teaching social skills, in real time, that particularly suited the children. Professionals should be connecting their families on many levels of need.

If there is a conference occurring in town, ask the speakers to announce your desire to form a group for a particular purpose. Professionals are in key positions to connect people with others who share similar struggles. People can stretch resources and help divide the work when they work together. It is wonderful to come to a place where people can describe their own path of progress and provide both support and information.

Budget Time to Work on Problems

Many problems are complex and will require a variety of appointments, assessments, and interventions. Help families to understand that, rather than feeling overwhelmed and always guilty about whether "enough" is being done, they should designate a certain amount of time per week to work on developing resources, getting assessments, consulting with specialists, and working on interventions. This time period should translate into a written, current, and ongoing to-do list. The "time keepers" should specifically enter each item on the list and the amount of time allotted for it into the overall schedule.

After the amount of pre-decided time is up, they must move on, whether the list has been completed or not. An important part of budgeting time is including both a starting and a stopping point. Families typically need to work about four to eight hours a week on therapies or resources. When this allotted time is completed, they must be encouraged to move on to other tasks and move off that list, both mentally and physically. The resilient family has other vital interests and activities. Siblings still need time and attention, friendships need cultivation, and hobbies can be enjoyed. Professionals must advocate for and support all of the client family's needs, not just their therapeutic needs.

Professionals are so interested in their specialty area that they need to be careful of what they are modeling. The client family should not feel a need to be as current on the literature as the therapist is, unless they are in the same profession. Instead, professionals should give concrete guidelines around the amount of time and energy devoted to learning about and focusing on the problem area that is "enough."

> For example, a family said to me, "We have child care, so we were planning to attend a weekend conference in trauma."
> The family had already steeped themselves in information. I replied, "You have child care? Leave town and take time off for yourselves! Sleep in. Go for a walk! You are over budget on this issue!"

This principle also applies to siblings. Often the healthier siblings of a troubled child are not getting adequate time. The family has rallied to work on a problem of a family member, but they have not achieved a balance of spending time *not* working on the problem. Encourage parents to take time with the siblings, processing all of the issues of their lives. Their little day-to-day successes and struggles need careful and sensitive attention. When these issues come up in sessions, it is often the first time that children have talked about what their struggles are in a clear way. Professionals can help them with support and clarity, but are also in a position to encourage alterations in the family that make a difference.

Children who had been dragged to a variety of appointments came in to see me without their brother. "We want him to do better," they explained, "but all we do is go to appointments."

I spoke with their parents about this imbalance, and we worked on a solution. Their father began to leave the office earlier and work from home, while the mother took the child to his appointments, so that the other children did not have to deal with waiting rooms to the degree that they had been. It took some effort, but this change helped the other children feel that family life did not center around one child. The significant issue was not just the waiting room. Instead it was the misperception that the parents did not care about everybody in the family. The other children saw that their parents were caring and responsive as the family made a change.

Reflect on an Optimistic Trajectory— and Then Work Backwards

Families who are raising children should have a sense of what success looks like and feels like for this specific child. They need to have a specific reality-based future point. Often families of children with special needs will need the objectivity of their social workers and/or therapist to form realistic expectations and set a path toward realistic goals for their children.

A projected age of 25 years old is a good benchmark age. Working backwards, help families figure out what will have to happen to ensure the best likelihood of that positive development for their child by the time he reaches 25. (The working backward approach allows for a "long-eye" perspective on parenting and resources.) What areas do parents need to cultivate to get to that point? What areas are completely outside of their control? Who can contribute in the areas that the parents cannot? Will there need to be another living or schooling situation?

> A man said, "I knew that my son's bipolar disorder was going to be a bear to live with since my wife was the target of his anger when he had troubles. So, I thought that if he could get into a job training program that he would get support to launch. Otherwise, I was pretty sure that he would end up getting kicked out of our house. This would derail community college or vocational training. He now has a vocation. He makes good money and has a work ethic. Sometimes he is great to have visit, sometimes not. But he can keep a job and live on his own."

This parent got practical information from the National Alliance for the Mentally Ill and attended a local workshop series for parents. He used the information in order to make a successful plan for his son. He highly recommended the workshop series for other parents with children or teens with serious mental illnesses. While this example was that of a self-starter, professionals can share such stories with groups, asking group members to develop a "long-eye" strategy with their parents. Parents have asked me, "Tell me some success stories. What works?"

Parents have formed organizations or teamed with organizations that give information on specific issues or specific disorders like FASD and ADD. They develop information to guide them over the life span. Professionals should be looking at the long-term best for their clients, participating in providing adoption-related resources for today's families.

Help Families to Feel That
They Are Coping

This is especially problematic in families whose children have prenatal exposure or executive dysfunction issues. The family routines need to be maintained for best results. I was talking to a parent who is raising children with FAS and who is an expert in FAS. She said. "I must get off of the phone. It is time for the bedtime routine to begin. They do so much better if I run it on time, the same way, every day."

Professionals can help parents by supplying an idea of what a "normal" day looks like for families like theirs. It is fine to use words like "overstimulated," but they need to have that broken down into how many activities, or how many changes, their children can tolerate.

> Collette, a mother of an 8-year old said, "We know that only one event a day is our boy's limit. He spends so much energy holding things together at school that he needs a half-hour nap when he gets home. If we go to the store, that is our activity. If we also have Scouts, then we have a melt-down. And whose fault is it? He's doing a lot better. But we know our limits now that we know about his processing load and PTSD. We just did not know what that meant to our schedule before. I used to haul him all over town. I thought that I was helping his development by taking him to the zoo and the science center. I would get mad because he was balking and making us late. I was furious when he raged. Now we get compliments on his behavior because we are working within his limits."

Encourage Stress Reduction as a Family

Children who have experienced neglect and trauma are stressed children. Their families, then, experience high stress levels, as well. Everyone in the family should be able to work on stress reduction, using deep breathing, slower pacing at home, positive routines, and pleasant hobbies. Professionals should at the very least teach breathing to parents and the children they treat. Siblings may learn it from the parents.

Professionals should ask about the leisure times for families. Refreshing vacations are a critical part of stress management.

> Some parents arrange several types of vacations. They plan a short one for themselves so that they can really get a break, one for the whole family, and camps for some children so that they can get extra time with other children.

I ask about vacations at times because it seems that they may go awry. For example, sometimes parents have children who need predictable schedules. The family may be planning to travel with grandparents who expect to dictate the schedule and invite many relatives to visit. By being forewarned, parents can call grandparents about their special situations, making a different arrangement. This way, everyone really does get a vacation.

Professionals can help to support family stress reduction. Stress reduction includes positive events and making plans that create opportunities for recreation. Parents and professionals sometimes have to modify existing opportunities or create new ones. Others are a natural.

> For example some parents have described horse camps as a great match for their whole family.

> Recently I asked a non-profit group if they would run a small camp for two teens that needed a smaller, organized group. The non-profit used a staff ratio of 2:1. The parents got a break, as did the siblings. The non-profit group plans to do the camp again, increasing its scope, since it turned out positively.

> Julie Gelo and her NOFAS group in the Puget Sound area run a camp for children and families who have a member with FASD (fetal alcohol spectrum disorder). A parent said, "This was the first time that I could relax, knowing that all the activities were appropriate for our son and well-supervised. We were refreshed and nurtured when we got home." (See the Resource List.)

Families who are not ready for these groups at one point will be at another point. It can be a process of doing some inside the family work first, and then getting ready for the support and help outside of the family.

Areas of Mastery Must Be Recognized and Enhanced

Families who have mastery issues tend to be resilient families. As families begin to master new areas critical to their family, they feel a sense of competence. Sometimes, however, families don't recognize their own successes. Professionals should point them out.

A parent said to me, "When you told me that I was a good parent, I began to believe it! I looked at some materials on FASD and realized that I was hitting all of the areas. The things that we were working on in therapy did not change anything at first. You did not blame me like I thought you would. You told me that progress would require some different approaches. You changed your approach and gave me different instructions. Now my daughter has improved. I feel confident and my husband and I are working as a unit instead of arguing."

Resilient families do no always look successful along the way. They struggle. But as they master the challenges ahead, these families develop a sense of pride in their accomplishments. Professionals should normalize this struggle as part of the mastery process. Things often stop working for us before we decide that we have to change.

Families who begin parenting later in life can tap into other earlier areas of accomplishments for lessons. Professionals can help point out areas of competencies useful for the new challenge.

An older parent confided, "This parenting is much harder than my Ph.D., but I can use the lessons from that process. Focus, work hard, keep researching, don't give up."

Another parent in his 50s said, "When you suggested that I might be best-suited to this school IEP process, I was shocked. I have never done the school issues for my older children. But I've spent my career working with complex institutional problems. That was my training for our harder problem of working with the kids' school system. I handle school meetings with the same preparation. And, I've learned that when I step on toes in the school district, I never spoil the shine. That way I have friends in the district. I'm glad that I can use my experiences to help my children."

Professionals should diligently point out how life skills can generalize. After all, they have seen the minute bites that go into success many, many times. The families may be unfamiliar with the specific skills. In the vignette above, the parent understood how to approach institutional problems, a quality that the professional immediately recognized as crucial.

In working with an attorney, I noticed that she was a great explainer. She could communicate complex ideas aptly. She used her skills to explain life to her daughter and son. She helped her children move from quick response, impulsive girls to ones who could understand the "big picture," or, the context and meaning of information.

A parent who was an experienced teacher took over the problematic homework—and then moved on to the music lessons and chores. He had an organized and matter-of-fact manner. He was unflappable. Previously, this man had been doing laundry and driving to after school events. By looking at the needs of the family, he plugged in his skills where the family was bogging down.

These discussions are part of professional objectivity used on behalf of the family. The professional should never be telling the family how to run their family, but should notice family strengths and how best to use them to meet the current challenges.

Help Families to Appreciate How Their Experience Develops the Value of Compassion and Commitment to Others

We can get stuck going through life thinking only in terms of the welfare of "Me and Mine." As we understand how difficult life can be for people in our client loads, it gives us the opportunity to have compassion for others. We can model this for those clients as well. It is not unusual for some families of children with special needs to begin not only to promote the well-being of their children and families, but to promote the welfare of others at the same time. They begin to view the world differently and to try to offer the same compassion to others that they want the world to offer to their family or family member. This is definitely part of the "bounce forward" of resilience.

A man said, "Having two children with IEPs is a one-way ticket to reality." Over time he used this vision of reality to return to school to become a special education teacher for teens with learning disabilities.

Other parents have set up services in orphanages and have used their compassion to help other families.

Another woman said, "We do respite care for families. No one knew how to support us in our church or neighborhood when we adopted an abused child. We know what its like to never get a break. We provide that break to others now. When we were working with you years ago, you mentioned that we might be able to make a difference in this area someday. I remembered that."

The gift of a transformed experience of adversity is compassion for others who are in difficult circumstances. It promotes a sense of unity.

Assist Families in Thinking about What Is Really Important in Life and Living in Peace with That View

Our culture is so performance based that many activities are geared toward giving us our ratings. We have grades, batting averages, company worth, and family "buying power." Newsmagazines depict the idea of family with a family photo next to a square insert of their income; they define family as "consumers." Yet, we all start life and end life helpless, with our performance in between birth and the end of life rather irrelevant. We depend on our families foremost to believe in our worth.

Families are the refuge from this graded view of life. We depend on families to believe in our worth. In families, people are loved because of their intrinsic value. Families are set apart from the melee of competition and status, promoting a sense of peace and worth in all of the members. Adversity forces people to think through what really matters. Its reward is being able to live life with that knowledge.

The families with whom we are working can become so mired down in the difficulties facing them that they are unable to find and live these goals. Your support as a professional is vital in helping them to find a way to feel at peace.

Help Clients Find Spiritual Strength

During adversity people ask for help from outside of themselves to remove the problem, to deal with the problem, and to see the problem differently.

Many times parents will say that they initially neglected their spiritual lives because they were so busy, or because they were confused about the adversity. As one man said, "I think that God played a bad joke on us." Another father said, "When God sees me coming, He starts laughing." Yet another parent said, "Without our daughter, I'd still be immature spiritually. I have discovered things about myself, some pretty ugly things, which I really wished that I did not have to face. Ignorance and prejudice are ugly."

Often our clients' spiritual lives need to be transformed as part of their overall world change. Professionals are leery about bringing up spirituality, since we believe so strongly as a country in freedom of religion. Yet, the spiritual beliefs that people have make them feel loved, cared for, and resonant with God during times of prayer or meditation. They feel His companionship and presence as anchors in daily life.

> One parent said, "I think that God must be so sad about the way His children are being ignored. I really only cared about my children until I saw what being passed over and devalued did to my son. Now I say, "God, is that how you feel, too, when people ignore your children around the world?'
>
> "I ask God to give me strength to care for others and to let me see what His vision is for our family. It gives me hope. I glimpse at times that we were always meant to care for each other. It has helped me to see what I need to do, not because of guilt, but because I want to."

In closing this book I want to let the words of Nobel Peace Prize winner Archbishop Desmond Tutu shine through as a model for resilience built through adversity.

> "There must be moments when God has beheld the nobility of His human creatures, their compassion and generosity of others; when God has looked at the integrity and courage of those who have stood up to tyrants, who have been willing to die for their faith. When God has looked at the exploits of a Francis of Assisi, a Mother Theresa, a Martin Luther King, Jr., an Albert Schweitzer, a Nelson Mandela, He has said, 'No it was worth taking the risk. They have vindicated my faith in them.' And God has again rubbed His hands in divine self-satisfaction and said of what He has seen that it was not just good, but that it was all really very good" (Tutu, 1999).

We travel in noble company any moment of any day when operating with compassion, generosity, and courage.

Glossary

Abuse

> "Emotional abuse—emotional coercion or disparagement that interferes with a child's social and psychological development.

> "Physical abuse—inflicting bodily injury through excessive force or physically endangering a child through circumstances or activity.

> "Sexual abuse—active and passive sexual contact, as well as exposing a child to sexual acts or materials" (Wissow, 1995).

Affective dysregulation—an emotional state that is extreme in relationship to its triggering events or circumstances.

Asperger's Syndrome—a disorder that lasts over time, in which lack of understanding and responding to social cues, as well as repetitive and restricted patterns of behavior, interests, and activities cause severe impairment in social, school, or work settings. It is included in the spectrum of autistic spectrum disorders.

Attachment—"the organization of behaviors in the young child that are designed to achieve physical proximity to a preferred caregiver at times when the child seeks comfort, support, nurturance, or protection" (AACP, 2005).

> Secure Attachment—an exclusive attachment made between children and their contingent, sensitive caregivers, who provide nurture, comfort, buffering, shared exploration, and help. Parents represent a secure base for exploration.

> Insecure Attachment, Avoidant—an exclusive attachment to a caregiver who is dismissing of the child's needs, insensitive, or shaming. The child defends herself emotionally and limits expectations for nurture, exploration, and emotional help. Children may continue this style into the adoptive family.

Insecure Attachment, Resistant (Anxious)—an exclusive attachment to a caregiver who is not able to meet his child's needs emotionally or with accuracy. For example, the parent is preoccupied with his own issues from the past. Or, the child doubts that the parent knows how to calm her or meet her needs in a timely or effective manner.

Insecure Attachment, Ambivalent--the combination of traits described above in both types of insecure attachment. Children use the strategies for defense in turn, i.e. avoiding the parent and insisting on care, and then resisting the parent's efforts to calm and care for the child.

Disorganized/Disoriented Attachment—the most typical attachment style of maltreated children. These children cannot organize a strategy. They show attributes of trauma, with freezing in place and becoming frightened when asked for closeness. They use pieces of several types of attachment models listed above.

Attunement—the process of feeling in emotional synchronicity with another person. This involves sharing feelings and an understanding of those feelings.

Auditory Processing Disorder—a neurological disorder in which hearing is normal, but the brain has difficulty making sense of the information. It may lose some of the information heard or store it incorrectly. The person may not process information quickly enough to respond optimally.

Autism Spectrum Disorder—a neurological disorder that causes marked impairment in social interaction, communication, and a restriction of activity and interests. The impairment in communication is both verbal and nonverbal. These individuals have repetitive and stereotyped patterns of behavior and interests, showing inflexibility in interests and routines.

Conservation Withdrawal— an early form of dissociation (see definition, below) in which individuals "freeze" when enduring overwhelming amounts of fear or pain, i.e. during abuse.

Contingent Response—an action that is related and responsive to another's cue. For example, a contingent response to hunger is offering food.

Cortisol (CORT)—a corticosteroid hormone released by the adrenal gland, can be released in response to stress.

Disruption—the interruption of a placement before an adoption is legally finalized.

Dissociation—A disruption in processing or integrating the feelings or the meaning of events which occurs when an individual becomes massively overwhelmed by pain, fear, or trauma.

Dissolution—the termination of an adoption after it has been legally finalized. The adoption is dissolved legally.

Dysregulation—a condition which includes body responses moving into maladaptive functioning.

Emotional Dysregulation—feelings that are extreme in the context of the events or circumstances that produced these emotions.

Executive Function—the complex and related processes of maintaining effortful attention, starting and stopping mental operations, inhibiting impulses, accessing working memory, generalizing information, and coordinating multiple mental processes. These functions are significant to academic and social success.

Fetal Alcohol Spectrum Disorder (FASD)—"an umbrella term describing the range of effects that can occur in an individual whose mother drank alcohol during pregnancy. These effects may include physical, mental, behavioral, and/or learning disabilities with possible lifelong implications." As defined by the Families Moving Forward website. (Please see Reference List.)

Flashback—frightening memories, images, or feelings related to trauma that occur even though life events are no long traumatic.

Grief and Pathological Grief—Grief—the process of accepting the loss of a person, a place, an idea or an expectation and accepting the meaning of the loss to the sense of oneself; working through the losses and their emotion and meaning to the extent that the person can retain the positive memory of the lost person or idea and resolve the negative memories associated with that which has been lost. Pathological grief—a grief response in which the person remains highly reactive to reminders of the loss and does not resolve feelings toward that which is lost.

Homeostasis—the state of physiological and emotional balance.

Hypothalamic-pituitary-adrenal Axis (HPA)—regulatory interactions between the hypothalamus, pituitary gland, and the adrenal gland, that function in the stress response and maintaining homeostasis. The HPA axis is involved with stress, anxiety, and effortful attention.

Individualized Educational Plan (IEP)—a formal plan which identifies issues that interfere with a student's learning, or areas that need individual attention in order for the student to achieve academically. The plan attempts to remediate these issues. These may include services that range from resource room help to a self-contained classroom, from speech and language services to social skills groups. These are individualized plans developed for each student.

Oppositional defiant disorder (ODD)—a psychological disorder characterized by a pattern of negative and defiant behavior towards authority figures, resulting in arguments, hostility, grudges, and anger. About 40% of children develop this in conjunction with attention deficit disorder.

Maltreatment—one or more of the following: neglect, physical, emotional, and sexual abuse.

Memory

　　Explicit Memory—the part of the memory which stores facts and events and is consciously used; also called Declarative Memory.

　　Implicit Memory—the part of the memory which stores information such as perceptions, feelings, and motor movements that are used unconsciously; also called Nondeclarative Memory.

Mindsight—"The ability to perceive our own minds and the minds of others" (Siegel, Hartzell, 2003).

Mirror Neurons—cells in the brain that fire in response to both watching and doing a specific behavior. They are hypothesized to be in the emotional centers of the brain, giving immediate feedback as to the feelings of others.

Neglect—"a caregiver's failure to provide for basic needs and care, medical care, supervision, and/or support." (Wissow, 1995).

Post traumatic stress disorder (PTSD)—This anxiety disorder shows the development of symptoms after the exposure to extreme stressors that involve witnessing death, injury, threat to self or others, or learning about death, serious harm, or threat of death or injury of a family member. The symptoms include intrusive recollections of the events, avoidance of reminders of the events, affective dysregulation, emotional numbing, persistent anxiety, nightmares, exaggerated startle response, difficulty with sleep, and flashbacks. The symptoms must last longer than one month after the trauma.

Physical abuse—"the infliction of bodily injury through excessive force, or physically endangering a child through circumstances or activity." (Wissow, 1995).

Reactive attachment disorder (RAD)—markedly disturbed social relationship for a child's age, shown in most of the child's contexts, and presumably occurring due to maltreatment. Symptoms must have begun before the age of 5.

Reflective capacity—the range of abilities to step back from events and analyze them with a sense of perspective.

Resiliency—special strength in maintaining developmental gains and functioning after a negative stressor; or the development of endurance and mastery after stresses and challenges.

Section 504—a special education plan that provides an appropriate accommodation for a health impairment such as ADD, static encephalopathy, visual impairment, and so forth.

Sensory integration—the process by which the brain receives, organizes, and interprets information from the environment.

Sensory processing dysfunction—disruptions in the systems of taking information through the senses and interpreting, responding to this information in a timely and meaningful manner.

Sexual abuse—"active and passive sexual contact, as well as exposing a child to sexual acts or materials" (Wissow, 1995).

Somatization—a feeling of genuine physical distress caused by psychological issues.

Stress regulation—the process of meeting the challenge of a stressful event without becoming overwhelmed.

Stress response—the coordinated process of hormonal and biochemical events that restores homeostasis (physiological and emotional balance) and promotes survival during stress; for example, seeing a branch falling and being able to jump out of the way.

Stressor—anything that is viewed as a potential disruption of homeostasis (physiological and emotional balance). Stressors may be positive or negative, large or small.

Still-face—early evidence of a dissociative process in infants, who show a shocked, frozen face when in the presence of frightening or massively overwhelming events.

Trauma—an horrific and terrifying event or series of events that shatters the threshold of tolerance.

Acute trauma—the one-month period after a trauma in which people show intrusive recollections, shock, nightmares, avoidance of the trauma's reminders, and anxiety.

Chronic trauma—an ongoing reponse in which life is characterized by ongoing traumatic events, for example, being raised in a war zone, crack house, etc.

Complex trauma—exposure to multiple chronic traumatic events that begin in early childhood and occur within the family and community systems.These events shape early emotional development, stress systems, and the meaning of the self.

Traumatic stress—an anxiety disorder showing the development of symptoms after exposure to extreme stressors that involve witnessing death, injury, serious threat to self or others, or learning about death, serious harm, or threat of death or injury of a family member. The symptoms include intrusive recollections of the events, avoidance of reminders of the events, affective dysregulation, emotional numbing, persistent anxiety, nightmares, startle response, difficulty with sleep, and flashbacks. The symptoms must last longer than one month after the trauma to meet the criteria for PTSD, a month or less for acute stress. Traumatic stress may used as a term when children have chronic stress in their lives.

Child Dissociative Checklist (CDC)
Version 3.0

by Frank Putnam, M.D.
No copyright restrictions apply.

This instrument is designed to be used as clinical screening tool for the identification of potential dissociative pathology in children.

Date:_____

Age:_____

Sex: M   F

Identification:_____

Below is a list of behaviors that describe children. For each item that describes your child now or within the past 12 months, please circle 2 if the item is *very true* of your child. Circle 1 if the item is *somewhat or sometimes true* of your child. If the item is *not true* of your child, circle 0.

0 1 2   1.   Child does not remember or denies traumatic or painful experiences that are known to have occurred.

0 1 2   2.   Child goes into a daze or trance-like state at times or often appears "spaced out." Teachers may report that he or she "daydreams" frequently in school.

0 1 2   3.   Child shows rapid changes in personality. He or she may go from being shy to outgoing, from feminine to masculine, from timid to aggressive.

0 1 2   4.   Child is unusually forgetful or confused about things that he or she should know, e.g. may forget the names of friends, teachers or other important people, loses possessions or get lost easily.

0 1 2   5.   Child has a poor sense of time. He or she loses track of time, may think that it is morning when it is actually afternoon, gets confused about what day it is, or becomes confused about when something happened.

0 1 2   6.   Child shows marked day-to-day or even hour-to-hour variation in his or her skills, knowledge, food preferences, athletic abilities, e.g. changes in handwriting, memory for previously learned information such as multiplication tables, spelling, use of tools or artistic ability.

0 1 2   7.   Child shows rapid regression in age-level of behavior, e.g. a twelve-year-old starts to use baby-talk, sucks thumb or draws like a four-year old.

0 1 2   8.   Child has a difficult time learning from experience, e.g. explanations, normal discipline or punishment do not change his or her behavior.

0 1 2   9.   Child continues to lie or deny misbehavior even when the evidence is obvious.

0 1 2   10.   Child refers to him or herself in the third person (e.g. as she or her) when talking about self, or at times insists on being called by a different name. He or she may also claim that things that he or she did actually happened to another person.

0 1 2   11.   Child has rapidly changing physical complaints such as headache or upset stomach. For example, he or she may complain of a headache one minute and seem to forget all about it the next.

0 1 2   12.   Child is unusually sexually precocious and may attempt age-inappropriate sexual behavior with other children or adults.

0 1 2   13.   Child suffers from unexplained injuries or may even deliberately injure self at times.

0 1 2   14.   Child reports hearing voices that talk to him or her. The voices may be friendly or angry and may come from "imaginary companions" or sound like the voices of parents, friends or teachers.

0 1 2   15.   Child has a vivid imaginary companion or companions. Child may insist that the imaginary companion(s) is responsible for things that he or she has done.

0 1 2   16. Child has intense outburst of anger, often without apparent cause and may display unusual physical strength during these episodes.

0 1 2   17. Child sleepwalks frequently.

0 1 2   18. Child has unusual nighttime experiences, e.g. may report seeing "ghosts" or that things happen at night that he or she can't account for (e.g. broken toys, unexplained injuries.)

0 1 2   19. Child frequently talks to him or herself, may use a different voice or argue with self at times.

0 1 2   20. Child has two or more distinct and separate personalities that take control over the child's behavior.

This scale is helpful in understanding the range of dissociation. It is normal to see a difference between the scores of two parents rating the same child.

This scale is helpful in seeing the mild to severe effects of dissociation, from the effects of maltreatment up to and including Dissociative Identity Disorder.

Joyanna Silberg notes that a scores for children with Dissociative Identity Disorder were 24.5 with a standard deviation of 5.2 (1998, p. 352).

CDC Ratings

Groups	Age in years	Mean (average)	Standard Deviation
Normal	5-8 9-11 12-16	3.2 2.9 1.9	2.9 1.0 1.9
Maltreated	5-8 9-11 12-16	10.3 6.1 4.2	8.7 6.5 1.9
DDNOS (Dissociative Disorder Not Specified)	5-8 9-11 12-16	21.4 16.5 20.0	9.1 6.9 8.0

"The CDC has proven to be internally consistent, reliable over time, and generally able to discrimate children with pathological dissociation from those without...a score of 12 or higher is considered an indication of pathological dissociation, and further evaluation is warranted" (Putnam, 1997, p. 250-251).

Adolescent Dissociative Experience Scale (A-DES) Version 1.0.

Judith Armstrong, Ph.D.
Frank W. Putnam, M.D.
Eve Bernstein Carlson, Ph.D.

No copyright restrictions apply.

Directions

These questions ask about different kinds of experiences that happen to people. For each question, circle the number that tells how much that experience happens to you. Circle a "0" if it *never* happens to you, circle a "10" it it is *always* happening to you. If it *happens sometimes but not all of the time*, circle a number between 1 and 9 that bet describes how often it happens to you. When you answer, only tell how much these things happen when you have not had any alcohol or drugs.

Example:

0   1   2   3   ④   5   6   7   8   9   10
(Never)   (Always)

1. I get so wrapped up in watching TV, reading, or playing video games that I don't have any idea what's going on around me.

0   1   2   3   4   5   6   7   8   9   10
(Never)   (Always)

2. I get back tests or homework that I don't remember doing.

0   1   2   3   4   5   6   7   8   9   10
(Never)   (Always)

3. I have strong feelings that don't seem like they are mine.

0   1   2   3   4   5   6   7   8   9   10
(Never)   (Always)

4. I can do something really well one time and then I can't do it at all another time.

0   1   2   3   4   5   6   7   8   9   10
(Never)   (Always)

5. People tell me I do or say things that I don't remember doing or saying.

0   1   2   3   4   5   6   7   8   9   10
(Never)   (Always)

6. I feel like I'm in a fog or spaced out and things around me seem unreal.

0   1   2   3   4   5   6   7   8   9   10
(Never)   (Always)

7. I get confused about whether I have done something or only thought about doing it.

0   1   2   3   4   5   6   7   8   9   10
(Never)   (Always)

8. I look at the clock and realize that time has gone by and I can't remember what has happened.

0   1   2   3   4   5   6   7   8   9   10
(Never)   (Always)

9. I hear voices in my head that are not mine.

0   1   2   3   4   5   6   7   8   9   10
(Never)   (Always)

10. When I am somewhere that I don't want to be, I can go away in my mind.

0   1   2   3   4   5   6   7   8   9   10
(Never)   (Always)

11. I am so good at lying and acting that I believe it myself.

0   1   2   3   4   5   6   7   8   9   10
(Never)   (Always)

12. I catch myself "waking up" in the middle of doing something.

0   1   2   3   4   5   6   7   8   9   10
(Never)   (Always)

13. I don't recognize myself in the mirror.

0   1   2   3   4   5   6   7   8   9   10
(Never)   (Always)

14. I find myself going somewhere or doing something and I don't know why.

0   1   2   3   4   5   6   7   8   9   10
(Never)   (Always)

15. I find myself someplace and don't remember how I got there.

0   1   2   3   4   5   6   7   8   9   10
(Never)   (Always)

16. I have thoughts that don't really seem to belong to me.

0   1   2   3   4   5   6   7   8   9   10
(Never)   (Always)

17. I find that I can make physical pain go away.

0   1   2   3   4   5   6   7   8   9   10
(Never)   (Always)

18. I can't figure out if things really happened or if I only dreamed or thought about them.

0   1   2   3   4   5   6   7   8   9   10
(Never)   (Always)

19. I find myself doing something that I know is wrong, even when I really don't want to do it.

0   1   2   3   4   5   6   7   8   9   10
(Never)   (Always)

20. People tell me that I sometimes act so differently that I seem like a different person.

0   1   2   3   4   5   6   7   8   9   10
(Never)   (Always)

21. It feels like there are walls inside of my mind.

0   1   2   3   4   5   6   7   8   9   10
(Never)   (Always)

22. I find writings, drawings or letters that I must have done but I can't remember doing.

0   1   2   3   4   5   6   7   8   9   10
(Never)   (Always)

23. Something inside of me seems to make me do things that I don't want to do.

0   1   2   3   4   5   6   7   8   9   10
(Never)   (Always)

24. I find that I can't tell whether I am just remembering something or if it is actually happening to me.

0   1   2   3   4   5   6   7   8   9   10
(Never)   (Always)

25. I find myself standing outside of my body, watching myself as if I were another person.

0   1   2   3   4   5   6   7   8   9   10
(Never)   (Always)

26. My relationships with my family and friends change suddenly and I don't know why.

0   1   2   3   4   5   6   7   8   9   10
(Never)   (Always)

27. I feel like my past is a puzzle and some of the pieces are missing.

0   1   2   3   4   5   6   7   8   9   10
(Never)   (Always)

28. I get so wrapped up in my toys or stuffed animals that they seem alive.

0   1   2   3   4   5   6   7   8   9   10
(Never)   (Always)

29. I feel like there are different people inside of me.

0   1   2   3   4   5   6   7   8   9   10
(Never)   (Always)

30. My body feels as if it doesn't belong to me.

0   1   2   3   4   5   6   7   8   9   10
(Never)   (Always)

The group of normal controls had a mean score of 2.4 with a standard deviation of 1.4.

The group of abused teens had a mean score of 3.5 with a standard deviation of 1.8.

The group of nonabused teens had a score of 2.1 with a standard deviation of 1.6.

The groups of teens with dissociative disorders had a score of 4.9 with a standard deviation of 1.1.

A score of 4.0 or greater suggests pathological levels of dissociation (Putnam, 1997, p. 254.)

Other Anxiety and Trauma-Related Assessment Tools

Beck Anxiety Inventory for Youth and Beck Anger Inventory for Youth.
By the author of the adult Beck Depressions scale. These tools are
written at a 2nd grade level. They are available from

Harcourt Assessment, Inc.
19500 Bulverde Road
San Antonio, Texas 78259
Phone: 1-800-211-8378
Fax: 1-800-232-1223

Children's PTSD Inventory. Phillip Saigh. This is a tool to use for children
who need the questions asked of them. Order through PsychCorp at
1-800-211-8378.

Trauma Symptom Checklist for Children (TSCC.) John Briere. Great instrument for assessing trauma. Order from PAR, Inc. www.parinc.com
or 1-800-331-8378.

Exercises for Helping Parents to Help their Children with their Grief Issues

Ways to Support Your Own Child's Grief Process

Children will need emotional support, facts, someone to help them organize their thoughts and feelings, and information about how their losses affect their identities.

Setting the Emotional Tone:

1. Time where the parent is available and reflective.
2. Parent is sitting down.
3. No television or radio. Background music only.
4. Parent shows emotional energy.
5. Parent is not just interested in behaviors, but in the meaning behind the behaviors.
6. Parent is emotionally ready to comfort their children and help them to process losses. (Does not try to talk them out of their grief.)

Ways to Approach a Child:

1. Read stories that give children a chance to move into discussion.
2. Look through the lifebook.
3. Predict that parents will be there for child during toughest times.
4. Give the nonverbal message that you care. Mirror the child's body.
5. Normalize the extra effort that children have to go through. Use the metaphor of the chapter book. (Your life is like a chapter book: it has some sad chapters. Some of the best stories have sad chapters, but the later chapters can be happy and exciting.)

Issues for Children:

1. Sometimes the losses involve such huge feelings that children have a phobic reaction to the loss. They are afraid of the feelings becoming too large. Let children know that you will help share the load so they do not get overwhelmed.

465

2. Sometimes children want the former caregiver of whom they are afraid. They are afraid that wishes come true. (For example, missing an abusive parent or parent figure.) Let them know that you can wish for a person and yet stay safe. It is hard to love someone you cannot trust to keep you safe.

3. Sometimes the losses are the ways in which children stay connected to a birthparent. The children, in trying to stay connected, get lost in the losses. They need to find a different way to connect if that is the case. Find some ways that they can positively connect with the birthparent—shared interests, hair cut, etc.

4. Children can figure out that adoptive parents are supposed to be happy about the placement. They get confused. They think that parents do not want to hear about the loss part. While parents *do* tend to want to prematurely come back to the positive, let children know that you expect and can help them with their sadness.

5. Sometimes children's grieving can get overcome by the parents' own losses. Parents, instead of supporting grieving, describe their own issues, feelings, and perspectives. There is not enough room for the child's thoughts and feelings.

Make certain that you are following the child's lead and supporting his process.

Noticing Your Child's Grief:

1. **Be aware of the ages and stages and reminders**: birthdays, Mother's day, Kid of the Week, pregnant women, and first realization that they have identity conferred upon them by society. As one child heard a parent call out to her son during a ball game, "One more strike and you are going to be adopted."

2. **Irritability**. Nothing seems to please; they search for the lost someone or the lost piece of themselves. Grief is much more likely to be in stops and starts, often about a 4-8 week duration for intense bursts. In unresolved grief, and with a lot of neglect, there may be a dull ache and loneliness that is almost always present. There is an inability to get comfortable in one's own body.

3. **Feelings around the losses, meaning of the losses**. They wonder what the losses mean to their sense of self, and sense of the world. A boy said, "I thought that maybe I would be a sad boy all of my life! I did not know how long I would feel sad."

4. **Look for comments**. "The day I was born was the saddest day of my life. It was the day that I saw for the last time my birthmother's face," a girl said. Follow that up with discussion and comfort.
5. **Children may separate too much or cling too much**. They seem to need quiet time and withdraw. Alternately, some children will cling and get fearful.
6. **Some children seem to move into grief through disappointments**. Adults often get to grief through ideas and events. Children get there by feelings just as often. They may not have a lot of words.

When Grief Coincides with a Need for Behavior Shaping:

Teach emotional modulation. The message is, "It is okay to feel this way and I will help you. But, you may not kick the kid on the bus or say ugly things to me when you feel bad."

Good grieving has support. However, you do not give permission for the grieving child to allow their feelings to overtake the household. Sometimes children want to talk about birthparents at night so that they get to stay up longer. I have said, "At bedtime we will *not* be talking about missing your birthmother. We will have snuggle time in the morning at which time you are welcome to talk about your birthmother."

How to Help Children Grieve:

Set aside times that you are available for your child. The rule of thumb is to have an empty lap or an empty sofa seat next to you. Have a cozy throw next to you so that children can snuggle in.

Consider making a book with a page for each of the feelings or thoughts. Allow children to touch, manipulate and express their feelings. Often they want lots and lots of pictures to arrange, stamp, treasure, or tape on scenes.

Allow anger to surface as part of the grief process. Do not be afraid of strong feelings, Often they will express rage if they were neglected and abused. That clears the air for the grief to come through. Sometimes they have conflicted loyalties, so they do not want parents to hear some of their negative thoughts about birthparents. (This is a good time to make an appointment with a therapist.)

1. Use pieces of paper with different feelings written on them: lonely, angry, happy, excited, sad, nothing. Put out about 30 pens. The child can

arrange the number of pens to correspond with the amount of that feeling that they have. (This idea is credited to Claudia Jewett.) This helps them to express conflicted feelings.

2. Use one piece of paper and color the colors of their feelings. They can decide which colors mean which feelings.
3. Buy or make paper dolls to act out the scenes of their lives.
4. Supply facts. Put the facts on a timeline to help children to stay organized.
5. Have them talk about other losses in their lives if they intersect. They will say, "This reminds me of when someone told me that I did not look like my parents and asked me in front of the Girl Scout leader, 'What happened? Who did you take after?'"
6. Help them figure out how others perceive them. Will others love them when they are hurt? Do others just want a happy friend? Are their feelings of grief and loneliness acceptable in life. Help them to see that this is part of the human condition.
7. Make up a song with verses. Dance it out.
8. Use rituals to say goodbye. (Wish on a star.)
9. Use memorials, for example, contributing to an orphanage or a fund to give school supplies to neglected children.
10. Help children gain perspective. Not everything is an adoption loss. Many disappointments are simply part of life.

The goal is to help children with their "shadow figures," or birthparents, even if they have no contact with them, so that throughout their lives birthparents are giving children both a sense of their good wishes and permission to go on to love the people in their lives.

In essence, you are moving much more of the loss information into a place in which they can talk about it without experiencing an overwhelming amount of emotion. They are able to process the strong feelings and simultaneously feel some mastery. Allow them to reminisce, think about, and remember without getting overwhelmed with grief.

With support children and teens are able to develop a sense of themselves and their own histories so they become present-focused and more optimistic. They learn that they do not face life's difficulties alone. With support, they can incorporate their feelings and facts into an integrated and positive self-concept.

Exercises for Helping Parents with their Grief Issues

Parents find that as they help their children, they will often experience losses.

Parents' Loss:

Helplessness in taking away the loss.

Recognition that in spite of how hard you work, you cannot take away their pain.

Peer rejection, while a normal part of growing up, is common as a trigger for adoption loss issues. This tends to resurface the parents' own issues around rejection and acceptance, and even adoption-connected issues like infertility.

Children's grief reawakens the parent's own unresolved grief processes. Many of us are about one loss behind in our own grief process.

Loss of the "wished-for adoption, wished-for child," may emerge.

Impact on parent's mood is inevitable.

Children's grief changes the meaning of life for the parent. I am not sufficient to meet all of my children's needs.

How to Grieve:

Set aside time that is quiet.

Select modalities to help your process: writing, singing, walking, or talking to others in a support setting.

Use music, photo albums, and lyrics to set the mood.

Dignify the process of learning about yourself. Your needs and process are important.

Arrange for support.

Have confidence that you can work through grief.

Consider what is an "unacceptable" emotion. Why?

If you are numb from pain, write in lists of 20. 20 reasons why this parenting makes me tired, 20 reasons why I am in pain when I enter my child's school, etc.

Exercise to Help Begin Emotional Flow

Write about the following

I am a person who yearns for

If that were to happen, then I believe that I could

I long for the parenting that I always wished that I could have done. My image of myself in that parenting is that I would be:_____. That would make me feel

If I could change my world, I would ask for people to be more

The hardest losses for me to deal with for my child are

I do not like myself when

The loss that I feel that I have the hardest time sharing with anyone is

These are ideas to get ideas and feelings flowing. They help people to begin the processing necessary to move into resolution.

References

AACAP Official Action. (2005.) "Practice Parameter for the Assessment and Treatment of Children and Adolescents With Reactive Attachment Disorder of Infancy and Early Childhood." *Journal of the American Academy of Child and Adolescent Psychiatry,* 44(11), pp. 1206-1219.

AFCARS Report #13, Health and Human Services. (2006.) Administration for Children and Families, Administration on Children, Youth and Families, Children's Bureau, www.acf.hhs.gv/gprograms/cb, pp. 1-10.

Allen, Jon. G. (2001.) *Traumatic Relationships and Serious Mental Disorders.* NY: John Wiley & Sons, Ltd.

APA: Diagnostic and Statistical Manual of Mental Disorders, Fourth Edition, Text Revision (2000), p 46.

Ames, Elinor. (1997.) "The development of Romanian orphanage children adopted to Canada." Final report to the National Welfare Grants program: Human Resources Development Canada.) Burnaby, British Columbia: Simon Frazier University.

Ames, Elinor. (1996.) Conference presentation in Vancouver. B.C.

Barry, Catherine, and Lori Scialabba. (2006.) "Hearings on International Adoption Guidelines," House of Representatives International Relations Subcommittee on Human Rights, Washington, D.C. November 14, 2006.

Bates, Brady D. and Mary Dozier. (2002.) "The Importance of Maternal State of Mind Regarding Attachment and Infant Age at Placement to Foster Mothers' Representations of Their Foster Infants." *Infant Mental Health Journal,* 23(4), pp. 417-431.

Beck, Aaron. (1987.) *Cognitive Therapy of Depression.* New York: Guilford Press.

Belsky, Jay and R.M.Pasco Fearon. (2002.) "Early Attachment security, subsequent maternal sensitivity, and later child development: Does continuity in development depend upon continuity of caregiving?" *Attachment and Human Development,* 4 (3), December 2002, pp. 361-387.

Bird, Gloria, Rick Peterson and Stephanie Miller. (2002.) "Factors Associated with Distress Among Support-Seeking Adoptive Parents." *Family Relations,* 51(3), pp. 215-220.

Bloomquist, Michael. (2006.) *Skills Training for Children with Behavioral Problems—Revised Edition*. New York: Guilford Press.

Bowlby, John. (1980.) *Attachment and Loss: Vol. 3. Loss*. New York: Basic Books.

Bridges, K. M. B. (1932.) "Emotional development in early infancy." *Journal of Genetic Psychology*, 37.

Briere, John, and Catherine Scott. (2006.) *Principles of Trauma Therapy*. Thousand Oaks, CA: Sage Publications.

Briere, John. (2002a.) "The Revised Self-Trauma Model." Conference Presentation in Vancouver, B.C.

Briere, John. (2002b.) "Treating adult survivors of severe childhood abuse and neglect: Further development of an integrative model." In J.E.B. Myers, L. Berliner, J. Briere, C.T. Hendrix, T. Reid, and C. Jenny (Eds.) (2002.) *The APSAC Handbook on Child Maltreatment. 2nd Edition*. Newbury Park, CA: Sage Publications.

Briere, John. (2003.) "Trauma, Dissociation, and Attachment." Conference Presentation in Vancouver, B.C.

Cassidy, Jude. (2006.) "Attachment and Emotion in Infants and Adolescents." Conference presented in Spokane, WA.

Chaffin, Mark and Bill Friedrich. (2004.) "Evidence-based treatments in child abuse and neglect." *Children and Youth Services Review*, 26 (2004.) pp.1097-1113.

Chasnoff, Ira, Linda Schwartz, Cheryl Pratt, Gwendolyn Neuberger. (2006.) *Risk and Promise—a handbook for parents adopting a child from overseas*. Chicago: NTI Publications.

Cloitre, Marylene. (2003.) "Treatment of PTSD and Complex PTSD." Conference Presentation in Vancouver, B.C.

Cook, A., M. Blaustein, J. Spinazzola, and B. van der Kolk, (Eds.) (2003.) "Complex trauma in children and adolescents." National Child Traumatic Stress Network. http://htsn.org

Department of Homeland Security. (2007.) "Immigrant Visa Issued to Orphans Coming to U.S." http://travel.state.gov/family/adoption/stats/stats_451.html

Dozier, Mary. (2005.) "Challenges of Foster Care." *Attachment & Human Development*, 7(1), pp. 27-30.

Dozier, Mary, Kelly L. Cue, and Laura Barnett. (1994.) "Clinicians as caregivers: role of attachment organization in treatment." *Journal of Consulting and Clinical Psychology*, 62(4), pp. 793-800.

Dozier, Mary and Manni, M. (2002.) "Recognizing the special needs of infants' and toddlers' foster parents: Development of a relational intervention." *Zero to Three Bulletin*, 22, pp. 7-13.

Dozier, Mary, Melissa Manni, Kathleen M. Gordon, Elizabeth Peloso. (2006.) "Foster Children's Diurnal Production of Cortisol: An Exploratory Study." *Child Maltreatment*, 11(2), pp. 189-197.

Dozier, Mary, K. Albus, P.R. Fisher, and S. Sepulveda. (2002.) "Interventions for foster parents: Implications for developmental theory." *Development and Psychopathology*, 18, pp. 843-860.

Dozier, Mary, and Oliver Lindhiem. (2006.) "This Is My Child: Differences among Foster Parents in Commitment to Their Young Children." *Child Maltreatment*, 11(4), pp. 338-345.

Dozier, Mary, D. Dozier, and Melissa Manni. (2002.) "Attachment and Biobehavioral Catch-up." *Zero to Three*, April/May 2002, pp. 7-13.

Dozier, Mary, E. Higley, K.E. Albus, and A. Nutter. (2002.) "Intervening with foster infants' caregivers: Targeting three critical needs." *Infant Mental Health Journal*, 25, 541-554.

Fahlberg, Vera. (2012.) *A Child's Journey through Placement*. London: Jessica Kingsley Publishers.

Fahlberg, Vera. (1995.) Conference presentation. Seattle, Washington.

Feletti, V. J.; R. F. Anda; D. Nordenerg; D.F. Williamson;, A.M. Spitz Edwards; et al. (1998.) "Relationship of childhood abuse to many of the leading deaths in adults." Adverse childhood experiences (ACE) study. *American Journal of Preventative Medicine*, 14(4), pp. 245-258.

Fisher, Philip; Megan Gunnar; Patricia Chamberlain; and John Reid. (2000.) "Preventive Intervention for Maltreated Preschool Children: Impact on Children's Behavior, Neuroendocrine Activity, and Foster Parent Functioning." *Journal of Academy of Child and Adolescent Psychiatry*, 39(11).

Fonagy, Peter; Gyorgy Gergely; Elliot Jurist; Mary Target. (2002.) *Affect Regulation, Mentalization, and the Development of the Self.* New York: Other Press, pp. 343-371.

Fonagy, Peter; Allan Schore; L. Alan Sroufe; Daniel Stern. (2002b.) Panel Discussion at "Attachment: From Early Attachment through the Lifespan," UCLA, Tape available, call (310) 474-2505.

Fosha, Diana. (2004.) "Attachment through the Lens of Affect: Implications for Clinical Practice," article at conference presentation Seattle, Washington.

Fraiberg, Selma. (1977.) *Every Child's Birthright*. New York: Basic Books.

Freyd, Jennifer; Anne DePrince; and Eileen Zurbriggen. (2001.) "Self-reported Memory for Abuse Depends Upon Victim-Perpetrator Relationship." *Journal of Trauma and Dissociation*, 2(3). 2001.

Freyd, Jennifer. (2002.) Conference Presentation on Memory Tasks, Trauma and Betrayal. Paper describing this information by Anne P. DePrince and Jennifer Freyd, (2001.) "Memory and Dissociative Tendencies: The Roles of Attentional Context in Word Meaning in a Directed Forgetting Task." *Journal of Trauma and Dissociation*, 2(2)2001.

Friedman, Matthew. (1997.) Material from lectures at Conference, "Victims of Traumatic Loss." August, 1997, Whitefish, Montana.

George, C.; N. Kaplan; and M. Main. (1996) *Adult Attachment Interview Protocol (3rd Ed.)* Unpublished Manuscript. Write to Professor Mary Main, Department of Psychology, University of California at Berkeley, Berkeley, CA 94720.

Gindis, Boris. (2005.) "How to Identify and Address School-related Issues in Internationally Adopted Older Children." Presentation at FRUA Conference, October, 2005, Boston, MA. CD available at: (410)796-8940 or conferencerecordings.com

Gray, Carol. (1994.) *Comic Strip Conversations*. Future Horizons, Available through (817)277-0727.

Gray, Deborah. (2012.) *Attaching in Adoption: Practical Tools for Today's Parents*. London: Jessica Kingsley Publishers.

Greenspan, Stanley and Serena Wieder. (1998.) *The Child with Special Needs: Encouraging Intellectual and Emotional Growth*. Reading, Massachusetts: Addison-Wesley.

Grossman, Klaus, Karin Grossman, and Everett Waters, Eds. (2005.) "Attachment from Infancy to Adulthood: The Major Longitudinal Studies." In Sroufe, L.A.; Egeland, B.; Carlson, E.; & Collins, W.A. *Placing Early Attachment Experiences in Developmental Context*. New York: Guilford Press.

Gunnar, Megan R.; S.J. Morison; K. Chisholm, and M. Schuder.(2001.) "Salivary Cortisol Levels in Children Adopted from Romanian Orphanages." *Development and Psychology*, 13(3), pp. 611-628.

Gunnar, Megan R., and Carol Cheatham. (2003.) "Brain and Behavior Interface: Stress and the Developing Brain." *Infant Mental Health Journal*, 24(3), pp. 195-211.

Gunner, Megan R., and Bonny Donzella. (2002.) "Social regulation of the cortisol levels in early human development." *Psychoneuroendocrinology*, 27, pp. 199-220.

Gutstein, Steven E., and Rachelle Sheely. (2002.) *Relationship Development Intervention with Young Children.* London: Jessica Kingsley Publishers.

Hayes, Steven,; Victoria Follette, and Marsha Linehan, Eds. (2004.) *Mindfulness and Acceptance: Expanding the Cognitive-Behavioral Tradition.* New York: Guilford Press.

Hesse, Eric. (1999.) "The Adult Attachment Interview: Historical and Current Perspectives." In Cassidy, Jude and Shaver, Phillip, Eds. *Handbook of Attachment.* New York: Guilford Press.

Horowitz, Mardi, G. Bonanno, A. Holen.(1993.) "Pathological Grief: Diagnosis and Explanation." *Psychosomatic Medicine*, May-June, 1993, pp. 260-273.

Horowitz, Mardi, Ed. (1999.) *Essential Papers on Posttraumatic Stress Disorde.* New York: New York University Press.

Johnson, Dana. (2000.)"Long-term Medical Issues in Internationl Adoptees." *Pediatric Annals.* 29(4), pp. 234-41.

Johnson, Dana. (2003.) "International Adoptee Follow-up Studies," Presentation at JCICS conference, Washington, D.C. Contact International Adoption Center, Fairfax, VA. (703)970-2651.

LeCuyer, E.A.and G.M. Houck. (2006.) "Maternal limit-setting in toddlerhood: Socialization strategies for the development of self-regulation. *Infant Mental Health Journal*, 27, pp. 344 - 370.

MacKenzie, Patricia and Deborah Gray. (2007.) "Regulation, Arousal Levels, and Behavioral Indicators," collaboration for purposes of this book.

McAfee, Jeanette. (2002.) *Navigating the Social World.* Arlington, Texas:Future Horizons Inc. Order through (800)489-0727.

Mason, Patrick. (2003.) "Growth Curves and Precocious Puberty." Presentation at JCICS conference, Washington, D.C. Contact International Adoption Center, Fairfax, VA. (703)970-2651.

Miller, Laurie C. (2005.) "Functional Outcome and Quality of Life for Internationally Adopted Children from Eastern Europe." Presentation at FRUA Conference, October, 2005, Boston, MA. CD available at: (410)796-8940 or www.conferencerecordings.com

Nelson, Charles and Michelle Bosquet. (2000.) "Neurobiology of Fetal and Infant Development: Implications for Infant Mental Health," in *Handbook of Mental Health, Second Edition*. New York: Guilford Press.

Nelson-Gardell, D. and D. Harris, (2004.) "Child Abuse History, Secondary Traumatic Stress, and Child Welfare Workers." *Best Practice*, Winter, 2004, available through www.cwresource.org

O'Conner T.G., and M. Rutter, and the English and Romanian Adoptees Study Team. (2000.) "Attachment disorder behavior following early severe deprivation: Extension and longitudinal follow-up." *Journal of the American Academy of Child and Adolescent Psychiatry*, 39, pp. 703-712.

Pecora, Peter; Jason Williams; Ronald Kessler; A. Chris Down, et al. (2003.) "Assessing the Effects of Foster Care: Early Results from the Casey National Alumni Study." For a copy contact: Casey Research Program at www.casey.org

Pecora, Peter; Ronald Kessler; Jason Williams; et al.(2005.) "Improving Family Foster Care: Finding from the Northwest Foster Care Alumni Study." For a copy contact: Casey Research Program at www.casey.org

Pertman, Adam. (2005.) Remarks at FRUA National Conference, Boston, MA.

Price-Levine, Hilde. (2004.) "Transitions from Foster Home to Adoptive Home: Importance and Implications for Practice and Systemic Change." Advocacy Paper available from author at www.adoption-counselingservices.com

Putnam, Frank. (1999.) "Biological Effects of Child Abuse." Conference Presentation at the 4th Annual NW Conference on Trauma Disorders, Chelan, WA.

Putnam, Frank. (1997.) *Dissociation in Children and Adolescents*. New York: Guilford Press.

Pynoos, Robert. (1997.) Material from lectures at Conference, "Victims of Traumatic Loss," August, 1997, Whitefish, Montana.

Sapolsky, R.M. (1992.) St*ress, the Aging Brain, and the Mechanisms of Neuron Death*. Cambridge, MA: MIT Press.

Scaer, Robert. (2001.) *The Body Bears the Burden: Trauma, Dissociation, and Disease*. New York: Haworth Press.

Schroen, Susan. (1985.) *Here I am: A LifeBook Kit for Use with Children with Developmental Disabilities*. Available from www.spaulding.org

Schore, Allan N. (2002.) Material from lectures at Conference: Attachment: From Early Attachment through the Lifespan, UCLA, Tape available (310)474-2505.

Schore, Allan N. (2003.) *Affect Dysregulation and the Disorder of the Self.* NY: Norton Press.

Schore, Allan N. (2003.) *Affect Regulation and the Repair of the Self.* NY: Norton Press.

Siegel, Daniel. (2001.) "Towards an Interpersonal Neurology of the Developing Mind: Attachment Relationships, 'Mindsight,' and Neural Integration," *Infant Mental Health Journal,* 22(1-2), pp. 67-94.

Siegel, Daniel. (2002.) "Interpersonal Neurobiology of the Developing Mind." Material from lectures at Conference, Attachment: From Early Attachment through the Lifespan, UCLA, Tape available (310)474-2505.

Siegel, Daniel and Mary Hartzell. (2003.) *Parenting from the Inside Out.* New York: Tarcher/Putnam.

Silberg, Joyanna. (1998.) *The Dissociative Child.* Maryland: Sidran Press.

Solomon, Marion F. and Daniel Siegel, Eds. (2003.) *Healing Trauma: Attachment, Mind, Body, and Brain.* New York: W. W. Norton and Company.

Solomon, Judith and Carol George. (1999.) *Attachment Disorganization.* New York: Guilford Press.

Sroufe, L. Alan. (1995.) *Emotional Development.* Cambridge, UK: Cambridge University Press.

Sroufe, L. Alan. (2002.) "Attachment from Early Childhood Through the Lifespan." Conference Presentation at UCLA. Tape available (310)474-2505.

Sroufe, L. Alan; Elizabeth Carlson; Alissa Levy; and Bryon Egeland. (1999.) "Implications of attachment theory of developmental psychopathology." *Development and Psychopathology.* 11 (1999) pp. 1-13.

Sroufe, L.Alan; Byron Egeland; Elizabeth Carlson; and W.Andrew Collins. (2005.) *The Development of the Person.* New York: Guilford Press.

Stafford, B.; C. Zeanah; M. Scheeringa. (2003.) "Exploring Psychopathology in Early Childhood: PTSD and Attachment Disorders in DC: 0-3 and DSM IV." *Infant Mental Health Journal,* 24(3), pp. 398-409.

Stern, Daniel. (1985.) *The Interpersonal View of the Infant.* New York: Basic Books.

Stern, Daniel. (2004.) *The Present Moment in Psychotherapy and Everyday Life.* New York: W.W. Norton Press.

Stern, Daniel. (2002.) "Why Do People Change in Psychotherapy?" Presentation at Conference March 9-10, "Attachment: From Early Childhood through the Lifespan," UCLA Campus.

Taylor, Nicole, Alicia Gilbert, Gail Mann, and Barbara Ryan. (Draft, 2006.) *Assessment-Based Treatment for Traumatized Children: A Trauma Assessment Pathway Model*. Chadwick Center for Children and Families and Rady Children's Hospital and Health Center, San Diego. Book is available on-line.

Taylor, Steven. (2006.) *Clinician's Guide to PTSD A Cognitive Behavioral Approach*. New York: Guilford Press.

Teicher, Martin H. (2002.) "Scars That Won't Heal: The Neurobiology of Child Abuse." *Scientific American*, March, 2002, www.sciam.com, pp. 68-74.

Toth, Sheree. L., Angeline Maughan, Jody Todd Manly, Mary Spagnola, and Dante Cicchetti. (2002.) "The relative efficiency of two interventions in altering maltreated preschool children's representational models: Implications for attachment theory." *Development and Psychopathology*, 14, 877-908.

Tutu, Desmond. (1999.) *No Future without Forgiveness*. New York: Doubleday.

Tyrrell, Christine L., Mary Dozier, Gregory B. Teague, and Roger D. Fallot. (1999.) "Effective Treatment Relationships for Persons with Serious Psychiatric Disorders: The Importance of Attachment States of Mind." *Journal of Consulting and Clinical Psychology*, 67(5), pp. 725-733.

van der Kolk, Bessel. (2002.) Conference Presentation, "Foundations of Understanding Disorders of Extreme Stress." Vancouver, B.C.

van der Kolk, Bessel A. (1994.) "The Body Keeps the Score, Memory and the evolving psychobiology of post traumatic stress." *Harvard Review of Psychiatry*, 1(5), pp. 253-265.

van der Kolk, Bessel A.; Alexander C. McFarlane; and Lars Weisaeth, Eds. (1996.) *Traumatic Stress*. New York: Guilford Press.

van der Kolk, Bessel A., D. Pelcovitz, S. Roth, F. Mandel, A. McFarlene and J. Herman. (2002.) "Dissociation, Affect Dysregulation and Somatization: the Complex Nature of Adaptation to Trauma." Available through www.trauma-pages.com/vanderk5htm

Walsh, Froma. (2006.) *Strengthening Family Resilience*. New York, Guilford Press.

Waters, Everett and Marta Valenzuela. (1999.) "Explaining Disorganized Attachment," chapter in *Disorganized Attachment*. Eds. Solomon, Judith and George, Carol. New York: Guilford Press.

Wissow, L.S. (1995.) "Child Abuse and Neglect." *New England Journal of Medicine*, 332, pp. 1425-1431.

Wolfe, Vicky Veitch. (1998.) "Child Sexual Abuse." Mash, Eric and Russell Barkley Eds. Chapter in *Treatment of Childhood Disorders*. New York: Guilford Press.

Zeanah, Charles H., Ed.(2000.) *Handbook of Infant Mental Health. Second Edition*. New York: Guilford Press.

Zeanah, Charles H, Elizabeth Carlson, Anna Smyke, and Sebastian F. Koga. (2005.) "Attachment in Institutionalized and Community Children in Romania." *Child Development*, September/October 2005, 76(5) pp.1015-1028.

Resource List

Organizations, Newsletters, and Information Sites

This list gives resources that lead to other, more specific resources. For example, ATTACh gives locations of therapists who meet APSAC standards around the country.

Adoption Today
246 S. Cleveland Ave.
Loveland, CO 80537
(970)663-1185
(970)663-1186 FAX
http://www.adoption.org/adopt/adoption-today-magazine.php
This magazine published by the adoptive-parent-owned Louis & Co supports adoptive families. It is readable, enjoyable, and informative. The website above has great links to support groups, news, and information.

Adoptive Families
2472 Broadway, Suite 377
New York, NY 10025
(800)372-3300
www.adoptivefamilies.com
This excellent magazine, published by adoptive-parent-owned New Hope Communications, is a free-standing magazine carrying the same name as the magazine of the now defunct non-profit AFA.

Adoptive Families Association of British Columbia, AFABC
104th Avenue
Surrey, BC V3K1N9
(604) 588-7300
info@bcadoption.com
Publishes parent-friendly resources for families, and sponsors ongoing training for families and professionals. Includes a helpful representation by birthparents.

ARIS (Adoption Referral and Information Service)
Yolanda Comparan, MSW
(888)777-1538
www.adoptionreferralservice.com

ARIS is a model referral service connecting adoptive parents with therapists, educational specialists, physicians, and resources in the Puget Sound area in Washington State. It is free to parents. For information on how to set up similar programs, please contact the above number or website.

ATTACh, Association for Treatment and Training in the Attachment of Children
P.O. Box 533
Lake Villa, IL 60046
(847)356-7856
www.attach.org
This national organization, with a missions to promote prevention, diagnosis, and treatment for attachment issues, publishes a newsletter, has a code of conduct for mental health providers, has listings of therapists, and has a superb yearly national conference.

ChildTrauma Academy
Feigin Center, Suite 715
Texas Children's Hospital
6621 Fannin
Houston, TX 77030
www.childtrauma.org
This is an educational series for parents and caregivers. Bruce Perry, M.D., Ph.D. composes or edits materials. Material is practical and accurate. It gives parents access to work from some of the finest caliber professionals.

Center for Cognitive-Behavioral Assessment and Remediation
www.bgcenter.com
This is a website run by developmental psychologist Dr. Boris Gindis. It has many articles useful for educational planning, not exclusive to those adopted from Eastern Europe.

CHADD-Children and Adults with Attention Deficit Disorder
8181 Professional Place, Suite 201
Landover, M.D. 20785
(800)233-4050
(301)306-7070
(301)306-7090 FAX
www.chadd.org
This organization is a powerhouse with information about education, medication, home routines, counseling, and local support groups. Invaluable in giving information to advocate for school planning.

Child Information Gateway
http://www.childwelfare.gov/
Formerly the National Clearinghouse on Child Abuse and Neglect Information and the National Adoption Information Clearinghouse, Child Welfare Information Gateway provides access to information and resources to help protect children and strengthen families. Provides information about all aspects of adoption and about child abuse and neglect, including publications, referrals to services, and searches of its computerized information databases. A service of the Children's Bureau, Administration for Children and Families, U.S. Department of Health and Human Services.

FASD: Families Moving Forward
http://depts.washington.edu/fmffasd/
This is a program that is designed to help children with FASD and there families. "The FMF program has been offered as a home visiting intervention model. But these intervention techniques can likely also be used in mental health clinics, early intervention settings, child guidance centers, or in settings where FASD diagnosis is done. The FMF model is both "manualized" (has certain core components and a specific session flow) and "individualized" (has special optional components that different families can decide to do)."
This is information from their website, which can be accessed at the web address above.

Fostering Families Today
www.fosteringfamiliestoday.com
The magazine published by Louis & Co (publishers, as well, of *Adoption Today*), is packed with sound and well-written articles and graphically attractive as well. It is also helpful for later-placed adopted children. It is one of my favorite resources in the field.

FRUA (Friends of Russian and Ukrainian Adoption and Neighboring Countries)
PO Box 2944
Merrifield, VA 22116
www.frua.org
This organization is a powerhouse. Join and sign up for their Family Focus newsletter and make use of their dynamic on-line discussion group. Better yet, go to or order tapes from their national conference. You do not have to have adopted from Eastern Europe to appreciate these resources.

Gottman Institute
www.gottman.com
(888)523-9042.
These are the experts on marriages--and how to keep them working. They also sell a DVD format called the Art and Science of Love. There are Gott-man weekends as well as Gottman-trained professionals through their network.

FAS Times Quarterly Newsletter
PO Box 2525
Lynnwood, Wa 98036
This is a most helpful newsletter. US $20 family, US $30 professional.

Homebuilders
http://www.institutefamily.org/
This effective intervention model was developed by the Institute for Family Development for family preservation. It is a national model for effective and evidence-based treatment. For details visit the website.

The Iceberg
P.O. Box 95597
Seattle, WA 98145-2597
Iceberg_fas@yahoo.com
Supporting families with members with Fetal Alcohol Syndrome or Effects, this excellent newsletter combines stories, advocacy, and research findings.

International Adoption Clinic
Box 211 UMHC
420 Delaware Street SE.
Minneapolis, MN. 55455
www.med.umn.edu/peds/iac/
This organization directed by Dana Johnson, M.D., is on the cutting edge of medical, psychological, and social issues facing adopted children and their families

Kinship Center
www.kinshipcenter.org
This is a great source for adoption-related information. Sharon Kaplan Rosia and her colleagues are the inspiration behind these materials, covering important aspects of parenting and professional support.

National Council on Adoptable Children (NACAC)
970 Raymond Avenue, Suite 106
St. Paul, MN 55114-1149
1-800-470-6665
www.nacac.org
This organization has legal, ethical, and practice influences on children's adoption issues. It is a powerful advocacy organization and leads in improving adoption practices.

NOFAS
National Organization on Fetal Alcohol Syndrome
1815 H Street NW, Suite 750
Washington DC 200006
800-66 NOFAS
800-666-6327
This organization has local chapters. It disperses great information on FASD.

Pact, An Adoption Alliance
3450 Sacramento Street, Suite 239
San Francisco, CA 94118
Voice: (425)221-6957
Fax: (510)482-2089
www.pactadopt.org
An adoption placement and education service focused on placing children of color and supporting families raising adopted children of color either in-racially or transracially.

Raising Black and Biracial Children
RBC
1336Meadow View Lane, #1
Lancaster, CA 93534
RBCeditor@aol.com
This magazine supports the parenting of African American, interracial, transracial adoptive, and foster families. The format is enjoyable, the subject matter informative

Sibshops
http://www.siblingsupport.org/
The sibling support project has developed a national directory of these workshops designed to best support siblings of special needs children. The kids love them. Please see the website for a State-by-State directory.

Society of Special Needs Adoptive Parents Newsletter.
(604)687-3364
sanp@snap.bc.ca.
This provides the latest on special needs issues, including FASD. It is extremely practical. Quarterly, $25 (family) or $35 (group). SNAP also has a great, downloadable book on parenting children affected by FASD.

The Center for Adoption Medicine
University of Washington Pediatric Care Center
4245 Roosevelt Way NE
Seattle, WA 98105
(206)598-3006
email adoption@u.washington.edu
website http://www.adoptmed.org

TAPS (Transracial Adoptive Parent Support)
(888)448-8277
Birthparent Line (800)750-7590
This service organization specializes in services to children of color. Its programs are excellent and its website outstanding.

Books for Professionals, Parents and Children

Adopting the Hurt Child: Hope for Families With Special Need Kids. Gregory Keck and Regina Kupecky. (Colorado Springs: Pinon Press, 1995.) Great book for those adopting older (school age and up) or seriously troubled children. Also check out their companion book, *Parenting the Hurt Child.*

Adopting and Advocating for the Special Needs Child. L. Anne Babb and Rita Laws. (Westport: Bergin and Garvey, 1997.) A guide to important information and assistance for those adopting children with special needs.

All about Adoption. Marc Nemiroll and Jane Annunziata. (Washington, DC: Magination Press, 2004.) This children's book for ages 6-11 includes good information about children's feelings, adoptive families, and birthparents. It includes anxiety, older child adoption, and birthparent issues.

The Best Single Mom in the World: How I Was Adopted. Mary Zisk. (Chicago: Albert Whitman and Company, 2001.) Want a cheerfully illustrated read-aloud book for a single parent family? This is it.

Assessment-Based Treatment for Traumatized Children: A Trauma Assessment Pathway Model. Nicole Taylor, Alicia Gilbert, Gail Mann, Barbara Ryan. (Draft, 2006.) Chadwick Center for Children and Families and Rady Children's Hospital and Health Center, San Diego. Book is available online. This gives assessment tools, latest trauma models, and all the addresses to order tools or read more.

Borya and the Burps. An Eastern European Adoption Story. Joan McNamara. (Indianapolis: Perspectives Press, Inc., 2005.) This is a light-heartened book that helps little ones to visualize the movement from Eastern Europe to home. It's beautifully illustrated and fun to read.

Childhood Speech, Language, and Listening Problems: What Every Parent Should Know. Patricia Hamaguchi. (1995, 2001.)

Children's Adjustment to Adoption: Developmental and Clinical Issues. Anne B. Brodzinsky, Daniel W. Smith, David M. Brodzinsky. (Thousand Oaks, CA: Sage Publications, 1998.) This is a short but excellent professional summary of pertinent adoption issues.

Child with Special Needs: Encouraging Intellectual and Emotional Growth. Stanley Greenspan and Serena Wieder. (MA: Addison Wesley, 1998.) Sophisticated parents or professionals will appreciate this approach, which stimulates development.

The Challenge of Fetal Alcohol Syndrome: Overcoming Secondary Disabilities. Eds. Ann Streissguth and Johanthan Kanter. (Seattle: University of Washington Press. 1997.)

A Child's Journey through Placement. Vera Fahlberg, M.D. (London: Jessica Kingsley Publishers, 2012.) This beautifully written book is a treasure for professionals who are placing children or treating children. Dr. Fahlberg's wisdom and sensitivity shine through.

Connecting with Kids through Stories. 2nd edition. Denise Lacher, Todd Nichols, Melissa Nichols and Joanne C. May. (London: Jessica Kingsley Publishers, 2012.) This book employs storytelling to help children to change their narratives and schema of life. It gives a helpful guide to parents and to clinicians.

Creating Capacity for Attachment. Arthur Becker-Weidman and Deborah Shell, Eds. (Oklahoma City: Wood and Barnes Publishing, 2005.) This book is a lovely addition to the literature. It helps clinicians to develop their practice skills in areas of assessment, attunement, and treatment for children's with attachment issues.

Clinician's Guide to PTSD: A Cognitive Behavioral Approach. Steven Taylor. (New York: Guilford Press, 2006.) This is an well-written guide that will speed clinician's in their competence in using CBT.

Delivered from Distraction: Getting the Most out of Life with Attention Deficit Disorder. Edward Hallowell and John Ratey. (New York: Ballantine Books, 2005.) This book is a guide for many aspects of life. It is a great book for families with a member with ADD.

The Development of Romanian Orphanage Children Adopted to Canada: Final Report (Romanian Adoption Project.) Elinor Ames and Simon Fraser. (University, Burnaby, B.C. V5A 1s6 Canada, 1999.) Report available at above address by sending $10. This gives an in-depth study of children's attachment and social adjustment post-adoption, and is relevant to other children previously institutionalized.

Facilitating Developmental Attachment. Daniel A. Hughes. (Dunmore, Pennsylvania: Jason Aronson/Inghram Book Company, 2000.) Professionals and parents who are sophisticated readers will enjoy this well-written book. Hughes describes not only the foundations of emotional relationships with parents and children, but sensitive ways in which to build on those relationships.

Fetal Alcohol Syndrome and Fetal Alcohol Effects. Diane Malbin. (Minneapolis: Hazeldon Books, 1993.) Available: 1-800-328-9000.This is a booklet that is written for professionals, but quite useful to parents. It explains the variations in children's processing in a clear, succinct manner.

Filling in the Blanks: A Guided Look at Growing Up Adopted. Susan Gabel. (Indianapolis: Perspectives Press, Inc., 1988.) This book helps pre-teen children and early teens with work on identity formation. It helps them to phrase questions and discuss the meaning of their life story. Parents can use this themselves or bring it to counseling for discussion.

Fostering Changes: Myth, Meaning and Magic Bullets in Attachment Theory. Richard Delaney. (Oklahoma City: Wood and Barnes Publishing, 2006.) This book describes good techniques and an updated theoretical base as a way to help older children in foster homes. The book is practical and respectful.

Growing Up Again, Parenting Ourselves, Parenting Our Children. Jean Illsley Clarke and Connie Dawson. (New York: Hazeldon Books/Harper Collins. 1989. Revised 1998.) This book helps parents who lacked a good start themselves to give a good start to their children and enjoy parenting. Connie Dawson brings an adoption perspective to the book.

Healing Trauma: Attachment, Mind, Body, and Brain. Eds. Marion F. Solomon and Daniel Siegel. (W. W. Norton and Company, 2003.) This book includes the finest research and theory on the subject.

Helping Adolescents with ADHD & Learning Disabilities: Ready-to-Use Tips, Techniques, and Checklists for School Success. Judith Ph.D. Greenbaum, Geraldine Ph.D. Markel. (San Francisco, CA: Jossey-Bass 2001). This book is great in giving ideas for IEPs and school meetings. It helps parents and teens in school matters.

Inside Transracial Adoption. Gail Steinberg and Beth Hall. (Indianapolis: Perspectives Press, Inc., 2000.) This book explores the complexities of transracial adoption while equipping parents with practical and compassionate advice. To top it off, it is a good read!

International Adoption, New Kids, New Challenges. Dana Johnson, M.D. PhD. Available from the International Adoption Clinic, This pamphlet describes common challenges and sensible plans for parents.

Launching a Baby's Adoption: Practical Strategies for Parents and Professionals. Patricia Irwin Johnston. (Indianapolis: Perspective Press, Inc. 1997.) This book guides the process up to and through one year post-placement so that babies get off to an optimal start. Parent's inner work is sensitively described through case examples. Attention is given to some of the early problems of attachment that infants may have, and ways to help infants adjust. Sound adoption practice standards that emphasize honesty among all members of the triad make this a helpful addition to placement professionals, as well as parents.

Help is on the Way—A Child's Book about ADD. Marc Neniroff and Jane Annunziata. (Washington, DC: Magination Press, 1998.) This is a fun and readable book to use with children who have been diagnosed with ADD.

The Mulberry Bird. Anne Braff Brodzinsky. (Indianapolis: Perspectives Press, Inc., 1986, revised 1996.) Children who are in elementary school like this book. It is particularly helpful to children who have a history of poor care. The children use the metaphors to talk to parents.

Navigating the Social World. Jeanette McAfee. (Future Horizons, 2002.) (800)489-0727. This is a handbook for children who have difficulty with social relatedness. It includes exercises to build these capacities in the older child. I have used this in a guided way with late high school age coaches and preteen clients with excellent success.

Night Falls Fast. Kay Redfield Jamison. (New York: Alfred A. Knoff, 1999.) This brilliant psychiatrist writes about her client's and her own experiences with mood disorders. Hers is a moving account that gives hard-headed but necessary information about medication. Her previous book, *An Unquiet Mind*, (New York: Vintage Books, 1995) is also excellent in describing mood disorders.

Parenting Children Affected by Fetal Alcohol Syndrome—A Guide for Daily Living. Ministry for Children and Families, British Columbia. (1998.) Available as a free downloaded book from snap@snap.bc.ca., regularly updated and extremely practical guide to daily schedules and an understanding of approaches that work with prenatally exposed infants, children, and teens.

Parenting from the Inside Out. Daniel J. Siegel and Mary Hartzell. (New York: Penguin/Putnam, 2003.) This excellent book explores solid family relationships in a brain-based, attachment-friendly, but warm manner. Also available from these authors is a two disc DVD setfeaturing a 10 hour training with this same title.

Principles of Trauma Therapy. John Briere and Catherine Scott. (Thousand Oaks: Sage Publications, 2006.) This is an up-to-date treatment book that is theoretically sound and research-based. The work described is excellent, although it is mostly geared towards adults, it is still helpful in working with children and families.

Ready or Not, Here Life Comes. Mel Levine. (New York: Simon and Schuster, 2005.) Want to look ahead, making certain that children are prepared for the future? This book does just that, especially focusing on children with learning differences.

Relationship Development Intervention with Children, Adolescents, and Adults. Steven E. Gutstein and Rachelle K. Sheely. (London: Jessica Kingsley Publishers, 2002.)

Relationship Development Intervention with Young Children. Steven E. Gutstein and Rachelle K. Sheely. (London: Jessica Kingsley Publishers, 2002.) This book and the one above are the curricula for developing social skills. They are fantastic resources for schools.

Rising to the Challenge. Suzanne Ebel, Ed. (2005.) Available from pca@kirkofthehills.org. This book gives an inclusive model for schools. It is graphically wonderful and appropriate for school-age kids and teens and their teachers and parents.

Risk and Promise: A Handbook for Parents Adopting a Child from Overseas. Ira Chasnoff, Linda Schwartz, Cheryl Pratt, and Gwendolyn Neuberger. (National Training Institute, 2006.) Written by pros, this book is an excellent, up-to-date description of all the relevant areas parents need to understand. It is concise and readable.

Sam's Sister. Julet Bond. (Indianapolis: Perspectives Press, Inc. 2004.) This is a first—a read-aloud book about children whose birth sibling will be part of an adoptive family. This is great for children who are biologically related but living in different families.

Supporting Brothers and Sisters: Creating a Family by Birth, Foster Care and Adoption. Arleta James. (Sagamore Hills, OH: AJ Productions, 2006.) This six hour curriculum with accompanying DVD offers great tips for helping prepare siblings whose homes will be opened to a child in foster care or to be adopted. Available from the author at 1070 Fleetwood Drive Unit C, Sagamore Hills,OH 44133 or arletaj@aol.com

Skills Training for Children with Behavioral Problems—Revised Edition. Michael Bloomquist. (New York: Guilford Press, 2006.) This is an excellent guide for parents and professionals who want tools, charts, and practical suggestions for reducing anger, anxiety, through changes in thinking and reward systems. It helps the whole family with better self-control and helpful thoughts.

Taking Charge of ADHD. Russell A Barkley. (New York: Guilford Press, 1995, Revised 2005.)This author explains simply, but not superficially, what is going on with children with ADHD and what to do about it. Russell Barkley is not only a prolific writer and researcher, but he is a caring advocate for children and their families.

Tell Me Again About the Night I Was Born. Jamie Lee Curtis. (New York: Harper Collins, 1996.) This is a fun, read-aloud. It helps children to understand the excitement of adoptive parents in a concrete manner.

Tell Me A Real Adoption Story. Betty Lifton and Claire Nivola. (New York: Alfred Knopf Publishing, 1993.) Good book about identity formation and loss issues for ages 6-12.

Toddler Adoption: The Weaver's Craft. Revised edition. Mary Hopkins-Best. (London: Jessica Kingsley Publishers, 2012.) A guide to adjustment, attachment, learning issues and parenting for parents whose children arrive between ages one year and four years.

Treating Parent-Infant Relationship Problems. Arnold J. Sameroff, Susan McDonough, and Katherine Rosenblum, Eds. (New York: Guilford Press, 2004.) This book describes processes and research effective in early treatment of infants in the context of their families. It is a sensitive book for clinicians looking for models.

Twenty Life Transforming Choices Adoptees Need to Make. Sherrie Eldridge. Colorado Springs: Pinon Press, 2003.) This book reads like a novel, while addressing important issues in adoption in a heartfelt way. I love this book.

Wanting a Daughter, Needing a Son, Abandonment, Adoption, and Orphanage Care in China. Kay Ann Johnson. (St. Paul, MN:Yeong and Yeong Book Company, 2004.) This book gives a fact-filled and historical account of the circumstances around China's "one-child" policy. It helps parents to understand and to present the cultural and resources realities of adoption.

We See the Moon. Carrie A. Kitze. (EMK Press, 2003.) This is my favorite book for children adopted from China who are in early primary grades. The pictures and voices are evocative and open-ended. It's well-loved by children in therapy with me. The illustrations are extraordinary.

When the Brain Can't Hear. Teri Bellis. (New York: Pocket Books, 2002.) This is a book on auditory processing disorder that helps parents and professionals comprehend the impacts on their children and what they need to do.

When You Were Born in China. Sara Dorow. (St. Paul, MN: Yeong and Yeong, 1997.) This book shows not just the joys of adoption, but pictures from the orphanage, places were children might have been placed by birth-parents, China's jewels and poverty. It gives material so that children process their story realistically.

Zachery's New Home. Geraldine Blomquist and Paul Blomquist. (Washington DC: Magination Press, 1991, rev. 2001). This has been the children's all-time favorite about beginning to trust after abuse.

Index

493

About the Author

photo by Jasen Sasaki

A leader in her field, Deborah Gray is an innovative clinical social worker specializing in the areas of attachment, grief and trauma. Over the past 15 years, Gray has spent over 15,000 hours counseling adopted children, using successful techniques and strategies based in up-to-date research. As founder of Nurturing Attachments and a former therapeutic foster parent, Gray believes that parents should be empowered to meet the needs of their children. Her practical approaches to promoting attachment, shaping behavior and working through trauma and grief make her a sought-after presenter nationwide.

Gray received her graduate degrees from Syracuse University in 1981. She is a licensed social worker and mental health counselor living and practicing in the state of Washington. She is on the faculty of two graduate foster care/adoption therapy programs and the Trauma Certificate Program at the University of Washington. *Nurturing Adoptions* is Deborah Gray's second book. She is the author of *Attaching in Adoption: Practical Tools for Today's Parents*, published by Jessica Kingsley Publishers, as well as numerous articles.

Contact Deborah at deborahdgray@yahoo.com

Jessica Kingsley *Publishers*
London - Philadelphia - Sydney - Vancouver

Jessica Kingsley Publishers is a leading independent publisher with offices in London and Philadelphia, dedicated to publishing books that make a real difference to society and to individuals.

Visit our web site at www.jkp.com

If you have enjoyed reading Nurturing Adoptions, *you may be interested in reading:*

Attaching in Adoption
Practical Tools for Today's Parents
Deborah D. Gray
ISBN 978 1 84905 890 2

Toddler Adoption
The Weaver's Craft
Revised Edition
Mary Hopkins-Best
ISBN 978 1 84905 894 0

Adoption is a Family Affair!
What Relatives and Friends Must Know
Patricia Irwin Johnston
ISBN 978 1 84905 895 7

Creating Loving Attachments
Parenting with PACE to Nurture Confidence and Security in the Troubled Child
Kim S. Golding and Daniel A. Hughes
ISBN 978 1 84905 227 6

Connecting with Kids through Stories
Using Narratives to Facilitate Attachment in Adopted Children
2nd edition
Denise B. Lacher, Todd Nichols, Melissa Nichols and Joanne C. May
ISBN 978 1 84905 869 8